W9-AWR-159

Taking SIDES

Clashing Views on Controversial Economic Issues

Seventh Edition

Taking
SIDES

Clashing Views on Controversial Economic Issues

Seventh Edition

Edited, Selected, and with Introductions by

Thomas R. Swartz
University of Notre Dame
and
Frank J. Bonello
University of Notre Dame

The Dushkin Publishing Group, Inc.

This book is dedicated to the thousands of students who have persevered in the "Bonello/Swartz (B.S.)" introductory economics course sequence at the University of Notre Dame. It is also dedicated to our children and grandchildren. In order of their birthdates, they are:

Mary Elizabeth, Karen Ann, Jennifer Lynne, John Anthony, Anne Marie, Rebecca Jourdan, David Joseph, Stephen Thomas, Chelsea Margaret, Kevin Joseph, and Meghan Claire

Photo Acknowledgments

Part 1   New York Stock Exchange
Part 2   Pamela Carley/DPG
Part 3   United Motor Manufacturing

Cover Art Acknowledgment

Charles Vitelli

Library of Congress Cataloging-in-Publication Data

Main entry under title:
  Taking sides: clashing views on controversial economic issues/edited, selected, and with introductions by Thomas R. Swartz and Frank J. Bonello.—7th ed.
  Includes bibliographical references and index.
  1. United States—Economic policy—1971–1981. 2. United States—Economic policy—1981–1993. 3. United States—Economic policy—1993–. I. Swartz, Thomas R., *comp.* II. Bonello, Frank J., *comp.*
    HC106.7.T34   338.9—dc20
    1-56134-329-3   94-45959

 Printed on Recycled Paper

The Dushkin Publishing Group, Inc.

PREFACE

Where there is much desire to learn, there of necessity will be much arguing

——John Milton (1608–1674), English poet and essayist

Presented here are 20 debates on important and compelling economic issues, which are designed to stimulate critical thinking skills and initiate lively and informed discussion. These debates take economic theory and show how it is applied to current, real-world public policy decisions, the outcomes of which will have an immediate and personal impact. How these debates are resolved will affect our taxes, jobs, wages, educational system, and so on; in short, they will shape the society in which we live.

It has been our intent throughout each of the seven editions of *Taking Sides. Clashing Views on Controversial Economic Issues* to select issues that reveal something about the nature of economics itself and something about how it relates to current, everyday newspaper headlines and television news stories on public policy issues that deal with economic considerations (and almost all do these days). To assist the reader, we begin each issue with an *issue introduction*, which sets the stage for the debate as it is argued in the YES and NO selections. Each issue concludes with a *postscript* that briefly reviews the arguments and makes some final observations. The introduction and postscript do not preempt what is the reader's own task: to achieve a critical and informed view of the economic issue at stake. Certainly, the reader should not feel confined to adopt one or the other of the positions presented. The views presented should be used as starting points, and the *suggestions for further reading* that appear in each issue postscript offer additional resources on the topic. At the back of the book is a listing of all the *contributors to this volume*, which provides information on the economists, policymakers, political leaders, and commentators whose views are debated here.

Changes to this edition   This new edition of *Taking Sides* represents a considerable revision of this book. Nineteen of the 40 selections and 10 of the 20 issues are new. Thus, as we rush toward the dawn of the twenty-first century, this heavily revised book will help us understand the implications of a changing set of economic issues that were not part of our world just a few short years ago. The newly raised issues are: *Should We Encourage the Private Ownership of Guns?* (Issue 2); *Is Managed Competition the Cure for Our Ailing Health Care Industry?* (Issue 6); *Are More Prisons and Prison Beds the Answer to America s Rising Crime Rate?* (Issue 7); *Will the North American Free Trade Agreement Help the Macroeconomy?* (Issue 9); *Does the United States Need to Save More?* (Issue 10), *Is a Consumption Tax a Good Substitute for the Income Tax?* (Issue 11); *Does the United States Have an Income Distribution Problem?* (Issue

i

14); *Can We End Welfare as We Know It?* (Issue 15); *Should Pollution Be Put to the Market Test?* (Issue 19); and *Has Capitalism Defeated Socialism?* (Issue 20).

As with all of the previous editions, the issues in the seventh edition can be used in any sequence. Although the general organization of the book loosely parallels the sequence of topics found in a standard introductory economics textbook, you can pick and choose which issues to read first, since they are designed to stand alone. Note that we have modified Part 3, which is now entitled "The World Around Us." We hoped that this broader category would allow us to more fully represent the host of problems our society faces in this ever-changing world we live in.

A word to the instructor   An *Instructor's Manual With Test Questions* (multiple-choice and essay) is available through the publisher. The manual includes a grid that correlates the individual issues in this edition of *Taking Sides* with chapters of 10 standard textbooks often used in introductory economics courses. And a general guidebook, called *Using Taking Sides in the Classroom*, which discusses methods and techniques for integrating the pro/con approach into any classroom setting, is also available.

Acknowledgments   We have received many helpful comments and suggestions from our friends and readers across the United States and Canada. As always, their suggestions were very welcome and have markedly enhanced the quality of this edition of *Taking Sides*. If as you read this book you are reminded of an essay that could be included in a future edition, we hope that you will drop us a note. We very much appreciate your interest and help, and we are always pleased to hear from you.

Our special thanks go to those who responded with suggestions for the seventh edition:

Stephen R. Ball
Cleary College

Wesley H. Booth
San Antonio College

Bruce E. Cole
Colorado Northwestern
   Community College

Behrooz Farhangi
Antelope Valley College

R. N. Folsom
San Jose State University

James F. Hill
Valdosta State University

James Hoefler
Dickinson College

Nayyer Hussain
Tougaloo College

James G. Kent
Itasca Community College

Patricia Ledesma
University of Notre Dame

Khalid Mehtabdin
College of Saint Rose

Judd W. Patton
Bellevue College

Gerald Perselay
Winthrop University

Joseph F. Talarico
Rider College

Peter Replogle
Orange County Community
    College

Richard Trieff
Des Moines Area Community
    College

David F. Ruccio
University of Notre Dame

David Wells
Glendale Community College

Gerald Sazama
University of Connecticut

We are also indebted to David H. Dean, our editorial advisor at The Dushkin Publishing Group for this edition of the book. He provided excellent council and gave us much needed support as we approached our publication deadlines. Those who suffered most in the preparation of this manuscript were those who had to read Swartz's tortured handwriting—our typists: Cheryl Reed and Sherry Reichold. Finally we owe much to our graduate assistants here at the University of Notre Dame: Joseph A. Stevano and Matthew C. Weagle. They were always able to maintain a smile even when our requests to run to the library were outrageous.

To all those mentioned above, we owe a huge debt, many thanks, and none of the blame for any shortcomings that remain in this edition of *Taking Sides*.

Thomas R. Swartz
University of Notre Dame

Frank J. Bonello
University of Notre Dame

CONTENTS IN BRIEF

CONTENTS

Free-market economist Milton Friedman contends that the sole responsibility
of business is to increase its profits. Philosopher Christopher D. Stone insists
that considerations other than profit making sometimes take precedence in a
business.

Law professor Daniel D. Polsby alleges that gun-control laws, not guns, increase crime rates and violence. Emergency room physician Arthur L. Kellermann and his colleagues argue that gun ownership increases an individual's
risk of being murdered.

Doug Bandow, a former special assistant to President Reagan, argues that
the Nunn-McCurdy proposal on national service represents an objectionable
intrusion of the state into the affairs of individual members of society. Profes-

sor of sociology Charles Moskos supports this proposal, calling it "a GI Bill without the GI."

Associate professor of economics Randall K. Filer maintains that wage differentials between women and men simply reflect differences in workers' preferences for jobs with varying degrees of pleasantness. Associate professors of sociology Jerry A. Jacobs and Ronnie J. Steinberg argue that wage differentials cannot be explained by worker employment choices.

Journalist William Tucker suggests that there is a substantial correlation between rent controls and homelessness. Sociologist Richard P. Appelbaum and his research associates submit that Tucker's statistical analysis is flawed and that he ignores the real causes of homelessness.

President Bill Clinton's Council of Economic Advisers argues that Clinton's reform proposal will cure the ailing health care industry by building upon the existing "strengths of our market-based system." Social critic Elizabeth

McCaughey asserts that this bill will reduce the quality of medical care and eliminate personal choice.

Edwin W. Zedlewski, an economist with the National Institute of Justice, argues that investment in more prison capacity is wise social policy. Economist David F. Greenberg alleges that Zedlewski has significantly overestimated the benefits of putting more criminals in prison.

Political scientists John E. Chubb and Terry M. Moe believe that the United States would be better off relying upon "markets and parental choice" in the quest for quality education. Public school superintendent Bill Honig replies that privatizing public schools through a system of choice is both unnecessary and dangerous.

Gary Clyde Hufbauer and Jeffrey J. Schott, senior fellows at the Institute for International Economics, argue that the North American Free Trade Agreement (NAFTA) will lead to increased trade with Mexico and boost U.S. employment. Jeff Faux, president of the Economic Policy Institute, argues that NAFTA does not support the goals of justice and sustainable development.

Economics professor William D. Nordhaus believes that increased amounts
of saving and investment are necessary if the United States is to avoid a
substantial decrease in its standard of living. Sociology professor Fred Block
and economics professor Robert Heilbroner argue that the problem is not
how much the country is saving but that there is a lack of political leadership
and economic sense.

The Bush administration's Council of Economic Advisers argues that consumption taxes would "distribute the tax burden more fairly than income
taxes." The late Joseph A. Pechman, former president of the American Economic Association, argues that the substitution of a consumption tax for an
income tax is not justifiable.

Federal Reserve chairman Alan Greenspan believes that federal government
budget deficits, in the long run, hurt the economy. Economics professor
Robert Eisner believes that the real problems of the U.S. economy are not
budget deficits but a lack of expenditures on "human capital and in public
investment."

Alan S. Blinder, a member of the Board of Governors of the Federal Reserve System, maintains that the energy of the market can solve America's environmental problems. Social critic David Moberg argues that clear public policy and direct government intervention will have the most positive effects on the environment.

Publisher Malcolm S. Forbes, Jr., argues that capitalism "works better than any of us can conceive." David McReynolds, cochair of the Socialist Party–U.S.A., remains committed to socialism because it "emphasizes cooperation rather than competition."

INTRODUCTION

Economics and Economists: The Basis for Controversy

Thomas R. Swartz
Frank J. Bonello

> "I think that Capitalism, wisely managed, can probably be more efficient for attaining economic ends than any alternative system yet in sight, but that in itself it is in many ways extremely objectionable."
>
> —Lord John Maynard Keynes
> *The End of Laissez-Faire* (1926)

Although nearly 70 years have passed since Lord Keynes (1883–1946) penned these lines, many economists still struggle with the basic dilemma he outlined. The paradox rests in the fact that a free market system is extremely efficient. It is purported to produce more at a lower cost than any other economic system. But in producing this wide array of low-cost goods and services, problems arise. These problems—most notably a lack of economic equity and economic stability—concern some economists. Other economists choose to ignore or minimize these issues. These problems form the foundation of this book.

If the problems raised and analyzed in this book were merely the product of intellectual gymnastics undertaken by eggheaded economists, then we could sit back and enjoy these confrontations as theoretical exercises. Unfortunately, we are not afforded that luxury. The essays contained in this book touch each and every one of us in tangible ways. They are real-world issues. Some focus upon *macroeconomic* topics, such as the current state of the U.S. economy and the underlying causes, effects, and cures for inflation, unemployment, and recession. Another set of issues deals with *microeconomic* topics. We refer to these issues as "micro" problems not because they are small problems but because they deal with small economic units, such as households, firms, or individual industries. The third set of issues in this book deals with matters that do not fall neatly into the macroeconomic or microeconomic classifications. This third set includes two issues relating to the international aspects of economic activity, two issues involving pollution, and one issue regarding the relative merits of capitalism and socialism. This third set of issues touches on our future directly and forces us to consider whether or not we should make fundamental changes in our economic policies.

For each of the 20 issues considered in this book, we have isolated those areas that currently generate the most controversy among economists. In a few cases this controversy represents a confrontation between extreme positions. Here the views of the *free-market* economists are contrasted with the views of the *radical reformist* economists. In other cases the conflicts are not as extreme; they represent conflicts between one extreme and economists with more moderate persuasions. Finally, we could not ignore the conflicts that occur among economists who generally agree on other issues. Economists— even economists who identify strongly with the same philosophical perspective—rarely agree on all issues, and these otherwise like-thinking economists can differ on specific topics.

The underlying reason for this apparent disagreement among economists can be explained, at least in part, in terms of Lord Keynes's 1926 remark. How various economists will react to the strengths and weaknesses found in an economic system will depend upon how they view the relative importance of *efficiency, equity,* and *stability.* These are central terms, and we will define them in detail in the following pages. For now the important point is that some economists may view efficiency as the overriding quality. In other cases, the same economists may be willing to sacrifice the efficiency generated by the market in order to ensure increased economic equity and/or increased economic stability. Determining when efficiency should be given a high priority and when efficiency should give way to other considerations occupies a large portion of the professional economist's time.

Given this discussion of conflict, controversy, and diversity, it might appear that economists rarely, if ever, agree on any economic issue. It would be misleading to leave the reader with this impression. Economists rarely challenge the internal logic of the theoretical models that have been developed and articulated by their colleagues. But they will challenge either the validity of the assumptions used in these models or the value of the ends these models seek to achieve. For example, it is difficult to discredit the internal logic of the microeconomic models employed by the free-market economist; these models are elegant, and their logical development is persuasive. However, these models are also challenged. The challenges typically focus upon such issues as the assumption of functioning, competitive markets, and the desirability of perpetuating the existing distribution of income. In this case, those who support and those who challenge the operation of the market agree on a large number of issues, but they disagree most assuredly on certain issues that have dramatic implications.

This same phenomenon of agreeing more often than disagreeing is also true in the area of economic policy. In this area, where the public is more acutely aware of the differences among economists, these differences are not generally over the kinds of changes that will be brought about by a particular policy. Again, the differences more typically concern the timing of the change, the specific characteristics of the policy, and the size of the resulting effect or effects.

ECONOMISTS: WHAT DO THEY REPRESENT?

Newspaper, magazine, and television commentators all use handy labels to describe certain members of the economics profession. What do the headlines mean when they refer to the "Chicago School," the "Keynesians," the "Antitrusters," or the "Radical Economists"? What do these individuals stand for? Since we, too, use our own labels throughout this book, we feel obliged to identify the principal groups or camps in our profession. Let us warn you that this can be a misleading venture. Some economists—perhaps most economists—defy classification. They float from one camp to another, selecting a gem of wisdom here and another there. These are practical men and women who believe that no one camp has all the answers to all the economic problems confronting society. As a consequence, they may be ardent supporters of a given policy recommendation of one philosophical group but vocal critics of other recommendations emanating from the same philosophical group.

Recognizing this limitation, four major groups of economists can be identified. These groups are differentiated on the basis of three criteria: how they view efficiency relative to equity and stability; what significance they attach to imperfectly competitive market structures; and how they view the evolution of an economic society. Before describing the views of the four groups based on these criteria, it is essential to understand the meaning of certain terms to be used in this description.

Efficiency, equity, and stability represent goals for an economic system. An economy is *efficient* when it produces those goods and services that people want and when it does so without wasting scarce resources. *Equity* in an economic sense has several dimensions. It means that income and wealth are distributed according to accepted principles of fairness: that those who are unable to care for themselves receive adequate care, and that mainstream economic activity is open to all persons. *Stability* is viewed as the absence of sharp ups and downs in business activity, in prices, and in employment. In other words, stability is marked by steady increases in output, little inflation, and low unemployment.

When the term *market structures* is used, it refers to the number of buyers and sellers in the market and the amount of control they exercise over price. At one extreme is a *perfectly competitive market*, where there are so many buyers and sellers that no one has any ability to influence market price. But one seller or one buyer could obviously have great control over price. This market structure, which we call *pure monopoly*, and other market structures that result in some control over price, are grouped under the broad label of imperfectly competitive markets. *Imperfect competition* is a situation where the number of market participants is limited and, as a consequence, the participants have the ability to influence price. With these terms in mind, we can begin to examine the various schools of economic thought.

Free-Market Economists

One of the most visible groups of economists, and perhaps the easiest group to identify and classify, is the *free-market economists*. These economists believe that the market, operating freely without interference from government or labor unions, will generate the greatest amount of well-being for the greatest number of people.

Economic efficiency is one of the priorities for free-market economists. In their well-developed models, *consumer sovereignty* (consumer demand for goods and services) guides the system by directly influencing market prices. Not only does the distribution of economic resources caused by these market prices result in the production of an array of goods and services that are demanded by consumers, but this production is also undertaken in the most cost-effective fashion. The free-market economists claim that, at any point, some individuals must earn incomes that are substantially greater than those of other individuals. They contend that these higher incomes are a reward for greater efficiency or productivity, and they also maintain that this reward-induced efficiency will result in rapid economic growth that will benefit all persons in the society. They might also admit that a system driven by these freely operating markets will be subject to occasional bouts of instability (slow growth, inflation, and unemployment). However, they maintain that government action to eliminate or reduce this periodic instability will only make matters worse. According to the free-market economist, government should play a minor role in the economic affairs of society.

Although the models of free-market economists are dependent upon functioning, competitive markets, the lack of these competitive markets in the real world does not seriously jeopardize their position. First, they assert that large-sized firms are necessary to achieve low per-unit costs; that is, a single large firm may be able to produce a given level of output with fewer scarce resources than a large number of small firms. Second, they suggest that the benefits associated with the free operation of markets are so great compared to government intervention that even a second-best solution of imperfectly competitive markets still yields benefits far in excess of government intervention. Lastly, the free-market economists clearly view the market as the highest form of economic evolution. The efficiency of the system, the simplicity of the system, the power of the system, and—above all—the personal freedoms inherent in the system demonstrate its superiority.

These advocates of the free market have been given various labels over time. The oldest and most persistent label is *classical economists*. This is because the classical economists of the eighteenth century, particularly Adam Smith (1723–1790), were the first to point out the virtues of the market. Smith captured the essence of the system with the following words:

> Every individual endeavors to employ his capital so that its produce may be of greatest value. He generally neither intends to promote the public interest nor knows how much he is promoting it. He intends only his own security, only his

own gain. And he is in this led by an invisible hand to promote an end which was no part of his intention. By pursuing his own interest he frequently promotes that of society more effectively than when he really intends to promote it.

—Adam Smith
The Wealth of Nations (1776)

Since free-market economists and those who echo their views resist most forms of government intervention, they are sometimes referred to as *conservatives* or *libertarians*. These labels are as much political labels as they are economic characterizations. It must be recalled that the classical economists of the eighteenth century not only embraced the political philosophy of laissez-faire (roughly translated to leave it, the economy, alone) but also developed a set of economic theories that were totally consistent with this political theory. These "political economists" were, as a result, called libertarians because they espoused political and economic policies that maximized personal liberties. The nineteenth-century libertarians are not to be confused with twentieth-century liberals. Modern-day liberals, as we shall explain shortly in more detail, are often willing to sacrifice some freedoms in the marketplace in order to ensure the attainment of other objectives.

Still other labels are sometimes attached to the free-market economists, such as *monetarists*, the *Austrian School*, *public choice* economists, *Chicago School* economists, *rational expectations* economists or *Friedmanites*. Among the modern-day practitioners of free-market economics, the most notable is Nobel laureate Milton Friedman (b. 1912), formerly of the University of Chicago. He and others argue that the government's attempts to promote economic stability through the manipulation of the money supply actually cause more instability than would have occurred if the government had not intervened. Therefore, these monetarists advocate a policy that would allow the money supply to grow at a reasonable, steady rate.

In the 1980s a new group of free-market economists was formed called the *supply-siders*. These economists, led by Arthur Laffer, also believe strongly in the market. What makes them unique is the specific proposals they offer to reduce government intervention in the economy. They contend that reductions in marginal tax rates will stimulate private activity.

Supporters of rational expectations are also a relatively new group of free-market economists. They claim that government monetary and fiscal actions will have no effect on economic activity unless the actions are unanticipated; that is, unless the government's actions are surprises. They argue that since the government is unlikely to consistently surprise the public, monetary and fiscal policies will not have much effect on economic activity.

Before turning our attention to the other major camps of economists, we should note that the free-market economists have been very successful in influencing the development of economics. Most introductory economic textbooks present major portions of the basic theoretical concepts of the free-market economists, especially in those chapters dealing with microeconomics. It is because of their influence over long periods of time that so many labels are used to describe them, so much is written about them, and so much is written by these conservative economists. The free-market position is represented in a substantial number of the 20 issues that are considered in this book.

Liberal Economists

Another significant group of economists in the United States can be classified as *liberal economists*. Liberal in this instance refers to the willingness to intervene in the free operation of the market. These economists share with the free-market economists a great respect for the market. However, the liberal economist does not believe that the explicit and implicit costs of a freely operating market should or can be ignored. Rather, the liberal economist maintains that the costs of an uncontrolled marketplace are often borne by those in society who are least capable of bearing them: the poor, the elderly, and the infirm. Additionally, liberal economists maintain that the freely operating market sometimes results in economic instability and the resultant bouts of inflation, unemployment, and slow or negative growth. Liberal economists believe that economic efficiency is highly desirable, but they find the attainment of economic efficiency at any cost to be unacceptable.

Consider for a moment the differences between free-market economists and liberal economists at the microeconomic level. Liberal economists take exception to the free market on two grounds. First, liberal economists find a basic problem with fairness in the marketplace. The market is driven by the forces of consumer spending, but there are those who, through no fault of their own (they may be aged, young, infirm, or physically or mentally handicapped), may not have the wherewithal to participate in the economic system. Others, however, perhaps because they have inherited wealth, not only have the ability to participate in the system, but they may also have the ability to direct the course of that system. Second, the unfettered marketplace does not and cannot handle spillover effects, or what are known as *externalities*. These are the third-party effects that may occur as a result of some action. For example, will a firm willingly compensate its neighbors for the pollutants it pours into a nearby lake? Will a truck driver willingly drive at 55 miles per hour and, in the process, reduce the highway accident rate? Liberal economists think not. These economists are therefore willing to have the government intervene in these and other, similar cases.

The liberal economists' role in macroeconomics is more readily apparent. Ever since the failure of free-market economics during the Great Depression of the 1930s, *Keynesianism* (another label for liberal economics) has become widely known. In his 1935 book *The General Theory of Employment, Interest, and Money*, Lord John Maynard Keynes laid the basic groundwork for this school of thought. Keynes argued that the history of freely operating market economies was marked by periods of recurring recessions, sometimes very deep recessions that we call *depressions*. He maintained that government intervention through its fiscal policy—government tax and spending power—could eliminate, or at least soften, these sharp reductions in economic activity to move the economy along a more stable growth path. Thus, for the Keynesians, one of the extremely objectionable aspects of a free-market economy is its inherent instability. Their call for active government participation is in sharp contrast to the policies of the free-market economists who argue that economic stability (growth, employment, and prices) can be achieved only if government intervenes less and not more.

Liberal economists are far more concerned about the existence of imperfections in the marketplace than are their free-market counterparts. These economists may agree that the imperfectly competitive firms can achieve some savings because of their large size and efficiency, but they assert that, since there is little or no competition, the firms are not forced to pass these cost savings on to consumers. Thus, liberal economists—who in some circles are labeled *antitrusters*—are willing to intervene in the market in two ways. In some cases they are prepared to allow some monopolies, such as public utilities, to exist, but they contend that these monopolies must be regulated by the government. In other cases they maintain that there is no justification for monopolies, and they are prepared to invoke the powers of antitrust legislation to break up existing monopolies and/or prevent the formation of new monopolies.

Unlike the free-market economist, the liberal economist does not believe that the free marketplace is the highest form of economic evolution. By definition, the liberal economist asserts that the highest form of economic evolution is a *mixed economy*—an economy where market forces are tempered by government intervention. These economists do not advocate extensive government planning and/or government ownership of productive resources. But they are not willing to allow the market to operate on its own. They maintain that the immense power of the marketplace properly tempered with government intervention can improve the economy's equity and stability.

During the 1960s and up to the middle 1970s, liberal economics dominated economic policy in the United States. In the late 1970s, however, there was a reemergence of free-market economics, and during the 1980s, free-market economics dominated public policy decisions. A similar pattern prevailed in the United Kingdom. Recent moves in the former Soviet Union and Eastern European countries toward free-market economics reflect a desire, in part, for greater economic efficiency. But economic policy has a way of shifting in response to prevailing economic problems. To understand the full spectrum of policy choice, we must examine the ideas of mainstream critics and radical reform economists.

The Mainstream Critics
There are a number of economists who are vocal critics of the ideas of both free-market and liberal economics but who do not fall into the category of radical reformists. Some of these economic critics might be labeled as *institu-*

tionalists, others as *structuralists,* and still others are *post-Keynesians.* They run the gamut from Thorstein Veblen (1857–1929) and his critique of conspicuous consumption to John Kenneth Galbraith (b. 1908) and his views on industrial structure. These economists find mainstream or traditional economics—free-market and liberal economics—to be eloquent theories that do not conform to reality. Unfortunately, to date, the mainstream critics have not developed their own unified set of economic propositions or laws that they can offer as a substitute for traditional economics.

So what are the criticisms offered by these economists? One point of attack is the simplified assumptions employed in traditional models. The critics maintain that the traditional models may explain how economic actors would behave if these actors behaved in a rational, self-interested manner and if these actors lived in a competitive world. However, the critics assert that consumers and business firms do not always act this way. Behavior is more complex. It is shaped by institutions and circumstances that are continuously changing. The critics also see the world in which we live as a dual-economy world. One part of that world is competitive; another, larger, part of the world is dominated by a few firms that have the power to set prices.

Some of the mainstream critics have concentrated their efforts on the structure of corporations as economic institutions. These economists, sometimes referred to as *structuralists,* examine the economic planning undertaken by these large economic units. They explore the impact that these large economic units have on inflation, employment, income distribution, and efficiency, as well as the role they play in international affairs. The institutionalists recognize that large corporate entities engage in massive economic planning that affects the entire society, and they also analyze alternative forms of regional and economic planning undertaken by government.

One reasonably cohesive group of mainstream critics are the *post-Keynesians.* These economists are post-Keynesians because they believe that, as the principal economic institutions have changed over time, they have remained closer to the spirit of Keynes than the liberal economists have. The key aspect of Keynes, as far as the post-Keynesians are concerned, is his assertion that "expectations of the future are not necessarily certain." Post-Keynesians assert, among other things, that the productivity of the economic system is not significantly affected by changes in income distribution; that the system can still be efficient without competitive markets; that conventional fiscal policies cannot control inflation; and that "incomes policies" are the means to an effective and equitable answer to the inflationary dilemma. (This characterization of post-Keynesianism is drawn from Alfred S. Eichner's introduction in *A Guide to Post-Keynesian Economics* [M. E. Sharpe, 1978].)

In spite of the fact that the mainstream critics lack an integrated theory, it is useful to articulate their position on our three criteria and to contrast these with those of the free-market economists and the liberal economists. On the basis of our first criterion—the relative importance of economic efficiency, equity, and stabilization—the mainstream critics differ dramatically. By rejecting the assumptions of rationality and self-interest, they maintain that whatever you set as your highest priority—be it efficiency, equity, or stability —you cannot achieve it using the abstract models of traditional economics. Indeed, they believe that the market as it exists in its concentrated form today leads to inefficiency, inequity, and inherent instability.

The second and third criteria further distinguish the mainstream critics from the other schools of economics. According to the mainstream critics, economics is in a constant state of evolution. At one time—perhaps when Adam Smith and his fellow classical economists were formulating their basic models—the economy could be legitimately characterized as competitive. At that time, free-market economics reflected reality and, therefore, could explain that reality. Today, functional competition rarely exists, and a new body of theorems and concepts must be developed to explain this present reality. At some future date, another set of economic institutions will develop and yet another body of theorems and concepts will be needed. The mainstream critics attach great importance to the existence of imperfect competition and to the process of economic evolution. The mainstream critics know that new theories must be developed to explain today's reality of imperfect competition, and they know that the economy is always in a state of evolution.

Radical Reformist Economists

As we move further and further away from the economics of the free market, we encounter the *radical reformist economists,* or the *Left.* These economists, who spring from several theoretical foundations, share a belief that the market and the capitalist system, no matter how well disciplined, is fatally flawed. They argue that the "visible hand" of public interest must replace the "invisible hand" of self-interest: the fundamental institutions of private ownership, with their inherent concentration of economic and political power, must be replaced by government or some other form of communal ownership of productive resources. Such changes are the means to the greater economic good and true political democracy.

This does not mean that all private ownership will cease to exist at some distant moment in time. Rather, many radical reformists maintain that it is the private ownership of the 1,000 largest firms that causes the basic problems for the capitalist economy. Therefore, in order to redress these problems, the private ownership of these 1,000 firms must eventually fade away. As a result, not all property must be owned collectively. Only the most radical of the Left would go that far.

As was the case with the other three broad clusters of economists, there is much diversity within this fourth cluster of economists. One group of economists within this cluster contains the radical, political economists who often focus upon microeconomic issues. They are concerned with issues such as the abuses that may result from *administered prices*—prices that can be administered or set by a firm because of the firm's monopoly influence in the marketplace. Another identifiable subgroup is the *Marxists.* Their lineage can be traced to the nineteenth-century philosopher-economist Karl Marx (1818–1883).

Ironically, Marx himself shares his economic roots with the free-market economists. Before writing his most impressive work, the three volumes of *Das Kapital,* Marx studied the work of the classical economists and incorporated a basic tenet of their works—David Ricardo's labor theory of value—into his own work. But unlike free-market economics, which Marx prophesied would fall of its own weight, Marx laid the foundation for *socialism.* In spite of the changes that have taken place in Eastern Europe, socialism (where some form of public ownership of the means of production is substituted for private ownership) is still prevalent throughout much of the world. Thus, we in North America cannot afford to ignore this group of economists.

Note that socialism may take many forms. It varies from the democratic socialism of the United Kingdom and other Western European countries to the radical, largely unreformed socialism of China. The one common characteristic is public ownership of the means of production. However, the extent of this public ownership varies dramatically among the socialist countries.

Although it may be difficult to classify the different subgroups of radical reformist economists, we can differentiate them from the other broad classifications of economists on the basis of our three criteria. In terms of the first criterion—the relative importance of economic efficiency, equity, and stabilization—the radical reformists are clearly set apart from their nonradical counterparts. Not only do they set a much higher value on equity and stability when compared to the free-market economists, but they have also developed a set of economic models that attempts to ensure the attainment of equity and stability. The radical reformists assert that the economic efficiency of a market economy is based on exploitation and the concentration of economic and political power; therefore, the market system is fundamentally flawed. These flaws result in unacceptable inequities and other economic outcomes that are incompatible with the common good.

The radicals are concerned by the existence of imperfect competition. For them the current reality is an immense concentration of economic power that is a far cry from Adam Smith's world of competitive markets. Today, in their view, the market economy operates to benefit a few at the expense of the masses. Firms with monopoly power control the economy. They administer prices. They are the invisible hand that guides the economy to their benefit.

Some of the radicals, who might be called *vulgar* Marxists, predict the demise of the market economy as we know it. They see capitalism as a necessary step in the evolution of economic systems: capitalism is needed to raise the economy out of the chaos of a feudal society. But after capital has been accumulated and a modern economy is developed, the basic inequities and instabilities will bring the market economy to its knees and socialism will emerge. Socialism itself is not the end of the evolutionary process. Socialism will eventually give way to *communism*—where government is nonexistent and everyone works according to their ability and receives according to their needs.

Of course, not all radical reformist economists are vulgar Marxists. There is a significant group, perhaps best represented by those who have published their research results over the years in the *Review of Radical Political Economics*, that might be labeled as *contemporary* Marxists. These economists examine issues that have been largely ignored by mainstream economists—issues such as war, sexism, racism, imperialism, and civil rights. In their analysis of these issues, they borrow from and refine the work of Marx. In the process, they emphasize the role of class in shaping society and the role of the economy in determining class structures. Most do not see socialism as evolving automatically, and they certainly do not see communism emerging at the end of an evolutionary process. Rather, these economists see a need to encourage explicitly the development of some form of socialism for North America, for only then will the greatest good for the greatest number be ensured.

What would these radical reformists say about the changes taking place in the former Soviet Union and other Eastern European countries? They would argue that these events are not evidence of the superiority of capitalism and the end of socialism. They believe the changes reflect the abuse of socialist practices and a despotic form of government. As these countries experiment with markets, they will encounter many problems that will lead them back to socialism, but there will be a new, democratic socialism rather than the despotic socialism from which they have emerged.

Before we turn to the next section, we must warn the reader to interpret these labels with extreme care. Our categories are not hard and fast, and there is little that is black and white in these classifications. This does not mean that there is no value to these classifications—only that there are gray areas concerning these definitions. However, this basic "map" of economic theories is an important key to understanding the philosophical backgrounds of the individual authors of the issues included in this volume.

Before moving ahead to the issues, it is useful to repeat the themes developed in the preceding section. First, there is much disagreement among economists and others on economic problems. There is, however, rhyme and reason to this disagreement. In large measure the disagreement stems from various ideologies that these individuals may espouse. Indeed, the differences that exist between individual economists and groups of economists can be defined in terms of their respective views of efficiency, equity, and stability; on the relative merits of imperfect competition; and on the place of the market economy in the evolutionary process of economic systems.

Second, the identification of causes, effects, and cures for economic problems must be undertaken at the practical level. At this level, sharp distinctions tend to disappear, and actions may be recommended by certain individuals that seem inconsistent with their ideology. Here the economist must sacrifice ideological purity for practical solutions. The science of economics must deal with real-world problems or it loses its meaning for most people.

THE ISSUES

It is not difficult to identify major problems in the American economy. Each month the news media discuss in detail the newly released statistics that reveal the success or failure of policies designed to reduce inflation and unemployment. Each day it seems that some businessperson, or labor leader, or consumer advocate, or public official releases a new proposal that will remedy pollution, improve the quality and the safety of products or the workplace, reduce unemployment and inflation, or halt and reverse the decay of our cities. Thus, the difficulty in developing this book was not in identifying real and important economic problems or in locating alternative views on those problems. The difficulty was one of selecting only issues from what, at times, appeared to be an endless list of problems and views on those problems.

We have selected 20 issues that represent a broad cross section of the conflicts that society faces. We have provided this generality in three different ways. First, the issues include eight microeconomic discussions, seven macroeconomic, and five issues dealing with matters beyond the domestic economy. Second, within each set of issues, the range of topics is broad. For example, within the microeconomic set there are issues that represent basic disagreements among economists on specific policy topics (such as rent controls) as well as broader disagreements that reflect ideological differences (such as the responsibilities of business in modern society). The third dimension concerns the ideologies of the views that are presented; the list of authors includes well-regarded academic economists, politicians, journalists, business leaders, and labor leaders. These individuals represent the far Right, the far Left, and many positions in between. Although the ideologies are sometimes tempered by practical considerations, the basic ideological positions are apparent.

A summary of several of the issues may serve to indicate the extent of this generality. This discussion will also demonstrate the interplay that exists between basic philosophy and practical considerations in arriving at a real-world solution or position on an economic problem.

One of eight microeconomic issues is: *Is Choice a Panacea For the Ills of Public Education?* Most Americans are aware of the problems with public education. They are bombarded with news stories of high school graduates who cannot read, with reports on how American students rank last in mathematical and scientific knowledge compared to students from other industrialized nations, and with statistics of low Scholastic Aptitude Test scores. The question is what to do about the problem.

One alternative is to get government out of the education business. This would be the solution offered by the far-right, extreme, free-market economists. They argue that there is already a significant private sector that educates American youth and that this sector produces superior educational outcomes. Moreover, the conservatives argue that the gains from increased education are basically private: more education means a better job and greater income. Because the gains from education are private, education should be financed privately and not by the government. In this fashion the consumers would demand quality education from the producers, and competition would force the producers into supplying quality education.

But this is an extreme position. Less extreme, free-market economists and liberal economists believe that there are substantial externalities or spillover effects associated with education. An educated person is more likely to make better political decisions; an educated person is also less likely to engage in criminal activity or became dependent on the welfare system. Moreover, private financing of education is problematic. Unlike financing the purchase of a car or a house, the person consuming education is unable to earn income and pay back the loan while the product is being consumed, and the educational loan can only be repaid after the education has been completed. And what if there is a default in loan payments? A car or a house can be repossessed, but what is to be repossessed when someone defaults on an educational loan? For these reasons economists, liberals, and less extreme, free-market economists believe in public education.

Given widespread support for public education and for government financing of this industry, the problem of improving educational outcomes remains. One alternative is to retain the current financing procedures and introduce internal reforms, such as competency testing, increased spending, smaller class sizes, increased teacher requirements, decentralized administration, magnet schools, and so on. Another alternative—initially developed by free-market economists but increasingly accepted by liberals—is to create more competition among the educational producers and among schools in order to improve the quality of their product. This would be accomplished by providing students and their parents with a choice as to which schools they would attend. Under this system, students and parents would be issued vouchers, which the students and parents would present to the school of their choice. These vouchers would represent the dollar votes of educational consumers. All schools would strive to produce the highest quality educational product in order to attract the highest number of students and earn the highest number of vouchers.

Mainstream critics and radical reformists have their views on this issue as well. The mainstream critics might argue that the current problems in public education are a manifestation of larger social problems. Quality education requires parental involvement, a stable home environment, and economic rewards for school graduates that are competitive with the economic rewards of criminal activity. Without changes in these areas, all efforts for educational reform will fail.

Radical reformist economists would argue that inferior public education and superior private education are the logical consequences of a capitalist economy. Only the privileged can afford private education, and by sending their children to private schools where they will obtain a superior education, the privileged parents will ensure their children a privileged position in the future. Only educational reform that guarantees equal opportunity and equal access will generate quality education for all.

One of the macroeconomic issues is: *Should the Federal Reserve Target Zero Inflation?* Free-market economists generally believe that the macroeconomy will produce solid economic growth, low inflation, and full employment. They admit that there may be short periods of recession or rapid inflation. However, they believe that these undesirable deviations will be of short duration, and the economy will quickly right itself. Government stabilization policies are the source of, and not the solution to, macroeconomic problems: efforts to raise and lower taxes, to increase or decrease government spending, to increase or decrease interest rates, or to increase or decrease the money supply in an effort to resolve macroeconomic problems will only make the problems worse. Thus, the government should not attempt active stabilization policies, and both monetary and fiscal policy should be passive. Passive fiscal policy means that the government should balance its budget with the levels of spending and taxation set at the lowest possible levels. Passive monetary policy means that the Federal Reserve System, the government agency responsible for monetary policy, should concentrate on achieving price stability or zero inflation. According to the group of free-market economists known as monetarists, the Federal Reserve System can achieve this outcome by simply allowing the money supply to increase the same rate as output.

Liberal economists, on the other hand, argue that the free-market position oversimplifies the problem. Some liberal economists, building on the analysis that John Maynard Keynes presented during the 1930s, argue that the economy is inherently unstable rather than inherently stable. It is not self-correcting. Once in a recession, the economy—without government assistance in the form of expansionary monetary and fiscal policies—will be unable to restore full employment. Other liberal economists accept the proposition that free-market economies are self-correcting. They support active stabilization policies on the grounds that such government actions can shorten the periods of recession and inflation and increase the length of business expansions. The liberal economists admit that the government may make mistakes in the process of executing stabilization policies, but even with mistakes, the overall performance of the economy with active stabilization policies would be better than the overall performance of the economy without active stabilization policies. And, they further argue, unemployment is a much more serious problem than inflation. Thus, they conclude that the Federal Reserve should target employment rather than price stability when executing active monetary policy.

Mainstream critics and radical reformist economists have taken positions on this issue. The mainstream critics side with the liberals, agreeing that the macroeconomy as presently constituted is inherently unstable. The mainstream critics, however, would argue that it might be more appropriate to attack macroeconomic problems through institutional changes rather than through active monetary and fiscal policies. By adopting, for example, a tax-based income policy, the inherent instability of a market economy could be reduced. Radical reformers would agree with the liberals and the mainstream critics on the systemic instability of capitalism: the systemic instability is just another example of the inherent contradictions of a market economy. In a class society, recessions and periodic high unemployment are a means by which the dominant class of business capitalists can maintain its position of power over the lower class of ordinary workers. Radical reformers believe that the inherent instability of a capitalist economy can only be resolved by a transformation of economic and social relations—by restructuring society from organizations based on competition and conflict to organizations based on cooperation and common interests.

One of the international issues deals with economic relations between Japan and the United States: *Is Japan a Threat to America's Economic and National Security?* Each month, newspapers report the most recent data regarding the United States–Japan trade balance. We see ads for Japanese products in all the media, some even indicating that the Japanese products are made in the United States. News stories of "Japan bashing" by Americans and of "America bashing" by Japanese hit the front pages and the television news.

It is not hard to summarize the views of free-market economists on United States–Japan economic relations. They believe that unrestricted free trade is the best policy; it will generate the greatest amount of well-being for the greatest number of people. So regardless of what the Japanese do in terms of their domestic markets, the United States should not protect American firms from Japanese competition. U.S. protection would prevent Americans from exercising their economic freedom, forcing them to pay higher prices for both domestic and foreign goods, and slowing down the adjustment of American firms to higher quality–lower cost products. Japanese investment in the United States is also beneficial: it creates jobs and provides American workers with greater capital. Japanese protection only hurts the Japanese, forcing Japanese consumers to pay higher prices for goods. All of these arguments for free trade go back to classical economists Adam Smith and David Ricardo (1772–1823).

Although liberal economists are firm believers in free trade, accepting the concept of comparative advantage first formalized by Ricardo in the early nineteenth century, they are concerned that trade be fair as well as free. They believe that economic conditions can be altered by government action and that comparative advantage can therefore be manipulated by government intervention. Thus, the liberal economists feel that actions by the American government to level the playing field are justified.

There is another difference between free-market and liberal economists in this area. Liberals support government programs designed to assist workers who are displaced by free trade. The larger society gains from free trade and should be willing to use some of those gains to assist, in the interest of equity, those whose lives have been disrupted by trade. Free-market economists worry that such assistance may delay the adjustment process and thereby promote inefficiency. This is why government activity under trade-assistance legislation was significantly reduced during the free-market Reagan administration.

What are the positions of the mainstream critics and radical reformers on this issue? Mainstream critics focus on industrial structure as shaped by an industrial policy. They believe that certain changes in the American economy —changes such as a preoccupation with finance rather than with production—explain the decline in America's international economic position. They believe that in an era of increasing global integration, each country needs an industrial policy where government targets specific industries for special assistance. The radical reformists see the decline in America's international position as the logical consequence, again, of a capitalist society. Other countries that stress mutual cooperation of government, business, and labor cannot help but outperform countries where various segments of society are seen as adversaries. They would add that the U.S. preoccupation with maintaining itself as the world's foremost military power has also contributed to America's international economic decline. Thus, because it is a cooperative society and because it has avoided unnecessary military expenditures, it is no surprise that Japan has attained such a lofty position in international economic affairs.

SUMMARY

It is clear that there is no shortage of economic problems that demand solutions. There is also no shortage of proposed solutions. The 20 issues included in this volume will acquaint you with some of these economic problems, for which there are at least two proposed solutions for each problem. Here, we hope to provide the reader with new insights by presenting the differences and similarities of these alternative remedies.

If this introduction has served its purpose, you will be able to identify common elements in the proposed solutions to the different problems. For example, you will be able to identify the reliance on the forces of the market advocated by free-market economists as the remedy for several economic ills. This introduction should also help you understand why there are at least two proposed solutions for every economic problem: each group of economists tends to interpret a problem from its own philosophical position and to advance a solution that is grounded in that same philosophical framework.

Our intention is not to connect persons to one philosophic position or another. We hope instead to generate discussion and promote understanding. To do this, not only must each of us see a proposed solution, but we must also be aware of the foundation that supports that solution. With greater understanding, meaningful progress in addressing economic problems can be achieved.

PART 1

Microeconomic Issues

Our lives are profoundly affected by economic decisions made at the microeconomic level. These decisions are made on such diverse questions as those regarding profit motives of business firms, the health care industry, requirements for national service, rent controls, and choice in public education, among others.

- Are Profits the Only Business of Business?

- Should We Encourage the Private Ownership of Guns?

- Is National Service at Odds With American National Interest?

- Are Women Paid Less Than Men Because Their Working Conditions Are More Favorable?

- Are Rent Controls the Cause of America's Homelessness?

- Is Managed Competition the Cure for Our Ailing Health Care Industry?

- Are More Prisons and Prison Beds the Answer to America's Rising Crime Rate?

- Is Choice a Panacea for the Ills of Public Education?

ISSUE 1

Are Profits the Only Business of Business?

YES: Milton Friedman, from "The Social Responsibility of Business Is to Increase Its Profits," *The New York Times Magazine* (September 13, 1970)

NO: Christopher D. Stone, from "Corporate Accountability in Law and Morals," in Oliver F. Williams and John W. Houck, eds., *The Judeo-Christian Vision and the Modern Corporation* (University of Notre Dame Press, 1982)

ISSUE SUMMARY

YES: Free-market economist Milton Friedman contends that the sole responsibility of business is to increase its profits.

NO: Philosopher Christopher D. Stone insists that the time for corporate social responsibility has come and considerations other than profit making sometimes take precedence in a business.

Every economic society—whether it is a traditional society in Central Africa, a fossilized planned economy such as Cuba's, or a wealthy capitalist society such as those found in North America, Western Europe, or the Pacific Rim —must address the basic economic problem of resource allocation. These societies must determine *what* goods and services they can and will produce, *how* these goods and services will be produced, and *for whom* these goods and services will be produced.

The *what, how,* and *for whom* questions must be answered because of the problem of scarcity. Even if a given society were indescribably rich, it would still confront the problem of scarcity—in the case of a rich society, "relative scarcity." It might have all the resources it needs to produce all the goods and services it would ever want, but it could not produce all these things simultaneously. Thus, even a very rich society must set priorities and produce first those goods and services with the highest priority and postpone the production of those goods and services with lower priorities. If time is of the essence, this society would determine *how* these goods and services should be produced. And since this wealthy society cannot produce all it wants instantly, it must also determine *for whom* the first bundle of goods and services will be produced.

Few, if any, economic societies are indescribably rich. On the other hand, there are many examples of economic societies that face grinding deprivation daily. In these societies and in all the societies that fall between poverty

2

and great affluence, the *what, how,* and *for whom* questions are immediately apparent. Somehow these questions must be answered.

In some societies, such as the Amish communities of North America, the answers to these questions are found in tradition: Sons and daughters follow in their parents' footsteps. Younger generations produce *what* older generations produced before them. The methods of production—the horsedrawn plow, the hand-held scythe, the use of natural fertilizers—remain unchanged; thus, the *how* question is answered in the same way that the *for whom* question is answered—by following historic patterns. In other societies, such as self-sustaining religious communities, there is a different pattern of responses to these questions. In these communities, the "elder" of the community determines *what* will be produced, *how* it will be produced, and *for whom* it will be produced. If there is a well-defined hierarchical system, it is similar to one of the former stereotypical command economies of Eastern Europe.

Although elements of tradition and command are found in the industrialized societies of Western Europe, North America, and Japan, the basic answers to the three questions of resource allocation in these countries are determined by profit. In these economic societies, *what* will be produced is determined by what will yield the greatest profit. Consumers, in their search for maximum satisfaction, will bid for those goods and services that they want most. This consumer action drives the prices of these goods and services up, which, in turn, increases producers' profits. The higher profits attract new firms into the industry and encourage existing firms to increase their output. Thus, profits are the mechanism that ensures consumers get what they want. Similarly, the profit-seeking behavior of business firms determines *how* the goods and services that consumers want will be produced. Since firms attempt to maximize their profits, they select those means of production that are economically most efficient. Lastly, the *for whom* question is also linked to profits. Wherever there is a shortage of goods and services, profits will be high. In the producers' attempts to increase their output, they must attract factors of production (land, labor, and capital) away from other economic activities. This bidding increases factor prices or factor incomes and ensures that these factors will be able to buy goods and services in the open marketplace.

Both Milton Friedman and Christopher D. Stone recognize the merits of a profit-driven economic system. They do not quarrel over the importance of profits. But they do quarrel over whether or not business firms have obligations beyond making profits. Friedman holds that the *only* responsibility of business is to make profits and that anyone who maintains otherwise is "preaching pure and unadulterated socialism." Stone, on the other hand, contends that there are occasions when a corporation should "select a course that voluntarily subordinates profit maximization to the realization of some other value that is not the organization's."

YES   Milton Friedman

THE SOCIAL RESPONSIBILITY OF BUSINESS IS TO INCREASE ITS PROFITS

When I hear businessmen speak eloquently about the "social responsibilities of business in a free-enterprise system," I am reminded of the wonderful line about the Frenchman who discovered at the age of 70 that he had been speaking prose all his life. The businessmen believe that they are defending free enterprise when they declaim that business is not concerned "merely" with profit but also with promoting desirable "social ends; that business has a social conscience" and takes seriously its responsibilities for providing employment, eliminating discrimination, avoiding pollution and whatever else may be the catchwords of the contemporary crop of reformers. In fact they are—or would be if they or anyone else took them seriously—preaching pure and unadulterated socialism. Businessmen who talk this way are unwitting puppets of the intellectual forces that have been undermining the basis of a free society these past decades.

The discussions of the "social responsibilities of business" are notable for their analytical looseness and lack of rigor. What does it mean to say that "business" has responsibilities? Only people can have responsibilities. A corporation is an artificial person and in this sense may have artificial responsibilities, but "business" as a whole cannot be said to have responsibilities, even in this vague sense. The first step toward clarity in examining the doctrine of the social responsibility of business is to ask precisely what it implies for whom.

Presumably, the individuals who are to be responsible are businessmen, which means individual proprietors or corporate executives. Most of the discussion of social responsibility is directed at corporations, so in what follows I shall mostly neglect the individual proprietor and speak of corporate executives.

In a free-enterprise, private-property system, a corporate executive is an employee of the owners of the business. He has direct responsibility to his employers. That responsibility is to conduct the business in accordance with their desires, which generally will be to make as much money as possible while conforming to the basic rules of the society, both those embodied in law and those embodied in ethical custom. Of course, in some cases his employers may have a different objective. A group of persons might establish a corporation for an eleemosynary purpose —for example, a hospital or a school. The manager of such a corporation will not have money profit as his objective but the rendering of certain services.

In either case, the key point is that, in his capacity as a corporate executive, the manager is the agent of the individuals who own the corporation or establish the eleemosynary institution, and his primary responsibility is to them.

Needless to say, this does not mean that it is easy to judge how well he is performing his task. But at least the criterion of performance is straightforward, and the persons among whom a voluntary contractual arrangement exists are clearly defined.

Of course, the corporate executive is also a person in his own right. As a person, he may have many other responsibilities that he recognizes or assumes voluntarily—to his family, his conscience, his feelings of charity, his church, his clubs, his city, his country. He may feel impelled by these responsibilities to devote part of his income to causes he regards as worthy, to refuse to work for particular corporations, even to leave his job, for example, to join his country's armed forces. If we wish, we may refer to some of these responsibilities as "social responsibilities." But in these respects he is acting as a principal, not an agent; he is spending his own money or time or energy, not the money of his employers or the time or energy he has contracted to devote to their purposes. If these are "social responsibilities," they are the social responsibilities of individuals, not of business.

What does it mean to say that the corporate executive has a "social responsibility" in his capacity as businessman? If this statement is not pure rhetoric, it must mean that he is to act in some way that is not in the interest of his employers. For example, that he is to refrain from increasing the price of the product in order to contribute to the social objective of preventing inflation, even though a price increase would be in the best interests of the corporation. Or that he is to make expenditures on reducing pollution beyond the amount that is in the best interests of the corporation or that is required by law in order to contribute to the social objective of improving the environment. Or that, at the expense of corporate profits, he is to hire "hard-core" unemployed instead of better-qualified available workmen to contribute to the social objective of reducing poverty.

In each of these cases, the corporate executive would be spending someone else's money for a general social interest. Insofar as his actions in accord with his "social responsibility" reduce returns to stockholders, he is spending their money. Insofar as his actions raise the price to customers, he is spending the customers' money. Insofar as his actions lower the wages of some employees, he is spending their money.

The stockholders or the customers or the employees could separately spend their own money on the particular action if they wished to do so. The executive is exercising a distinct "social responsibility," rather than serving as an agent of the stockholders or the customers or the employees, only if he spends the money in a different way than they would have spent it.

But if he does this, he is in effect imposing taxes, on the one hand, and deciding how the tax proceeds shall be spent, on the other.

This process raises political questions on two levels: principle and consequences. On the level of political principle, the imposition of taxes and the expenditure of tax proceeds are governmental functions. We have established elaborate constitutional, parliamentary and judicial provisions to control these functions, to assure that taxes are imposed so far as possible in accordance with the preferences and desires of the public—after all, "taxation without representation" was one of the battle cries of the American Revolution. We have a system of checks and balances to separate the legislative function of imposing taxes and enacting expenditures from the executive function of collecting taxes and administering expenditure programs and from the judicial function of mediating disputes and interpreting the law.

Here the businessman—self-selected or appointed directly or indirectly by stockholders—is to be simultaneously legislator, executive and jurist. He is to decide whom to tax by how much and for what purpose, and he is to spend the proceeds—all this guided only by general exhortations from on high to restrain inflation, improve the environment, fight poverty and so on and on.

The whole justification for permitting the corporate executive to be selected by the stockholders is that the executive is an agent serving the interests of his principal. This justification disappears when the corporate executive imposes taxes and spends the proceeds for "social" purposes. He becomes in effect a public employee, a civil servant, even though he remains in name an employee of a private enterprise. On grounds of political principle, it is

intolerable that such civil servants—insofar as their actions in the name of social responsibility are real and not just window-dressing—should be selected as they are now. If they are to be civil servants, then they must be selected through a political process. If they are to impose taxes and make expenditures to foster "social" objectives, then political machinery must be set up to guide the assessment of taxes and to determine through a political process the objectives to be served.

This is the basic reason why the doctrine of "social responsibility" involves the acceptance of the socialist view that political mechanisms, not market mechanisms, are the appropriate way to determine the allocation of scarce resources to alternative uses.

On the grounds of consequences, can the corporate executive in fact discharge his alleged "social responsibilities"? On the one hand, suppose he could get away with spending the stockholders' or customers' or employees' money. How is he to know how to spend it? He is told that he must contribute to fighting inflation. How is he to know what action of his will contribute to that end? He is presumably an expert in running his company—in producing a product or selling it or financing it. But nothing about his selection makes him an expert on inflation. Will his holding down the price of his product reduce inflationary pres- sure? Or, by leaving more spending power in the hands of his customers, simply divert it elsewhere? Or, by forcing him to produce less because of the lower price, will it simply contribute to shortages? Even if he could answer these questions, how much cost is he justified in imposing on his stockholders, customers and employees for this social purpose?

What is the appropriate share and what is the appropriate share of others?

And, whether he wants to or not, can he get away with spending his stockholders', customers' or employees' money? Will not the stockholders fire him? (Either the present ones or those who take over when his actions in the name of social responsibility have reduced the corporation's profits and the price of its stock.) His customers and his employees can desert him for other producers and employers less scrupulous in exercising their social responsibilities.

This facet of "social responsibility" doctrine is brought into sharp relief when the doctrine is used to justify wage restraint by trade unions. The conflict of interest is naked and clear when union officials are asked to subordinate the interest of their members to some more general social purpose. If the union officials try to enforce wage restraint, the consequence is likely to be wildcat strikes, rank-and-file revolts and the emergence of strong competitors for their jobs. We thus have the ironic phenomenon that union leaders—at least in the U.S.—have objected to Government interference with the market far more consistently and courageously than have business leaders.

The difficulty of exercising "social responsibility" illustrates, of course, the great virtue of private competitive enterprise—it forces people to be responsible for their own actions and makes it difficult for them to "exploit" other people for either selfish or unselfish purposes. They can do good—but only at their own expense.

Many a reader who has followed the argument this far may be tempted to remonstrate that it is all well and good to speak of government's having the responsibility to impose taxes and determine expenditures for such "social" purposes as controlling pollution or training the hard-core unemployed, but that the problems are too urgent to wait on the slow course of political processes, that the exercise of social responsibility by businessmen is a quicker and surer way to solve pressing current problems.

Aside from the question of fact—I share Adam Smith's skepticism about the benefits that can be expected from "those who affected to trade for the public good"—this argument must be rejected on grounds of principle. What it amounts to is an assertion that those who favor the taxes and expenditures in question have failed to persuade a majority of their fellow citizens to be of like mind and that they are seeking to attain by undemocratic procedures what they cannot attain by democratic procedures. In a free society, it is hard for "good" people to do "good," but that is a small price to pay for making it hard for "evil" people to do "evil," especially since one man's good is another's evil.

I have, for simplicity, concentrated on the special case of the corporate executive, except only for the brief digression on trade unions. But precisely the same argument applies to the newer phenomenon of calling upon stockholders to require corporations to exercise social responsibility (the recent G.M. crusade, for example). In most of these cases, what is in effect involved is some stockholders trying to get other stockholders (or cus- tomers or employees) to contribute against their will to "social" causes favored by the activists. Insofar as they succeed, they are again imposing taxes and spending the proceeds.

The situation of the individual proprietor is somewhat different. If he acts to reduce the returns of his enterprise in order to exercise his "social responsibility," he is spending his own money, not someone else's. If he wishes to spend his money on such purposes, that is his right, and I cannot see that there is any objection to his doing so. In the process, he, too, may impose costs on employees and customers. However, because he is far less likely than a large corporation or union to have monopolistic power, any such side effects will tend to be minor.

Of course, in practice the doctrine of social responsibility is frequently a cloak for actions that are justified on other grounds rather than a reason for those actions.

To illustrate, it may well be in the long-run interest of a corporation that is a major employer in a small community to devote resources to providing amenities to that community or to improving its government. That may make it easier to attract desirable employees, it may reduce the wage bill or lessen losses from pilferage and sabotage or have other worthwhile effects. Or it may be that, given the laws about the deductibility of corporate charitable contributions, the stockholders can contribute more to charities they favor by having the corporation make the gift than by doing it themselves, since they can in that way contribute an amount that would otherwise have been paid as corporate taxes.

In each of these—and many similar —cases, there is a strong temptation to rationalize these actions as an exercise of "social responsibility." In the present climate of opinion, with its widespread aversion to "capitalism," "profits," the "soulless corporation" and so on, this is one way for a corporation to generate goodwill as a by-product of expenditures

that are entirely justified in its own self-interest.

It would be inconsistent of me to call on corporate executives to refrain from this hypocritical window-dressing because it harms the foundations of a free society. That would be to call on them to exercise a "social responsibility"! If our institutions, and the attitudes of the public make it in their self-interest to cloak their actions in this way, I cannot summon much indignation to denounce them. At the same time, I can express admiration for those individual proprietors or owners of closely held corporations or stockholders of more broadly held corporations who disdain such tactics as approaching fraud.

Whether blameworthy or not, the use of the cloak of social responsibility, and the nonsense spoken in its name by influential and prestigious businessmen, does clearly harm the foundations of a free society. I have been impressed time and again by the schizophrenic character of many businessmen. They are capable of being extremely far-sighted and clear-headed in matters that are internal to their businesses. They are incredibly short-sighted and muddle-headed in matters that are outside their businesses but affect the possible survival of business in general. This short-sightedness is strikingly exemplified in the calls from many businessmen for wage and price guidelines or controls or incomes policies. There is nothing that could do more in a brief period to destroy a market system and replace it by a centrally controlled system than effective governmental control of prices and wages.

The short-sightedness is also exemplified in speeches by businessmen on social responsibility. This may gain them kudos in the short run. But it helps to strengthen the already too prevalent view that the pursuit of profits is wicked and immoral and must be curbed and controlled by external forces. Once this view is adopted, the external forces that curb the market will not be the social consciences, however highly developed, of the pontificating executives; it will be the iron fist of Government bureaucrats. Here, as with price and wage controls, businessmen seem to me to reveal a suicidal impulse.

The political principle that underlies the market mechanism is unanimity. In an ideal free market resting on private property, no individual can coerce any other, all cooperation is voluntary, all parties to such cooperation benefit or they need not participate. There are no "social" values, no "social" responsibilities in any sense other than the shared values and responsibilities of individuals. Society is a collection of individuals and of the various groups they voluntarily form.

The political principle that underlies the political mechanism is conformity. The individual must serve a more general social interest—whether that be determined by a church or a dictator or a majority. The individual may have a vote and a say in what is to be done, but if he is overruled, he must conform. It is appropriate for some to require others to contribute to a general social purpose whether they wish to or not.

Unfortunately, unanimity is not always feasible. There are some respects in which conformity appears unavoidable, so I do not see how one can avoid the use of the political mechanism altogether.

But the doctrine of "social responsibility" taken seriously would extend the scope of the political mechanism to every human activity. It does not differ in philosophy from the most explicitly collectivist doctrine. It differs only by professing to believe that collectivist ends can be attained without collectivist means. That is why, in my book "Capitalism and Freedom," I have called it a "fundamentally subversive doctrine" in a free society, and have said that in such a society, "there is one and only one social responsibility of business—to use its resources and engage in activities designed to increase its profits so long as it stays within the rules of the game, which is to say, engages in open and free competition without deception or fraud."

NO

Christopher D. Stone

CORPORATE ACCOUNTABILITY
IN LAW AND MORALS

During the past decade, along with a perceived growth in corporate power and the increased publicity given to corporate misconduct, there has been renewed interest in corporate social responsibility as an antidote. Indeed, to say that corporations should be socially responsible sounds at once so laudable and so limp that the notion has won broad support from both leaders within the corporate community and critics hammering from without. Corporate social responsibility is something we need, something whose "time has come"—but no one is being especially clear as to what it *is*. Exactly what are socially responsible corporations supposed to do, and why?

Certainly, in the space of these remarks, a complete and satisfactory set of answers is not forthcoming. But I hope to provide a few basic observations that are precise enough to steer the debate in a more productive direction. Specifically, I set out with an attempt to define the grounds under dispute: where do the proponents and opponents of corporate social responsibility agree, and where are they at odds?...

I. THE PROFITS POSITION VS. VOLUNTARISM

Some of the confusion in the corporate-social-responsibility literature begins with its choice of the term itself. To say that one is advocating "corporate social responsibility" is highly misleading, if it suggests that those who disagree favor corporations being irresponsible, in the sense of indifferent to the satisfaction of human wants. In truth, there probably exists, between the two camps—those who favor and those who oppose the talk about corporate social responsibility—some differences as to what each would regard as the ideal society. But I suspect that the differences between them are less significant than the common bonds. Both groups want to see a productive and sober use of society's resources. Neither wants to see people going around unfed, much less poisoned by toxic wastes. Hence, the basic dividing line is not

From Christopher D. Stone, "Corporate Accountability in Law and Morals," in Oliver F. Williams and John W. Houck, eds., *The Judeo-Christian Vision and the Modern Corporation* (University of Notre Dame Press, 1982). Copyright © 1982 by University of Notre Dame Press. Reprinted by permission. Some notes omitted.

over ends, but means. Those who demur to "corporate social responsibility" believe by and large, that corporations are most likely to satisfy human wants when they are seeking profits within the bounds of collectively agreed-upon constraints in the form of legal rules. By contrast, the "responsibility" advocates believe that the social welfare requires corporate managers to give some consideration to social-moral concerns that are not adequately captured in the profits-law signals.

In order not to "load" the issue in favor of the proponents, I will temporarily[1] drop the term "responsibility," and divide the contending camps into advocates of the *profits position,* and advocates of *voluntarism.* The issue can be put as follows: Is society generally better off if corporate managers decide among alternative courses of action on the basis of which choice promises to be most profitable? or should they, in certain defined circumstances, select a course that voluntarily subordinates profit maximization to the realization of some other value that is not the organization's? It is the first of these positions that I term the profits position; the second is what I shall call voluntarism....

One reason why the distinction between the profits position and voluntarism is not more clearly drawn in the literature is that it is so often unclearly drawn in practice. In many situations in which the corporate managers, scanning the unknowable future, decide a concrete case, several alternatives will hold equal promise of yielding the most profit (or providing the corporation whatever else it may be seeking to maximize). Of course, it would be easy to argue that at least in these cases, in which the managers face an array of alternatives equally

promising from the perspective of profits, they ought to select from the group that choice which ranks best from some moral perspective. However, I do not want to be diverted by this set of cases (although it may possibly turn out to be a large and significant group), because to get at the fundamental issue, we have to postulate situations in which the conflict between the profits position and voluntarism appears clear-cut.

Making the conflict clear-cut is not easy, however, even in an illustration. Part of the problem stems from the fact that what is "morally" the right thing to do—considering the things the voluntarist wants the manager to account for—often comes out the same as "good business" considered simply from the vantage of profits. Consider, for example, a company that is considering "pulling up stakes" from the community that has been dependent upon it for many years, without giving warning, in order to head off community countermeasures. Obviously, the decision can be seen to raise considerations not only of ethics, but of profits, inasmuch as the proposed action has an adverse effect on profits—through loss of goodwill, jeopardization of government contracts, increase in wage costs necessary to retain employees in a firm with a "bad name," and so on. However, there is a firm conceptual distinction that we have to keep in mind. If the company looks to the unfavorable public reaction *as evidence of strongly held moral values,* and decides against the action *on those grounds,* we would be justified in labeling its decision voluntarist. If, on the other hand, it considers the unfavorable publicity only through the lens of, and to the extent of, *the impact on corporate profits,* to be weighed in the balance with the moving vans and all the other costs of the move out of town, then the company's decision would be animated not by voluntarism, but by the profits position, as we are employing the term.

Let us proceed to examine the theoretical foundation for each view: first, for the profits position, then—by way of rejoinder—for the voluntarist.

II. THE CASE FOR THE PROFITS POSITION

Voluntarism has broad appeal. For no one—perhaps the new breed of business executives coming out of the management schools, in particular—likes to believe that there is nothing to their job beyond making money. In fact, however, the case for the managers to set their sights on profits, and therefore benefit the entire society, has considerably broader appeal than most of the corporate responsibility advocates—both in and out of business—generally acknowledge. In fact, the case for the profits position has in its favor three arguments, all with—and this has to be emphasized—strong moral appeal. Each of these arguments would seem to place the burden of rebuttal on the voluntarists.

(1) *The Market Argument.* First, the voluntarists have to account for the presumptive capacity of the market both to produce and to allocate resources in a way that is morally superior to alternative social arrangements. In general, businesses make profits, or fail, in proportion to how adequately the goods and services they provide benefit society. This is not a presumption that is rebutted by showing —what I assume to be obvious to everyone—that the pursuit of profits leads to "excesses" that most of us oppose. For the issue that divides the advocates of the

profits position from the voluntarists is one of selecting alternative *systems.* The profits defender may respond that, whatever the failings of profits-oriented managerialism, voluntarism, established as a general principle of managerial orientation, would engender more "evil"—less social product, and less equitable distributions of what is produced. The managers, the way this point is ordinarily put, are trained to manage businesses. They are neither social accountants, nor politically accountable.

(2) *The Law "Corrections."* But the profits position need not stand or fall upon the much-vaunted, and often exaggerated virtues of "the market system" per se. Even the most diehard "market" advocate recognizes the need for occasional political action to keep certain abuses in check. If, under prevailing market conditions, a certain course of corporate conduct that society collectively disapproves of turns out to be profitable, society can "correct" the market signals through law. Consider, for example, a firm that finds it profitable—under pure market conditions—to dump its toxic wastes into the handiest marsh. If this state of affairs is widely disapproved of, society can make the firm civilly liable for all the damages its wastes cause. The conduct having been made that much less profitable by the prospects of damage suits, the company is induced to respond by installing pollution-abatement devices, or by redesigning its production processes so that the wastes are recycled. If, even in the face of this level of "correction," the pollution continues in an amount society deems "still too much," a second and even third level of "corrections"—in the form of punitive damages and criminal fines—can be superimposed on the civil damages.[2]

The point is that there is a politically legitimate response to undesired corporate conduct which does not involve uprooting the managers from their orientation to profits. If the course of conduct that the market makes profitable is the "wrong" one, the law is available to make the course of conduct less profitable, in proportion to society's aversion to it. In this manner, the corporate managers do not have to weigh independently the costs and values of different courses of conduct. ("Is *this* much pollution, at *these* costs, more valuable than *this* level of pharmaceutical production, at *these* costs?") That weighing process is left to society, through the agreed-upon, democratic decision procedures.

(3) *The Promissory-Agency Argument.* Third, the voluntarists have to account for the managers' obligation to their shareholders as an independent basis for the profits position. Here, the argument is not that social welfare, as such, obligates the managers to pursue profits, but that their principal obligations are to the shareholders, who are presumed to prefer profits. This argument is ordinarily garbed in the language of "agency," which is something of a misstatement, since in some technical legal sense, the directors are not the pure "agents" of the shareholders.[3] And certainly there is no express promise to maximize profits running from the managers to the shareholders. Indeed, shareholders do not typically buy their shares directly from the corporation, through the managers, at all; most shareholders have purchased their shares from prior stockholders through impersonal market transactions in which nothing is said but "buy" and "sell."

Nonetheless, a colorable, if not quite so rigorous, argument can be made to the same effect, based on an implied promise in the circumstances, fortified by rightful expectancies and reliance. The "top" managers of the corporation, the directors, are elected by the shareholders. The shareholders have come, through tradition, to expect the managers to resolve ambiguities on their behalf. These expectancies have even found sanction in the rules of fiduciary duties, which recognize the priority of the investors' claims. And, in purchasing their shares, the investors have, in anticipation of the superiority of their claims, paid more for their shares than they would have otherwise. Thus, while a strong, literal agency-promise basis of obligation is missing, a case remains that the shareholders have a moral right to expect the managers to give their interests preference.

In summary of the profits position, the voluntarist has a hard row to hoe. He must be prepared to identify circumstances in which the corporation ought to subordinate profit maximization to the advancement of some exogenous value in the face of (1) the presumptive capacity of market signals to express collective desires, (2) the presumptive capacity of society to "correct" for any defects in these market signals by providing appropriate liability rules, and (3) the not unreasonable preference that the managers, at the least, resolve any lingering ambiguities in favor of the investors.

III. THE COUNTERARGUMENTS OF THE VOLUNTARISTS

In my view, none of the arguments is adequate to displace the need for the corporation to take into account values exogenous to the corporation's "self-interest." Let me take up the third argument—the promissory/agency argument—first.

Even if we were prepared to infer from the circumstances that the managers made a constructive "promise" to the shareholders to give priority to their claims, the inference would hardly settle the issue. As a moral matter (which is what we are discussing here), the practice of making promises provides for the justifiable breaking of them in certain circumstances. It is sometimes morally justifiable to break promises in the furtherance of higher social and moral interests. Hence, promises—or the assumption of an agency role—can advance moral arguments, by way of creating prima facie cases in favor of conduct, but few of us believe that a promise or agency, per se, can put an end to moral discussion. Moreover, promises always have to be interpreted; we have to decide what a promise *means*, before we even reach the question of whether to *follow it*. Thus, even if managers were to make—as I observed they do not—an express promise to their shareholders to "maximize your profits," I am not persuaded that the ordinary investor would interpret it to mean "maximize *in every way you can possibly get away with*, even if that means polluting the environment, breaking the law if you will not get caught," etc. Nor if there *were* a promise that could be interpreted as such a commitment, would I lightly suppose there to be a moral argument that it must be kept.

In the last analysis, the strength of the profits position turns not on the promissory-agency claims, but on a combination of the first two arguments. Indeed, the issue over which the profits supporter and the voluntarist divide is one of the most fundamental in any

society; the *ability* and *desirability* of law as a means of organizing human conduct. The profits position comes down to a strong—but I think overly strong—preference for law as the way to "correct," i.e., restrict the incidence of, profitable, but undesired behavior. The voluntarist wants to allow for, even to foster, alternative self-imposed constraints. It is largely because I, although a lawyer, harbor misgivings about our society's increasing reliance on law, that my own sympathies are divided.

Why might one harbor misgivings about law as a control device? First, as to the *abilities* of the law to transmit the desired signals to corporate managers, there are several serious drawbacks. There are, to begin with, the problems of what I call information gap and time lag. To illustrate, the first clues as to the existence of some corporate-connected hazards will often reach corporate managers before they reach, and can be acted upon by, the authoritative lawmaking bodies. For example, scientists in a company's laboratory are likely to suspect, and be able to evaluate, the dangers that some new product poses, long before governmental agencies get wind of them. In these circumstances, there would seem to be a strong case for the managers, at the least, to notify the appropriate agencies so as to set the lawmaking machinery in motion. Observe that such a moral obligation seems defensible whether or not the disclosure is the most profitable course for the managers to pursue, and even if the supplying of the data is not required by law. One can also imagine extending the argument to maintain not only that the managers should notify lawmakers, but that they should hold some particularly hazardous courses of action in abeyance until the legislative process has had a reasonable time to react. In other words, one might well take the basic presumption of the profits position—that anything profitable goes until the law says clearly "no" —and reverse it in some circumstances: one does not hazard some things (destruction of the ozone layer) unless and until the law clearly says "yes."

Moreover, it seems weak to argue that the corporation's obligations do not extend beyond *obeying* the law, when corporations are exerting so much influence on the laws that they are subject to. The voluntarist may be concerned to affect corporate behavior in the lawmaking process. The profits advocate is tempted to respond that the lawmaking context need present no exception to his general formula. After all, the participation of corporations in lawmaking can be made subject to its own laws—of lobbying, political contributions, and so on: let corporations maximize profits within *those laws*.

But this response has several defects. To begin with, it is somewhat circular, inasmuch as the political participation laws about corporate lobbying, and so on, are themselves subject to corporate influence. Moreover, even if the legislature were willing to enact tough restrictions on corporate political speech, it is not free to do so. Any legal constraints that touch on participation in the lawmaking process are themselves subject to superior constitutional restrictions, i.e., the First Amendment's guarantees of free speech, and the right to petition the government. As a consequence, even if we assume, for purposes of argument, that the law can provide a relatively acceptable response to abuses of commercial advertising for which First Amendment restrictions are less stringently applicable,[4] the law cannot—and ought not—be as restrictive when the corporation is engaged in political participation. When the corporation is acting as citizen, and not touting its products, we are committed to deal with it less through law, and more through trust. In this context, the case can be made that the managers are committed, reciprocally, to react in kind: to exercise self-restraint that is in some measure *voluntary*; to bring into the legislative and administrative process their own grievances about "overregulation," and their own expertise—surely; but in doing so, to temper pure profit seeking with some measure of civic responsibility.

A further inadequacy of law (hence, a further toehold for voluntarism) is apparent when we shift from a consideration of features of lawmaking (above), to features of corporations as targets of the law. There are special reasons to doubt the adequacy of law when corporations are its target. Most obviously, some of the sanctions that society deems appropriate penalties for truly heinous wrongdoing, such as imprisonment and the death penalty, are simply unavailable when the corporation is the law's quarry. Other skepticism stems from the fact that the incentives of "the corporation"—which the law typically threatens—are distinct both from those of the managers, on the one hand, and the shareholders, on the other. The salaries of the managers are likely to be relatively unscathed by fines and damage awards that fall on the corporation.

The defect in law reliance vis-à-vis the shareholders is a consequence of limited liability. Suppose, for example, a company engaged in making toxic substances. The law's sanctions—the civil- and criminal-liability rules aimed at the corporation—may pose a threat to the corporate coffers of, say, $100 million, if the company recklessly skimps on safety measures with the result that communities are endangered. But if the catastrophe happens, and the penalties are invoked, the losses will be so severe that the company will fail. In this event, the shareholders—those who stand behind the firm—are, by virtue of limited liability, immune from personal judgment. Hence, in many of the most threatening situations, the law's threats are hollow: no one will have to pick up the tab.

Thus there is considerable reason to doubt that the law can provide a complete and reliable set of rules for constraining corporate misconduct. Something more is needed.

Not only is the profit position insensitive to the limits of the law as an *effective* constraint on corporate misconduct, it makes questionable assumptions about the *desirability* of law as a control device. That is, even if (contrary to the assumptions above) the legislators were adequately informed and competent, the legislative process was unaffected by corporate influence, the rules of limited liability were not in question, and so on, there would be lingering reasons to search for some other control techniques.

It must be kept in mind that there are a number of techniques by which social behavior is constrained; the law is only one of them, sometimes reinforcing, sometimes supplementing, other, less authoritative social constraints. If we turn to ordinary human conduct, for example, we find it continuously being given direction and hedged by customs, manners, mores, and so on. All these "looser" controls derive their source of authority not from the threat of the state's force, but through the internalized dynamics associated with feelings of shame, guilt, anxiety about the censure of others. Indeed, when it comes to ordinary mortals, these dynamics shoulder the largest brunt of social control: we rely on people acting *responsibly*. We would certainly think it odd for anyone to suggest that people ought to do whatever their id impulses tell them to do, within the bounds of what the law specifically condemns. The burden would seem to be on the profits advocate to tell us why it should be otherwise with corporations.

This, I think, is the central burden that the profits advocates have failed even to acknowledge. And it is not an easy burden to meet....

It often appears, too, that the further the law goes in laying down precise "bright-line" standards of permissible and impermissible conduct, the more it may tempt people to press their behavior to the very bounds of what is allowed. Clear legal rules may induce more unwanted activity than no rules at all.[5] Indeed, we might say that the most serious "costs" of a law-ridden society involve the toll such reliance exacts from its citizens, measured in moral timbre. One thinks of the Confucians' objection to the codification of laws: "A litigious spirit awakes, invoking the letter of the law, and trusting that actions will not fall under its provisions.[6]

I cannot trace out how each of these infirmities may serve to shift some of our reliance on law to a reliance on morals and manners. But let me give an illustration to suggest some of the connections. Let us suppose that a majority of voters today would prefer that people do not smoke in public places. Yet, in recent referendums, the voters have consistently refused to ban smoking in public places by law. In my view, it would be a mistake to interpret these refusals to ban smoking as a vote in favor of letting anyone who wants to smoke do so whenever and wherever they want to. On the contrary, I suspect that what is being expressed is a preference *against law*, a decision to relegate the matter of smoking control to a complex social code of morals and manners. The minority who want to smoke are allowed to smoke so far as the law is concerned. But underneath, control is being relegated to a network of conventions. These include "mandates" that, before lighting up, the smoker look around to see if others are smoking; he is not to smoke if no one else is doing so; he is to make an inquiry of his neighbors to measure the intensity of feelings in the circumstances ("do you mind if I smoke?"); he is to adjust, flexibly, by finding a table as far away from nonsmokers as possible, or ideally situated, considering air circulation. Thus certain adjudicatory responsibilities fall, not on the judge, but on the maître d'.

In this context, more people may smoke, and more may be offended by smoke than otherwise. But notice the savings in enforcement costs and the quality of personal conduct and human interchange that are fostered. And might there not be some value in the fact that nonsmokers can feel that those who are resisting their impulses to smoke are doing so because they *care*, not because the law compels them?

In all events, if we look closely at the smoking example, and the pattern of control based on morals and manners, I think we will find that something is going on that is more complicated than what the term voluntarism suggests, i.e., something more than simply asking the smoker voluntarily to forgo his desire to smoke.

IV. RESPONSIBLE REFLECTION

I want now to argue that the flavor of this something extra *is* best captured by the term responsibility, which, while dropped earlier to avoid "loading" the issue, is therefore appropriate to reintroduce at this point. For when we begin to analyze what is going on, one can identify two separate, although related sets of techniques, both of which involve "responsibility" in different senses.

The first sense of responsibility—which I will call R_1—emphasizes following prescribed rules of conduct. It is in this sense that we judge someone "responsible" who follows the law, who abides by the rules—legal and moral —of his social office (as judge, prosecutor, or citizen). The second sense of responsibility—R_2—emphasizes cognitive process, reflection, how one goes about deciding, particularly when no special, clear-cut prescriptions of the R_1 sort are available. That the two senses of responsibility are separable is easy to demonstrate, inasmuch as the same act can, depending upon which sense one employs, be either "responsible" or "irresponsible." For example, a judge in Nazi Germany who carried out the orders of his superiors might be seen as "responsible" in sense R_1—in that he carried out the orders of his superiors, according to rules and the dictates of his office; and yet, we might say of him also that he was "irresponsible" in the sense—R_2—that he inadequately reflected as an autonomous, moral human being....

Let us take, as an example that illustrates the misgivings of the profits supporters, a product safety case. Suppose that the managers of an automobile company are considering a design that will entail 3.4 fatalities from impact on crash per 100 million vehicle miles traveled (the current industry average). If they alter the designs slightly, incorporating a stronger, heavier frame at a cost of $500 per car, the projected fatalities would be reduced by approximately 10 percent, to 3 per 100 million vehicle miles. What guidance can responsible reflection, as I have described it, provide in these circumstances?

To begin with, a moral rule that required the managers, in essence, to put themselves in the place of the consumers would hardly be calculated to yield an unambiguous decision. If, as we are assuming, the decision to add the extra safety costs will reduce profits, there is already some rather good evidence that if the managers were in the consumers' place they would reject the marginal increases in safety at the marginal costs of providing it. True, this probability of what the consumers want does not settle the matter. Thinking about one's responsibilities sometimes produces paternalistic action—that is, sometimes we feel that we are morally obligated to do something in the interest of someone else in disregard of their own preferences, such as a parent or the state sometimes exercises on the behalf of a child. The argument might take the form that if the consumers *really knew*, as vividly and in the detail that our test data indicates— e.g., how much more solidly the proposed design resists impact—they would decide in its favor.

But this is hardly a strong reed to lean on, particularly since we recognize that, in a decision like this, the consumers are not the only other group whose place the managers ought responsibly "to stand in." There are many people other than the consumers who are variously and often conflictingly affected by the decision to strengthen or not to strengthen the car.

For example, the increased weight of the car will reduce fuel efficiency. This will translate into an adverse impact not only on consumers; if the managers are to put themselves "in the place of" the society at large, they will have to think about the implications for increased dependency on oil, and for inflation. The new design would also contribute to inflation through increased demand for steel and labor, and consequent higher auto prices. Moreover, the additional coal and steel required to strengthen the cars will exact its toll in injuries among coal workers and steelworkers: how are the managers to feel if they put themselves in the places of these workers, balancing off the effect of increased wages, increased inflation, and increased injuries?

I think that this exercise is significant in reminding us that in many cases a "responsible" corporate decision, even one undertaken in the best of faith, is going to be indecisive, and the presumption for profits, when all is said and done, quite rightly remains. But the example is also, in its way, misleading. Much of what corporate responsibility advocates, such as myself, are seeking is not reducible to a binary decision such as whether to trade off $500 per car for 0.4 lives per 100 million miles traveled. What the responsibility advocates should be concentrating on is a *concern for safety*, and the willingness to design *an ongoing, internal corporate system* that advances safety concerns.

A corporation that consistently and fairly considers safety factors will undoubtedly come up with many possibilities of trade-offs that are, like the example employed above, in a range too ambiguous to overcome the profits presumption. But over time a company that sets up such a system may also discover the possibility of trade-offs that resist casuistry. For example, a company may come up with a lighter, safer, material that can save thousands of lives with virtually no increase in costs. To this, the profits defenders will respond that profit considerations alone will be enough to provide the incentives; "responsibility" is not required to institute such research since "safety sells." But such a response misses an important legal rub. Under present law, the very fact that a company undertakes to give thorough consideration to safety risks may operate to intensify corporate liability, should there be accidents, and encourage law suits seeking to exact criminal and punitive damages. Hence, it may not be *profitable* for a company to give full and responsible consideration to safety; but I would be prepared to argue that—profitable or no—a company should be obligated to press ahead in its safety research beyond the dictates of law-corrected market signals. This is particularly so when we consider that the company is the most efficient investigator of safety problems; it presumably can learn more about the problem and its solution, at less cost, than the rest of us.

Moreover, the auto-safety case we have just examined is not the only paradigm with which the responsibility advocate may be concerned. Many other cases seem to lie beyond the capacity of all but the most diehard profits defenders to complexify. In these situations, it is possible that "responsible" reflection will unearth several defensible decisions. But it is wrong to suppose that, once a multiplicity of defensible outcomes has been identified, we have no choice but to throw up our hands and revert to profits. Any one of the "responsible" outcomes

may be clearly preferable to the outcome dictated by profits.

NOTES

1. Later in the text I will restore the term "responsibility" to the debate, but only after I have demonstrated the important sense that responsibility captures, while terms like "voluntarism" and "altruism" do not.

2. I assume that most opponents of corporate social responsibility would agree that, once some form of conduct has been criminalized by the legislature, the managers ought not to engage in it, even if, though criminal, it remains profitable —either because conviction is unlikely, or because the profits to be made for lawbreaking exceed the penalties. David Engel has argued, however, that the presence of the criminal-liability rule ought not, in and of itself, preclude the corporation from performing the forbidden act, if doing so is profitable. He argues that there are only a few crimes so heinous as to be unacceptable under any circumstances; many fines are like business expenses. Where some form of criminal conduct is not absolutely clearly condemned by strong consensus in all cases, the managers would wrongly arrogate legislative power if they desist from a profitable course of lawbreaking. Suppose for example, a company that from some course of conduct will earn $12,000 and be fined $10,000; the $10,000 fine may represent a collective judgment that the social cost of the unlawful act is, say $2,000 (supposing that the legislature in setting the penalty of $10,000 assumed that the chances of getting caught were 1 in 5). Not to violate the law would be withholding goods or services the society values at $12,000 in exchange for avoiding a $2,000 cost, a course of conduct for which, Engel points out, there is no clear-cut consensus. Engel, "An Approach to Corporate Social Responsibility," *Stanford L. Rev.*, 32 (1979):1.

3. Most significantly, while a true principal is free to discharge his agent at will, the shareholders are subject to a complex body of constraints on recalling the directors from office, between terms of election, without "cause."

4. See *Virginia State Board of Pharmacy v. Virginia Citizens Consumer Council* 425 U.S. 748 (1976), holding that commercial advertising, while not as protected from interference as other forms of speech, is not wholly outside the protection of the First Amendment, either.

5. It is important to remember, however, that when the law gets involved in people's lives, especially where severe criminal penalties are involved, there are moral and constitutional reasons

to provide clear rules in the service of "fair warning" and the restricting of governmental abuse.

6. The quote is attributed to Shu Shiang, criticizing the codification of the criminal law on mental cauldrons on the view that "since all crimes cannot be prevented" their Confucian ancestors had "set up the barrier of righteousness (*i*)... [and] treated ... according to just usage (*li*)," quoted in J. Needham, *Science and Civilization in China*, 2 (Cambridge: Cambridge University Press, 1956), 521.

POSTSCRIPT

Are Profits the Only Business of Business?

Friedman dismisses the pleas of those who argue for socially responsible business action on the grounds that these individuals do not understand the role of the corporate executive in modern society. Friedman points out that the executives are responsible to the corporate owners, who expect these executives to do everything in their power to earn the owners a maximum return on their investment. If the corporate executives take a "socially responsible" action that reduces the return on the owners' investment, they have spent the owners' money. This, Friedman maintains, violates the very foundation of the American political-economic system: individual freedom. He believes that no individual should be deprived of his or her property without his or her permission. If the corporate executives wish to take socially responsible actions, they should use their own money; they should not prevent the owners from spending their money on whatever social actions they might wish to support.

In Stone's view, corporations have a responsibility to consider the welfare of society even when there are no explicit laws governing their action. Laws are simply ineffective in controlling corporate conduct that is profitable but harmful to society at large. Stone does not believe that the special relationship that exists between shareholders and managers obligates these managers to maximize profits "in every way you can possibly get away with."

Perhaps no single topic is more fundamental to microeconomics than is the issue of profits. Many pages have been written in defense of profits, such as Milton and Rose Friedman's *Free to Choose: A Personal Statement* (Harcourt Brace Jovanovich, 1980). Other works have also added much to this discussion. A classic reference is Frank H. Knight's *Risk, Uncertainty, and Profits* (Kelly Press, 1921). Friedrich A. Hayek, the author of many journal articles and books, is a guru for many current free marketers. There are a number of other books and articles, however, that are highly critical of the Friedman-Knight-Hayek position, including Christopher D. Stone's *Where the Law Ends: Social Control of Corporate Behavior* (Harper & Row, 1975). Others who challenge the legitimacy of the notion that markets are morally free zones include Thomas Mulligan, "A Critique of Milton Friedman's Essay 'The Social Responsibility of Business Is to Increase Its Profits,'" *Journal of Business Ethics* (1986); Daniel M. Hausman, "Are Markets Morally Free Zones?" *Philosophy and Public Affairs* (Fall 1989); and Andrew Henley, "Economic Orthodoxy and the Free Market System: A Christian Critique," *International Journal of Social Economics* (vol. 14, no. 10, 1987).

ISSUE 2

Should We Encourage the Private Ownership of Guns?

YES: Daniel D. Polsby, from "The False Promise of Gun Control," *The Atlantic Monthly* (March 1994)

NO: Arthur L. Kellermann et al., from "Gun Ownership as a Risk Factor for Homicide in the Home," *The New England Journal of Medicine* (October 7, 1993)

ISSUE SUMMARY

YES: Law professor Daniel D. Polsby alleges that guns do not increase crime rates or violence in the streets but that the "proliferation of gun-control laws almost certainly does."

NO: The research of emergency room physician Arthur L. Kellermann and his colleagues suggests that gun ownership increases an individual's risk of being murdered rather than providing that person with self-protection.

In 1992 crimes committed with handguns increased by almost 50 percent over the previous five-year annual average. In that year, handguns were used in 931,000 violent crimes. It may be because of statistics such as these that the Brady Bill—federal legislation requiring a five-day waiting period and a background check for individuals wishing to purchase guns—was passed by Congress in November 1993 after numerous attempts to pass gun-control legislation were defeated by the powerful pro-gun lobby during the previous seven years.

The pro-gun interests in the United States are well articulated by the National Rifle Association (NRA) and its members. This organization boasts a membership in excess of 3.3 million, and it claimed liquid assets of more than $90 million in 1990. Throughout its existence, the NRA has effectively blocked nearly every attempt at governmental control over private ownership of guns. Traditionally, the NRA and others have defended their position on the grounds that legislation in this area would violate the "right to bear arms," which they allege is protected by the Second Amendment to the Constitution.

However, in recent years public opinion has increasingly turned against the gun lobby. Also, society has begun to question whether or not the Second Amendment is applicable to private gun ownership. The amendment in full states: "A well regulated Militia, being necessary to the security of a free

State, the right of people to keep and bear Arms, shall not be infringed."
Many argue that the NRA's constitutional argument is rendered invalid by
the reference to a "well regulated Militia." Most legal scholars maintain that
the Supreme Court's 1939 decision in *United States v. Miller* still stands as the
appropriate interpretation of the Second Amendment. Here the Court ruled
that the intent of the amendment was to ensure a collective right having "some
reasonable relationship to the preservation or efficiency of a well-regulated
militia." The Court did not rule that individuals have a right to keep and bear
arms. Indeed, lower courts have turned to the *Miller* decision to *uphold, not
strike down* gun-control legislation.

The most recent Supreme Court ruling in this area came in 1980, when the
Court reaffirmed that attempts to control the use of guns through legislative
action "do not trench upon any constitutionally protected liberties." It is
noteworthy that both Warren E. Burger, the chief justice at that time, and
the current chief justice William H. Rehnquist, both conservatives, joined the
majority of the Court in this interpretation.

If there is no constitutional prohibition against gun control, what are the
costs and benefits of private ownership of handguns? The NRA has long
argued that handguns are necessary for self-protection. The NRA's new advertising slogan, "Refuse to Be a Victim," is directed toward getting that
message across to women, who as a group have traditionally been more opposed to gun ownership than men. The arguments of those opposed to gun
control goes far beyond this, however. This becomes clear in the essay by
Daniel D. Polsby, which follows. Polsby raises fundamental economic questions about the demand for guns, the sources of the supply of guns, and the
elastic characteristics of both supply and demand.

In large measure, the purpose of Polsby's selection is to respond to the
medical community, which has challenged the NRA's contention that guns are
an important means of self-protection. In this regard, Arthur L. Kellermann
and his associates argue that guns are more likely to result in injury to a
member of a gun-owning household than they are to protect the household
from intruders.

YES

Daniel D. Polsby

THE FALSE PROMISE OF GUN CONTROL

During the 1960s and 1970s the robbery rate in the United States increased sixfold, and the murder rate doubled; the rate of handgun ownership nearly doubled in that period as well. Handguns and criminal violence grew together apace, and national opinion leaders did not fail to remark on the coincidence.

It has become a bipartisan article of faith that more handguns cause more violence. Such was the unequivocal conclusion of the National Commission on the Causes and Prevention of Violence in 1969, and such is now the editorial opinion of virtually every influential newspaper and magazine, from *The Washington Post* to *The Economist* to the *Chicago Tribune*. Members of the House and Senate who have not dared to confront the gun lobby concede the connection privately. Even if the National Rifle Association [NRA] can produce blizzards of angry calls and letters to the Capitol virtually overnight, House members one by one have been going public, often after some new firearms atrocity at a fast-food restaurant or the like. And last November they passed the Brady bill.

Alas, however well accepted, the conventional wisdom about guns and violence is mistaken. Guns don't increase national rates of crime and violence —but the continued proliferation of gun-control laws almost certainly does. Current rates of crime and violence are a bit below the peaks of the late 1970s, but because of a slight oncoming bulge in the at-risk population of males aged fifteen to thirty-four, the crime rate will soon worsen. The rising generation of criminals will have no more difficulty than their elders did in obtaining the tools of their trade. Growing violence will lead to calls for laws still more severe. Each fresh round of legislation will be followed by renewed frustration.

Gun-control laws don't work. What is worse, they act perversely. While legitimate users of firearms encounter intense regulation, scrutiny, and bureaucratic control, illicit markets easily adapt to whatever difficulties a free society throws in their way. Also, efforts to curtail the supply of firearms inflict collateral damage on freedom and privacy interests that have long been considered central to American public life. Thanks to the seemingly never-ending war on drugs and long experience attempting to suppress prostitution and pornography, we know a great deal about how illicit markets function and how costly to the public attempts to control them can be. It is essential that we make use of this experience in coming to grips with gun control.

The thousands of gun-control laws in the United States are of two general types. The older kind sought to regulate how, where, and by whom firearms could be carried. More recent laws have sought to make it more costly to buy, sell, or use firearms (or certain classes of firearms, such as assault rifles, Saturday-night specials, and so on) by imposing fees, special taxes, or surtaxes on them. The Brady bill is of both types: it has a background-check provision, and its five-day waiting period amounts to a "time tax" on acquiring handguns. All such laws can be called scarcity-inducing, because they seek to raise the cost of buying firearms, as figured in terms of money, time, nuisance, or stigmatization.

Despite the mounting number of scarcity-inducing laws, no one is very satisfied with them. Hobbyists want to get rid of them, and gun-control proponents don't think they go nearly far enough. Everyone seems to agree that gun-control laws have some effect on the distribution of firearms. But it has not been the dramatic and measurable effect their proponents desired.

Opponents of gun control have traditionally wrapped their arguments in the Second Amendment to the Constitution. Indeed, most modern scholarship affirms that so far as the drafters of the Bill of Rights were concerned the right to bear arms was to be enjoyed by everyone, not just a militia, and that one of the principal justifications for an armed populace was to secure the tranquillity and good order of the community. But most people are not dedicated antiquitarians, and would not be impressed by the argument "I admit that my behavior is very dangerous to public safety, but the Second Amendment says I have a right to do it anyway." That would be a case for repealing the Second Amendment, not respecting it.

FIGHTING THE DEMAND CURVE

Everyone knows that possessing a handgun makes it easier to intimidate, wound, or kill someone. But the implication of this point for social policy has not been so well understood. It is easy to count the bodies of those who have been killed or wounded with guns, but not easy to count the people who have avoided harm because they had access to weapons. Think about uniformed police officers, who carry handguns in plain view not in order to kill people but simply to daunt potential attackers. And it works. Criminals generally do not single out police officers for opportunistic attack. Though officers can expect to draw their guns from time to time, few even in big-city departments will actually fire a shot (except in target practice) in the course of a year. This observation points to an important truth: people who are armed make comparatively unattractive victims. A criminal might not know if any one civilian is armed, but if it becomes known that a large number of civilians do carry weapons, criminals will become warier.

Which weapons laws are the right kinds can be decided only after considering two related questions. First, what is the connection between civilian possession of firearms and social violence? Second, how can we expect gun-control laws to alter people's behavior? Most recent scholarship raises serious questions about the "weapons increase violence" hypothesis. The second question is emphasized here, because it is routinely overlooked and often mocked when noticed; yet it is crucial. Rational gun control requires understanding not only the relationship between weapons and violence but also the relationship between laws and people's behavior. Some things are very hard to accomplish with laws. The purpose of a law and its likely effects are not always the same thing. Many statutes are notorious for the way in which their unintended effects have swamped their intended ones.

In order to predict who will comply with gun-control laws, we should remember that guns are economic goods that are traded in markets. Consumers' interest in them varies. For religious, moral, aesthetic, or practical reasons, some people would refuse to buy firearms at any price. Other people willingly pay very high prices for them.

Handguns, so often the subject of gun-control laws, are desirable for one purpose—to allow a person tactically to dominate a hostile transaction with another person. The value of a weapon to a given person is a function of two factors: how much he or she wants to dominate a confrontation if one occurs, and how likely it is that he or she will actually be in a situation calling for a gun.

Dominating a transaction simply means getting what one wants without being hurt. Where people differ is in how likely it is that they will be involved in a situation in which a gun will be valuable. Someone who *intends* to engage in a transaction involving a gun—a criminal, for example—is obviously in the best possible position to predict that likelihood. Criminals should therefore be will-ing to pay more for a weapon than most other people would. Professors, politicians, and newspaper editors are, as a group, at very low risk of being involved in such transactions, and they thus systematically underrate the value of defensive handguns. (Correlative, perhaps, is their uncritical readiness to accept studies that debunk the utility of firearms for self-defense.) The class of people we wish to deprive of guns, then, is the very class with the most inelastic demand for them —criminals—whereas the people most likely to comply with gun-control laws don't value guns in the first place.

DO GUNS DRIVE UP CRIME RATES?

Which premise is true—that guns increase crime or that the fear of crime causes people to obtain guns? Most of the country's major newspapers apparently take this problem to have been solved by an article published by Arthur Kellermann and several associates in the October 7, 1993, *New England Journal of Medicine.* Kellermann is an emergency-room physician who has published a number of influential papers that he believes discredit the thesis that private ownership of firearms is a useful means of self-protection. (An indication of his wide influence is that within two months the study received almost 100 mentions in publications and broadcast transcripts indexed in the Nexis data base.) For this study Kellermann and his associates identified fifteen behavioral and fifteen environmental variables that applied to a 388-member set of homicide victims, found a "matching" control group of 388 nonhomicide victims, and then ascertained how the two groups differed in gun ownership. In interviews Kellermann made clear his belief that owning a handgun markedly increases a person's risk of being murdered.

But the study does not prove that point at all. Indeed, as Kellermann explicitly conceded in the text of the article, the causal arrow may very well point in the other direction: the threat of being killed may make people more likely to arm themselves. Many people at risk of being killed, especially people involved in the drug trade or other illegal ventures, might well rationally buy a gun as a precaution, and be willing to pay a price driven up by gun-control laws. Crime, after all, is a dangerous business. Peter Reuter and Mark Kleiman, drug-policy researchers, calculated in 1987 that the average crack dealer's risk of being killed was far greater than his risk of being sent to prison. (Their data cannot, however, support the implication that ownership of a firearm causes or exacerbates the risk of being killed.)

Defending the validity of his work, Kellermann has emphasized that the link between lung cancer and smoking was initially established by studies methodologically no different from his. Gary Kleck, a criminology professor at Florida State University, has pointed out the flaw in this comparison. No one ever thought that lung cancer causes smoking, so when the association between the two was established the direction of the causal arrow was not in doubt. Kleck wrote that it is as though Kellermann, trying to discover how diabetics differ from other people, found that they are much more likely to possess insulin than nondiabetics, and concluded that insulin is a risk factor for diabetes.

The New York Times, the Los Angeles Times, The Washington Post, The Boston Globe, and the Chicago Tribune all gave prominent coverage to Kellermann's study as soon as it appeared, but none saw fit to discuss the study's limitations. A few, in order to introduce a hint of balance, mentioned that the NRA, or some member of its staff, disagreed with the study. But readers had no way of knowing that Kellermann himself had registered a disclaimer in his text. "It is possible," he conceded. "that reverse causation accounted for some of the association we observed between gun ownership and homicide." Indeed, the point is stronger than that: "reverse causation" may account for most of the association between gun ownership and homicide. Kellermann's data simply do not allow one to draw any conclusion.

If firearms increased violence and crime, then rates of spousal homicide would have skyrocketed, because the stock of privately owned handguns has increased rapidly since the mid-1960s. But according to an authoritative study of spousal homicide in the American Journal of Public Health, by James Mercy and Linda Saltzman, rates of spousal homicide in the years 1976 to 1985 fell. If firearms increased violence and crime, the crime rate should have increased throughout the 1980s, while the national stock of privately owned handguns increased by more than a million units in every year of the decade. It did not. Nor should the rates of violence and crime in Switzerland, New Zealand, and Israel be as low as they are, since the number of firearms per civilian household is comparable to that in the United States. Conversely, gun-controlled Mexico and South Africa should be islands of peace instead of having murder rates more than twice as high as those [in the United States]. The determinants of crime and law-abidingness are, of course, complex matters, which are not fully understood and certainly not explicable in terms of a country's laws. But gun-control enthusiasts, who have made capital out of the low murder rate in England, which is largely disarmed, simply ignore the counterexamples that don't fit their theory.

If firearms increased violence and crime, Florida's murder rate should not have been falling since the introduction, seven years ago, of a law that makes it easier for ordinary citizens to get permits to carry concealed handguns. Yet the murder rate has remained the same or fallen every year since the law was enacted, and it is now lower than the national murder rate (which has been rising). As of last November 183,561 permits had been issued, and only seventeen of the permits had been revoked because the holder was involved in a firearms offense. It would be precipitate to claim that the new law has "caused" the murder rate to subside. Yet here is a situation that doesn't fit the hypothesis that weapons increase violence.

If firearms increased violence and crime, programs of induced scarcity would suppress violence and crime. But —another anomaly—they don't. Why not? A theorem, which we could call the futility theorem, explains why gun-control laws must either be ineffectual or in the long term actually provoke more violence and crime. Any theorem depends on both observable fact and assumption. An assumption that can be made with confidence is that the higher the number of victims a criminal assumes to be armed, the higher will be the risk—the price—of assaulting them. By definition, gun-control laws should make weapons scarcer and thus more expensive. By our prior reasoning about

demand among various types of consumers, after the laws are enacted criminals should be better armed, compared with noncriminals, than they were before. Of course, plenty of noncriminals will remain armed. But even if many noncriminals will pay as high a price as criminals will to obtain firearms, a larger number will not.

Criminals will thus still take the same gamble they already take in assaulting a victim who might or might not be armed. But they may appreciate that the laws have given them a freer field, and that crime still pays—pays even better, in fact, than before. What will happen to the rate of violence? Only a relatively few gun-mediated transactions —currently, five percent of armed robberies committed with firearms—result in someone's actually being shot (the statistics are not broken down into encounters between armed assailants and unarmed victims, and encounters in which both parties are armed). It seems reasonable to fear that if the number of such transactions were to increase because criminals thought they faced fewer deterrents, there would be a corresponding increase in shootings. Conversely, if gun-mediated transactions declined—if criminals initiated fewer of them because they feared encountering an armed victim or an armed good Samaritan—the number of shootings would go down. The magnitude of these effects is, admittedly, uncertain. Yet it is hard to doubt the general tendency of a change in the law that imposes legal burdens on buying guns. The futility theorem suggests that gun-control laws, if effective at all, would unfavorably affect the rate of violent crime.

The futility theorem provides a lens through which to see much of the debate. It is undeniable that gun-control laws work—to an extent. Consider, for example, California's background-check law, which in the past two years has prevented about 12,000 people with a criminal record or a history of mental illness or drug abuse from buying handguns. In the same period Illinois's background-check law prevented the delivery of firearms to more than 2,000 people. Surely some of these people simply turned to an illegal market, but just as surely not all of them did. The laws of large numbers allow us to say that among the foiled thousands, some potential killers were prevented from getting a gun. We do not know whether the number is large or small, but it is implausible to think it is zero. And, as gun-control proponents are inclined to say, "If only one life is saved . . ."

The hypothesis that firearms increase violence does predict that if we can slow down the diffusion of guns, there will be less violence; one life, or more, *will* be saved. But the futility theorem asks that we look not simply at the gross number of bad actors prevented from getting guns but at the effect the law has on *all* the people who want to buy a gun. Suppose we succeed in piling tax burdens on the acquisition of firearms. We can safely assume that a number of people who might use guns to kill will be sufficiently discouraged not to buy them. But we cannot assume this about people who feel that they must have guns in order to survive financially and physically. A few lives might indeed be saved. But the overall rate of violent crime might not go down at all. And if guns are owned predominantly by people who have good reason to think they will use them, the rate might even go up.

Are there empirical studies that can serve to help us choose between the futility theorem and the hypothesis that guns increase violence? Unfortunately, no: the best studies of the effects of gun-control laws are quite inconclusive. Our statistical tools are too weak to allow us to identify an effect clearly enough to persuade an open-minded skeptic. But it is precisely when we are dealing with undetectable statistical effects that we have to be certain we are using the best models available of human behavior. . . .

ADMINISTERING PROHIBITION

Assume for the sake of argument that to a reasonable degree of criminological certainty, guns are every bit the public-health hazard they are said to be. It follows, and many journalists and a few public officials have already said, that we ought to treat guns the same way we do smallpox viruses or other critical vectors of morbidity and mortality—namely, isolate them from potential hosts and destroy them as speedily as possible. Clearly, firearms have at least one characteristic that distinguishes them from smallpox viruses: nobody wants to keep smallpox viruses in the nightstand drawer. Amazingly enough, gun-control literature seems never to have explored the problem of getting weapons away from people who very much want to keep them in the nightstand drawer.

Our existing gun-control laws are not uniformly permissive, and, indeed, in certain places are tough even by international standards. Advocacy groups seldom stress the considerable differences among American jurisdictions, and media reports regularly assert that firearms are readily available to anybody anywhere in the country. This is not the case. For example, handgun restrictions in Chicago and the District of Columbia are much less flexible than the ones in the United Kingdom. Several hundred thousand British subjects may legally buy and possess sidearms, and anyone who joins a target-shooting club is eligible to do so. But in Chicago and the District of Columbia, excepting peace officers and the like, only grandfathered registrants may legally possess handguns. Of course, tens or hundreds of thousands of people in both those cities—nobody can be sure how many—do in fact possess them illegally.

Although there is, undoubtedly, illegal handgun ownership in the United Kingdom, especially in Northern Ireland (where considerations of personal security and public safety are decidedly unlike those elsewhere in the British Isles), it is probable that Americans and Britons differ in their disposition to obey gun-control laws: there is reputed to be a marked national disparity in compliance behavior. This difference, if it exists, may have something to do with the comparatively marginal value of firearms to British consumers. Even before it had strict firearms regulation, Britain had very low rates of crimes involving guns; British criminals, unlike their American counterparts, prefer burglary (a crime of stealth) to robbery (a crime of intimidation).

Unless people are prepared to surrender their guns voluntarily, how can the U.S. government confiscate an appreciable fraction of our country's nearly 200 million privately owned firearms? We know that it is possible to set up weapons-free zones in certain locations —commercial airports and many courthouses and, lately, some troubled big-city high schools and housing projects. The sacrifices of privacy and convenience, and the costs of paying guards, have been thought worth the (perceived) gain in security. No doubt it would be possible, though it would probably not be easy, to make weapons-free zones of shopping centers, department stores, movie theaters, ball parks. But it is not obvious how one would cordon off the whole of an open society.

Voluntary programs have been ineffectual. From time to time community-action groups or police departments have sponsored "turn in your gun" days, which are nearly always disappointing. Sometimes the government offers to buy guns at some price. This approach has been endorsed by Senator Chafee and the *Los Angeles Times*. Jonathan Alter, of *Newsweek*, has suggested a variation on this theme: youngsters could exchange their guns for a handshake with Michael Jordan or some other sports hero. If the price offered exceeds that at which a gun can be bought on the street, one can expect to see plans of this kind yield some sort of harvest—as indeed they have. But it is implausible that these schemes will actually result in a less-dangerous population. Government programs to buy up surplus cheese cause more cheese to be produced without affecting the availability of cheese to people who want to buy it. So it is with guns....

The solution to the problem of crime lies in improving the chances of young men. Easier said than done, to be sure. No one has yet proposed a convincing program for checking all the dislocating forces that government assistance can set in motion. One relatively straightforward change would be reform of the educational system. Nothing guarantees prudent behavior like a sense of the future, and with average skills in reading, writing, and math, young people can realistically look forward to constructive employment and the straight life that steady work makes possible.

But firearms are nowhere near the root of the problem of violence. As long as people come in unlike sizes, shapes, ages, and temperaments, as long as they diverge in their taste for risk and their willingness and capacity to prey on other people or to defend themselves from predation, and above all as long as some people have little or nothing to lose by spending their lives in crime, dispositions to violence will persist.

This is what makes the case for the right to bear arms, not the Second Amendment. It is foolish to let anything ride on hopes for effective gun control. As long as crime pays as well as it does, we will have plenty of it, and honest folk must choose between being victims and defending themselves.

NO

Arthur L. Kellermann et al.

GUN OWNERSHIP AS A RISK FACTOR FOR HOMICIDE IN THE HOME

Homicide claims the lives of approximately 24,000 Americans each year, making it the 11th leading cause of death among all age groups, the 2nd leading cause of death among all people 15 to 24 years old, and the leading cause of death among male African Americans 15 to 34 years old. Homicide rates declined in the United States during the early 1980s but rebounded thereafter. One category of homicide that is particularly threatening to our sense of safety is homicide in the home.

Unfortunately, the influence of individual and household characteristics on the risk of homicide in the home is poorly understood. Illicit-drug use, alcoholism, and domestic violence are widely believed to increase the risk of homicide, but the relative importance of these factors is unknown. Frequently cited options to improve home security include the installation of electronic security systems, burglar bars, and reinforced security doors. The effectiveness of these protective measures is unclear, however.

Many people also keep firearms (particularly handguns) in the home for personal protection. One recent survey determined that handgun owners are twice as likely as owners of long guns to report "protection from crime" as their single most important reason for keeping a gun in the home. It is possible, however, that the risks of keeping a firearm in the home may outweigh the potential benefits.

To clarify these issues, we conducted a population-based case–control study to determine the strength of the association between a variety of potential risk factors and the incidence of homicide in the home....

RESULTS

Study Population
There were 1860 homicides in the three counties [from which samples were taken] during the study period. Four hundred forty-four (23.9 percent) took place in the home of the victim. After we excluded the younger victim in

19 double deaths, 2 homicides that were not reported to project staff, and 3 late changes to a death certificate, 420 cases (94.6 percent) were available for study.

Reports on the Scene

Most of the homicides occurred inside the victim's home. Eleven percent occurred outside the home but within the immediate property lines. Two hundred sixty-five victims (63.1 percent) were men; 36.9 percent were women. A majority of the homicides (50.9 percent) occurred in the context of a quarrel or a romantic triangle. An additional 4.5 percent of the victims were killed by a family member or an intimate acquaintance as part of a murder–suicide. Thirty-two homicides (7.6 percent) were related to drug dealing, and 92 homicides (21.9 percent) occurred during the commission of another felony, such as a robbery, rape, or burglary. No motive other than homicide could be established in 56 cases (13.3 percent).

The great majority of the victims (76.7 percent) were killed by a relative or someone known to them. Homicides by a stranger accounted for only 15 cases (3.6 percent). The identity of the offender could not be established in 73 cases (17.4 percent). The remaining cases involved other offenders or police acting in the line of duty.

Two hundred nine victims (49.8 percent) died from gunshot wounds. A knife or some other sharp instrument was used to kill 111 victims (26.4 percent). The remaining victims were either bludgeoned (11.7 percent), strangled (6.4 percent), or killed by other means (5.7 percent).

Evidence of forced entry was noted in 59 cases (14.0 percent). Eighteen of these involved an unidentified intruder; six involved strangers. Two involved the police. The rest involved a spouse, family member, or some other person known to the victim.

Attempted resistance was reported in 184 cases (43.8 percent). In 21 of these (5.0 percent) the victim unsuccessfully attempted to use a gun in self-defense. In 56.2 percent of the cases no specific signs of resistance were noted. Fifteen victims (3.6 percent) were killed under legally excusable circumstances. Four were shot by police acting in the line of duty. The rest were killed by another member of the household or a private citizen acting in self-defense.

Comparability of Case Subjects and Controls

… Interviews with a matching control* were obtained for 99.7 percent of the case interviews, yielding 388 matched pairs. Three hundred fifty-seven pairs were matched for all three variables, 27 for two variables, and 4 for a single variable (sex). The demographic characteristics of the victims and controls were similar, except that the case subjects were more likely to have rented their homes (70.4 percent vs. 47.3 percent) and to have lived alone (26.8 percent vs. 11.9 percent)….

Univariate Analysis

Alcohol was more commonly consumed by one or more members of the households of case subjects than by members of the households of controls. Alcohol was also more commonly consumed by the case subjects themselves than by their matched controls. Case subjects were reported to have manifested behavioral correlates of alcoholism (such as trouble at work due to drinking) much more

*[Controls were matched with the case subjects according to sex, race, age, and neighborhood of residence.—Eds.]

often than matched controls. Illicit-drug use (by the case subject or another household member) was also reported more commonly by case households than control households.

Previous episodes of violence were reported more frequently by members of case households. When asked if anyone in the household had ever been hit or hurt in a fight in the home, 31.8 percent of the proxies [who were interviewed as representatives of] the case subjects answered affirmatively, as compared with only 5.7 percent of controls. Physical fights in the home while household members were drinking and fighting severe enough to cause injuries were reported much more commonly by case proxies than controls. One or more members of the case households were also more likely to have been arrested or to have been involved in a physical fight outside the home than members of control households.

Similar percentages of case and control households reported using deadbolt locks, window bars, or metal security doors. The case subjects were slightly less likely than the controls to have lived in a home with a burglar alarm, but they were slightly more likely to have controlled security access. Almost identical percentages of case and control households reported owning a dog.

One or more guns were reportedly kept in 45.4 percent of the homes of the case subjects, as compared with 35.8 percent of the homes of the control subjects.... Shotguns and rifles were kept by similar percentages of households, but the case households were significantly more likely to have a handgun.... Case households were also more likely than control households to contain a gun that was kept loaded or unlocked.

Multivariate Analysis

Six variables were retained in our final conditional logistic-regression model: home rented, case subject or control lived alone, any household member ever hit or hurt in a fight in the home, any household member ever arrested, any household member used illicit drugs, and one or more guns kept in the home. Each of these variables was strongly and independently associated with an increased risk of homicide in the home. No home-security measures retained significance in the final model. After matching for four characteristics and controlling for the effects of five more, we found that the presence of one or more firearms in the home was strongly associated with an increased risk of homicide in the home....

Stratified analyses with our final regression model revealed that the link between guns and homicide in the home was present among women as well as men, blacks as well as whites, and younger as well as older people. Restricting the analysis to pairs with data from case proxies who lived in the home of the victim demonstrated an even stronger association than that noted for the group overall. Gun ownership was most strongly associated with homicide at the hands of a family member or intimate acquaintance.... Guns were not significantly linked to an increased risk of homicide by acquaintances, unidentified intruders, or strangers. We found no evidence of a protective benefit from gun ownership in any subgroup, including one restricted to cases of homicide that followed forced entry into the home and another restricted to cases in which resistance was attempted. Not surprisingly, the link between gun ownership and homicide was due entirely to a strong association between gun ownership and homicide by firearms. Homicide by other means was not significantly linked to the presence or absence of a gun in the home.

Living in a household where someone had previously been hit or hurt in a fight in the home was also strongly and independently associated with homicide, even after we controlled for the effects of gun ownership and the other four variables in our final model.... Previous family violence was linked to an increased risk of homicide among men as well as women, blacks as well as whites, and younger as well as older people. Virtually all of this increased risk was due to a marked association between prior domestic violence and homicide at the hands of a family member or intimate acquaintance....

DISCUSSION

Although firearms are often kept in homes for personal protection, this study shows that the practice is counterproductive. Our data indicate that keeping a gun in the home is independently associated with an increase in the risk of homicide in the home. The use of illicit drugs and a history of physical fights in the home are also important risk factors. Efforts to increase home security have largely focused on preventing unwanted entry, but the greatest threat to the lives of household members appears to come from within.

We restricted our study to homicides that occurred in the home of the victim, because these events can be most plausibly linked to specific individual and household characteristics. If, for example, the ready availability of a gun increases the risk of homicide, this effect should be most noticeable in the immediate environment where the gun is kept.

Although our case definition excluded the rare instances in which a nonresident intruder was killed by a homeowner, our methodology was capable of demonstrating significant protective effects of gun ownership as readily as any evidence of increased risk....

Four limitations warrant comment. First, our study was restricted to homicides occurring in the home of the victim. The dynamics of homicides occurring in other locations (such as bars, retail establishments, or the street) may be quite different. Second, our research was conducted in three urban counties that lack a substantial percentage of Hispanic citizens. Our results may therefore not be generalizable to more rural communities or to Hispanic households. Third, it is possible that reverse causation accounted for some of the association we observed between gun ownership and homicide—i.e., in a limited numbers of cases, people may have acquired a gun in response to a specific threat. If the source of that threat subsequently caused the homicide, the link between guns in the home and homicide may be due at least in part to the failure of these weapons to provide adequate protection from the assailants. Finally, we cannot exclude the possibility that the association we observed is due to a third, unidentified factor. If, for example, people who keep guns in their homes are more psychologically prone to violence than people who do not, this could explain the link between gun ownership and homicide in the home. Although we examined several behavioral markers of violence and aggression and included two in our final logistic-regression model, "psychological confounding" of this sort is difficult to control for. "Psychological autopsies" have been used to control for psychological differences between adolescent victims of suicide and inpatient controls with psychiatric disorders, but we did not believe this approach was practical for a study of homicide victims and neighborhood controls. At any rate, a link between gun ownership and any psychological tendency toward violence or victimization would have to be extremely strong to account for an adjusted odds ratio of 2.7.

Given the univariate association we observed between alcohol and violence, it may seem odd that no alcohol-related variables were included in our final multivariate model. Although consumption of alcoholic beverages and the behavioral correlates of alcoholism were strongly associated with homicide, they were also related to other variables included in our final model. Forcing the variable "case subject or control drinks" into our model did not substantially alter the adjusted odds ratios for the other variables. Furthermore, the adjusted odds ratio for this variable was not significantly greater than 1.

Large amounts of money are spent each year on home-security systems, locks, and other measures intended to improve home security. Unfortunately, our results suggest that these efforts have little effect on the risk of homicide in the home. This finding should come as no surprise, since most homicides in the home involve disputes between family members, intimate acquaintances, friends, or others who have ready access to the home. It is important to realize, however, that these data offer no insight into the effectiveness of home-security measures against other household crimes such as burglary, robbery, or sexual assault. In a 1983 poll, Seattle homeowners feared "having someone break into your home while you are

gone" most and "having someone break into your home while you are at home" 4th on a list of 16 crimes. Although homicide is the most serious of crimes, it occurs far less frequently than other types of household crime. Measures that make a home more difficult to enter are probably more effective against these crimes.

Despite the widely held belief that guns are effective for protection, our results suggest that they actually pose a substantial threat to members of the household. People who keep guns in their homes appear to be at greater risk of homicide in the home than people who do not. Most of this risk is due to a substantially greater risk of homicide at the hands of a family member or intimate acquaintance. We did not find evidence of a protective effect of keeping a gun in the home, even in the small subgroup of cases that involved forced entry.

Saltzman and colleagues recently found that assaults by family members or other intimate acquaintances with a gun are far more likely to end in death than those that involve knives or other weapons. A gun kept in the home is far more likely to be involved in the death of a member of the household than it is to be used to kill in self-defense. Cohort and interrupted time-series studies have demonstrated a strong link between availability of guns and community rates of homicide. Our study confirms this association at the level of individual households.

Previous case–control research has demonstrated a strong association between the ownership of firearms and suicide in the home. Also, unintentional shooting deaths can occur when children play with loaded guns they have found at home. In the light of these observations and our present findings, people should be strongly discouraged from keeping guns in their homes.

The observed association between battering and homicide is also important. In contrast to the money spent on firearms and home security, little has been done to improve society's capacity to respond to the problem of domestic violence. In the absence of effective intervention, battering tends to increase in frequency and severity over time. Our data strongly suggest that the risk of homicide is markedly increased in homes where a person has previously been hit or hurt in a family fight. At the very least, this observation should prompt physicians, social workers, law-enforcement officers, and the courts to work harder to identify and protect victims of battering and other forms of family violence. Early identification and effective intervention may prevent a later homicide.

POSTSCRIPT

Should We Encourage the Private Ownership of Guns?

The real issue here is whether or not the firearms industry should go unregulated. Advocates of regulation note that many consumer goods that appear to be far less dangerous than handguns are regulated. If everyday items such as children's toys, over-the-counter drugs, and small kitchen appliances are regulated, why are handguns left unregulated? Surely, more individuals are maimed and killed each year by handguns than by many of the goods that society now regulates.

The NRA would be quick to point out that regulation of the gun industry is not the answer. Indeed, they might argue that the answer is to deregulate all consumer goods. This is the position taken by Jacob Sullivan, the managing editor of *Reason*. In a recent article in *National Review* (February 7, 1994), Sullivan takes great care to show how ineffective regulation such as the Brady Bill will be. Waiting periods and background checks, he argues, will not stop the Colin Fergusons of the world. (Ferguson shot 23 people, fatally wounding 6 of them, on a New York train running from Manhattan to Hicksville on the Long Island Railroad.) Ironically, according to Sullivan, these gun regulations would not have even stopped John Hinckley, who attempted to assassinate President Ronald Reagan and seriously wounded and permanently handicapped Reagan's press secretary James Brady, for whom the Brady Bill is named.

Polsby and other spokespersons for the NRA's position assert that gun control would disarm the law-abiding citizenry and leave the "bad guys" with a monopoly on guns. Kellermann and others within and outside of the medical field, however, find that the cost paid for gun ownership is too high: There are too many accidental shootings; there are too many successful gun-related suicides; and there are too many friends and family members shot in the heat of passion. For Kellermann, guns are too efficient in killing people.

There has been much written about the firearms industry and gun control, particularly after Congress passed the Brady Bill in November 1993. For background, see Jonathan Alter, "How America's Meanest Lobby Ran Out of Ammo," *Newsweek* (May 16, 1994); Frank Lalli, "The Cost of One Bullet: $2 Million," *Money* (February 1994); and Owen Ullmann and Douglas Harbrecht, "Talk About a Loaded Issue," *Business Week* (March 14, 1994). For a good discussion on the limitations of gun control, see David B. Kopel, "Hold Your Fire: Gun Control Won't Stop Rising Violence," *Policy Review* (Winter 1993). And to hear from another member of the medical community, read the editorial by Jerome P. Kassirer entitled "Guns in the Household," which appeared in the October 7, 1993, issue of *The New England Journal of Medicine* along with the Kellermann article.

Finally, we should call your attention to the latest struggle by the NRA: to gain the support of women. In magazines such as *Women and Guns* (published by the Second Amendment Foundation) and in an ad campaign entitled "Refuse to Be a Victim," which has appeared in women's journals such as *Woman's Day* and *Redbook*, the NRA has urged women to "declare your independence from the tragic fear that has become the shameful plague of our times." For a discussion of this campaign, see Sally Chew, "The NRA Goes Courting," *Lear's* (January 1994).

ISSUE 3

Is National Service at Odds With American National Interest?

YES: Doug Bandow, from "National Service: Unnecessary and Un-American," *Orbis: A Journal of World Affairs* (Summer 1990)

NO: Charles Moskos, from "Rebuttal: Necessary and American," *Orbis: A Journal of World Affairs* (Summer 1990)

ISSUE SUMMARY

YES: Doug Bandow, a former special assistant to President Reagan, argues that the Nunn-McCurdy proposal on national service represents an objectionable intrusion of the state into the affairs of individual members of society—an intrusion that will weaken our future military preparedness.

NO: Professor of sociology Charles Moskos, who advises the conservative-leaning Democratic Leadership Conference, characterizes this proposal as "bold legislation" and "a GI Bill without the GI."

In the spring of 1989, eight separate national service bills were introduced before Congress by such legislators as Senator Claiborne Pell (D-Rhode Island), Senator Barbara A. Milkulski (D-Maryland), Representative Morris K. Udall (D-Arizona), Representative Leon E. Panetta (D-California), Senator Edward M. Kennedy (D-Massachusetts), and Senator Dale Bumpers (D-Arkansas). Of these bills, none was more important than the Citizenship and National Service Act that was introduced by Senator Sam Nunn (D-Georgia) and Representative David McCurdy (D-Oklahoma) and whose merits are debated in this issue.

All of these proposals, to a greater or lesser extent, are patterned after the immensely popular "GI Bill" that was made available to veterans of World War II. (GI is an informal term used to describe a member or former member of the military—particularly enlisted members. It came into general usage during World War II and originally was an abbreviation for galvanized iron, but it was also taken as an abbreviation for government issue.) Members of the military who served during the war were given the opportunity to attend colleges, universities, or other training facilities after they were discharged from service. They were provided a tuition grant plus a living allowance. This program generated tens of thousands of first-generation college graduates, and the United States has reaped benefits from the human capital created by this public policy.

The Nunn-McCurdy Plan, like the GI Bill, would provide vouchers that could be used to offset the expenses of a college education. This plan, however, broadens the coverage in several ways. In addition to using the vouchers to cover the cost of a college education, the vouchers could be used as a down payment on a home. Secondly, participants could earn their vouchers in military service or in civilian service. That is, a participant would be required to engage in one or two years of full-time civilian service or two years active plus six years reserve service in the military. While in national service, the participant would earn a nominal income of $100 per week, which would include health insurance.

For fiscal year 1989, 6 million students in the United States received federal aid totaling approximately $9 billion. The Nunn-McCurdy bill directly challenges the premise of the existing system of educational grants and subsidized loans that are currently in place. This system is designed to provide equal access for all citizens to postsecondary educational opportunities with a minimum number of restrictions or conditions. The new system would explicitly tell high school graduates that if they want a college education paid for by society, then they have to serve society. After a five-year phase-in period, education grants-in-aid would be conditional on national service.

The Bush administration took steps in the direction of implementing a program of national service by creating the White House Office on National Service, which was given the responsibility of initiating a program called Youth Engaged in Service to America.

The bills introduced in Congress and presidential initiatives are signals that national priorities may be changing. But should they? Should the federal government tie government financial support for higher education to national service? It appears that policymakers in the executive and congressional branches of government support this as a wise decision. However, others, including many in the education community, even if they support the positive aims and good intentions of this legislation, are concerned that the proposed legislation will undermine the national commitment to equal educational opportunities.

In the following selections, Doug Bandow and Charles Moskos discuss the problems and strengths of national service legislation. In assessing the merits or lack thereof of national service for young people, you might also want to see if you can relate what you may have already learned in your economics course about the operations of the labor market and about human capital theory to this debate.

YES

Doug Bandow

NATIONAL SERVICE: UNNECESSARY AND UN-AMERICAN

The U.S. government inaugurated an All-Volunteer Force (AVF) in 1973, despite the skepticism of the Pentagon and many in Congress. After almost two decades, it has proven its success by providing an above average group of young Americans to fill the military's ranks. In fact, despite some problems in the late 1970s, the AVF is now delivering a higher quality force than ever was acquired through conscription....

CRITICISMS OF THE ALL-VOLUNTEER FORCE

Though the idea of freedom has attenuated greatly in America over the past 150 years, a majority of Americans probably still associate national service only with military service. Consequently, military service remains a key selling point of national service proposals, and criticism of the AVF therefore remains a leading basis for proposing national service.

Typically, four charges are levelled against the AVF: that the annual cohort of volunteers is not large enough; not smart enough; not representative of America; and not idealistic. Let us consider each argument in turn.

Not enough volunteers. The first criticism says that the AVF cannot withstand the coming of the "baby bust" generation. Since 1979, the pool of eighteen-year-olds has been shrinking and it will continue to do so until 1992. Moreover, the number of eighteen- to twenty-four-year-olds will decline throughout the 1990s. The DLC [Democratic Leadership Council] and its allies believe that these demographic changes present the United States with a crisis requiring dramatic action.

Demographics, though, are not decisive. The eighteen-year-old cohort peaked in 1979; yet that was the last year the services failed to meet their objectives. By the end of the 1980s, the Pentagon had endured more than two-thirds of the total expected population drop (which will end in 1992), all the while meeting its goals and increasing the quality of its recruits. As for the shrinking eighteen- to twenty-four-year-old pool, the Pentagon estimates

From Doug Bandow, "National Service: Unnecessary and Un-American," *Orbis: A Journal of World Affairs* (Summer 1990). Copyright © 1990 by The Foreign Policy Research Institute. Reprinted by permission. Notes omitted.

that there will be more than 7.3 million males eligible to serve in 1996, of whom the Pentagon will need to recruit only 5 percent.

Moreover, these estimates, made barely three years ago, are now out of date. Events in the Soviet Union and Eastern Europe are almost certain to reduce sharply the size of the military. In November 1989, the services drafted plans to cut overall manpower levels by 250,000, more than one-tenth of the force. The army, the most personnel-intensive service, proposed dropping three of eighteen active-duty divisions and reducing the number of reserve divisions from ten to nine. The result would be to slash 135,000 of 769,000 active-duty soldiers, roughly 18 percent of its force. Only two months later, in January 1990, Defense Secretary Richard Cheney announced that the Pentagon expected to dismantle not four but five of its twenty-eight active and reserve army divisions.

Not smart enough. The AVF, it is said, does not attract enough qualified volunteers to handle the military's increasingly complex weapons. This charge is hard to sustain. Reviewing everything from family background to educational aspirations to SAT scores suggests that the military is attracting high-quality recruits. In fact, the Pentagon's performance has been superlative. In FY 1989, 92 percent of its recruits were high school graduates, compared to 75 percent of the general youth population. While only 69 percent of civilian youth score in the top three (of five) categories of the Armed Forces Qualification Test (AFQT), 94 percent of new enlistees did so last year. Furthermore, the military has maintained these excellent results throughout the 1980s despite a lengthy economic recovery.

That current recruits are smarter than average has led some hawks to conclude that there is no security justification for national service. As Representative G.V. "Sonny" Montgomery (Democrat of Mississippi) testified before his colleagues in early 1989: "We're in great shape and should not tamper with the effective tools we've given the military."

Not sufficiently representative. The DLC complains in its book on national service that "Americans should be concerned that our armed forces today are not representative of society as a whole," that the poor and minorities are carrying a disproportionate share of the burden of defense. Specifically, what they mean is that not enough white, middle-class youths are serving. The DLC argues that minorities comprise roughly 38 percent of army personnel and 30 percent of all servicemen, compared to just 14 percent of the civilian labor force. The DLC believes that "an unrepresentative army undermines the civic ethic of equal sacrifice."

Obviously, few if any critics of AVF are concerned about unrepresentativeness as such. Few of them are troubled that women make up well under half of America's forces. No one has decried the absence of a proportionate number of handicapped people, nor the services' failure to incorporate a socially typical number of those who score in the lowest category of the AFQT. And, frankly, there would probably be little criticism from national-service advocates were whites overrepresented.

The critics' selectivity points to a conceptual problem: their notion that all civic roles should be shared equally. Wealthy people tend to pay more in taxes. Construction workers are overwhelmingly male. The Irish, for many years, bore a disproportionate "burden" of New York City's policing duties. And nonurban residents are overrepresented in the military. Should all such roles be shared equally? As long as rich and poor, black and white, men and women, ethnic groups, and regional groups face different situations in life, they are likely to assume certain social roles disproportionately. To think that it should be otherwise is simply to advocate an equality of result that is alien to America.

Anyway, the DLC overstates its case, once again. First, it uses overall Pentagon figures. Minorities reenlist in higher numbers than whites, something that would not be affected by national service. Second, civilian labor force statistics are incorrectly cited. Bruce Chapman of the Hudson Institute points out that when the DLC compares figures for minority eighteen- to twenty-one-year-olds, it uses 26.9 percent for the military and 17.8 percent for the civilian population. Yet the latter figure does not include Hispanics, who comprise 9.5 percent of the relevant population. Thus, although blacks are overrepresented in the military, (during FY 1989, 22 percent of new recruits were black, compared to 14 percent of the corresponding youth population), Hispanics, Asians, and other minority groups are underrepresented. As a result, the overall percentage of minorities in the military roughly matches their percentage in the population as a whole.

As for rich whites serving: They always have and always will, although trying to measure their participation is difficult. Using zip codes and average family incomes, a 1977 Rand Corporation report, conducted during a relatively difficult recruiting period, found that while 1.06 percent of all sixteen- to twenty-one-year-olds came from families in the top 1 percent of income, 0.34 percent of those joining the military did. Moreover, while 5.13 percent of all sixteen- to twenty-one-year-olds came from families in the 95 to 99 percentiles of income, 2.67 of those joining the military did. Thus, as one might expect, the wealthy are somewhat less likely to serve; but still many do join. The Rand report concluded that "military service apparently continues to be viewed as an alternative employment option for a very broad cross section of American society, from the wealthiest to the poorest."

Not idealistic. Proponents of mandatory service hold that the AVF has, in [Charles] Moskos's words, moved "from citizen soldier to economic man," placing an undue emphasis on marketplace values. That is, the AVF has fostered an "it's just a job" mentality. Moskos goes so far as to argue that "the most far-reaching consequence of the AVF is that it ultimately reduces recruiting an armed forces to a form of consumerism, even hedonism, which is hardly a basis for the kind of commitment required in a military organization."

Moskos's critique deserves to be taken seriously. Although military surveys consistently find that many servicemen joined to serve and to fulfill a sense of duty, much of the armed services' recruiting certainly seems pitched to the casual job hunter—learn a skill, earn some money, travel the world. That said, however, even Moskos acknowledges that many of the changes we see in the military are tied to social trends. In other words, no job ought to be "just a job," but any job can be "just a job." It depends on the individual and the value he places on his performance as a worker. Thus, a particularly serious problem of "ticket-punching" exists among some military officers, who of course would be unaffected by national service.

No doubt, the military would be stronger if it better emphasized its institutional uniqueness and its history as a high calling. But this seems contrary to Moskos's proposal of flooding the field with "young people who serve short terms in the military at less than market wages." Anyway, in the late 1980s, there has been an upsurge of idealism and activism on the part of the young without a new federal program. Those trends are likely to affect military recruiting; moreover, the down-sizing of the force will allow the military to choose a larger portion of enlistees who take duty seriously.

In sum, critics of the AVF have failed to make a convincing case. Nonetheless, national service advocates continue to believe that the military has a problem, and that their new national service program is the answer.

NATIONAL SERVICE PROPOSALS

Nearly a dozen different pieces of legislation concerning national service are now circulating in Washington. Some mirror the president's [Bush] "Thousand Points of Light" initiative, and would simply hand out federal money to promote volunteerism. Others encourage part-time civilian service along the lines of the National Guard, providing financial assistance in return for weekend civilian service. The Citizen Corps program advocated by [Senator Sam] Nunn [Democrat of Georgia], Representative David McCurdy (Democrat of Oklahoma), Moskos, and the DLC, seems to be the only attempt to employ national service in a way that would significantly affect the military.

The Citizen Corps program would create a Corporation for National Service to implement a civilian service program administered through state and local councils. (Military service would be handled by the Pentagon.) Federal financial aid for education would be conditioned on one or two years of service; and completion of the program would be rewarded with a voucher usable for education or a home purchase. In this way, national service advocates say, their program would bring in more recruits and more upper-income white recruits.

Moreover, Moskos predicts that "a citizen soldier option would dramatically lower per capita manpower costs" in two ways. It would attract college-bound youths with lower attrition rates than today's recruits; and the program would pay "citizen soldiers," serving only two years, less than "professional soldiers."

But Moskos and his allies may well be wrong on all counts. National service is likely to raise costs and hurt the services.

First, despite the DLC's desire to employ inexpensive, semivolunteer "citizen soldiers," use of an education/housing voucher would result in higher net annual benefits for the two-year enlistees than for longer-term enlistees. As Walter Oi of the University of Rochester points out, the tax-free voucher could easily be "cashed out" through home buybacks, with the result that a national service participant would end up with pay "63 percent higher than that paid to a regular enlisted man or woman." Instead of appealing to middle- and upper-class youths on the basis of something other than money, national service would in this way encourage enlistments from all income levels precisely because of the material incentives offered. (Moskos's version of the voucher, which could not be used to purchase a home, would be less subject to abuse.)

Second, with a plethora of two-year enlistment terms, training and turnover expenses would be much greater. In its official response to the Nunn-McCurdy national service proposal, the Defense Department warned:

Because of the large influx of 2-year enlistments, the training base (and associated costs) would have to expand markedly. In addition, unit training work loads, personnel turbulence, and attrition experienced in active and Reserve operational units would all increase. Minimum overseas tour lengths would need to be cut, sharply increasing permanent change of station costs. The combined effect of these factors would drive sharp accession and end strength increases, disrupt unit cohesion, weaken esprit and morale, reduce individual proficiency and compromise unit readiness.

Third, the advantages of the two-year plan would induce many career-minded recruits to take the "citizen" option, further upsetting the balance between short- and long-term enlistments. Pay and benefits for professionals would probably have to rise to encourage reenlistment and to maintain an adequate career force. All told, the research firm Syllogistics estimates, costs could rise between $1.1 billion and $9.2 billion annually. (See Table 1.)

Clearly, the impact of the plan on professionals is critical. The DLC appears to view a more experienced force as a detriment, citing as a possible source of savings the "reduction in the number of soldiers in higher pay grades." But not only is that saving illusory, an older force (in addition to being more effective) can actually offer significant savings

Table 1

Military-Related Costs of National Service FY 1985 Career Mix

	Estimated Cost Increases (Millions of Dollars)	
Element	Trained Man-year Method*	Productivity-weighted Man-year Method**
Savings from Cutting Regular Army Pay	(8316)	(8316)
Tax Loss from Cutting Regular Army Pay	433	433
Citizen Corps Pay (Net Taxes)	5320	9314
Reenlistment Bonuses	382	382
G.I Bill	(1629)	(1629)
Citizen Corps Educational Voucher	4605	8063
Additional Training	341	983
Total	1136	9230

*Trained man-year method merely preserves a force with equal years of training.
**Productivity weighting recognizes that an additional year of training is often worth more than an earlier year of training.

Source: Syllogistics, Inc., "The Effects of National Service on Military Personnel Programs," September 1988, pp. 6–19.

through efficiency. In fact, a decade ago, manpower experts Martin Binkin and Irene Kyriakopoulos urged the Pentagon to "take steps to improve retention among certain experienced personnel, thereby reducing the demands for new volunteers and for the resources now devoted to maintaining a relatively large pool of nonproductive employees. These steps not only would allow the nation to field more effective armed forces but could save money as well."

Fourth, one needs to keep in mind that potential savings from the personnel costs of new recruits are always going to be small, simply because most personnel spending goes for careerists, civilians, and retirees. When the DLC's book, *Citizenship and National Service*, compares personnel costs in 1964 and 1986 and blames the rise on the termination of conscription, something is clearly wrong. Barely one-tenth of personnel costs is now attributable to soldiers serving in their first two years (the ones who replaced draftees). Any added expense from increasing their pay is more than offset by eliminating the costs of conscription, lowered turnover, and lowered reenlistment incentives. (The rise was in fact due largely to increased costs associated with career soldiers, civilians, and retirees.)

Fifth, the military is today the one large-scale government service program that provides educational benefits; national service is therefore likely to draw people away from the military rather than encourage them to enlist. Thomas Byrne of the (private) Association of the U.S. Army complains, "We don't want high-caliber people who might otherwise join the Army off planting trees instead." It makes no sense to create a federal civilian service program to compete with the armed services for young men.

If the decision is made to use education aid to increase the number of young people enlisting in the military, there is a much simpler method. The government need only adopt the principle of "earned benefits" advocated by national service proponents—but apply it more selectively. That is, federal educational aid could still be conditioned on service, but on military service alone. No service, no aid. Such an approach would implement the sensible philosophical point advanced by Nunn and his colleagues, that educational subsidies are not an entitlement, and would also avoid creating a civilian program to compete with the military.

Lastly, what would national service do for a volunteer military thought to emphasize a "just-a-job" attitude? Moskos has observed that "we must encourage a general attitude, a cast of mind, an outlook." And that is true—in the military and in every other line of work. But many of today's servicemen already serve for less than a civilian market wage. Naval personnel who work long hours on aircraft carriers handling multimillion-dollar aircraft make no more than supermarket clerks. They —like many doctors, lawyers, journalists, teachers, entrepreneurs, and other citizens—have chosen their profession for reasons of personal fulfillment.

Would national service pull in more patriots in place of time-servers? No, an educational voucher would tend to attract people who want to go to college. Indeed, because "citizen soldiers" would get greater benefits under the voucher system than career soldiers, the scheme could create an entire class of recruits who joined solely because of the material rewards and who looked forward only to getting out and using their vouchers.

THE MORAL ARGUMENT

If national service has so little to commend it, why does the specter haunt us still? It seems likely that most of those who advocate national service are driven by something more than practical considerations. Like Edward Bellamy and William James, they appear to possess an intense dislike of America's individualist, bourgeois political culture.

Former representative Paul McCloskey, who introduced a mandatory national service program in 1979, observed that "the privilege of being an American justifies a duty to serve the country a year or two in one's youth." This implies that the government is the grantor, rather than the protector, of rights—fundamentally misconstruing the American view of the relationship between the individual and the state. It is a privilege to be an American only because it is a stroke of luck to live in a society that respects individual rights more than most other societies. But the rights of a free man are not a benefit or privilege bestowed by the government. The contrary views—that the status of freedom is a gift from the king, or the state, or society, and therefore something for which one must pay homage—reflects the view of feudalism, of fascism, and of socialism.

Of course, free individuals should defend themselves and their communities. But in a free society this decision must be a personal moral choice, not a legal duty imposed from above. Individuals operating within the informal social and community networks that surround them should be the ones to decide how best to fulfill their social obligations. As Daniel Webster asked: "Who will show me any constitutional injunction, which makes it the duty of the American people to surrender everything valuable in life, and even life itself... whenever the purposes of an ambitious and mischievous government may require it?"

Today, most advocates of national service say that their schemes are voluntary. But many of these advocates openly admit that they prefer national service to be involuntary. And in a sense, they are right. For if national service is in fact a duty owed to the country, why should it not be enforced, just as contractual obligations are enforced? Indeed, it must be enforced, since those who most need to learn to obey will not volunteer. Once this logic of "duty" takes hold, Washington will not long foot the huge bill for a "public service" army it can employ on the cheap.

Moreover, why stop the process at national service? Charles Moskos wants young people to act as prison guards, teachers, and in a host of other roles. Why not conscript them? William James wanted to draft men to do everything from wash windows to serve on fishing fleets in December. That may be going a bit far, but surely defense of the local community is not much less compelling than defense of the country. Why not conscript people for a "home guard" in the police and fire departments? Why not compel them to participate in neighborhood watch associations? This would bring in mature adults, otherwise not so easily lured from home and career. And if this sounds absurd, remember the DLC argument that "in a democracy... citizenship requires not just sharing burdens, but sharing them equally."

In the end, the DLC gets one part right, asserting that "No obligation is more fundamental to citizenship than that of preserving our free institutions." Just so, and the conclusion is obvious: no obligation is more fundamental than opposing national service.

NO

Charles Moskos

REBUTTAL: NECESSARY AND AMERICAN

Doug Bandow has done a great service by highlighting key issues in the current debate on national service. He focuses on the national service proposal introduced by Senator Sam Nunn, Representative Dave McCurdy, and other congressional Democrats. This bold legislation, shaped by the Democratic Leadership Council's study, *Citizenship and National Service*,[1] would establish a voluntary national service program aimed primarily at young people between the ages of eighteen and twenty-six.

By presenting a program of national service embracing both military and civilian dimensions, the DLC study broke new ground. The military side would include two tracks: one a new lower-paid "citizen-soldier" track, offering short enlistments coupled with generous post-service educational benefits, the other a professional soldier track—basically the system as it presently exists. The civilian side would consist of an entirely new youth service, which would focus on conservation work and social services, and which would be administered mainly through state governments, local agencies, and voluntary associations.

The linchpin of the proposal lies in its extension to civilian service of the GI Bill established after World War II. The basic principle of that original GI Bill was to provide education or job training in return for military service. Under one DLC proposal, young people who perform one or two years of service, either military or civilian, would become the main recipients of federal student aid. This moves away from the present program under which the government gives $9 billion each year in loan subsidies and grants to college students without asking anything in return—in effect, a GI Bill without the GI. By linking service to student aid, the DLC proposal incurred the wrath of the higher education establishment and its paleo-liberal allies on Capitol Hill.

Libertarians take issue with national service for different reasons, of course. As well articulated by Bandow, these concerns center around three core contentions: (1) A national service plan will hurt (or at least will not significantly improve) the all-volunteer force (AVF); (2) The nonmilitary roles envisioned

From Charles Moskos, "Rebuttal: Necessary and American," *Orbis: A Journal of World Affairs* (Summer 1990). Copyright © 1990 by The Foreign Policy Research Institute. Reprinted by permission.

by national service plans are unneeded, or better met in other ways; (3) The concept of national service is un-American.

NATIONAL SERVICE AND THE AVF

Critics of the marketplace AVF (and I am one) focus their arguments on the army, the largest of the services, the one that formerly relied most on draftees, and the bellwether of the AVF. Of the many practical criticisms that have been lodged against AVF, Bandow presents rebuttals to four of the commonest: its poor quality; its unrepresentativeness; its high costs; and its difficulties in hiring and firing people.

Not smart enough. When it comes to the relation between quality and length of service, Bandow echoes an article of faith held by the Office of the Secretary of Defense (OSD)—that longer enlistments are nearly always preferable to shorter ones. But this dogma does not stand up to scrutiny. The effectiveness of soldiers is based on ability and training, not on time in a grade. Every study of combat soldiers supports this conclusion.[2] Army data show that two-year soldiers, compared with longer enlistees, are twice as likely to score in the upper aptitude categories and much less likely to be removed from the army for disciplinary causes. The army command structure is quite happy with its two-year enlistees. Why does Bandow want to change a winning formula?

Also, Bandow's use of accession figures to demonstrate the quality of the enlisted force is misleading. Rather than focusing on recruits alone, one ought to look at the total enlisted membership brought into the army under AVF. And here the picture is different. Even in the late 1980s, the best years in AVF history, the percentage of the army's enlisted personnel in the top two mental categories was lower than the percentage of the total population in those categories. The reason for this is that today's noncommissioned officers (NCOs) entered the army in the late 1970s, when the quality of recruits was at rock bottom. Thus, we now have a situation where the aptitude scores of privates are much higher than those of their sergeants. For example, 5 percent of recruits fall into the lowest test level compared with 26 percent of staff sergeants.

Not sufficiently representative. To argue, as does the 1977 Rand report Bandow cites, that the military was "viewed as an alternative employment option… from the wealthiest to the poorest" is laughable. In 1977, one-third of all army entrants were black and close to half of the white males were high school dropouts. To see this as a representative army takes some leap of imagination. Surely, Bandow recognizes that the representativeness issue does not center on creating a mirror of the civilian population (i.e., proportionate numbers of handicapped, mentally ill, and so forth). It centers, rather, on unrepresentativeness that affects the fighting capabilities of the armed forces. Is there any level of unrepresentativeness that would disturb Bandow?

Costs. When calculating the costs of a national service plan, Bandow displays a faulty comprehension of military manpower, for he ignores the concept of a Total Force—reserves as well as active forces. When reserve components are included in military manpower analysis, savings occur in training costs even with short-term enlistments, if these are tied to reserve obligations. This is precisely what the DLC proposal stated. Indeed, in 1989, Army Chief of Staff Carl E. Vuono supported an enlistment option of two years in the active force, two years in the ready reserve, and two years in the standby reserve. That military manpower trends, for both budgetary and strategic reasons, are moving toward greater reliance on reserve components makes the case for the citizen-soldier component of the DLC proposal all the more timely.

In support of his contention that long-term enlistments are less expensive than short-term enlistments, Bandow also perpetuates another OSD myth—that the AVF has proven less expensive than conscription.... [A] look at dollar figures (given in constant 1990 values) shows the real changes in military personnel costs since the advent of the AVF. In 1964, the last year of the peacetime draft, average personnel costs for each active-duty soldier were $22,500; this compares with $35,600 in 1990. The contrast in total manpower costs is enormous. The total bill in 1964 for the active-duty force was $55.1 billion, in 1990 it came to $73.9 billion. In other words, even though there are a half million fewer soldiers on active duty, the AVF costs $18 billion more! Nor does this include the extra $10 billion a year now paid to civilians or the skyrocketing retirement costs. Whatever arguments there are against the draft, cost savings is not one of them.[3]

Hiring and firing. The contention that the DLC proposal and the Nunn-McCurdy bill would hurt military recruitment by drawing young people into civilian work is foolishness. To require service from college youth who now receive federal education benefits without a service requirement can only create an unparalleled reservoir of potential military recruits. The Syllogistics study cited by Bandow, which suggested that a national service plan might require higher pay to bring in military re-cruits, never addressed the specifics of the Nunn-McCurdy bill and is irrelevant to the discussion at hand. A 1989 study by Juri Toomepuu, of the United States Army Recruiting Command, concludes that the Nunn-McCurdy bill would be an unprecedented boon for recruitment.[4] To this date, Toomepuu's analyses have never been publicly rebutted by anyone, including Doug Bandow, and indeed efforts to repress the study were partially successful: the study was not publicly available until reporters acquired copies through the Freedom of Information Act —too late to have an impact on the Nunn-McCurdy bill in Congress.

Obviously, as Bandow rightly points out, we now face a new environment for military manpower. As we enter the post-cold war era, the immediate issue is one of "downsizing," rather than recruitment. But here again AVF has created problems. Reductions would be demoralizing for the military under any scenario, but a career-heavy force makes them immeasurably worse. The AVF is smaller today, compared to what it would have been with a draft, entirely owing to the paucity of lower-ranking enlisted members and junior officers. In effect, the AVF emptied the military of privates and lieutenants—and this is now making necessary draconian reductions of the career force. Of the army's proposed 200,000-man reduction, 80,000 will be through "involuntary retirement."[5] Of course, there was nothing inevitable about having an AVF top-heavy with career soldiers. But this was the path favored by OSD with its resistance to the concept of the citizen-soldier.

Finally, let it be said, Bandow is quite right to note the current success of AVF recruitment. But he fails to mention that the OSD fought the two major recruitment initiatives of the 1980s—the army's two-year enlistment and GI Bill educational benefits.

NATIONAL SERVICE AND CIVILIAN NEEDS

The practical argument for national service is that it can be a means of providing services that the government cannot afford and in which the private sector finds no profit. For example, the most pressing social problem in the United States may be that citizens over the age of eighty-five constitute the fastest growing segment of the population. Already 1.4 million people live in nursing homes; as many as one-third of these people could live at home if someone helped them get outside the house and ran errands for them. In Germany, such services to the elderly are performed by young men in lieu of serving as draftees in the military, and the system operates successfully. Studies show that each youth server in the German system performs labor with a net worth of more than $21,000 a year.[6]

Such youths in short-term service are an effective and humane way to meet the needs of an aging population. If a young person were attracted to such service under the provisions of the DLC proposal, would Bandow oppose it? Does he favor the present system of federal student aid, which requires no payback of service? Youth servers would also be less expensive than the market or conventional bureaucracy in meeting the needs of the elderly. Or can Bandow think of better and cheaper ways to meet such needs?

There is another consideration. With the cutback in military manpower, a major and honorable avenue for deprived youth to escape a dead-end existence is being cut off. A national service program would be a way to recapitulate the military's record in salvaging impoverished youths through new forms of civilian youth corps.

Proponents of national service must always answer a simple question. Is national service more likely to achieve its purpose, and at less cost, than some other means? If the answer is no, then I will categorically state that national service is not appropriate. If it is yes, will Doug Bandow support national service?

NATIONAL SERVICE AND AMERICAN IDEALS

Only a simplistic reading of American history could ignore recurring connections between citizen duties and rights —the militia system of the colonial and early republican era, the "common defense" and "general welfare" provisions of the Constitution, the mandatory public schools of the Northwest Ordinances, the twentieth-century drafts in both peace and war, the military training requirements of the land grant colleges, the CCC of the New Deal, the alternative service provisions for conscientious objectors, the GI Bill, the Peace Corps and VISTA, the Solomon Amendment requiring draft registration for federal student aid, and the more than twenty local and state youth corps in the contemporary period. The history of the United States shows that notions of civic obligation periodically expand and contract—and that the solutions of one period are as American as those of another.

For example, scholars consistently stress the crucial role of the militia in the War of Independence.[7] But because of his unalloyed opposition to the citizen soldier, Bandow seems not to appreciate this or the strong militia tradition that followed. From the origins of the American nation onward, the ideal of the citizen soldier has coexisted with the need for the professional soldier; although the proper balance of these two has been a perennial dilemma. George Washington favored a small regular army *and* a militia of male citizens. Today, Title 10 of the U.S. Code reiterates the tenet that every physically sound and mentally fit male between eighteen and forty-five years of age is part of the unorganized militia of the United States.

Perhaps most telling, though, is Bandow's perception of the DLC proposal as a stalking horse for a full-scale mandatory program. This is a serious point. But the transition from the comprehensive but nonmandatory system of the Nunn-McCurdy bill to a compulsory program would be a momentous step—one that would require widespread support. Such support would exist only if the comprehensive program were widely viewed as a great success. It seems perverse to argue against a voluntary national service program on the grounds that it might prove too successful.

Political theorists as well as ordinary citizens are showing a growing appreciation of citizens' obligations and the importance of shared values. For example, four out of five Americans favor a volunteer youth corps at the federal level. And support even for mandatory service is high, with 55 percent favoring such a program for young men and 44 percent for young women.[8] This new interest in the duties of citizens results from the inadequacies of Marxism, with its materialistic analysis and collectivist prescrip-

tions, and the inadequacies of libertarianism, which offers a similar materialist analysis but with an insistent stress on the individual.

We may be on the verge of a breakout from those "left versus right" mindsets. Advocacy of national service is the political center reasserting itself. In this sense, national service is quintessentially American.

NOTES

1. Democratic Leadership Council (DLC), *Citizenship and National Service* (Washington, D.C.: Democratic Leadership Council, 1988). Will Marshall, president of the Progressive Policy Institute, was the primary author of this study. By way of full disclosure: both the DLC proposal and the Nunn-McCurdy legislation incorporated ideas from my book, *A Call to Civic Service* (New York: The Free Press, 1988).

2. "Soldier Performance Research Project," a report issued by the U.S. Army Training and Doctrine Command, August 31, 1989. For a summary of the literature, see Juri Toomepuu, *Soldier Capability —Army Combat Effectiveness*, vol. 1, Main Report (Ft. Benjamin Harrison, Ind.: U.S. Army Support Center, April 1981).

3. Although studies sponsored by the Department of Defense consistently find that a draft would cost more than the volunteer force, studies done outside conclude—with equal consistency—that a draft would result in budgetary savings of over $7 billion annually. For one example of the latter, see the General Accounting Office, *Military Draft: Potential Impacts and Other Issues* (Washington, D.C.: Government Printing Office, March 1988).

4. Juri Toomepuu, *Effects of a National Service Program on Army Recruiting* (Fort Sheridan, Ill.: U.S. Army Recruiting Command, February 1989).

5. *The Washington Post*, May 14, 1990.

6. Juergen Kuhlmann, "National Service Policy and Programs: The Case of West Germany," in Donald J. Eberly and Michael W. Sherraden, eds., *The Moral Equivalent of War?* (Westport, Conn.: Greenwood Press, 1990).

7. For example, John Shy, *A People Numerous and Armed* (New York: Oxford University Press, 1976); Charles Royster, *A Revolutionary People at War* (New York: The Free Press, 1984).

8. Gallup Poll, January 24, 1988.

POSTSCRIPT

Is National Service at Odds With American National Interest?

In this debate, two conservatives battle over the advisability of dramatically altering how tuition support is provided for needy college-bound youths without unduly disturbing the supply of talented young men and women that is needed to maintain military preparedness. Currently, these two public policies are uncoordinated even though they draw their "recruits" from the same age cohort.

Moskos argues that those who enter both the military and institutions of higher learning will benefit by the introduction of "national service." In Moskos's view, this program provides a unique opportunity to join together and to underscore the *duties and the rights* of America's youth; this is "quintessentially American."

Obviously Bandow does not share this view. Although he, too, is concerned with the rights and the obligations of young Americans, he fears that this voluntary program will evolve into a mandatory national service. In this case, government would be seen as the "grantor, rather than the protector of rights." In Bandow's opinion, this would fundamentally misconstrue "the American view of the relationship between the individual and the state."

Much has been written and will continue to be written about national service as Congress continues to address this issue. One source of further information is a volume prepared by the Democratic Leadership Council (DLC), a group of Democrats who are attempting to attract the political right back to their party. See their monograph *Citizenship and National Service: A Blueprint for Civic Enterprise* (May 1988). A second group to contact for information is the National Service Secretariat, a Washington, D.C.–based group that sponsors the Coalition for National Service. Since 1986, this nonprofit organization has acted as a clearinghouse for information; additionally they sponsored the Wingspread Conference in July 1988, which articulated an action agenda for the 1990s. See *National Service: An Action Agenda for the 1990s* (The National Service Secretariat, 1988). Other sources are the written statements prepared by those who have testified before the Committee on Education and Labor concerning the topic "Citizenship and National Service." These hearings were held during the spring of 1989. Coverage has appeared in the *Chronicle of Higher Education* (March 15, 1989), the *Wall Street Journal* (October 16, 1989), and, on a continuing basis, in *Experiential Education*, a publication of the National Society for Internships and Experiential Education. One other source might be of value: Charles Moskos's *A Call to Civic Service —National Service for Country and Community* (Free Press, 1988).

In response to new legislative efforts introduced in Congress in January 1990 that called for a national service corps, Janet Lieberman, a spokesperson for the U.S. Student Association, declared that the measures are a "step backward for student aid." The U.S. Student Association argues that measures to provide college students who volunteer for national service with vouchers for education expenses or the purchase of a first home discriminate against lower-income students. They charge that low-income students should be guaranteed access to college, and they feel that the provision linking national service to student aid might discourage such students from attending college.

ISSUE 4

Are Women Paid Less Than Men Because Their Working Conditions Are More Favorable?

YES: Randall K. Filer, from "Occupational Segregation, Compensating Differentials, and Comparable Worth," in Robert T. Michael et al., eds., *Pay Equity: Empirical Inquiries* (National Academy Press, 1989)

NO: Jerry A. Jacobs and Ronnie J. Steinberg, from "Compensating Differentials and the Male-Female Wage Gap: Evidence from the New York State Comparable Worth Study," *Social Forces* (December 1990)

ISSUE SUMMARY

YES: Associate professor of economics Randall K. Filer maintains that comparable worth policies are unnecessary since wage differentials simply reflect differences in workers' preferences for jobs with varying degrees of pleasantness.

NO: Associate professors of sociology Jerry A. Jacobs and Ronnie J. Steinberg argue that empirical evidence proves that wage differentials cannot be explained by worker employment choices.

The term *comparable worth* may be relatively new, but the problem that it is intended to address has plagued the U.S. economy for many years: Women are and have been paid less than men for work activities that have *comparable* characteristics. As Randall K. Filer notes, "Median weekly earnings of full-time female workers over age 16 have risen from 61 percent of those for men in 1978 to 71 percent of male earnings in the second quarter of 1987." Although this marks a clear and considerable improvement in the economic well-being of women wage earners over this 10-year period, and a remarkable improvement over the differentials in wages that existed as recently as 25 years ago, there still exists an apparent 30 percent penalty for being female in the labor markets.

This is not a problem that has been ignored by public policymakers. In 1917 the federal government created the War Labor Board in part to handle charges of sex discrimination in the war industries. The board ordered that the wages of women should equal the wages paid to men when the services rendered were equal. During World War II the War Labor Board again attempted to establish the basic concept of equal pay for equal work. This time the board was less successful. A few corporations, notably Westinghouse and General Electric, persisted in setting different wages for men and women doing equal work.

Although lobbying efforts for federal legislation that would guarantee equal pay for equal work continued throughout the 1940s and 1950s, this right was not established by Congress until 1963, when the Equal Pay Act was passed. The following year, Congress took yet another step toward closing the wage gap by enacting Title VII of the Civil Rights Act, which broadly prohibited employment discrimination based upon race, color, national origin, religion, or sex. The net result of these two major legislative initiatives was to establish clearly the right of women to "equal pay for substantially equal work."

Yet more than 25 years after these laws were passed, large wage differentials between men and women still exist. Although the laws have eliminated most of the blatant forms of wage discrimination that existed where women and men doing the same jobs were paid at different rates, the laws have done little to address the wage discrepancies that continue to exist between pay for work traditionally considered to be "women's work" and pay for "men's" jobs.

Proponents of comparable worth argue that on the basis of objective criteria —job skill requirements, job responsibilities, education, training, and experience levels needed—many low-paying jobs that by tradition have been held by women are as demanding as some high-paying jobs that have been predominately held by men. These proponents go on to argue that the only way to correct these wage differences is to objectively judge each job classification and correct for any sex-biased differences that are uncovered.

In 1981, the Supreme Court issued a decision in *Washington County v. Gunther* that appears to make it possible to bring comparable worth cases to the courts. Additionally, two-thirds of the states have introduced or are attempting to introduce comparable worth legislation, while six states have implemented explicit forms of comparable worth programs for their public employees. Lastly, a number of trade unions are bringing this issue to the bargaining table.

Some comparable worth policies have caused concern among many free-market economists. This is the case for Randall K. Filer. He argues that if poorly conceived policies are put in place, they can only "lead to distortions in resource allocation and the creation of inefficiencies." Other researchers, such as Jerry A. Jacobs and Ronnie J. Steinberg, find that the wage differentials found in the marketplace reflect the relative economic and political power that male workers have as compared to female workers.

YES

Randall K. Filer

OCCUPATIONAL SEGREGATION, COMPENSATING DIFFERENTIALS, AND COMPARABLE WORTH

In surveying the relative positions of men and women in the labor market, two facts stand out. First, wage differences between the two sexes are substantial. Second, differences in occupational structure are significant; men and women are concentrated in different occupations and heavily female occupations tend to be lower paying. Recent years have seen substantial shifts in both of these factors. Median weekly earnings of full-time female workers over age 16 have risen from 61 percent of those for men in 1978 to 71 percent of male earnings in the second quarter of 1987. Thus, in the past 10 years approximately 25 percent of the difference in male and female earnings has been eliminated. At the same time, although there are methodological difficulties in measuring changes in the degree of occupational sex segregation over time, numerous recent studies have documented that the degree of sex segregation in occupations has declined since at least 1970 (and probably since 1960).[1] ...

Despite these improvements in the relative economic position of women over the past few years, significant differences in occupational distributions and earnings between the sexes persist. There are important policy implications to be derived from an understanding of why these differences exist. To the extent that they arise from unequal opportunities caused by unfair hiring or promotional practices, the economy has failed to make appropriate use of human resources and has created inefficiencies. In this case there is justification for intervention to facilitate greater sex equality in the labor market. On the other hand, to the extent that sex differences in occupational structure and earnings arise from differences in individual productivity or choices, despite equal labor market opportunity, interventions to change either employment or earnings patterns would lead to distortions in resource allocation and the creation of inefficiencies.

POSSIBLE CAUSES OF
SEX DIFFERENCES

The observed pattern of the genders being concentrated in different occupations, coupled with lower average wages in the occupations that are heavily female, is consistent with a number of possible explanations that have been proposed by economists. Those explanations provide the framework for the analysis in this paper.

Differences in Productivity

It may be that one gender has lower average levels of productivity and has concentrated in occupations in which it has a comparative advantage. Primary among the factors that may contribute to differences in productivity between typical men and women is past work experience. Previous research has established that between one-quarter and one-half of the gender gap in wages may be due to differences in the extent of previous employment (Corcoran, 1979; Mincer and Ofek, 1982; Mincer and Polachek, 1978; Sandell and Shapiro, 1978).

Physical differences may also contribute to differing occupational comparative advantages and overall productivity. In one setting, Hoffmann and Hoffman (1987) found that upper body strength and lifting requirements limited women's bidding on and accepting "male" jobs even though they were actively encouraged to do so by their employer. Similarly, several authors (e.g., Daymont and Andrisani, 1984; Filer, 1983; Greenfield et al., 1980) have observed that women and men in the labor market have substantially different personality patterns with respect to such characteristics as empathy and aggression, which may lead to different job

choices and, consequently, different reward structures.[2]

Differences in Utility Functions

Men and women may make rational choices in the job market based on differences in utility functions that create differing preferences for certain types of work and other duties. For example, some evidence indicates that women attach greater importance to various forms of attractive working conditions and that men place relatively greater emphasis on incomes (Forgionne and Peters, 1982; Harvey, 1986; Murray and Atkinson, 1981). Such a difference in preferences, coupled with the fact that the market forces employers to pay compensating differentials to those workers who fill jobs with relatively unattractive working conditions, will, even given equal productivity, result in women being concentrated in lower paying but otherwise more attractive jobs. Evidence presented in Filer (1985) suggests that such compensating differentials may be responsible for up to one-quarter of earnings differences between men and women.

Much of the literature regarding differences between men and women in labor market preferences starts with the fact that there are differences in home duties. Filer (1985) reports that jobs typically held by women are those from which it is easier to take time off for personal reasons and are typically located closer to their homes.[3] Others (O'Neill, 1983, 1985; Waite and Berryman, 1985) have pointed out that female-dominated jobs require less overtime, are less likely to have rotating shifts, and are more likely to be part time. All of these findings are consistent with women assuming responsibility for child rearing.

Perhaps the most frequently advanced reason why differing home responsibilities might lead to occupational segregation comes from the fact that women tend to have more discontinuous work histories. This should lead them to choose jobs that require little firm-specific human capital and in which there is relatively little atrophy of skills when not in use....

Employers may respond to a greater propensity of women to leave the labor force by investing less in training women and being less likely to promote women (see Lazear and Rosen, 1989). Such theories of "statistical discrimination" rest on the inability of employers to distinguish between those women who will remain on the job and those who will leave. They do not, however, explain why women, who presumably know whether they intend to leave their employer to assume responsibilities at home, do not negotiate contingent claims contracts insuring employers against lost investments. Finally, Becker (1985) provides a theoretical rationale for why differing home duties will result in men providing greater levels of effort on the job.

Discrimination

If lower wages for one group are not the result of lower productivity and are not fully compensated by nonwage aspects of the job, the labor market is not in equilibrium and members of the group receiving lower wages should move into higher wage occupations. The absence of such equilibrating movement (and thus a stability over time in the extent of occupational sex segregation) would suggest that women have been involuntarily denied access to certain occupations (see Bergmann, 1974; Blau, 1984; Madden, 1975; Stevenson, 1984). Obviously, such conscious denial of access to occupations, whether through the actions of employers, other workers, customers, or legislative action, would create occupational segregation.[4] This could explain lower wages for women through one of two mechanisms. "Crowding" of women into a limited number of jobs could artificially increase supply and depress wages (see Bergmann, 1974; Johnson and Solon, 1984). Alternatively, employers may consciously take the sex composition of jobs into account when setting pay levels (see England et al., 1982; Treiman and Hartmann, 1981).

If discriminatory differences in occupational structures are not being eliminated by labor market mobility, some structural barrier must be preventing such movement. This would suggest two possible courses of action. Either the barrier(s) to mobility may be removed so that rational mobility decisions on the part of workers will create equality of compensation, or the occupational distribution may be taken as fixed and an attempt made to raise wages in jobs heavily filled by women.[5]

It is the latter policy that has come to be known as "comparable worth." Advocates of comparable worth call for pay to be administratively set so that differences in wages (or full compensation, including the value of fringe benefits) not based on differences in productive skills, effort, responsibility, and working conditions are eliminated. An excellent review of the development and implementation of the concept of comparable worth is presented in Weiler (1986).

ANALYTIC FRAMEWORK

This paper investigates the extent to which there exist differences in the wages paid in various occupations that are not related to levels of effort and responsibility, working conditions, or the productive characteristics of incumbents in them, but which are related to the sex composition of the occupation. Much recent work has applied a similar procedure to micro-level data, regressing individual wages on personal characteristics and the percentage of women in an individual's occupation.[6] Studies such as England (1982, 1985), England et al. (1986), Ferber and Lowry (1976), Jusenius (1977), and Stevenson (1975) have found a negative relationship between the proportion of female workers in an occupation and its average wage.

Other studies (Aldrich and Buchele, 1986; England et al., 1982; Fuchs, 1971; Treiman et al., 1984) have used occupations as the unit of analysis, regressing average wages in an occupation (either separately for men and women or combined) on a set of explanatory variables as well as the occupation's sex composition. These studies have been handicapped by their ability to include, at most, a small subset of the factors encompassed in an occupation's "effort, responsibility, working conditions and productive requirements." ...

RESULTS

The first column in Table 1 reports the estimated impact on the wages in a job if it were to move from 0 percent female to 100 percent female as estimated from a combined sample of men and women. Columns two and three show results for men and women separately. Differences between them and column one represent the extent to which women's lower wages *within* occupations bias the gender effect when it is estimated using a combined sample. To calculate the impact of gender composition on wage differentials, one must calculate the change in wages that would occur if each occupation exactly mirrored the proportion female in the work force. Forty-two percent of the workers in the 5 percent census sample were women. The average man was in a job that was 23 percent female and the average woman was in a job that was 68 percent female.

Adding Demographic and Personal Characteristics

The first row of Table 1 shows the estimated effect of a job's being 100 percent female on the wages of full-time workers in that job if no other characteristics of either the worker or the job are taken into account. The most standard adjustment is to recognize that men and women do not, on average, bring the same levels of productive attributes to the labor market. Census data provide a limited set of personal and demographic characteristics that may capture these productivity differences and can be included in the regression. Among them are racial group, marital and citizenship status, education, and crude measures of the type of employer. In addition, estimated actual work experience ... was included in this specification. Results from this estimation are reported in the second row of Table 1. Increased femaleness of an occupation still implies significantly lower wages after controlling for these characteristics. Moving from being 100 percent male to being entirely female would, according to these estimates, bring a reduction of $1.92 an hour in average wages for women and $1.38 an hour for men. The relationship is significant for both sexes, although, unlike results found by other

Table 1

Estimated Coefficients of Gender Composition on Wages, All Full-Time, Full-Year Workers

| | Estimated Coefficient[a] (Standard Error) | | |
| | Men and Women | | |
Equation Specification	Combined	Women Only	Men Only
Gender composition only	−4.41	−1.73	−2.32
	(.38)	(.25)	(.42)
Gender composition and	−3.30	−1.92	−1.38
demographic variables	(.30)	(.19)	(.32)
Gender composition, demographic	−3.13	−1.59	−1.29
variables, and union coverage,	(.30)	(.19)	(.32)
Gender composition, demographic	−1.70	0.30	0.31
variables, union coverage,	(.31)	(.24)	(.32)
effort, responsibility, and			
working conditions (maximum R²)			
Gender composition, demographic	−1.35	−0.55	0.18
variables, union coverage,	(.50)	(.37)	(.53)
effort, responsibility, and			
working conditions (all variables)			

[a]The estimated impact of an occupation shifting from entirely male to entirely female composition. Multiply by the difference in the femaleness of the job held by the typical woman and that held by the typical man to obtain the estimated gender contribution to the gross wage differential.

researchers, it appears to be stronger for women than for men.

It is often asserted that one reason women earn less than men is their lower participation in unions that obtain higher than competitive wages. The third row of Table 1 reports estimated gender coefficients for an equation including personal characteristics and the proportion of the occupation covered by a collective bargaining agreement. There is some support for the hypothesis that lack of female participation in unions contributes to the estimated gender impact on wages. When unionization is added, the gender impact in the female equation falls by almost 20 percent.

Due to space considerations, coefficients on other variables are not reported in full.[7] In general, however, they are as expected. Education effects are some-what stronger than found in micro-level studies. An additional year of schooling is estimated to result in between 51 and 76 cents an hour in additional earnings. Estimated union effects are consistent with those from micro-level studies. The estimated benefits to joining unions are substantially greater for women than for men. This raises the question of why women's unionization rates have traditionally been lower then men's. The answer may lie in discrimination within unions, higher costs to women in joining unions, or the fact that women must amortize organizational costs over shorter expected periods of job tenure.

No relationship was found between the imputed average level of experience of women in an occupation and its wages. For men, a positive relationship was found.... Results regarding the impact of the ethnic composition of an occupation on its wages will be discussed below.

Adding the Full Set of "Comparable Worth" Factors

Even after the addition of census demographic characteristics, the effect of the proportion female in an occupation on its average wages remains substantial. We can turn now to the extent to which this is a statistical bias resulting from the omission of significant characteristics that are correlated with the proportion female in an occupation but which advocates of comparable worth recognize as compensable in their own right, such as a job's working conditions and levels of effort and responsibility.

The results of two versions of the "complete" comparable worth specification are presented. The fourth row of Table 1 contains estimates of the gender impact from an equation constrained to include the variables discussed in the previous section plus the job characteristics that maximized the adjusted R^2 of the linear hedonic wage equation for men and women combined (since there were slight differences in the set that was entered for the sexes separately).[8] [R^2 refers to the percentage of the variation in the wage rate that is explained by the independent variables in the equation.—Eds.] The reader is cautioned, however, that where there are several measures relating to any comparable worth factor, patterns of multicollinearity make interpretation of any one coefficient impossible. It is only the effect of the full set taken jointly that has meaning. What is of interest here is not the coefficients in and of themselves (for a discussion of their meaning see Filer, 1987), but rather the impact that their inclusion has on estimates of the effect of gender composi-

tion on wages in an occupation. Finally, the last row of Table 1 reports the result when all 225 job characteristics were entered into the wage equation.

The impact of adjusting for compensable job characteristics is striking. Once compensating differentials for a job's effort, responsibility, fringe benefits, and working conditions are taken into account there *is no significant relationship between an occupation's gender composition and its wages* for either men or women. What appears to be an effect in the combined equation results from lower wages for women within each occupation, which, to the extent that they represent other than legitimate compensation practices, can be addressed by equal employment laws but which are immune to comparable worth adjustments.

Some of the results for other variables in this equation are worthy of note. For a more thorough analysis, the reader is referred to Filer (1987). The pattern of the census variables remains the same. There is an approximately 25 percent reduction in the estimated impact of education on wages, although this coefficient is still highly significant. Examining comparable worth concepts such as effort and responsibility is complicated by the fact that there are several related and highly intercorrelated measures of each. When taken as a group (say by assuming a change of one standard deviation in each), the results suggest that occupations requiring more effort or responsibility, exposure to worse working conditions, or longer commutes pay higher wages for both men and women; while those with higher levels of fringe benefits, more interaction with other people, or employment in smaller establishments can pay lower average wages.[9] ...

Changes in Sex Composition

To what extent are mobility patterns of women consistent with a labor market moving toward an equilibrium resulting in equality of wages? Women can be expected to enter those jobs for which pay is greatest for women, no matter what the extent of any discriminatory pay gap in that occupation.

Women can also be expected, all else being equal, to enter those jobs for which there is the least degree of penalty for being female. The size of such a potential gap can be estimated by comparing the actual earnings of women in an occupation with the earnings they would be predicted to have if they were rewarded in the same manner as men (the sum of the average levels of independent variables for women times the coefficients for men). If these predicted earnings are equal to their actual earnings, women in the occupation are being exactly compensated for their productive attributes, effort, responsibility, and working conditions faced. If predicted earnings exceed actual earnings, women are being undercompensated in that occupation (i.e., there is a discriminatory gap). The greater the gap, the greater should be the incentive for women to move out of that occupation and into ones in which they do not face such a disadvantage. Finally, if predicted earnings are lower than actual earnings, the incentive goes in the opposite direction, the discriminatory gap favors women, and women should desire to enter the occupation.

Thus, if occupational mobility is serving to equalize wages between men and women, a positive relationship between actual wages paid to women in an occupation and the movement of women into that occupation should be found as well as a negative relationship between the gap between predicted and actual wages and the rate of growth of female employment. Both of these results are seen. The correlation between the percentage of increase in the proportion of workers in an occupation who were women before 1970 and 1980 and its average wage in 1980 was .24, a result that is statistically significant at a better than .0001 confidence level.... Thus, it would appear that movements of women in the 1970s were in directions consistent with improving their labor market status. One can only speculate that the greater shifts of the current decade will be seen to have furthered this tendency when the 1990 census becomes available.

SUMMARY AND CONCLUSIONS

The results of this analysis should serve to give pause before the United States rushes to adopt the complex legal remedy of comparable worth to deal with a perception of gender effects on wages. Although the methodology has limitations, it provides a framework designed to capture far more gender effects than could be removed by the comparable worth laws advocated in the United States. Yet, even in this most favorable case, the results provide no evidence that once legitimate influences on wages (e.g., an occupation's effort, responsibility, fringe benefits, and working conditions) are taken into account there remains any detectable effect of its sex composition on the wages of either men or women in that occupation.

To the extent that such effects have been claimed from other studies, they may be due to an inability to include more than a limited array of job characteristics. When the characteristics included more fully capture the nature of the job rather than being limited by either data availability or the researcher's prior beliefs, the labor market appears to reward job attributes and worker productivity and not the race or sex of the worker.

NOTES

1. The methodological difficulties arise from changes over time in the categories into which occupations are classified (England, 1981).

2. It should be noted that nothing has been said about how these personality differences may have arisen. Some maintain that they are innately linked to biological differences between the sexes; others believe they are the result of childhood conditioning. The reality is probably some combination of these and other sources.

3. Such locational differences contribute to wage differentials because commuting time is a negative characteristic that must be compensated for and because, by restricting the opportunity set from which a job may be chosen, individuals who desire to work close to home limit their ability to seek out their highest productivity and highest paying match. Occupational segregation will result from the fact that workers who desire employment close to home will only be available to those industries that are well suited to decentralized production in residential areas. Firms requiring large work forces (therefore having to draw workers from a wide geographic area) or not able to locate in residential neighborhoods (due to the need to be in a central place or because of production externalities) will tend to have a disproportionate share of male workers. To the extent that such firms are (as would appear likely) better paying establishments, this segregation will also contribute to wage differentials.

4. It is an unanswered question to what extent observed patterns of occupational segregation result from impositions from outside the labor market. An obvious example is the law preventing women from serving in combat specialties in the armed forces. Until very recently, many states had protective legislation that limited the exposure of women to hazardous working conditions and restricted the schedules and number of hours women could work.

It has been very difficult to develop models of how denial of access can be stable over time and not create incentives for nondiscriminatory employers (including women themselves) to employ women

in the previously denied occupations. Indeed, most models of discriminatory actions on the part of employers lead to firm segregation rather than occupational segregation, a result consistent with the finding of Bielby and Baron (1984) that segregation among firms is generally greater than that across occupations.

5. These policies are, to a certain extent, mutually exclusive. If policies are enacted to raise wages in women's occupations to a level commensurate with their productivity and working conditions, this reduces the incentive for women to move into jobs previously held by men.

6. See Polachek (1987) for an explanation of why this procedure is unable to distinguish adequately between human capital and occupational sex segregation explanations for sexual differences in earnings.

7. They are available from the author.

8. As an alternative method of data reduction, factor analysis was tried on the full set of raw variables. Even when rotated in several alternative ways, however, a large number of factors were required to capture even a moderate portion of the complexity in the data. Given the pattern of loadings on the factors, it proved difficult to assign any meaningful interpretation to them. An attempt was then made to group the variables on an ad hoc basis into 25 distinct sets based on what they apparently measured and then extract factors only within each set. Results from this experiment were highly ungratifying, and the resulting factors were of little use in explaining average wages in occupations. Thus, the decision was reached to retain variables in their raw form and reduce the number of variables used through a stepwise procedure.

9. Fringe benefits are one of the clearest cases for which compensating differentials theory suggests that wages will adjust to job characteristics. For example, a job that provides health coverage can attract workers at a lower wage than one that does not provide health benefits since workers will not have to pay for them out of pocket. Although one might alternatively add fringe benefits to wages to obtain a measure of full compensation, there are difficulties with this approach. Since fringe benefits are typically offered as a take-it-or-leave-it package, there can be no assumption that any given worker values them at their full cost to the employer (e.g., consider the value of maternity leave to a single man). Thus, the value of a fringe benefit package to employees is best established not by accounting costs but rather by the wage reductions workers are willing to accept in order to obtain the package.

NO

Jerry A. Jacobs and
Ronnie J. Steinberg

COMPENSATING DIFFERENTIALS AND THE MALE-FEMALE WAGE GAP: EVIDENCE FROM THE NEW YORK STATE COMPARABLE WORTH STUDY

Though the sex gap in wages has declined somewhat in recent years, it remains substantial. In 1986, the earnings of women working full time were 64% of those of comparably employed men. Measured human-capital characteristics explain only a small proportion of this difference. One prominent line of inquiry attempting to explain gender-based earnings inequality has focused on the concentration of women in relatively low-paying occupations. Approximately one-fifth of the sex gap in wages has been associated with sex segregation of occupations, and, when industrial segregation is also considered, the proportion of the wage gap resulting from sex segregation increases to 36%. Thus the low wages associated with female-dominated occupations are not primarily the result of sex differences in measurable human-capital traits. Jacobs has further proposed that sex segregation is not simply the result of early-life socialization but rather a consequence of a life-long system of social control that channels and rechannels women into female-dominated fields.

Since human-capital and socialization explanations have proven insufficient in explaining occupational segregation, research interest has been increasingly directed to the role of organizational personnel policies and practices. The comparable worth movement has made such a shift in its focus on compensation practices in its attempt to elevate the relative pay of female-dominated occupations by correcting for the undervaluation of "women's work."

Though most researchers have accepted as a given that women's work is more poorly paid than men's in jobs requiring similar education and experience, Randall Filer's prominent article in the National Research Council's *Pay Equity: Empirical Inquiries* (1989) maintains that female-dominated occupations in fact are not underpaid. He frames his argument in terms of the

From Jerry A. Jacobs and Ronnie J. Steinberg, "Compensating Differentials and the Male-Female Wage Gap: Evidence from the New York State Comparable Worth Study," *Social Forces*, vol. 69, no. 2 (December 1990). Copyright © 1990 by University of North Carolina Press. Reprinted by permission. Notes and references omitted.

economic "compensating differentials" hypothesis, suggesting that women work in "lower paying but otherwise more attractive jobs" and concluding that the wage gap can be accounted for by the wage premium paid to men because of undesirable working conditions in their jobs. The implication is that the wage gap that flows from sex segregation is the legitimate result of job differences. Filer holds that sex segregation of occupations is largely voluntary because of differences in "tastes" regarding the importance of working conditions. Wages between female- and male-dominated occupations differ because women choose to take a larger proportion of their total compensation package in nonpecuniary amenities, whereas men opt for a larger proportion of their benefits in wages.

If correct, the conclusion that women's work is not undervalued would be significant, not only for our understanding of the processes of sex segregation but also for our assessment of policy efforts such as comparable worth. Filer is well aware of the policy relevance of his findings. "The results," he cautions, "should serve to give pause before the United States rushes to adopt... comparable worth to deal with a perception of gender effects on wages."

In this article we examine Filer's argument directly by testing the proposition that differences in undesirable features of work between male- and female-dominated occupations account for the sex gap in wages. We argue that the compensating differentials argument is flawed both empirically and conceptually. We first review studies that offer compensating differentials as an explanation of the gender gap in wages and then examine in detail the compensation associated with a wide array of working conditions

found in New York State government employment. Specifically, we test whether male-dominated jobs are characterized by more unfavorable working conditions than female-dominated jobs and whether these differences translate into wage differentials that account for the gender gap in wages. In addition, we compile pertinent data on this thesis from a number of comparable worth studies.

We conclude by suggesting that our results are consistent with a power-based perspective on intraorganizational wage-setting. We hold that the ability of workers to obtain compensating differentials depends on the politics of the workplace —that workers receive extra compensation for working in unfavorable or dangerous conditions only when they are powerful enough to insert this claim directly into their labor contract.

This article contributes to related research literature and policy discussions in several respects. First, it adds to the small body of research on the possible contribution of working conditions to the gender gap in wages. It also broadens one's understanding of the role of working conditions in wage determination by examining a wide set of job attributes in a unique data set drawn from the New York State Comparable Pay Study.

Further, the evidence presented contributes to the general question of the role of preferences as an explanation for occupational sex segregation. The compensating differentials hypothesis is the economists' version of the view that women bring different goals and values with them into the labor market. Sociologists and social psychologists have also argued that socialization results in such work-oriented differences in traits, although Jacobs has found that such differences do not account for the persistence of occupational segregation. An examination of the impact of job characteristics on wages will shed light on whether women's preferences are responsible for their lower pay. Finally, this analysis will contribute to a vigorous, ongoing policy debate regarding the legitimacy and significance of comparable worth as a strategy for decreasing the sex gap in wages.

COMPENSATING DIFFERENTIALS

The idea that workers receive extra compensation for toiling under unfavorable conditions originated with Adam Smith. In *Wealth of Nations,* Smith's first postulate concerning wage variation is that "the wages of labor vary with the ease or hardship, the cleanliness or dirtiness, the honourableness or dishonourableness of the employment." Smith held that workers doing physically onerous or dirty jobs receive extra compensation for their troubles, whereas those employed in the "honourable professions are 'under-recompensed.'" Simply stated, he reasoned that an undesirable feature of a job reduces the supply of individuals interested in that job and that anything that reduces the supply of workers increases the wage employers must pay to fill that position.

Contemporary economists refer to this phenomenon as a "compensating differential" whereby an observed difference in the wages between two jobs may represent monetary compensation for a countervailing differential in working conditions. This reasoning would hold, for example, that garbage collectors are likely to be paid more than bus drivers.... This wage premium is paid because the former position is less pleasant and consequently requires an added wage incentive to induce prospective employees to pursue this line of work. The assumption is that the "utility" of the higher wage to the marginal worker is just sufficient to compensate for the unpleasantness (and associated "disutility") of the less desirable job. While high-income positions may have better working conditions than low-income ones, among jobs with similar entry requirements, higher wages should be observed in jobs with less desirable working conditions. Though most often discussed by economists, the compensating differentials logic is consistent with the logic of the functional theory of stratification.

Can the compensating differentials hypothesis predict which specific job characteristics will be positively rewarded and which negatively? The preferences of the "marginal" worker are considered crucial in determining which working conditions will be associated with a wage premium. Since no one knows who the marginal worker is or what his or her preferences are, in principle it is impossible to predict which job characteristics will be positively or negatively valued. As Robert Smith notes in his review of recent literature on compensating differentials, "Given the variety of human preferences, it is doubtful that [job] characteristics ... can be claimed, a priori, to be disagreeable at the margin."

Nonetheless, the operationalization of undesirable working conditions has largely rested on plausible assertions relying on face validity. In their reviews of ten articles, all focusing on exclusively male samples, both Brown and Smith cite a common list of job conditions economists have isolated as undesirable. These are work requiring heavy physical labor; work involving noise, temperature extremes, dirt, or hazardous materials; repetitive work; fast-paced work;

work involving low autonomy; stressful work; job insecurity; work with machines; and work involving risk of injury or death. The implicit assumption is that most workers prefer secure jobs that are clean and safe and do not involve extreme noise and temperature, and in which there is sufficient autonomy to regulate the pace of one's work. In practice, most empirical research selects a subset of these job characteristics, asserts their undesirability, and leaves it up to the reader to judge the reasonableness of such an evaluation.

Empirical evidence on the compensating differentials hypothesis remains mixed despite its illustrious pedigree. In his review of compensating differentials literature, Robert Smith concludes that, except for jobs that involve risk of injury or death, working conditions such as those involving heavy physical labor, low autonomy, or a fast pace often produce negative wage effects instead of the positive ones predicted by the compensating differentials hypothesis. Brown also reports that the literature contains an "uncomfortable number" of exceptions to the predictions of this hypothesis. Nevertheless, the logic of compensating differentials has recently been employed as an explanation for the difference in pay between male- and female-dominated jobs.

COMPENSATING DIFFERENTIALS AND THE WAGE GAP

Randall Filer has advanced the most serious empirical effort to demonstrate the importance of working conditions in explaining the sex gap in wages. Filer asserts that both men and women assess the undesirable features of jobs uniformly but act differently in making job choices, with men attaching more

importance to wages and benefits and women to "interpersonal and other nonwage aspects of the job." He further maintains that women are paid less because they work in more pleasant jobs. In his words,

> Once compensating differentials for a job's effort, responsibility, fringe benefits, and working conditions are taken into account, there is no significant relationship between an occupation's gender composition and its wages for either men or women.

Filer is not especially concerned with specifying which job characteristics are undesirable *a priori*. Instead, he states, "No preconceived notions of whether these characteristics are 'good' or 'bad' are required. The data will tell us how the marginal worker evaluates them." In other words, if a job characteristic is positively compensated, it must be undesirable. Thus Filer's identification of job characteristics that require a wage premium is decidedly *post hoc*.

Filer's 1985 article analyzes a national sample of men and women from the 1977 Quality of Employment Survey [QES] to estimate the effects of 28 different job characteristics, controlling for individual variation in education and experience. Based on a sample of 250 women and 350 men employed in jobs that pay hourly wages, he finds that women generally report more favorable working conditions than men. Further, Filer concludes that, depending on the equation, between 31% and 65% of the gender gap in wages is attributable to differences in job characteristics.

However, closer scrutiny reveals that Filer's estimate of the wage gap attributable to working conditions is based on little statistically reliable evidence.

Because of his small sample size, few of the coefficients for job attribute variables Filer reports are statistically significant, raising questions about whether a given job characteristic can be viewed as a basis for compensation. Specifically, only 7 of the 28 coefficients for working conditions are statistically significant for men, and a mere 4 for women. Further, in our reanalysis of the QES data, the introduction of a simple control for occupation substantially reduces the number of coefficients that remain significant and in the direction predicted by the compensating differentials hypothesis. Yet, for purposes of decomposing the sex gap in wages, Filer treats all of these coefficients as if they were meaningful and precise. Since the decomposition of the wage gap sums up the effects of a large number of statistically insignificant coefficients associated with particular job attributes, we consider the analysis suspect. . . .

Finally, we are skeptical about the impact of compensating differentials on the wage gap because evidence suggests that compensation typically offered for working conditions constitutes a small fraction of workers' wages. Aldrich and Buchele note, for example, that skills are typically fourteen times as important as working conditions in the job evaluation systems they examined.

Nevertheless, the conclusion that female-dominated jobs are not underpaid once associated working conditions are taken into account strikes at the heart of the justification for comparable worth. Because this argument is receiving considerable play in policy circles and among economists, a careful examination of the compensating differentials hypothesis is warranted.

COMPENSATING DIFFERENTIALS: A TEST

For the compensating differentials logic to account for the wage gap between men and women, three things must be true. First, male-dominated positions must feature less desirable working conditions than female-dominated jobs. A fair test of this premise would involve measuring a wide array of job characteristics found in both male- and female-dominated jobs. While certain undesirable working conditions are concentrated in male-dominated jobs, occupations dominated by women may have their own set of undesirable working conditions. Previous research on compensating differentials has focused almost exclusively on undesirable working conditions typically found in male-dominated jobs.

Second, jobs must receive a wage premium for such undesirable employment conditions. After controls for entry requirements such as education are introduced, undesirable working conditions should have a positive association with wages. If there were no wage bonus for undesirable working conditions, the presence of such conditions in male-dominated occupations would not be able to account for the male-female pay gap.

Third, the sex gap in earnings attributable to working conditions must be shown to account for a substantial portion of the difference in pay between male- and female-dominated jobs. In other words, one must show statistically that little or no sex composition effect persists once working-conditions measures are controlled.

. . . [T]he data from the New York State Comparable Pay Study, which include more variegated measures of job attributes than any survey data of which we are aware, constitute an excellent testing ground for assessing the compensating differentials model. . . .

RESULTS

Distribution of Job Attributes by Sex-Type of Job

Our first test of the compensating differentials hypothesis assesses whether white male-dominated jobs are characterized by more undesirable working conditions than female-dominated jobs. . . .

If we based our test simply on the working-conditions summary index, we would find that male-dominated jobs have somewhat more undesirable attributes than those dominated by women. This result is not surprising—we note ... the connection of this index to conventional measures of hazards historically associated with male-dominated blue-collar jobs. However, when we disaggregate this measure, we find that female-dominated jobs are more likely to be noisy and to involve cleaning others' dirt, whereas jobs dominated by men are likelier to involve working in hot or cold conditions, exposure to fumes, risk of injury, and strenuous physical activity.

Yet, as expected, other undesirable characteristics are concentrated in female-dominated positions, which are more likely to involve working with difficult clients and sick or dying patients as well as less autonomy and more repetition. Male-dominated jobs, on the other hand, are likelier to involve communication with the public and (slightly) more stress.

The productivity-related job content of male- and female-dominated jobs also vary White male-dominated jobs involve such desirable features as managerial, supervisory, and fiscal responsibilities. Because these are productivity-related job attributes rather than working conditions *per se*, we do not consider these measures tests of the compensating differentials thesis.

Thus the first premise of the compensating differentials explanation of women's low wages receives mixed support at best. On the basis of some 25,000 employee reports on job content and conditions associated with 1,605 different jobs held by approximately 170,000 workers, we find that in New York State female-dominated jobs involve somewhat *different* (and not necessarily fewer) undesirable working conditions than jobs dominated by men. Since we don't know how seriously employees view each of these items, this analysis by itself is not definitive. But these data do suggest that male-dominated jobs do not have a monopoly on undesirable working conditions. Yet, as Barry discovered, compensation may be made for undesirable working conditions in male-dominated jobs though it may not be in jobs dominated by women. We now examine how each of these working-conditions items relates to wage structure.

Job Attributes and Wages

A second test of the compensating differentials argument examines whether additional wages are paid for jobs that involve undesirable working conditions. In other words, for the compensating differentials thesis to be an accurate predictor of wage premiums, undesirable job attributes would have to be associated with premiums, net of other compensable job attributes such as experience and educational requirements and managerial and supervisory responsibility. . . .

Of the 14 job-characteristic measures considered, the signs of 10 are contrary to the prediction of the compensating differentials model. Only 4 of the measures have the expected positive effect on wages for undesirable working conditions: stress, fumes, handling sick patients, and unexpected problems. Of these, only handling sick patients is statistically significant.

In the analysis restricted to statistically significant variables, we find that jobs that involve working in hot, cold, or noisy conditions, cleaning others' dirt, engaging in strenuous physical activity, and even risking injury—the most direct measure of on-the-job hazard—are each associated with lower wages than are other jobs. Incumbents in jobs with these attributes earn less than those in other jobs with similar educational, writing, and experience requirements, and at similar levels of time, effort and supervisory responsibility. Repetitive work and being told what to do are also negatively compensated. For only one job measure—dealing with sick or dying patients—is there evidence of positive compensation associated with an undesirable job characteristic. Ironically, since this attribute is found disproportionately in female-dominated jobs, it cannot explain the gap between men's and women's wages. To do so, other positively compensated attributes would have to be concentrated in male-dominated occupations.

We next test for interaction effects between sex composition of the job and undesirable working conditions to determine whether the latter might be compensated for in either male- or female-dominated jobs but not across-the-board.... In general, the sign of each of the working-conditions measures is the same for both male- and female-dominated jobs: traits that are negatively valued for male-dominated jobs are also negatively valued for female-dominated jobs. The exceptions run counter to what would be predicted by the compensating differentials explanation of the gender gap. Male-dominated jobs seem to be more heavily penalized than jobs dominated by women for undesirable working conditions that are strenuous jobs. Indeed, we find that in New York State employees in white male-dominated jobs are actually negatively compensated for the two job conditions that have conventionally been most associated with the compensating differentials argument: risk of injury and work involving strenuous physical activity. Similarly, female-dominated jobs are more heavily penalized for repetitious work, an attribute more prevalent in these jobs.

As a final test, we repeat this analysis for the jobs included in each of the three collective bargaining units. In New York State government employment, each of the bargaining units represents a "natural" break in job groupings. One union, for example, represents clerical, operational, and nonprofessional institutional service jobs; a second bargains for entry-level positions requiring a bachelor's degree and/or the so-called women's professions; a third unit represents nonunionized managerial and professional employees. We carried out this analysis because we suspected that, while compensating differentials might not account for wage differences between a heavy equipment operator and an assistant commissioner of the Office of General Services, they might explain wage differences between nonexempt male- and female-dominated jobs in which the differences in wages are less extreme.

The results indicate that, with one interesting exception, compensating differentials do not explain these differences. Within each bargaining unit, most undesirable working conditions are associated with lower wages, controlling for all other job attributes. The exception is that, among the lowest-tier jobs, which include craft and construction workers, risk of injury becomes positively associated with wages. This is worth highlighting, since it foreshadows our discussion of the complexities of assuming that compensating differentials, as opposed to political manipulation, are the basis for wage-setting practices.

Explaining the Sex Gap in Wages
The third test of the compensating differentials explanation determines whether the difference in pay between women and men can be accounted for by the wage effects of undesirable working conditions. We find that the explanation fails to meet this test as well: net of all factors examined, the proportion of women in a job continues to depress the wage associated with it. Therefore, even when these content and context factors are taken into account, the greater the presence of women in a job, the lower the salary accorded it. The percent minority does not remain statistically significant once job-content controls and other job characteristics are included in the analysis. But a detailed test of whether the race gap in wages is accounted for by the compensating differentials thesis is beyond the scope of this article.

First we note that working conditions explain only a small proportion of the variance in wages in New York State. Productivity-related variables account for 86% of the variation in salary grades, and adding working conditions

to the analysis adds only 3% to the explained variance. This suggests that working conditions are unlikely to account for the substantial sex gap in wages in this employment system. Our findings are consistent with those of Aldrich and Buchele, indicating the small weight accorded to working conditions relative to skills in existing job-evaluation systems. We summarize the practical significance of our results by considering the results of three hypotheticals which indicate how much impact working conditions has on the sex gap in wages.

What would happen to wages for female-dominated jobs if the sex bias in wage-setting were removed? Specifically, how much change would we observe in wages associated with female-dominated jobs if the negative effect of sex composition of occupations were removed? Note that this is the sex composition effect that remains after both productivity and working-conditions measures are controlled.... In this model, a 100% change in the percent female with a job reduces its associated wage by 2.56 salary grades. Since the average female-dominated job is held by 85% women, removing this presumably discriminatory effect would increase the wages for female-dominated jobs by 2.18 salary grades, or 18% of its base pay. The ratio of wages for female-dominated jobs to white male-dominated jobs would increase from 61.5% to 72.3%. Thus using this equation as the basis for a comparable worth remedy would result in a 27.9% reduction in the gap between the wages for male- and female-dominated jobs.

Second, what would be the effect on wages for female-dominated jobs if these jobs were characterized by the same working conditions as male-dominated ones? We hold the education, experience, and responsibility measures for female-dominated jobs constant and substitute men's means for the working-conditions variables in calculating the salary grade of female-dominated jobs. This substitution results in a *reduction* in wages for these jobs from an average salary grade of 12.12 to 11.87, or 60.4% of the salary of white male-dominated jobs. If women in the New York State Civil Service worked in conditions more like those in which men do, their wages would *decline* slightly, since working conditions generally have negative effects on wages: since men have somewhat higher levels of these negatively valued job attributes, substituting their levels for women's reduces women's remuneration relative to men's

Third, what would be the effect of eliminating the negative effect of working conditions on wages of both men and women? On the face of it, it makes no sense for employees to lose money for performing unpleasant tasks or tolerating undesirable conditions. If we removed the negative effect of all working conditions, what would be the effect on the wages of female-dominated jobs relative to those of white male-dominated jobs?

...We find that the average salary grade of female-dominated jobs increases substantially from 12.12 to 17.35. At the same time, the average salary grade of white male-dominated jobs rises from 19.66 to 23.63. While the absolute increase is similar, it constitutes a larger fraction of women's wages. Thus we find that the wages of both women and men would increase as a result of such a program but that women's wages would increase more than men's. The ratio of the salary grade of female-dominated jobs to white male-dominated jobs would increase

from 61.6% to 73.4%. Most of this change, it should be noted, is caused by the removal of the sex composition of jobs: only a slight positive increment results from the "zeroing out" of negatively valued working conditions.

Even though incumbents in some female-dominated jobs receive a relative salary advantage because they deal with sick and injured patients, their salaries are deflated because of their tendency to clean up after others and to work in noisy settings. Repetition and being told what to do also contribute to a reduction in their wages. In New York State government employment, therefore, removing the negative impact of the range of undesirable working conditions found in jobs would slightly improve women's wages relative to men. Once again, these results are inconsistent with the predictions of a compensating differentials approach to the sex gap in wages, since that approach predicts wage bonuses and not wage penalties for working in undesirable conditions.

Corroborating evidence was culled from a number of state and local comparable worth studies, all of which have explicit measures of working conditions as well as productivity-related job-content measures. Though these studies, which are often methodologically sophisticated and professionally conducted, have not found their way into the research literature and were not constructed to test the compensating differentials thesis, they do constitute direct evidence of the effect of working conditions on wages. Each study measures job content differently and each controls for different variables....

These studies generally find that undesirable working conditions *negatively* related to wages after appropriate controls are introduced. Only 6 of the 22 working conditions coefficients... are in the positive direction predicted by the compensating differentials thesis. In 3 of the studies, the results are entirely inconsistent with compensating differentials. Moreover, the evidence indicates that, while productivity-related and other job characteristics account for some of the gender gap in wages, female-dominated positions remain undervalued even after these effects are removed.

DISCUSSION

The three basic tests of the compensating differentials argument fail to receive support in this analysis. The results are directly at odds with the compensating differentials explanation of the gender gap in wages. Male-dominated positions do not have a monopoly on undesirable working conditions. There are countless undesirable features of work, and many of these are concentrated in female-dominated jobs. Further, in general, neither men nor women are positively compensated for working in unpleasant or unsafe conditions. The majority of the measures of undesirable working conditions have a negative effect on wages, net of education, experience, responsibility, and other productivity-related job attributes. We did find that trade and construction workers receive some additional compensation for risk of injury on the job relative to those in the same bargaining unit, and that health workers receive additional compensation for working with sick or injured patients. As we will elaborate below, we view these exceptions to be grounded in particular political circumstances rather than an indication of some general economic imperative requiring the compensation of workers in undesirable settings. As

a rule, undesirable working conditions have been penalized in the compensation policy of the New York State government. Finally, a significant negative gender coefficient remains in all the equations estimated. Thus, even after all the factors considered are taken into account (factors that explain 90% of the variance in wages), women's work remains significantly undervalued. Each of the links in the compensating differentials chain fails to receive support in our analysis. Putting women in jobs with the same working conditions as men would not reduce the sex gap in wages, while eliminating the perverse effects of working conditions on wages would benefit women slightly more than men.

We have even deeper problems with the compensating differentials approach. We believe that the general pattern of wage penalties associated with undesirable working conditions, as well as the occasional wage premium, can be explained by a model of wage determination that begins not with preferences but with an analysis of the politics of wage determination in a firm or an organization. The ability of specific groups of employees to obtain additional compensation for working in undesirable conditions depends on their ability to legitimate a claim of entitlement and their power to insert this claim into their organization's compensation policy. Once a claim has been inserted into the compensation practices of enough employers in a local labor market and not found to be economically deleterious, it becomes institutionalized into most wage structures in that local labor market....

Recent experience with comparable worth initiatives is especially instructive in that they reveal the way political arrangements affect efforts to reform the wage structure. Steinberg shows that in New York State one of the motives for undertaking a comparable worth study was to satisfy a long-standing union demand that clerical jobs be reclassified upward. During the New York study, decisions about the definition of female-dominated jobs and jobs held by a disproportionate number of minorities, the nondiscriminatory pay standard, and job-content factors and factor weights were the subject of lengthy and often heated negotiations between management, labor, and the feminist proponents conducting the study. The poststudy implementation of wage adjustments was filled with political manipulation and conflict, which included unilateral managerial reworking of the statistical analysis to minimize equity adjustments and threats to one union of wage cuts in the male-dominated jobs it represented.

In Oregon, Acker found that managers and unions were able to reproduce class and gender hierarchy in the wage structure even during an initiative whose goal was a substantial reduction in such inequalities. After more than four years of intense conflict among labor, management, and feminists, only feminists fell short of their goals for modifying the wage structure. The general power resources and specific access to decision making available to labor and management was simply not open to feminists.

We maintain that workers' efforts to receive supplemental compensation for working in undesirable conditions generally involves a process of conflict in a context of unequal power similar to what is being observed in comparable worth initiatives. Workers are not without power, however, and one source of power not often discussed in the literature is the legitimation of employee

demands by recourse to an argument that carries compelling face validity. Risk, noise, and other negative job attributes can be translated into wages most often when workers are powerful enough to introduce such issues into discussions regarding wages, often through unions or other workplace pressure groups, and when there is a basis for constructing a plausible and effective rationale.

This process at the organizational level parallels the one that occurs in the political arena when employees demand that the state intervene in the setting of the terms and conditions of their employment contract. Given a commitment to laissez-faire, the state would only intervene in circumstances regarded as "extraordinary," where the legal assumption of bargaining equality was visibly violated. During the Progressive Era, for example, labor standards legislation specifying working hours or prohibiting nightwork was extended to women, minors, and males who succeeded in arguing that they worked in physically dangerous conditions. Thus men who worked in underground mines obtained statutory rights to an 8-hour day, whereas men who worked in bakeries were denied such rights because their jobs were not viewed as dangerous. Even women's rights were limited by the industry or occupation in which they worked: it took decades of vigorous political action by women to extend the right to a 48-hour work week from manufacturing to retail sales. The labor standard laws extended to women were the result of a conscious strategy by groups such as the National Consumers League, collaborating with unions, to use the ideology of women's biological inferiority as a power resource to extend to them rights legally denied men. In general, the inclusion of particular types of work under the umbrella of protection was the result of the political success of these unions in defining specific types of work as deserving this designation, as workers failed to achieve a universal entitlement to protection.

Thus a political or what might be called "negotiated" model of wage determination does not assume that undesirable working conditions automatically translate into wages, even if there is a shortage in the supply of workers. In the case of labor shortage, a number of outcomes is possible. Employers might raise wages to attract a larger pool of workers, in which case a number of other categories of workers may also obtain wage increases on grounds of equity or by attempting to show that they are also in great demand. Alternatively, the tasks involved might be redefined to minimize or alleviate the shortage. In a large bureaucratic setting with an elaborate division of labor, those with power have been known to reorganize their work to have tasks that are viewed as "dirty" or "routine" handled by others. A labor shortage might present itself as an opportunity to a group endeavoring such a strategy. We suggest that power arrangements will affect the conditions of work, its content, and its assessment for purposes of compensation. Indeed, from the perspective of the sociology of work, undesirable working conditions may be a sign of lack of power, indicating that the job is unlikely to receive high wages.

Future research needs to develop specific independent measures of power that can be employed to empirically explain wage patterns that cannot be explained by the imperatives of economic efficiency and utility maximization underlying the compensating differentials perspective. Comparable worth efforts may be a strategic vantage point for such case studies because the political struggles over comparable worth raise questions regarding what makes a job "deserving" of additional compensation. Study of such initiatives can also inform us of the conditions under which employees will actually obtain wage increases once they are viewed as underpaid.

Authors are listed alphabetically and share authorship equally. An earlier draft of this article was presented at the American Sociological Association Meetings, Atlanta, August 1988. The research assistance of Tahmina Ferdousi is greatly appreciated. We thank Paula England, Lois Haignere, David Karen, Janice Madden, Patricia Roos, Leo Rigsby, and Helen Remick for their comments and suggestions.

POSTSCRIPT

Are Women Paid Less Than Men Because Their Working Conditions Are More Favorable?

This issue allows us to examine how labor markets work. It provides us an opportunity to test our understanding of economic theory and to observe how researchers test hypotheses. Because of the sophisticated statistical/econometrics techniques employed in these two essays, we might miss the basic economic argument that takes place here. That would be unfortunate, since the wage differentials that currently exist in the labor market may be imposing a substantial financial burden on female workers. If the differentials are justifiable, then the comparable worth legislation that is currently in place creates a windfall gain to some female workers, an economic distortion in the labor markets, and an unnecessary burden on taxpayers.

Filer provides evidence to support this latter set of conclusions. His research suggests that women are attracted to occupations that have more "pleasant" job characteristics than those jobs that are dominated by men. Since the female-dominated occupations are more pleasant, their compensation is lower than the less pleasant but more highly paid male-dominated occupations.

Jacobs and Steinberg reject this conclusion. Their research implies that women simply do not have sufficient *power* to demand and receive the compensation that they are entitled to in a workplace that is dominated by male workers. They conclude that compensating differentials depend on the politics of the workplace. If workers are relatively strong, they can negotiate extra compensation for tolerating dangerous or unpleasant working conditions. If they are weak, which historically has been the case for women, they suffer the consequences of lower wages.

Much has been written about the advisability and inadvisability of comparable worth. An excellent introduction to this topic by an advocate of comparable worth is in Helen Reinick, ed., *Comparable Worth and Wage Discrimination* (Temple University Press, 1984). The opposition's arguments are well argued in E. Robert Levernash, ed., *Comparable Worth: Issues and Alternatives* (Equal Employment Advisory Council, 1980). An extremely readable and informative set of congressional hearings is found in Hearings before the Subcommittees on Human Resources, Civil Service, and Compensation and Employee Benefits, Committee on Post Office and Civil Service, *Pay Equity: Equal Pay for Work of Comparable Worth*, 97th Congress, 2d session (1982).

Finally we should note that you can follow the Filer–Jacobs/Steinberg debate in the professional literature. Filer provides a final "Comment" in the December 1990 issue of *Social Forces*. His work in turn is critiqued by James P. Smith in an essay entitled "Commentary," which can be found in Robert T. Michael, Heidi Hartman, and Bridget O'Farrell, eds., *Pay Equity: Empirical Inquiries*, (National Academy Press, 1989).

ISSUE 5

Are Rent Controls the Cause of America's Homelessness?

YES: William Tucker, from "How Housing Regulations Cause Homelessness," *The Public Interest* (Winter 1991)

NO: Richard P. Appelbaum et al., from "Scapegoating Rent Control: Masking the Causes of Homelessness," *Journal of the American Planning Association* (Spring 1991)

ISSUE SUMMARY

YES: Journalist William Tucker analyzes the problem of homelessness across the United States and suggests that rent controls and homelessness are correlated.

NO: Sociologist Richard P. Appelbaum and his research associates submit that Tucker's statistical analysis is flawed and that he ignores the real causes of homelessness: poverty, the lack of affordable housing, and inadequate support services for those who suffer from mental illness and alcoholism.

Most principles of economics textbooks spend some time discussing rent controls and how they distort the operation of the market system. Most use rent controls as an example of a price ceiling, which is a legal maximum on the price that may be charged for a commodity. The objective of rent control is, of course, to protect the consumer from high rents. However, supply and demand analysis suggests that, as a result of rent controls, an excess in the quantity demanded for rental housing occurs. This in turn forces landlords to ration the limited supply of rental units on some nonprice basis (personal habits, family size, and length of residence in the community, for example). With the imposition of rent controls, the market is not allowed to reach its equilibrium level, and a "net loss" to society is assumed to result as consumers are forced to pay a high price for the relatively small quantity that suppliers of housing units make available to the market.

Some textbooks go beyond discussing the efficiency implications of these market interferences and examine the historical experiences of New York City, Boston, Los Angeles, San Francisco, Washington, D.C., and other U.S. cities that have experimented with rent controls. These textbooks generally assume that purely competitive market conditions, which are necessary to utilize a supply and demand analysis, are or would be present in these housing markets if there were no rent controls. They conclude that these well-meaning governmental interventions in housing markets have left those in search of affordable housing worse off than if the market were allowed to operate on its own. They allege that renters hold on to apartments because rents are low, while at the same time these low rents discourage landlords from maintaining, upgrading, and/or investing in new units. Thus there are simply fewer housing units on the market.

It is only in recent years, however, that homelessness has been linked to the imposition of rent controls. This connection can be directly traced to the research findings of William Tucker.

In the early 1980s, under pressure from groups charged with the responsibility to provide social services to the homeless, the Reagan administration began to count the number of homeless persons. In 1984, the U.S. Department of Housing and Urban Development issued a study entitled "Report to the Secretary on the Homeless and Emergency Shelters," which estimated that the national homeless population was somewhere between 250,000 and 350,000 persons. (This study forms the statistical foundation for the Tucker selection in this debate.) This estimate and the Reagan administration's hands-off policy to deal with this problem came under intense attack. Groups such as the Coalition for the Homeless in New York and the Committee for Creative Non-Violence in Washington, D.C., estimated that this population was in reality between 2 and 3 million persons in 1984.

Who are these people who find themselves homeless? (*Homeless* refers to an individual who regularly has no place to sleep and must seek refuge in a shelter or remain on the streets after nightfall.) Besides the mentally ill who have not found adequate community care following deinstitutionalization and the drug and alcohol addicts, there are: low-income families who have been evicted for nonpayment of rent; the unemployed; those who have lost their benefits from federal or state welfare or unemployment programs; battered women; and individuals and families that have been displaced by condominium conversions, gentrification, and urban renewal.

It seems reasonable to ask, why has the market not responded by providing "affordable housing" for these people? If we are to believe Tucker, it is because of rent controls. Prospective landlords do not believe that they can earn a financial return sufficient to compensate them for the risk that they must bear. Richard P. Appelbaum and his research team reject Tucker's analysis and his conclusion, largely on the basis of a systematic statistical critique of the Tucker study.

YES

William Tucker

HOW HOUSING REGULATIONS CAUSE HOMELESSNESS

The problem of homelessness in the 1980s has puzzled liberals and conservatives alike. Both have tended to fit the problem into their preconceived views, without looking at what is new and different about the phenomenon.

For liberals, the issue has been fairly straightforward. Homelessness, they say, stems from a lack of government effort and compassion. Reacting almost reflexively, liberals have blamed homelessness on federal spending cuts and the heartlessness of the Reagan administration. The most commonly cited figure is that budget authorizations for the Department of Housing and Urban Development (HUD) were cut 75 percent in the Reagan years, from $32 billion in 1981 to $8 billion in 1988. Everything else is presumably self-explanatory. This compelling logic has even been repeated in the *Wall Street Journal*.

Conservatives, on the other hand, have taken two approaches. Either they deny the problem's existence or they assert that homelessness is almost always the result of personal pathologies. On the first count, it has often been argued (as in Martin Morse Wooster's June 1987 *Reason* article, "The Homeless: An Adman's Dream") that homelessness is really no worse than it ever was, but that the problem has been exaggerated to justify increases in government spending. On the other, conservatives have also argued that most of the homeless are insane, alcoholics, or drug addicts, and that their personal failings make it impossible for them to find housing, even when it is available.

UNPERSUASIVE EXPLANATIONS

But these arguments, whether liberal or conservative, do not really hold up under close scrutiny.

The most obviously flawed explanation lies in the figures that seem to indicate a massive federal cutback in housing assistance. There has been no such cutback. Federal low-income housing assistance actually *increased* from $5.7 billion in 1980 to $13.8 billion in 1988. The number of households receiving low-income housing assistance also rose, going from 3.1 million to 4.2 million during the same period.

The commonly cited "cutback" from $32 billion to $8 billion is the figure for HUD's future authorizations. This figure has nothing to do with actual housing assistance, however, since it only indicates the amount of money that Congress authorized HUD to spend in the future. These authorizations often run forty years in advance—and much of the money is never spent anyway.

The reason for this cutback has been the changeover from a program centered around public-housing construction to one centered around housing vouchers. When Congress authorizes a unit of new public housing, it must include all future mortgage payments, running decades ahead. In authorizing a housing voucher, Congress pledges money for only five years—the lifetime of the voucher.

In addition, vouchers provide the same housing at only half the price. A unit of public housing costs the federal government $8,000 a year, while a voucher costs only $4,000. Thus, twice as many people can be reached with the same amount of money. This is why HUD has been able to extend housing aid to more low-income people without an equivalent increase in spending.

But if the liberal argument about "spending cuts" is based largely on a misunderstanding of the budgetary process, the conservative argument that homelessness has not really increased at all seems equally ill-founded.

There were indeed homeless people long before 1980, and their numbers have always been difficult to count. But it is hard to ignore the almost unanimous reports from shelter providers (many of them old-line conservative church groups) that the problem has been getting steadily worse since 1980. The anecdotal evidence is also abundant. Anyone who has walked the streets of New York or Washington over the last decade knows that there are more beggars sitting on the sidewalks and sleeping on park benches than there were ten years ago.

Although many of the homeless are obviously alcoholics, drug addicts, and people who are clinically insane, large numbers appear only to be down on their luck. The most widely accepted statistical breakdown was first proposed in a 1988 Urban Institute paper: "Feeding the Homeless: Does the Prepared Meals Provision Help?" According to authors Martha Burt and Barbara Cohen, one-third of the homeless can be categorized as released mental patients, one-third as alcoholics and drug abusers, and one-third as people who are homeless for purely economic reasons.

Thus the component of homeless people who are not affected by personal pathologies is large. It should also be noted that being a chronic alcoholic or drug addict does not condemn a person to living in the streets. Even "winos" or "stumblebums" were able to find minimal housing in the past.

And so paradoxes remain. How can we have such a large homeless population at a time when rental vacancy rates are near postwar highs? How can there be plenty of housing but not enough "affordable housing"? In short, how can there be scarcity in the housing market when so much housing is still available?

VARIATIONS AMONG HOUSING MARKETS

These paradoxes can be resolved when we recognize that the housing market is not a national market but is instead the sum of many regional and local markets. Rental vacancy rates probably serve as the best measure of the availability of affordable housing, since most poor people rent. These rates vary widely from city to city. During the 1980s, rental vacancy rates in Dallas and Houston were rarely below 12 percent—a figure that is about twice what is considered a normal vacancy rate. At the same time, housing has been absurdly scarce in other cities. New York has not had vacancy rates over 3 percent since 1972. San Francisco had normal vacancy rates during the 1970s, but they plunged to 2 percent during the 1980s, where they remain today.

Since the poor tend to be limited in their mobility, vacancy rates significantly affect their ability to find housing. Although southern and southwestern cities claim to receive a regular seasonal migration of homeless people during the winter months, there is little evidence that people are moving from city to city to find housing. Other factors, like work opportunities, proximity to family members, and sheer inertia, seem to dominate people's choice of locale.

What should be far more mobile is the capital that builds housing and has created such a superabundance in specific cities. If it is difficult to find tenants for new apartments in Dallas and Phoenix, why don't builders shift to Boston or San Francisco, where housing is desperately needed?

Once we start asking this question, the impediments in the housing market suddenly become visible. It is obviously not equally easy to build housing in all cities. In particular, the local regulatory climate has a tremendous impact on the housing supply. Dallas and Houston are free-wheeling, market-oriented cities with little or no zoning regulation and negligible antigrowth sentiment. They have been able to keep abreast of hous-ing demand even as their populations grew rapidly. Boston and San Francisco, on the other hand, have highly regulated housing markets. Both are surrounded by tight rings of exclusionary suburbs, where zoning and growth-control sentiment make new construction extremely difficult. In addition, both have adopted rent control as a way of "solving" local housing shortages. As a result, both have extremely high housing prices and extremely tight rental markets. The median home price in each approaches $200,000, while in Dallas and Phoenix the median price is below the national median of $88,000.

Thus it makes little sense to talk about a national housing market's effect on homelessness. Local markets vary widely, and municipal regulation seems to be the deciding factor.

This is what has misled both liberals and conservatives. Conservatives look at the national superabundance of housing and conclude that local problems do not exist. Liberals look at local shortages and conclude that there is a national housing problem. In fact, housing shortages are a local problem created by local regulation, which is the work of local municipal governments.

It is not surprising, then, to find that homelessness varies widely from city to city, with local housing policies once again the decisive factor. These conclusions are supported by research that I conducted in 1988: I calculated comparative rates of per-capita homelessness for various cities, using the homelessness figures for the largest thirty-five cities investigated in the 1984 *Report to the Secretary of Housing and Urban Development on the Homeless and Emergency Shelters.* I also added fifteen other large cities that were not included in the initial HUD survey.

I then subjected the comparative rates of homelessness to regression analysis, in order to look for possible associations with other factors.

Among the independent variables that I considered were the local unemployment rate, the poverty rate, city size, the availability of public housing, the median rent, annual mean temperature, annual rainfall, the size of the minority population, population growth over the past fifteen years, the rental vacancy rate, the presence or absence of rent control, and the median home price in the metropolitan area surrounding each city.

Of all these variables, only four showed a significant correlation: the median home price, the rental vacancy rate, the presence of rent control, and the size of the minority population. The first three formed an overlapping cluster, with the median home price being the strongest predictor (accounting for around 42 percent of the variation, with a chance of error of less than .001 percent). The size of the minority population added about another 10 percent. The total predictive value for both factors was 51 percent, with a margin of error below .00001 percent.

When combined on a single graph (see Figure 1), the figures for the forty cities for which all of the relevant data are available show a strong trendline for median home prices; the cities with rent control are predominantly clustered in the top right-hand quadrant. Of the four major cities with minority populations of more than 60 percent, the two with rent control (Newark and Washington) are right on the trendline, while the two without it (Miami and Detroit) are the sole "outliers"—cities whose rates of homelessness do not seem to correspond with their positions in correlation with median home prices.

Altogether, these data suggest that housing variables are a better indicator of homelessness than are the traditional measures of unemployment, poverty, and the relative size of a city's public housing stock. High median home prices are usually found in cities with strict zoning ordinances and a strong no-growth effort. Cities with a tight ring of exclusionary suburbs (such as Boston, New York, Washington, San Francisco, and Los Angeles) have high home prices. Strangely enough, most have also adopted rent control.

At the same time, rent control is closely correlated with low rental vacancy rates. Every city in the country with rent control (except Los Angeles) has a vacancy rate below 4 percent, while the average for cities without rent control is over 8 percent.

When viewed historically, these low vacancy rates are obviously the result of rent control rather than its cause. When most of these cities adopted rent control in the 1970s, all had vacancy rates around the norm of 6 percent. Rather than being spurred by low vacancies, the rent-control ordinances that swept the East and West Coasts during the 1970s were advertised as a response to inflation. The housing shortages came later. (New York, on the other hand, has had rent control since 1943, when it was imposed as part of World War II price controls. Vacancy rates stood at 10 percent in 1940, but have never been above 5 percent since the war ended; they have been below 3 percent since the late 1960s.)

Given these facts, the most plausible explanation of the relation of homelessness to high median home prices, low rental vacancies, and the presence

Figure 1

Homelessness in Forty American Cities, Correlated with Rent Control, Size of Minority Population, and Median Home Price

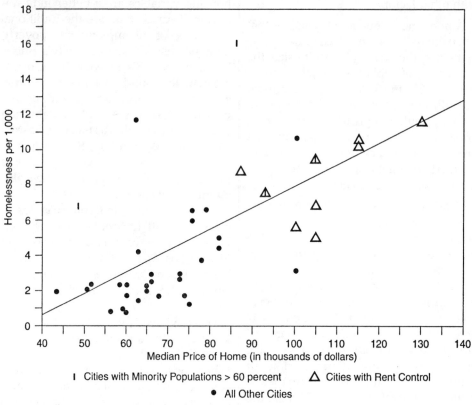

(R = .649; P < .0001)

of rent control seems to be what might be called "intense housing regulation." Many cities, such as San Francisco, Berkeley, and Santa Monica, have adopted rent control as part of municipal efforts to slow growth and stop development. These efforts are often aimed against new housing construction, particularly of apartments and rentals.

Since most communities that adopt no-growth ordinances usually like to think of themselves as liberal-minded, they do not like to admit to limiting housing opportunities for low-income people. So

they try to compensate by imposing rent control, which they claim "protects" tenants from rising rents.

But of course rent control makes things only worse, by causing vacancy rates to decline and apartments to become much harder to find. The words of Assa Lindbeck, the Swedish socialist (and now chairman of the Nobel Prize Committee for Economics) can hardly be improved upon:

The effects of rent control have in fact been exactly what can be predicted from the simplest type of supply-and-demand analysis—"housing shortage" (excess demand for housing), black markets, privileges for those who happen to have a contract for a rent-controlled apartment, nepotism in the distribution of the available apartments, difficulties in getting apartments for families with children, and, in many places, deterioration of the housing stock. In fact, next to bombing, rent control seems in many cases to be the most efficient technique so far known for destroying cities.

ATTACKS ON GROWTH AND SRO'S

Perhaps the best place to see this syndrome at work is in the San Francisco area, which has some of the country's most intense and innovative housing regulation and is also generally considered to be the center of some of the nation's worst homelessness.

It may be hard to believe, but housing prices in California in 1970 were no higher than the national average—even though the state experienced astonishing population growth during the 1950s and 1960s. It was not until the wave of environmental regulation and no-growth sentiment emerged in the 1970s that housing prices began to climb. Throughout California, the increase in home prices has consistently outpaced the national average over the last two decades. By 1988, the median price for a home stood at $158,000 there, in contrast to the nationwide figure of $88,000. In the highly regulated San Francisco Bay area, the median was $178,000, more than twice the national median.

California also experienced a wave of rent-control ordinances in the 1970s. Berkeley adopted rent control in 1971, shortly after imposing a "neighborhood preservation ordinance" that all but prohibited new development. The ordinance was eventually overturned in the California courts in 1975. Then in 1978, Howard Jarvis made an ill-fated promise that Proposition 13 would lower rents by reducing property taxes. When rent reductions failed to materialize, angry tenants in more than a dozen cities retaliated by adopting rent control.

As a result, housing in highly regulated metropolitan regions around San Francisco, San Jose, and Los Angeles has become very scarce. At the same time, homelessness has become a pronounced problem. Santa Monica, which imposed rent control in 1979 as part of an intense antidevelopment campaign, has become the homelessness capital of the West Coast.

Once growth control, tight zoning, and rent control are in place, even middle-class people may have trouble finding housing. A municipality in effect becomes a closed community, open only to its current residents (who either experience remarkable run-ups in the value of their homes or live at rents far below market) and people with strong inside connections. Mark Kann's 1986 book *Middle Class Radicalism in Santa Monica*, which generally praised the city's housing policies, speaks of a "woman who tried to get a Santa Monica apartment for more than a year without success[;] ... she broke into the city, finally, by marrying someone who already had an apartment there."

No-growth ordinances and rent control have not, of course, been embraced everywhere; but city administrations have often produced comparable results through intense housing-code enforcement, designed to drive "undesirable" housing (and the people who live in it) out of their jurisdictions.

In *New Homeless and Old: Community and the Skid Row Hotel,* Charles Hoch and Robert Slayton have traced the disappearance of the single-room occupancy (SRO) and "cubicle" hotels that once provided cheap housing to thousands of marginal tenants in downtown Chicago. Over 8,000 of these hotel rooms—still available to Chicago's low-income transients in 1963—have disappeared, leaving barely 2,000 today. These lost accommodations were all supplied by the private market. Although remarkably inexpensive (often costing only $2 a night), these rooms offered residents exactly what they wanted—security and privacy. Most of the hotels had elaborate security systems, with desk clerks screening visitors and protecting residents from unwanted ones. In addition, the cheap hotels were usually convenient to stores and public transportation, allowing low-income residents with few family connections to lead frugal but relatively dignified lives.

What happened to these old SRO hotels? Almost without exception, they became the target of urban-renewal efforts and municipal campaigns to "clean up downtown." Intense building-code enforcement and outright condemnation drove most of them out of business. Strict zoning ordinances have since made it virtually impossible to build replacements. Hoch and Slayton conclude:

We do not believe that the demise of Skid Row and the SRO hotels was the inevitable result of market forces, or that Skid Row residents embodied peculiar social and psychological characteristics that produced deviant and pathological social behavior.... [Instead,] this loss was the result of decades of antagonism from civic and business leaders, legitimated from the 1950s on by social scientists, and incorporated into dramatic change-oriented programs like urban renewal.

Nor have these policies abated today. Despite the hue and cry over the loss of SRO hotels, their replacement is still generally forbidden by zoning ordinances. In Los Angeles, there is a movement afoot to close down SRO hotels—even those subsidized by the city government—because they are not built to withstand earthquakes. Peter Smith, president of the New York City Partnership for the Homeless, comments: "It's essentially illegal for private developers to build SRO hotels in New York anymore."

RESTRICTING DEVELOPMENT

What is causing homelessness, then, is the familiar phenomenon of government regulation. This regulation tends to escape the attention of the public and the enthusiasts of deregulation, because it is done at the local rather than the state or national level.

The truth is that cities and towns do not always welcome new development. At bottom, even the most enthusiastic advocates of progress would often prefer to see their own neighborhoods remain just as they are. People will usually settle for higher-priced housing, because it raises the value of their own homes; but few want tenements, rentals, or other forms of "low-income" housing.

Through regulation, most cities and towns hold a tight rein on their housing markets. Suburbs are particularly exclusionary, zoning out everything but high-priced single-family homes (which require large lot sizes), and prohibiting the rental of rooms or apartments. Cities themselves, although sometimes offering rhetorical welcomes, often play the same exclusionary games.

An example can be seen in Takoma Park, Maryland, a nineteenth-century "streetcar suburb" of Washington, D.C., which until recently had a long history of tolerant housing policies. Takoma Park is a hodgepodge of two-, three-, and four-family homes within easy commuting distance of Washington. During World War II, homeowners rented attics and spare bedrooms to wartime officials who could not find housing in Washington. This tradition continued after the war, when many returning GI's sought housing while attending nearby Columbia Union College. Many homeowners permanently converted their homes to two- and three-family units.

During the 1970s, however, a group of homeowners living in a recently constructed, more suburban part of the city asked Montgomery County to enforce a sixty-year-old zoning ordinance that prohibited rentals in single-family zones. (Zoning is controlled by county governments in Maryland.) After a long dispute, the city council adopted a compromise in 1978, which permitted anyone who was renting before 1954 to continue to do so for another ten years. In 1988 the reprieve expired, however, and evictions began. More than six hundred tenants were forced to leave their homes.

THE APPEAL OF UTOPIANISM

It is important to realize that housing regulations are to blame for a lot of homelessness. But at the same time, we must acknowledge the impulses that make people want to intervene in the housing marketplace.

About a year ago, I spent a few days in San Francisco's Market Street dis-trict, a notorious skid row. Although not particularly dangerous, the surroundings were decidedly unpleasant. Weather-beaten young men, each of whom seemed to have his entire worldly belongings wrapped in a sleeping bag, lounged along the sidewalks. Ragged holdovers from the sixties perched on public monuments, performing drunken imitations of rock singers. Veterans of motorcycle gangs weaved past timid pedestrians, carrying on garrulous arguments with their equally disheveled girlfriends. Along the side streets, tattoo parlors jostled with cheap cafeterias, pornography shops, and the inevitable flophouse hotels.

It is easy enough to imagine some ambitious politician surveying the scene and deciding that it was time to "clean up Market Street." Such campaigns have occurred all over the country and have inevitably produced the disjuncture that we now find between the supply of housing and the price that poor people can afford to pay for it.

Yet distasteful as it may seem, skid rows play a crucial role in providing the poor and near-poor with cheap housing. Not everyone can live in suburban subdivisions or high-rise condominiums. To provide for everyone, we also need rooms for rent, fleabag hotels, tenements, trailer parks—and the "slumlords" who often run them. Although usually imagined to be rich and powerful, these bottom-rung entrepreneurs almost always turn out to be only slightly more affluent than the people for whom they are providing housing.

In the utopian dreams of regulators and "housing activists," such landlords are always eliminated. They are inevitably replaced by the federal government and the "non-profits," orchestrated by the city planners and visionary architects who would "tear down the slums" and replace them with "model tenements" and the "garden cities of tomorrow."

It is not wrong to have such visions. But let us do things in stages. Let us build the new housing *first*—and only then tear down the old "substandard" housing that is no longer needed. If we let the best become the enemy of the good—or even the barely adequate—the homeless will have nothing more substantial to live in than the dreams of the housing visionaries themselves.

NO Richard P. Appelbaum et al.

SCAPEGOATING RENT CONTROL: MASKING THE CAUSES OF HOMELESSNESS

The U.S. Congress has recently considered legislation that would withhold federal housing funds from the numerous locales that have adopted rent control. Such legislation is supported by HUD [Department of Housing and Urban Development] Secretary Jack Kemp, who strongly believes that rent control is partly responsible for discouraging badly needed investment in rental housing. Sixteen states currently have laws that restrict the ability of localities to enact rent control, while another 29 have been targeted for such laws by the National Apartment Owners' Association and the National Multi-Housing Council. While the belief that rent control has adverse consequences for housing markets has long been advanced by housing economists, a new claim has recently emerged in support of anti-rent control legislation: the assertion that rent control should be dismantled because it is the chief underlying cause of homelessness. The evidence for this claim can be traced to a single study by journalist William Tucker (1987a, 1987b, 1989a, 1989b). Since homelessness is such a visible national issue, local rent regulations —affecting millions of tenants nationwide—are more vulnerable to federal anti–rent-control legislation than at any time in the recent past....

Despite the widespread attention it has received, Tucker's research is seriously flawed. The link between rent control and homelessness it purports to demonstrate does not withstand serious scrutiny. Given the political context in which the research appears, the following critique of Tucker's thesis is doubly important. Unchallenged, Tucker's work represents a serious threat to local rent control by linking it with a national problem of high concern. Pointing the finger at rent control can only divert attention from a serious effort to uncover and address the actual causes of homelessness.

The growth of homelessness during the 1980s is not linked with the efforts by a handful of local governments to regulate skyrocketing rents. Homelessness is directly related to the overall level of poverty, to the availability of affordable housing, and to the accessibility of support services for people

From Richard P. Appelbaum, Michael Dolny, Peter Dreier, and John I. Gilderbloom, "Scapegoating Rent Control: Masking the Causes of Homelessness," *Journal of the American Planning Association*, vol. 57, no. 2 (Spring 1991). Copyright © 1991 by The American Planning Association. Reprinted by permission. Notes and references omitted.

suffering from mental illness or alcoholism. It is no accident that the number of homeless Americans increased dramatically during the 1980s. The past decade has witnessed growing poverty, especially among the "working poor"; a decline in low-rent housing, including sharp cuts in federal low-income housing assistance; and a failure to adequately serve the deinstitutionalized mentally ill. As a result, since the early 1980s the homeless population has increased between 20 and 25 percent a year, according to the U.S. Conference of Mayors annual surveys (1989, 2). Moreover, the profile of the homeless population includes a growing number of families with young children, as well as individuals with jobs (U.S. Conference of Mayors 1989).

This assessment of the underlying causes of America's homeless problem would seem to suggest fairly straightforward remedies directed at increasing the wages of America's working poor, expanding the supply of affordable housing, and providing residential and social support programs for the nation's mentally ill. A comprehensive examination of the evidence gives no support to the claim that rent control is the root cause of homelessness in the United States....

THE EFFECT OF RENT CONTROL ON INVESTMENT IN RENTAL HOUSING

Two hundred cities and counties currently have some form of rent regulation. This group includes over 100 communities in New Jersey, as well as cities and counties in Massachusetts, New York, Virginia, Maryland, Alaska, Connecticut, and California. Most of these ordinances were first enacted in the early 1970s. Approximately 10 percent of the nation's rental housing stock is estimated to be covered by some form of rent control (Baar 1983). Current rent control measures can be categorized as *moderate*, in comparison with the more *restrictive* rent control that was in effect in New York City during the immediate postwar period.

Moderate rent controls permit rent increases sufficient for the landlord to maintain an adequate return on investment, while protecting tenants against rent gouging. All ordinances currently in effect are moderate in nature. Such controls typically peg annual rent increases to increases in the landlords' costs, and exempt newly constructed rental units from controls altogether. They also often require adequate maintenance as a condition for annual rent adjustments: tenants in buildings that are inadequately maintained can appeal their rent increases. Some rent control laws permit vacated units to be temporarily decontrolled so that rents can be raised to market levels for incoming tenants, after which they are recontrolled. Moderate rent controls thus contain a number of provisions explicitly designed to encourage both construction of new rental housing and maintenance of existing units.

In a few highly inflationary California housing markets, some controls are coupled with an additional provision: they exclude increased mortgage costs from the formulas relating landlords' costs and allowable rent increases. This provision is designed to discourage speculation in rental housing. Under such an exclusion, a landlord who has incurred increased capital costs (either through recent purchase or through refinancing to obtain equity capital) cannot pass the higher financing costs through to tenants in the form of rent increases.

In sum, current rent controls contain provisions that are intended to guarantee the landlord a fair and reasonable rate of return on investment, while protecting the interests of tenants by preserving affordable housing. Maintenance is strongly encouraged; newly built units are not controlled at all.

Nonetheless, critics continue to argue that rent control discourages investment in rental housing. According to Tucker (1987a, 1987b, 1989a), for example, localities that enact rent control rob landlords of their rightful returns. So deprived, landlords cut costs. Maintenance suffers; buildings are abandoned. Badly needed new units are never constructed. Although rents may be lowered in the short run, the argument goes, housing scarcity eventually results. Scarcity, in turn, causes homelessness. In posh areas like Santa Monica, Cambridge, or the Upper West Side of Manhattan, yuppies squeeze out low income tenants in the fight for scarce apartments. In blighted areas like the South Bronx, buildings are abandoned, and eventually razed by arsonists or government bulldozers. Either way, says Tucker, the poor are relegated to the streets and shelters.

This analysis is not original to Tucker; on the contrary, it is shared by a number of housing economists as well as many people in the real estate community. For example, ten years ago a national survey of economists found virtually unanimous agreement that "a ceiling on rents reduces the quantity and quality of housing available" (Kearl et al. 1979). These conclusions are not based on empirical studies, but on theoretical assumptions about how housing markets are supposed to operate. The real estate lobby has been highly effective in communicating this analysis to its members and the media. Major news organizations, including the *Wall Street Journal* and *Forbes* magazine, have editorialized against rent controls (Gilderbloom 1983).

Numerous empirical studies have been conducted on the effects of moderate rent control on rental housing investment; none support the views just described. A comprehensive review ... finds that such controls have not caused a decline in construction, capital improvements, maintenance, abandonment, or demolition of controlled units relative to noncontrolled ones. This is because of the nonrestrictive nature of moderate controls, which, as we have seen, guarantee landlords a fair and reasonable rate of return. Rent controls eliminate extreme rent increases, particularly in highly inflationary markets, but they do not eliminate the profits necessary to encourage investment in private rental housing (Gilderbloom 1984, 1986; Heffley and Santerre 1985; Mollenkopf and Pynoos 1973; Daugherbaugh 1975; Vitaliano 1983). In particular, the vacancy decontrol-recontrol provision in some localities results in significantly higher average rents than those that would occur in the absence of such a provision (Gilderbloom and Keating 1982; Hartman 1984; Clark and Heskin 1982; Rydell 1981; Los Angeles Rent Stabilization Division 1985). While moderate rent control is successful in eliminating exorbitant rent increases, its impact on redistributing income from landlords to tenants clearly depends on the degree to which market conditions would otherwise have led to rent increases that greatly exceed the allowable rent levels.

RENT CONTROL AND HOME-LESSNESS: TUCKER'S ANALYSIS

Tucker's study is the first to look at the impact of rent control on homelessness. In order to support his argument that rent control produces homelessness by discouraging investment and thereby creating housing scarcity, Tucker sought to show that cities with rent control had lower vacancy rates and greater homelessness than cities without rent control.

For his primary data set, Tucker relied on the single comparative study of homelessness that had been done at the time of his study—the HUD survey of homelessness in 60 metropolitan areas (1984). HUD had conducted a random sample of 20 cities in each of three size strata (50,000– 250,000; 250,000–1,000,000; and over, 1,000,000). For each city, HUD telephoned people they labeled "knowledgeable informants" and asked for their estimates of the homeless street population in their areas. (Shelter estimates were more accurately obtained from information provided by shelter operators.) The various estimates for each locale were then combined into an average figure that was weighted to reflect the presumed reliability of the different sources. Tucker took the HUD estimates for the 40 metropolitan areas in the two largest strata. He then computed a homeless rate for each city by dividing HUD's estimate of the total number of homeless by the population of the core city for each metropolitan area.

Tucker did not rely exclusively on HUD's random sample of places; rather, he modified the HUD sample in several ways. First, he dropped six cities from among HUD's 40 metropolitan areas over 250,000 in population: Day-ton, Davenport, Colorado Springs, Scranton, Raleigh, and Baton Rouge. These six places were reportedly eliminated because of "the great difficulty in determining local vacancy rates" (Tucker 1989a, 5, n. 4). For unexplained reasons, Tucker then added to his list one of HUD's smallest (under 250,000) metropolitan areas—Lincoln, Nebraska. He also mistakenly classified Hartford as a city with rent control. Finally, he added 15 additional cities "to include some notable HUD omissions" (1987a, 1); he does not explain how these cities were selected out of thousands of possible places across the United States. Since these cities were not a part of HUD's original study, Tucker developed his own homeless estimates by making telephone calls to unspecified informants in each city. This misguided sampling methodology yielded a final list of 50 places for his analysis.

Once he had obtained his list of places, Tucker identified factors that might be important determinants of homelessness. He originally chose rates of poverty, unemployment, public housing availability, and rental housing vacancy; total population; mean annual temperature; and the presence (or absence) of rent control. Two additional variables—population growth rate and mean annual rainfall—are employed in a recent study (1989a) but apparently not in the original studies (1987a, 1987b); nonetheless, the appendix in the recent study reports only the seven original variables. High rates of poverty and unemployment are indicative of an economically marginal population, and therefore should be associated with greater homelessness. Public housing availability, on the other hand, provides one form of protection against homelessness, and so should be associated with lower rates.

Low vacancy rates indicate scarcity in the private rental housing market, and —according to Tucker—should be associated with both rent control and homelessness. Larger, faster-growing places may well attract the unemployed with the lure of jobs, thereby contributing to homelessness in such cities. Finally, locales with warm temperatures and low rainfalls have an obvious appeal to the homeless.

Having selected these key variables, Tucker employed them in two- and three-variable regression equations predicting homelessness. While his results vary somewhat among his various reports, he generally found that the only variables that made any substantial difference in the rate of homelessness were the local vacancy rate and rent control—and that the latter statistically accounts for much of the impact of the former. In fact, Tucker found that rent control by itself explains fully 27 percent of the difference in homelessness among cities; when combined with mean temperature, it accounts for 31 percent. According to these findings, homeless people are attracted to cities with hospitable climates; when such places have rent control, increased housing scarcity is assumed to result, and —with it—greater homelessness.

In evaluating Tucker's findings, it is important to bear in mind that he classified only 9 of the 50 cities as having any form of rent control at all. Since all of the cities had homeless problems to varying degrees, it is obvious that rent control cannot be the principal cause of homelessness, as Tucker contends. Miami, with the highest rate of homelessness in the cities under study, does not currently have rent control. Nor does St. Louis, which ranks second. Nor does Worcester, which ranks fourth. The fact that three out of four places with the most severe homeless problems lack rent control would seem to provide a prima facie case for rejecting Tucker's claim out of hand.

The first major difficulty in Tucker's study lies with his use of HUD's measure of homelessness (1984) as his key variable. According to two congressional hearings that examined HUD's methods in detail, that measure was highly unreliable. HUD relied on what it called "knowledgeable informants"—police departments, social service agencies, shelter staffs—who simply *guessed* at the numbers of homeless people in the 60 areas HUD reviewed. There was no actual count of the number of homeless in the streets, park benches, abandoned cars, and elsewhere—and certainly no estimate of the "invisible" homeless temporarily living in overcrowded apartments with friends or relatives. Although the guesses were mainly for downtown neighborhoods, HUD acted as if they applied to much larger metropolitan areas—Rand McNally marketing areas (RMAs), areas with four or five times as many people. This method, not surprisingly, produced very low rates of homelessness for the metropolitan areas HUD studied, since they guaranteed that homeless people outside the downtown areas would be excluded from the study. Tucker's principal variable, therefore, substantially undercounts the homeless.

The second major problem results from the questionable procedures by which Tucker arrived at his 50 cities, which —as will be demonstrated in the next section of this article—skew his results towards his foregone conclusions. As noted above, he began with HUD's random sample of 40 medium and large metropolitan areas, added one smaller HUD metropolitan area, selectively eliminated six places, and then added 15 others of his own choosing. Since only five of HUD's cities were among the more than 200 places with rent control, Tucker made certain that three rent-controlled cities were included among those he added. But sampling problems are compounded by the fact that the three rent-controlled cities he added are already presumably included in HUD's homeless estimates: Newark and Yonkers are part of the New York City metropolitan area, while Santa Monica is part of Los Angeles.

Tucker's third major error is his failure to consider the possibility that high rents might themselves be a chief cause of homelessness, while at the same time causing tenants to demand rent control. In other words, his reported correlation between rent control and homelessness might be an artifact of the association of both with high rents. He nowhere looks at the possible causal effect of rent on homelessness....

WHY DO WE HAVE A HOMELESSNESS PROBLEM?

The United States now faces the worst housing crisis since the Great Depression. The underlying problem is a widening gap between what Americans can afford to pay and what it costs to build and operate housing. In this situation, the poor are the most vulnerable to joining the ranks of those without a home.

The number of poor Americans, now about 33 million people, is growing, and the poor are getting poorer (Center on Budget and Policy Priorities 1988, 1; Children's Defense Fund 1989, 16–26, 100–106, 115; U.S. Joint Economic Committee of Congress 1988, ch. VII). The

largest increase is among the "working poor"—people who earn their poverty on the job because of low wages. Among the "welfare poor"—primarily single mothers and their children—Aid to Families with Dependent Children (AFDC) and other benefits have declined far below the poverty level. These are people who are only one rent increase, hospital stay, or layoff from becoming homeless. In fact, a recent report by the U.S. Conference of Mayors (1989, 2) found that almost one-quarter of the homeless *work*, but simply have wages too low to afford permanent housing.

The plight of the poor is worsened by the steadily rising housing costs that have plagued the economy throughout the past decade (see U.S. Comptroller General 1979 for an early announcement of the housing crisis). On one hand, rising homeownership costs have forced many would-be first-time buyers into the status of reluctant long-term renters, greatly increasing pressures on the rental housing market. Homeownership rates have been declining steadily since 1980, particularly among first-time homebuyers. Among households where the head was under 25, for example, ownership has declined from 23.4 percent to 15.1 percent of all households, a drop of 36 percent; for those headed by someone aged 25 to 34, the decline has been from 51.4 percent to 45.1 percent, or 12 percent (Apgar 1988, 24). In 1973, it took 23 percent of the median income of a young family with children to carry a new mortgage on an average-priced house. Today, it takes over half of a young family's income (Children's Defense Fund 1988, 57).

On the other hand, renters confront chronic production shortages and rising rents. Between 1970 and 1983 rents tripled, while renters' income only doubled. As a result the average rent-income ratio grew from roughly one-quarter to one-third; the proportion of tenants paying 25 percent or more income into rent increased from one-third to one-half. By 1985, close to one out of every four renters paid over half of their income for housing costs. Eleven million families now pay over one-third of income on rent; 5 million pay over half.

The problem is especially acute for the poor, who are now competing with the middle class for scarce apartments. It is estimated that by 1985 there was a national shortage of some 3.3 million affordable units for households earning under $5,000—an increase of more than 80 percent since 1978 (Leonard et al. 1989, 9). Among the nation's nearly 7 million poor renter households, 45 percent spent more than 70 percent of their income on housing in 1985; 65 percent paid more than half; while 85 percent—some 5.8 million households—paid more than the 30 percent officially regarded as "affordable" under current federal standards. The median tenant household paid almost two-thirds of its income on rent (Leonard et al. 1989, 1–2). The typical young single parent pays 81 percent of her meager income just to keep a roof over her children's heads (Children's Defense Fund 1988, 59).

Despite the severity of these problems, less than one-third of poor households receive any kind of housing subsidy (Leonard et al. 1989, 27; U.S. Congressional Budget Office 1988, 3). This housing subsidy level is the lowest of any industrial nation in the world. Some 6 to 7 million low-income renter families receive no housing assistance whatsoever, and are therefore completely at the mercy of housing markets that place them immediately at risk of being homeless. And,

while the number of poor families has risen during the 1980s, the number of low-rent private apartments has plummeted as a result of rising rents, urban redevelopment activities, condo conversions, and arson. Between 1974 and 1985, the number of privately owned, unsubsidized apartments renting for less than $300 (measured in 1988 dollars) fell by one-third, a loss of nearly 3 million units (Apgar et al. 1989, 4). The swelling waiting lists of even the most deteriorated subsidized housing projects are telling evidence of the desperation of the poor looking for affordable homes.

The already existing shortages of affordable private housing were worsened considerably by the short-sighted actions of the Reagan administration. The 1986 Tax Reform Act, for example, removed many of the tax benefits that previously made it profitable for the private sector to rent housing to poorer families. It is estimated that the loss of tax shelters for housing will eventually reduce the value of income property by 20 percent, forcing compensating rent increases of 25 percent by the early 1990s. The National Association of Home Builders predicted that rental housing construction would decline by half as a direct result (Furlong 1986, 16); an MIT market simulation predicted an eventual loss of 1.4 million units (Apgar et al. 1985, 1).

The Reagan administration's budget cutbacks virtually eviscerated publicly owned and subsidized housing, all but eliminating the already small federal commitment to providing housing for the poor. Not only were safety net programs cut in general, but housing was selected to bear the brunt of budgetary retrenchment. Between 1981 and 1989 federal expenditures for subsidized housing declined by four-fifths, from $32 billion to

$6 billion. Total federal housing starts declined from 183,000 in 1980 to 20,000 in 1989 (Low Income Housing Information Service 1989). The administration even proposed to sell off 100,000 units of public housing, an effort that was stymied largely because public housing tenants were too poor to afford their units. A number of specific programs, including several directed at the needs of the homeless, were "zeroed out" in the 1989 budget. It should be pointed out that, as severe as these measures may appear, President Reagan's proposed cuts were still deeper: philosophically committed to ending federal involvement in housing altogether, he was prevented from doing so only by the lobbying efforts of low-income housing advocates before a Democrat-controlled Congress. A single statistic tells the story in unambiguous terms. When President Reagan came to office in 1981, the federal government spent seven dollars on defense for every dollar on housing. When he left office in 1989, the ratio of dollars spent was 46 to one.

In sum, declining incomes at the bottom have converged with rising housing costs to produce a potentially explosive situation, which unwise short-term federal policies have served to worsen. Rent control plays no role in this unfolding tragedy. According to one estimate (Clay 1987, i), by 2003 "the gap between the total low-rent housing supply (subsidized and unsubsidized) and households needing such housing is expected to grow to 7.8 million units," representing an affordable housing loss for nearly 19 million people. This figure represents the probable constituency of the homeless, as the United States moves into the twenty-first century.

On its own, rent control can't solve the housing crisis. It is merely one tool available to local governments for confronting skyrocketing rents and a shortage of affordable housing. Tucker's study does not demonstrate what it sets out to do, and so cannot be used to justify a scapegoating of rent control for the mounting tragedy of homelessness.

AUTHOR'S NOTE

We would like to thank Jon Lorence and William Bielby for giving us special assistance in the analysis of this data. Carrie Donald, Gary Dworkin, Neal King, and Bob Nideffer also provided important technical assistance. Special thanks go to Kevin Quinn and the staff of the Economic Policy Institute, who published an earlier version as a briefing paper. Authors are listed in alphabetical order.

POSTSCRIPT

Are Rent Controls the Cause of America's Homelessness?

This is a debate where the protagonists defend their positions with reasoned arguments and statistical evidence. But note, the provision of statistical evidence can itself be subject to challenge. Your task here is to bring critical questions to bear on the statistics used as you untangle the conflicting claims made in these two essays. Which essay provides the most reasonable set of assumptions? Which analysis employs data that are least subject to question? Which set of conclusions is justifiable?

These are not easy questions to answer. Yet if we do not attempt to systematically examine the assumptions, data, economic theories, and conclusions of empirical studies such as those of Tucker and Appelbaum et al., we would simply allow our uninformed preconceptions to determine which argument we would accept as the foundation for the public policy we endorse. If we lean toward the conservative, free-market camp, we might be inclined to accept unquestioningly Tucker's analysis, since it suggests that government interferences in the market rent controls cause the social problem of homelessness. If, on the other hand, we find ourselves sympathetic toward the liberal, institutional, or even the radical view of economics, we would tend to accept without question the Appelbaum et al. work, since they suggest that the interference-free market fails to provide affordable housing to the large majority of individuals and families who find themselves homeless. By now we hope we have convinced you that a knee-jerk reaction is never correct. That means that, on occasion, we must reject the arguments of some researchers, even if we want to believe them.

To help you make this determination, we suggest that you look at other published work in this area. In the anti–rent control camp you will find noted housing authority Anthony Downs, *Residential Rent Controls: An Evaluation* (Urban Land Institute, 1988). You will also find other works published by Tucker, since his work provides the empirical foundation for the anti–rent control camp. See, for example, *The Excluded Americans: Homelessness and Housing Policies* (Regnery Gateway, 1990) and *The Source of America's Housing Problem: Look in Your Own Back Yard*, Policy Analysis Series, no. 127 (Cato Institute, February 6, 1990). On the other side we suggest that you read some of the other work published by Appelbaum and Gilderbloom. Among other contributions to this literature, Appelbaum has published *Rent Controls: Facts, Not Fiction* (California State Senate Rules Committee, 1990). Gilderbloom has also written widely in this area, including "Towards A Sociology of Rent," *Social Problems* (vol. 34, no. 3, 1987).

ISSUE 6

Is Managed Competition the Cure for Our Ailing Health Care Industry?

YES: Council of Economic Advisers, from *Economic Report of the President 1994* (Government Printing Office, 1994)

NO: Elizabeth McCaughey, from "What the Clinton Plan Will Do for You: No Exit," *The New Republic* (February 7, 1994)

ISSUE SUMMARY

YES: President Bill Clinton's Council of Economic Advisers argues that there is a health care crisis and that Clinton's "bold and comprehensive" reform proposal will cure this ailing industry by building upon the existing "strengths of our market-based system."

NO: Social critic Elizabeth McCaughey asserts that the American people "haven't been given a straight story about the Clinton health bill." She alleges that this bill will reduce the quality of medical care and eliminate personal choice.

Government is no stranger to the health care industry. For nearly 30 years the U.S. government has actively shaped both the supply and the demand for services in this industry. Although some trace governmental involvement back to the passage of the personal income tax in 1913, which excluded from taxation the market value of company-paid fringe benefits such as health insurance, most agree that the real impact of governmental involvement was not felt until the mid-1960s.

In an attempt to provide access to the U.S. health care system for the aged and often poverty-stricken retired population, Congress amended the Social Security Act in 1965 and created what is known as Medicare. A short time later, it extended these benefits to the non-aged poor by passing Medicaid. These two pillars of President Lyndon B. Johnson's War on Poverty brought about fundamental changes in the health care industry. Few deny that some of these changes were good. Indeed, large numbers of American citizens were provided with much-needed health care, which they could not have otherwise purchased. But few also deny that this government intrusion into the marketplace set in motion a tidal wave of price increases in the industry that are easily discernible three decades later.

For example, using 1982–1984 as our base for the Consumer Price Index (CPI=100), in 1965 all items in the CPI equaled 31.5. By 1993 all items in the CIP equaled 144.5. This suggests that overall prices in the U.S. have more than quadrupled since 1965. These general price increases, however, pale in comparison to the prices in the medical care sector: the medical care component of the CPI increased from 25.2 in 1965 to 201.4 in 1993. This represents an eight-fold increase in medical care prices, nearly twice the rate of inflation for the economy at large.

What went wrong? If we reexamine the Medicare/Medicaid legislation in light of our understanding of supply and demand and the concept of elasticity, then answering that question is not difficult. First, this legislation increased the effective demand for medical services by providing vouchers for those who could not afford to purchase medical services on the open market. Anytime demand increases and supply remains unchanged, we normally expect prices to increase. This is not the end of the story, since we expect long-run adjustments in the supply of medical services. Unfortunately, this is where policymakers went wrong. They anticipated that the long-run supply would be relatively elastic, while in fact it proved to be relatively inelastic. Prices increased sharply, and the quantity demanded increased by less than expected.

These increases in price and relatively small (but very significant) increases in consumption of medical services have had major consequences. Consider how much of the U.S. income is devoted to health care: In 1965 it equaled 5.9 percent. By 1992 it had skyrocketed to 14 percent. Some estimate that by the year 2000 it may reach 19 percent of the nation's total gross domestic product (GDP). What is even more distressing is that, in spite of paying more than $350 billion a year for health care in the United States, 15 percent of the population are still denied access to the country's medical care system.

Will President Bill Clinton's health care reform proposal stem the tide of rising medical costs and at the same time provide universal medical coverage? Or should we pay heed to Elizabeth McCaughey's warning that the Clinton health bill will have many negative effects on medical care in the United States?

YES   Council of Economic Advisers

HEALTH CARE REFORM

The United States spends far more per capita on and devotes a much larger share of its income to health care than does any other country. In 1993, one out of every seven dollars that Americans spent—14.3 percent of gross domestic product (GDP)—went to health services. In 1991, the most recent year for which comparable international data are available, the United States spent 13.2 percent of GDP on health care, while no other industrialized country spent more than 10 percent. Indeed the average for all the industrialized countries of the Organization for Economic Cooperation and Development (OECD) was only about 8 percent. Yet despite this massive commitment of resources, the United States insures a much smaller fraction of its population than do most other industrial countries, and ranks comparatively poorly on such important overall indicators of health outcomes as life expectancy and infant mortality. Tens of millions of Americans remain uninsured and live in constant fear of bankruptcy should they become ill. Tens of millions more have inadequate insurance or risk becoming uninsured if they lose their jobs.

For the lucky Americans who have comprehensive benefits and little worry about becoming uninsured, the current system buys care of high quality and provides genuine health security. For others less fortunate, the system works less well or not at all. And even the lucky suffer from the shortcomings of the current system, as the costs of covering services for the uninsured and some of the costs for those served by government programs are shifted onto hospitals and other providers and ultimately onto private sector insurance premiums.

Health care spending is not only high but growing rapidly. In almost every year of the last three decades, health care costs have increased at more than twice the rate of total income. In the 1980s, real per capita health care spending increased at an annual rate of 4.4 percent in the United States, compared with an average of only 3.2 percent in Canada, France, Germany, Japan, and the United Kingdom. Current projections indicate that, without reform, the

From Executive Office of the President, Council of Economic Advisers, *Economic Report of the President, Transmitted to the Congress, February 1994* (Government Printing Office, 1994).

United States will devote nearly 18 percent of its GDP to health care by the turn of the century.

At the level of the individual, the family, and the firm, the inexorable growth in health care spending means ever-increasing insurance premiums and ever-higher medical bills. And at the level of Federal and State and local governments, rising health care costs mean that health expenditures claim larger and larger budget shares, with less left over for essential competing demands like public safety, infrastructure maintenance and expansion, and improvements in education and training. Despite a sustained reduction in real discretionary spending, the Congressional Budget Office projects that escalating health care costs will be the dominant force pushing Federal Budget deficits back up as the 20th century nears its end.

The facts speak for themselves: The United States faces a health care crisis that demands a solution, both for the health of its citizens and for the health of its economy over the long run....

UNIVERSAL COVERAGE AND HEALTH SECURITY

Providing universal health coverage and security for all Americans is an essential objective of health care reform.... According to the Current Population Survey, over 15 percent of Americans —nearly 39 million people—were uninsured throughout 1992. That is one of the highest shares in the industrialized world. While some people remain uninsured for long periods of time, many more experience brief episodes during which they lack coverage, for instance when they lose a job. The Survey of Income and Program Participation (SIPP)

found that over three times as many people are uninsured at some time during a given year as are uninsured throughout the year. The SIPP estimates that more than one in four Americans were uninsured at some point in a 28-month period from 1987 to 1989.

The fact that so many people are uninsured at least some of the time means that the prospect of being uninsured may influence the behavior of a large number of Americans. As long as people can lose their health coverage simply by changing employment, health insecurity will remain a barrier to changing jobs or starting new businesses. An important rationale for universal coverage is therefore to increase mobility and employment opportunities for those who already have insurance but do not have health security.

Similarly, many people remain on welfare because they will lose their medicaid coverage if they take a job. Some estimates indicate that up to one-quarter of recipients of aid to families with dependent children (AFDC) would take a job if private health insurance equivalent to that provided by medicaid were available to them. A second rationale for universal coverage is thus to reduce the number of people on welfare and to further the Administration's goal of welfare reform.

A third rationale for universal coverage is to improve the health of the uninsured. The uninsured do use health care— they do not simply do without. It is estimated that those without insurance for all of 1994 will consume about $1,200 of medical care per capita—60 percent of which will be paid for by governments and private payers, not by the uninsured themselves (Figure 1). This expenditure is roughly half the over $2,300 per capita

Figure 1

Sources of Payment for Health Care by Insurance Status: 1994 Estimates

Uninsured All Year
(Per capita spending = $1,224)

Any Private Insurance
(Per capita spending = $2,332)

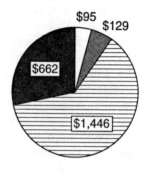

■ Out-of-Pocket   ▤ Insurance   ▦ Government   ☐ Bad debt, free care, and workers' compensation

Note: About 60 percent of care for the uninsured is financed by governments, other private payers, bad debt, free care, or workers' compensation.

Source: Department of Health and Human Services.

consumed by those who are currently insured.

While the uninsured do receive care, it is often neither timely nor appropriate. The uninsured are more likely than the insured to receive care in the emergency room, are less healthy when they are admitted to a hospital, and receive less treatment than people with similar diagnoses once admitted. Some studies indicate—and common sense suggests—that the health of the uninsured suffers as a result.

Indeed, without reform, the problem of adverse health outcomes for the uninsured is likely to worsen over time. Historically, governments and private payers have shouldered the burden of financing care for the uninsured. As health care costs continue to escalate, however, these payers may become less willing to bear this burden.

Perhaps surprisingly, providing universal health insurance to cover those currently uninsured will not require a large increase in total health expenditures. While the uninsured are poorer than the population as a whole, they are also younger and healthier. Almost all of the elderly already have insurance—through medicare. Among the nonelderly population, 24 percent of those with employer-sponsored insurance are between the ages of 45 and 64, compared with only 17 percent of the uninsured. Only 9 percent of the privately insured are between the ages of 18 and 24, compared with 18 percent of the uninsured. And while uninsured adults often perceive themselves to be in poorer

MORAL HAZARD AND ADVERSE SELECTION

All insurance markets face two potential problems. The first, called moral hazard, involves incentives. Insurance may encourage those who are covered to use insured services more than they otherwise would, or it may discourage the insured from taking steps to lower their need for such services. Insurance against any kind of risk—including health risks—always involves some element of moral hazard. When people use health services more than they would without insurance, the total amount insurers must pay increases, and they in turn must increase their prices. Furthermore, because individuals pay less than the full social cost of the services they receive, too much of society's resources will be devoted to such services.

The second problem is adverse selection. People who know that they are more at risk than others of falling ill are more likely to purchase health insurance. Therefore, insurers who set their prices at the average cost for the population as a whole are likely to discover that their prices do not cover their costs, because their customers are on average sicker than the population at large. To address this problem, insurers have incentives both to charge prices that exceed the cost of covering the average person and to select risks as best they can. The higher prices of insurance that result from adverse selection have the perverse effect of discouraging some healthy people from purchasing insurance. Because of the adverse selection problem, all people must be required to purchase insurance if each of them is to be charged the average cost of providing insurance.

general health than the population as a whole, they are less likely than the insured to have chronic conditions. Estimates that account for these demographic and health factors generally find that insuring the uninsured would increase national health spending by less than 10 percent.

A fourth rationale for universal coverage is to solve the "free rider" problem. At least some of the uninsured could afford to purchase insurance but choose to go without because they feel they do not need it, and because they know that if they do become sick they will be cared for on an emergency basis at little cost to themselves. For some, relying on such "free" catastrophic insurance can be more attractive than purchasing insurance in the private market. By requiring that all individuals pay something for coverage, health reform can help eliminate this problem.

Finally, ... universal coverage is essential if everyone in the population is to share equally in the costs of insurance [see box]. ...

CREATING A MORE EFFICIENT MARKET AND CONTAINING COSTS

... As already noted, the United States spends a larger share of its GDP on health

Figure 2

Health Expenditure and Life Expectancy in Industrial Countries

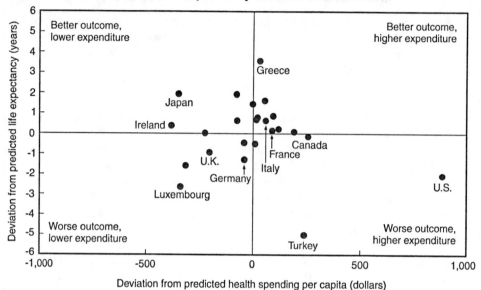

Deviation from predicted health spending per capita (dollars)

The United States spends more on health care yet has lower life expectancy than would be expected given its level of income.

Note: Health spending and life expectancy are deviations from what would be expected given per capita income. The sample consists of the member countries of the OECD.

Sources: Organization for Economic Cooperation and Development and the World Bank.

care than any other industrialized nation. If Americans valued medical care more than people in other countries do, this might not be cause for concern. But the facts suggest otherwise.

Although the fraction of national resources devoted to health care in the United States is partially explainable by our higher income, Figure 2 reveals that the United States is an outlier—we spend considerably more per capita on health care yet achieve a somewhat lower life expectancy than our higher income would predict. Nor can these differences be explained away by the age of the American population. In fact, the percentage of the population over 65 is lower in the United States than in most

of the other OECD countries. Since older people tend to use more medical care than younger people, the age distribution of the American population suggests that the United States should spend a smaller rather than a larger fraction of GDP on health care than do other industrialized countries.

It has been suggested that sociodemographic factors such as the greater prevalence of violence in American life may explain why health care spending in the United States is comparatively high. Existing research based on partial estimates suggests, however, that violent crime may add only about 2 percent to national health expenditures. No comparative studies have assessed whether vio-

Table 1

Distribution of Population and Health Spending by Spending Category, Estimates for 1994

Annual health spending (dollars)	Percent of population	Percent of spending
0	7.8	0.0
1–500	26.0	1.4
501–1,000	13.1	2.5
1,001–3,000	25.2	13.4
3,001–5,000	10.4	12.0
5,001–10,000	9.3	19.4
10,001–30,000	6.5	31.0
Over 30,000	1.6	20.3

Note: Health spending is in 1994 dollars. The estimates pertain to the noninstitutionalized population under the age of 65, excluding people who receive aid to families with dependent children or supplemental security income. The distribution presented is for health insurance units.

Source: Department of Health and Human Services.

lence is a more important determinant of health care spending in the United States than elsewhere.

... [T]he current system of insurance may also encourage some consumers to use more care or more-expensive care options than they would if they were forced to pay higher out-of-pocket costs for services. On the other hand, if consumer co-payments or deductibles were increased to reduce utilization, some of the value of insurance would be lost. Higher copayments might also discourage utilization of preventive services, with potentially adverse effects on health outcomes. Furthermore, even drastic increases in deductibles would provide only limited incentives. Table 1 shows that even if all families had a $5,000 deductible, only 29 percent of health dollars would be spent by individuals or families paying the full marginal cost of care.

Available evidence indicates that the weakness of effective competition in the health care marketplace results in substantial fraud and abuse as well as inappropriate care or care of equivocal value. Some estimates suggest that fraud and abuse may account for about 10 percent of total health care spending. And... as much as one-third of some common procedures may be performed in cases where they are inappropriate or of equivocal value on medical grounds.

There are often large differences in the amounts of medical care that people receive in different regions of the country, and even in different areas within the same region. These geographic differences may be evidence of resource misallocation. In 1989, for example, medicare physician payments per capita were 57 percent higher in Detroit than in New York City. Other research has found that the level of use of hospital beds in a community is determined primarily by the number of beds in that community. People in areas with more hospital beds are not any healthier than people who live in areas with fewer beds, but they are more likely to die in a hospital....

HEALTH CARE AND GOVERNMENT BUDGETS

The final problem in the current health care system is the growing burden it places on government finances. Because governments pay for such a large share of health spending, increases in health costs contribute directly to pressures on Federal, State, and local budgets. Public sector spending on health care grew over 2 percentage points faster than private sector spending in the 1970s, and at about the same rate as private sector spending in the 1980s. The result has been an increasing share of health spending by governments. In addition, ... health spending is growing four times as rapidly as any other component of the Federal budget. Over the two decades ending in 1991, Federal health spending increased from 9 percent to 21 percent of total Federal revenues. Similar changes have occurred in State and local government spending.

The Federal Government has responded to increasing health care costs in part by attempting to limit the reimbursement rates paid by public programs to health care providers. This approach in turn has resulted in the substantial shifting of costs to the private sector described earlier. In the absence of systemwide reform, the imposition of caps on Federal health care programs would either further aggravate the cost-shifting problem or gradually limit access to care.

Without health care reform, escalating health care costs will continue to confront the Federal Government—as well as State and local governments—with painful choices among additional taxes, cuts in spending on education and other programs that promote economic prosperity, or increases in budget deficits. As already noted, projected increases in Federal spending on medicare and medicaid are the main force behind a projected increase in the Federal deficit toward the end of this century.

THE ARCHITECTURE OF THE HEALTH SECURITY ACT

The Administration's approach to health care reform, while bold and comprehensive, builds on the strengths of the current market-based system. The Administration considered but rejected radical approaches such as a single-payer system or government-set health care prices in favor of restructuring the current system and relying on the forces of market competition. The Administration's framework preserves and expands consumer choice among providers and preserves the current employer-based system of health insurance. The Administration's plan also allows large firms to continue operating self-insured plans. Such firms generally provide comprehensive benefits, and many have managed to control health care spending. Indeed, the Administration's plan reflects many of the lessons learned from the experience of such firms.

Elements of Reform

To address the Nation's health care problems, meaningful reforms must address the four interrelated issues identified in the preceding discussion: universal coverage and health security; reform of the private insurance system; efficiency improvements and cost control; and sustained deficit reduction. The Health Security Act, which the Administration proposed in 1993, contains reforms that simultaneously meet these objectives....

Universal Coverage

The Health Security Act guarantees all Americans a health insurance package with a comprehensive set of benefits. The medicare program will be left largely unchanged, and medicare will remain the insurer for most Americans over the age of 65. Most medicaid recipients under 65 will be absorbed into the new system. With very few exceptions, all other Americans will receive their health insurance from the "health alliances" described below.

Universal coverage is essential for the reasons noted earlier. Comprehensive benefits are equally important if health security for all Americans is to be achieved. Some reform proposals promise universal coverage but guarantee coverage only for catastrophic expenses. In practice, people with high incomes may be able to afford additional coverage beyond catastrophic, but many other Americans cannot. Plans that guarantee only catastrophic coverage leave many people without genuine health security—subject to the risk that their insurance coverage will deteriorate if they lose their jobs, just when their incomes are falling.

Since the Administration's comprehensive benefits package includes a prescription drug benefit for the under-65 population, the Administration's proposal also calls for a comparable drug benefit to be added to the medicare program. In addition, the proposal includes funding for long-term care services, primarily to expand the amount of home- and community-based care....

Efficiency Improvements and Cost Savings

To encourage cost-consciousness decisions, the Health Security Act allows consumers a choice among several plans with identical benefits, gives them information about the quality of competing plans and their customers' satisfaction, and allows them to receive more of the savings if they choose a less expensive health plan. In addition, the act sets a limit on the growth of premiums in the alliances.

Promoting choice among health plans is essential to controlling costs. By encouraging plan choice, the act attempts to create a more efficient health care delivery system and thus lower overall spending.

The act's proposed limits on the allowable growth of premiums are intended to guarantee control over the growth of costs, in case enhanced private incentives fail to have the anticipated effect. These limits are an important safeguard because they reduce the risk to the government of runaway health spending.

Deficit Reduction

Over time, cost savings from the provisions just described and from reimbursement changes in public problems will provide budgetary savings for the Federal Government. As noted above, long-run success in keeping the Federal deficit under control is directly tied to success in reducing the growth rate of Federal health care spending. In the short term, the health Security Act entails some new Federal costs—discounts for the poor and for small and low-average-wage businesses, a new drug benefit for medicare, and coverage of long-term care. The savings from slowing the rate of growth of health care spending start right away, but they are small at first. Over time, these savings grow larger, and deficit reduction increases accordingly.

Maintaining Choice

The Health Security Act allows families, doctors, firms, and States to make significant choices about the nature of their involvement in the new health care system.

Households will get to choose their own doctors, and many families that currently have no choice over their health plan will be given several options. Doctors will get to choose the plan or plans in which they work, and may remain in the fee-for-service sector if they wish. Large firms may choose to form corporate alliances or to join regional alliances. And each State will be allowed to adjust its health care system to its particular circumstances—including the establishment of a single-payer system if it so chooses....

ECONOMIC EFFECTS OF THE HEALTH SECURITY ACT

The Health Security Act is certain to have impacts both on the overall American economy and on the health care sector in particular.

Macroeconomic Effects

One important concern about health care reform is its effects on employment. Because employer mandates to provide insurance may initially increase labor costs to firms that are not now providing or are underproviding insurance, fears have arisen that labor demand might decline as a consequence of reform.

In fact, however, changes in employer-paid health insurance costs can have several effects on workers other than changes in employment.... [T]he dominant effect of increases in health care costs in the past has been a reduction in the real wages received by employees.

Figure 3 shows projections of total employer health insurance payments with and without health reform. While reform will have different effects on different firms, total employer spending is essentially unchanged through 1998 and then declines relative to the baseline. This pattern reflects the balance of spending increases from the employer mandate and spending reductions from cost savings. Through 1998 these effects are roughly equal, resulting in little additional business spending. Between 1998 and 2000, the savings increase but there is no increase in spending. The result is a net savings in employer payments.

There are many things employers can do with the savings from reform: They can hire more workers, pay higher returns to shareholders, or increase employee compensation. Empirical evidence suggests, however, that as total employer payments fall over time, the likely result will be a corresponding increase in workers' wages. By the year 2000, wage and salary compensation could therefore increase by $20 billion to $30 billion, or about 0.6 percent of payroll.

Although reform is unlikely to lead to a large reduction in the demand for labor, it could affect the supply. Some individuals who work mainly to obtain health insurance may voluntarily leave the labor force after health reform is passed. Evidence from continuation of coverage (COBRA) laws passed by the Federal Government and many State governments suggests that the number of people deciding to retire is about 1 percent higher when they have the option to purchase coverage through their former employer after retirement. These estimates must be raised to account for the lower price of insurance under reform; with this

Figure 3

Business Spending on Health Insurance

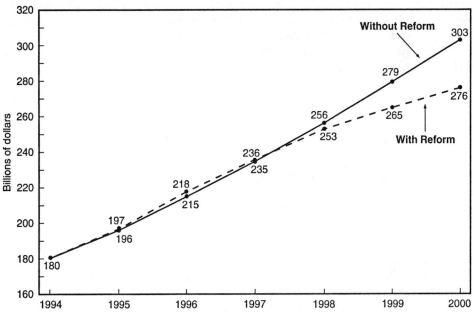

Business spending will increase slightly after reform but will fall below baseline by the end of the decade.
Note: Business spending is for services and populations that will be in regional or corporate health alliances.
Source: Administration estimates.

adjustment, it is estimated that about 350,000 to 600,000 additional people will be retired as a result of the provisions in the Health Security Act.

On the other hand, some welfare recipients are likely to decide to enter the labor force when health benefits become universal. A welfare recipient currently receiving medicaid benefits who then takes a job incurs a "tax" of two-thirds or more on earnings because of the resulting reduction in AFDC benefits, food stamps, and medicaid benefits. Once health care is guaranteed universally, the loss of income associated with leaving welfare should fall by up to 10 percentage points. A number of studies suggest that many more welfare recipients will decide to

work in response to these lower implicit tax rates.

Weighing all this evidence, several private sector economists have concluded, as has this Council, that the net effect of health reform on employment is likely to be small: at most plus or minus one-half of 1 percent of total employment. The reason is that a number of offsetting factors are in the plan, some of which will increase employment and some of which will reduce it. On net, these factors are likely to cancel out....

CONCLUSION

Reforming the Nation's health care system is integral to the health of both our citizens and our economy. One-seventh of the Nation's economy is currently characterized by weak competition, inadequate information, and inappropriate incentives. The Administration's health care reform proposal builds on the strengths of the current system while correcting its shortcomings. It preserves consumer choice and our employer-based private insurance system. It relies on enhanced market competition and improved incentives to provide health security for all Americans, slow rising health care costs, and address our long-run budget deficit problem.

NO

Elizabeth McCaughey

NO EXIT

If you're not worried about the Clinton health bill, keep reading. If the bill passes, you will have to settle for one of the low-budget health plans selected by the government. The law will prevent you from going outside the system to buy basic health coverage you think is better, even after you pay the mandatory premium. The bill guarantees you a package of medical services, but you can't have them unless they are deemed "necessary" and "appropriate." That decision will be made by the government, not by you and your doctor. Escaping the system and paying out-of-pocket to see a specialist for the tests and treatment you think you need will be almost impossible. If you walk into a doctor's office and ask for treatment for an illness, you must show proof that you are enrolled in one of the health plans offered by the government. The doctor can be paid only by the plan, not by you. To keep controls tight, the bill requires the doctor to report your visit to a national data bank containing the medical histories of all Americans.

If these facts surprise you, it's because you haven't been given a straight story about the Clinton health bill. Take two examples: on November 4, Leon Panetta, the director of the Office of Management and Budget, testified to senators that the bill does not "set prices" and "draw up rules for allocating care"; a month later Hillary Rodham Clinton assured a Boston audience that the government will not limit what you can pay your doctor. The text of the bill proves these statements are untrue.

The administration also says that the bill will not lower the quality of your medical care or take away personal choices you now make. This statement goes right to the issues that matter most. How true is it? To help you decide, here is a guide to the 1,364-page Health Security Act.

No effort is made here to compare the Clinton bill with the many alternatives offered by Republicans and other Democrats or to assess the nature and extent of the health care "crisis." The purpose is to answer one question: Under the Clinton bill, if you become ill, will you be able to get the treatment you need and make choices about your own health care?

The Law Will Make You Get Health Care Through Your "Alliance." Under the bill, unless you get Medicare, military benefits or veteran's benefits,

From Elizabeth McCaughey, "What the Clinton Plan Will Do for You: No Exit," *The New Republic* (February 7, 1994). Copyright © 1994 by The New Republic, Inc. Reprinted by permission of *The New Republic*. References omitted.

or you or your spouse work for a company with more than 5,000 employees, you must enroll in one of the limited number of health plans offered by the "regional alliance" where you live. Regional alliances are government-run monopolies that select health plans, collect premiums from residents and their employers and pay most of the money to HMOs and insurers. If you fail to enroll, or the plan you choose is oversubscribed, alliance officials will assign you to one. The goal is to curb health care spending by limiting what every American is allowed to pay for health insurance. Restricting how much people can pay for insurance limits how much money is in the pot to take care of them when they're sick.

The Health Care You Can Get Will Be Limited.   Under the bill, a National Health Board—seven people appointed by the president—will decide how much the nation can spend on health care beginning in 1996 (the baseline year). Based on that national budget, the board will set a budget for each region and a ceiling on what the average health plan in the region can cost. The bill outlaws plans that would cause a region to exceed its budget or that cost over 20 percent more than the average plan. After 1996, increases in health plan premiums will be strictly limited by an "inflation factor" based on the consumer price index.

Putting price controls on premiums to limit the amount of money in the health care system might wring out waste during the first year or two, but there is no doubt it will cause hardship later on. Seventy-seven million baby boomers will be reaching the age when they need more medical care. Increasing numbers of teen pregnancies and low-birth-weight babies

also will require more health dollars— $158,000 on average for each severely underweight newborn. Even the bill's authors anticipate that restricting the dollars available for health care in the teeth of these trends will produce grave shortages: the bill provides that when medical needs outpace the budget and premium money runs low, state governments and insurers must make "automatic, mandatory, nondiscretionary reductions in payments" to doctors, nurses and hospitals to "assure that expenditures will not exceed budget."

Above the threshold level of quality, alliance officials will approve health plans based on lowest cost, not highest quality, to stay under the premium ceiling set by the National Health Board, explains Cara Walinsky of the Health Care Advisory Board and Governance Committee, which advises 800 hospitals worldwide. That is why Anthony L. Watson, chief executive of the Health Insurance Plan (HIP) of Greater New York, is optimistic. If the Clinton bill passes, "New York is mine," he told *The New York Times.* "I'm going to be the lowest-cost plan." HIP, with a physician staff that is 57 percent foreign-trained, already has what that newspaper calls "the image of being the least desirable health care option for city workers and others who cannot afford anything more."

Staying With the Doctors You Use Now Will Be Hard.   Deciding for yourself when to see a specialist or get a second opinion and selecting the hospital you think is best will be even harder. The bill is designed to push people into HMOs, which restrict your choice of physicians and hospitals, and use gate-keepers to curb the use of specialists, expensive tests and costly high-tech treatments.

What most of us call fee-for-service (choose-your-own-doctor) insurance will be difficult to buy. The ceiling on premiums and the 20 percent rule will eliminate most fee-for-service plans, which tend to be more expensive than their pre-paid counterparts. Although the Clinton administration insists that Americans always will be able to choose fee-for-service insurance, experts such as Dr. John Ludden, medical director of the Harvard Community Health Plan, say that option will "vanish quickly."

Even where it is possible to buy fee-for-service insurance, it will be hard to find doctors practicing on that basis. According to Walinsky, the Clinton proposal contains "very strong incentives" against fee-for-service "on the consumer side but also on the provider side." Price controls on doctors' fees and other regulations will push doctors to give up independent practice and sign on with HMOs. We've been told that the government won't be putting price controls on doctors, but the bill limits what health plans can pay physicians and prohibits patients from paying their doctors directly. Alliance officials post a schedule of fees, and it is illegal for doctors to take more.

In addition, alliance officials set yearly limits on payments to fee-for-service doctors in each field of medicine, like cardiology or pulmonology. What if a flu epidemic causes pulmonologists to see more patients with breathing problems than the region's budget allows? The bill compels insurance plans to slash doctors' fees or cut off their payments entirely until the next year "to assure that expenditures will not exceed the budget."

HMOs Do the Job of Rationing. Under the Clinton bill, the federal government uses price controls on premiums to curb dollars paid into the health care system. Limiting how those dollars are spent is a job shared by alliance officials, who budget payments to doctors in the dwindling fee-for-service sector, and HMO administrators, who are expected to do the lion's share of health care rationing. Is "rationing" too strong a word? Not according to Ludden, whose HMO serves 570,000 people. He predicts that "price controls on premiums will drive us straight to rationing at bedside." Princeton Professor Paul Starr, a key designer of the Clinton plan, prefers to say that premium caps will induce "a different frame of mind" in both doctors and health care administrators. "They will have to manage under constraint."

* * *

HMOs already have a track record of tightly controlling a patient's access to physicians. At Kaiser Permanente, the first person a sick patient sees is the "advice nurse," who makes the decision whether a doctor is needed. In HMOs, the ratio of physicians to members averages 1 to 800, about half the ratio of physicians to the general population. Specialists are particularly hard to see.

Current HMO cost-cutting methods already are drawing criticism from Congress, government investigators and worried doctors. The Clinton bill's premium caps will compel HMOs to use even more stringent methods of limiting care, but the bill omits any safeguards to protect patients from abusive practices.

For example, missing from the bill is any effort to put a stop to "the withhold," the pervasive HMO practice of punishing doctors financially for providing care they believe their patients need. Almost all large, for-profit HMOs, including those operated by Aetna, Metlife, Oxford and Prudential (but not Cigna) withhold between 10 percent and 25 percent of a doctor's compensation until year's end, and return it only if the doctor has met HMO targets for limiting patient tests, referrals to specialists and hospitalizations. Doctors report that targets are so stringent that HMOs almost always keep part of the withhold, which means that what a doctor orders for a patient comes out of the doctor's own pocket at the end of the year.

The withhold has caused a surge in dangerous "hallway consultations," according to Dr. Alan Jasper, a pulmonologist and critical care specialist at St. Vincent's Medical Center in Los Angeles. Other doctors stop Jasper in the hospital corridors, describe the patient's breathing problem and seek a diagnosis, in order to avoid referring the patient for a specialty consultation and incurring points against the withhold. The danger, says Jasper, is that the other doctor might fail to mention a critically important aspect of the patient's condition.

The withhold motivates primary care doctors to take a "we'll see how you feel next week" or "let's try this first" approach, even if it means additional worry and needless suffering for the patient. At a Humana-owned HMO in San Antonio, for example, a 40-year-old woman with back pain was told by the orthopedist that she needed an MRI. But her primary care doctor rejected the specialist's request for the test, saying the patient would have to try something less expensive, and sent her for acupuncture, followed by months of hot packs and physiotherapy. When nothing worked, the gatekeeper authorized the MRI, which revealed the woman needed a lumbar dischetomy (disc removal), as the orthopedist had suspected. The story was related by the woman's surgeon, Dr. William V. Healey, a clinical professor at the University of Texas, who said the lesson was that HMO cost-cutting incentives, such as the withhold, fail to account for the graver cost—the months a patient is home from work, worried and in pain.

Another HMO cost-cutting strategy that makes doctors and patients worry is the utilization review—a sick patient must wait while the doctor telephones a utilization review company, describes the symptoms and medical history to a nurse or clerk seated at a computer terminal and hopes for an O.K. to proceed with tests and treatment.

Three hundred and fifty utilization review companies that claim to slash health care costs sell their services to HMOs, hospitals and others at a rate of $1 to $3 per patient reviewed. It's a $7 billion industry. Such "cookbook medicine" ignores the non-average, abnormally sick patient who may need more intense treatment than the computer program recommends. It also discounts the value of examining a patient, and ignores the physician's judgment and expertise. Dr. Jerome Groopman, head of oncology and hematology at the New England Deaconess Hospital in Boston, says, "It's an 800 number. They don't know me from Adam!"

"Horror stories abound" about utilization review, according to a 1993 report for the National Association of Attorneys General. Doctors' treatment plans are "rejected by inadequately trained personnel," according to the report, and utilization review companies refuse to give reasons for their decisions, even to doctors, because it is presumed doctors would figure out ways to get around the review guidelines once they were known.

Even when doctors' recommendations are ultimately approved, it can take weeks longer to diagnose and begin treating an HMO patient than a patient with fee-for-service insurance, Jasper explains, because of the successive delays in getting each test approved. One HMO patient with coughing trouble was given antibiotics by his primary care doctor, who thought the problem was pneumonia. The patient lost thirty-five pounds while waiting from October 27 to December 24 for an O.K. to see Dr. Jasper, then to have a CAT scan and lung biopsy, and finally to learn that the correct diagnosis was a lung fungal disease. Jasper said he could have had a fee-for-service patient on anti-fungal medicine within fourteen days, instead of nine weeks.

The Attorneys General report urges state lawmakers to look into curbing utilization review in HMOs. In contrast, the Clinton bill calls utilization review a "reasonable restriction" on patient care and expressly includes it as a requirement for doctors treating patients with fee-for-service insurance as well....

The Government Won't Protect You from HMO Abuses. If most Americans are moved into HMOs, who will ensure that they get good health care? The Clinton bill establishes two national boards to develop quality standards and depends on alliance officials in each state to enforce them. But history shows that federal and state officials have failed to protect patients from HMO abuses, even in small pilot programs.

In 1990 Florida newspapers printed lurid accounts of abuses by Humana Medical Plan, an HMO paid to care for the elderly under a small, experimental program to reduce Medicare costs.

Congress ordered an investigation of Humana's performance, and Janet Shikles, in charge of the probe for the General Accounting Office testified about the company's "failure to order appropriate diagnostic tests and failure to follow up on abnormal test results." *Consumer Reports* (August 1992) also investigated the shortcomings of the pilot Medicare-HMO program in Florida, and concluded that government oversight was "lackadaisical."

A nationwide investigation for Congress drew the same conclusion. Pointing out that only twenty-one of fifty-seven HMOs investigated received a passing grade, the late Senator John Heinz warned that the priority "has been to promote enrollment in HMOs and we have not given equal priority to monitoring what happens" to people "after they have enrolled."

Far from protecting patients in HMOs, the Clinton bill ties the hands of state lawmakers who want to pass protective legislation. Some states recently have enacted laws to safeguard choices patients want to make for themselves, such as which hospital or pharmacy to use. HMOs protest that these laws hobble cost containment, and the Clinton administration apparently agrees. The Clinton bill pre-empts state laws protecting patient choice.

You'll Get More Primary Care Than High-Tech Medicine, and That's Not Good News. Will patients get the care they need when gatekeepers limit their access to specialists and high-tech medicine, as the Clinton bill intends? The evidence strongly suggests that low-tech care will not be good enough. People with heart disease, for example, will suffer. HMOs already ration high-tech care to heart attack patients, according to a study in *The New England Journal of Medicine* (December 1993). HMO patients hospitalized with coronary heart disease (myocardial infarction, unstable angina, angina pectoris or ischemic heart disease) are 30 percent less likely to be given by-pass surgery or a coronary angioplasty (declogging of the arteries) than similarly sick patients with fee-for-service insurance. Another recent study by Duke University points to the consequences of such low-tech care. In the study, American heart attack patients who tended to be treated with three costly, high-tech procedures—catheterization (inserting a thin tube into the heart for diagnosis), angioplasty and bypass surgery—recovered far better than Canadian heart attack patients, who had less access to the procedures. American patients, who were twice as likely to undergo the procedures, tended to have a better quality of life after a heart attack. Canadians suffered more recurring pain, felt more depressed and were less able to go back to work and pick up their old activities. Dr. Robert Califf says the Duke study may help people understand "the implications of reducing services in a health care system."

Is it true that we need less care by specialists? Not according to the National Institutes of Health, which recently issued a warning that patients with many common conditions should be treated routinely by a renal (kidney) specialist. According to the NIH panel, primary care doctors frequently are overlooking the early signs of kidney failure and are hanging on to patients too long. Patients should be referred to specialists for dialysis sooner, said the NIH, before it is too late to save their lives. Twenty-five percent of kidney patients who don't receive dialysis until it is an emergency die. Dr. C. Craig Tisher, chairman of the NIH panel, warned that patients with high blood pressure, diabetes, weight problems and metabolism abnormalities should be regularly cared for by a renal specialist, not only a primary care doctor.

In the short run, the Clinton bill depends on HMOs to limit access to specialists and high-tech care. As a longer-term strategy to limit such care, the Clinton bill seizes control of medical education and requires that by 1998, no more than 45 percent of young doctors be permitted to go on to advanced training in a specialty. Specialty programs at leading medical schools will be downsized. Doctors in training will be assigned to the coveted specialty programs based partially on race and ethnicity, depending on how "underrepresented" each racial or ethnic group is "in the field of medicine in general and in the various medical specialties."

Restricting medical education by government fiat undoubtedly will reduce the consumption of expensive, cutting-edge care. Doctors who are not trained in sophisticated technology cannot use it. But preventing doctors from learning about the most advanced medical procedures is a lethal way to curb health care consumption. Keeping doctors uninformed could not possibly be an improvement.

Unwritten Rationing Rules. Under the Clinton bill, you are entitled to a package of basic benefits, but you can have them only when they are "medically necessary" and "appropriate." That decision will be made by the National Quality Management Council, not by you and your doctor. The council (fifteen presidential appointees) will establish "practice guidelines" to control "utilization" of health services. These guidelines will compel doctors to uniformly practice low-budget medicine. "There needs to be some point of reference for [health] plans to determine what is appropriate care," Starr said. "There is an enormous amount of excessive, inappropriate care." In Starr's view, the bill provides "high quality care." People who want access to more are asking for a "neurotic" level of care. What is most troubling about the practice guidelines is that they are not spelled out in the bill. Congress and the public are asked to approve the concept without knowing the content.

How rigorous will the standard of "medically necessary" and "appropriate" be? In other words, how much rationing based on cost-effectiveness will we have to endure? When a kidney transplant is needed, will the patient's age matter, as it does in Great Britain, where older patients are routinely denied high-tech treatments? Will patients with advanced AIDS be entitled to intensive care? Oregon's standard of appropriate care for needy residents excludes high-tech, life-sustaining procedures for advanced AIDS cases, as well as for extremely premature babies and advanced cases of certain cancers. Groopman, who treats cancer and AIDS patients, worries that decisions now made by the patient, doctor and family will be made by a council of "omniscient bureaucrats" who "are looking at two things: dollars and ideology."

Many organizations, including the American Medical Association, specialty medical societies and insurers already devise what they call "practice guidelines" to help physicians keep abreast of the most effective treatments. Ludden explained that "doctors appreciate guidelines" when they are recommendations, "but not when they become matters of law."

Many physicians who treat the HIV-positive population are troubled that the Clinton plan's practice guidelines will prevent them from trying new strategies to help desperate patients. Jasper recalls that he learned quickly "through the grapevine" that other doctors were achieving some success with treating pneumocystis pneumonia, an AIDS-related illness, with adjunctive corticosteroids. Mandatory practice guidelines would have stifled such innovation and prevented Jasper from keeping his patient alive. Similarly, Ludden recalls that at Harvard "we were using aerosol pentamidine" to treat an AIDS-related condition "eighteen months before any practice guideline would have regarded it as appropriate." The Clinton bill would hold changes in medical treatments to a slow-moving government timetable, putting many patients' lives at risk while the National Quality Management Council deliberates.

If You're Over 65, Good Luck. Another cost-cutting measure in the Clinton bill deprives people over 65 of access to new cures. The secretary of health and human services has the power to set a controlled price for every new drug, and to require the drug manufacturer to pay a rebate to the federal government on each unit sold to Medicare patients at market price instead of the controlled price. If a producer balks at paying the rebate, the secretary can "blacklist" the drug, striking it from the list of medications eligible for Medicare reimbursement. The proposed regulation threatens to keep a new drug such as Tacrine (a treatment for Alzheimer's) from older patients.

Under the bill, the secretary weighs the development costs and profit margin for the single drug, rather than the overall profitability of investing in new cures. Biotech investors point out that for every drug that reaches market, more than 1,000 others dead-end, with a 100 percent loss for investors. Limiting the price and profitability of the one drug in a thousand that succeeds will halt research into new cures, including drugs for ovarian and breast cancers now in the pipeline.

Before Signing On, You Should Know. The Clinton bill will prevent people from buying the medical care they need. Price controls on premiums will push most Americans into HMOs and pressure HMOs into sharply cutting access to specialists and effective, high-tech cures. Price controls on doctors' fees and regulations tying doctors' hands will curb the care physicians can give patients. Price controls on new drugs will keep people over 65 from getting the medications that can help them. Most important, government controls on medical education will limit what future doctors know, costing lives and suffering no one can calculate.

The administration often cites two statistics—America's relatively high infant mortality rate and its lower life expectancy—to support the need for the Clinton health bill. But these have almost nothing to do with the quality of American medical care. Both statistics reflect the epidemic of low-birth-weight babies born to teenage and drug-addicted mothers, as well as the large number of homicides in American cities and drug-related deaths.

* * *

In fact, if you are seriously ill, the best place to be is in the United States. Among all the industrialized nations, the United States has the highest cure rates for stomach, cervical and uterine cancers, the second highest cure rate for breast cancer and is second to none in treating heart disease. In other countries that spend less, people who are sick get less care, are less likely to survive and have a poorer quality of life after major illness. Consider what happens in Canada, whose health care system often is held up as a model for the United States. In Canada medical technology is rationed to dangerously low levels. The United States has 3.26 open-heart surgery units per million people; Canada has only 1.23 units per million. Cardiovascular disease is Canada's number one health problem, yet open-heart surgery units and catheterization equipment are kept in such short supply that the average wait for urgent (not elective) surgery is eight weeks. The shocking result is that in Canada, a cardiac patient is ten times as likely to die waiting in line for surgery as on the operating table. In the United States, there is no wait.

The choice is not between the Clinton bill and the status quo. Members of Congress should read this bill, instead of relying on what they hear, and then turn their attention to alternatives sponsored by Democrats and Republicans. These alternatives provide urgently needed reform of the health insurance industry, outlawing its worst abuses, without taking important decisions away from patients and their doctors and without depriving Americans of effective, high-tech medical care when they are seriously ill. Congress also should consider ways to provide insurance for those who cannot afford it, and level with the public about what universal coverage will cost. Whatever the price, ultimately, it will be less expensive than the consequences of the Clinton bill.

POSTSCRIPT

Is Managed Competition the Cure for Our Ailing Health Care Industry?

Clearly, there is continued support for some federal initiative in the area of health care. Voters want a change. In a *Wall Street Journal*/NBC News poll reported in June 1994, 71 percent of those surveyed responded that they wanted reform when asked, "Should Congress and the president continue their efforts to reform the health care system or leave it as it is now?"

There are several reasons for voter concern in this area. Some worry that they will lose their medical benefits that are provided by their employer. As the cost of this fringe benefit continues to accelerate, more and more employers are priced out of the system. Indeed, in May 1994, Secretary of Labor Robert Reich released a study indicating that only 61 percent of workers received medical coverage from their employers in 1993, compared to 66 percent in 1979. Others worry that living standards will be eroded as a greater share of the nation's income is pulled into the health care industry. And still others worry that hasty changes in the system will result in "socialized medicine," which will fatally wound America's capitalistic system.

President Bill Clinton argues that we "must make history" now, by reforming the nation's health care system. He maintains that piecemeal approaches will not work. For Clinton, a market-based system that preserves choice and is tied to an employer-based private insurance system is needed. McCaughey, in response, asserts that the "choice is not between the Clinton bill and the status quo." For her there are many other far more attractive alternatives that are less costly and that will not deprive Americans of effective medical care.

There have been volumes written about the pros and cons of the American health care system. You may wish to begin by reading the full text of the president's proposal as he outlined it in the *Economic Report of the President, February 1994*. His proposal is in part modeled after a managed competition plan put forth by Alain Enthoven and Richard Knonich in "A Consumer-Choice Health Plan for the 1990s," *The New England Journal of Medicine* (January 12, 1989). An alternative proposal is detailed by Michael D. Intriligator in "A Way to Achieve National Insurance in the United States," *American Behavioral Scientist* (July 1993).

There is by no means universal support for these far-reaching proposals. For some less optimistic views, see "Health Care Costs Are Going Down," by Fred Barnes, *The American Spectator* (February 1994); Bruce Bartlett, "Low-Rent Health," *National Review* (May 2, 1994); and Dick Armey and Newt Gingrich, "The Welfarization of Health Care," *National Review*, February 7, 1994).

ISSUE 7

Are More Prisons and Prison Beds the Answer to America's Rising Crime Rate?

YES: Edwin W. Zedlewski, from "When Have We Punished Enough?" *Public Administration Review* (November 1985)

NO: David F. Greenberg, from "The Cost-Benefit Analysis of Imprisonment," *Social Justice* (Winter 1990)

ISSUE SUMMARY

YES: Edwin W. Zedlewski, an economist with the National Institute of Justice, argues that investment in more prison capacity is wise social policy because the associated costs are more than compensated for by the value of the benefits society would enjoy.

NO: Economist David F. Greenberg alleges that many of the costs of imprisonment are excluded from Zedlewski's calculations and that he has significantly overestimated the benefits.

Few people feel totally safe walking the streets of urban America or even pitching a tent in a wilderness area. It is well known that the country is plagued by a terrifying crime rate. Crime reports in newspapers, on radio, and on television are daily reminders that nearly 6 million people in the United States annually suffer the effects of violent crimes—murder, rape, robbery, and aggravated assault. Another 29 million Americans suffer the effects of property crime—arson, burglary, and larceny/theft. Stated differently, the 1992 "crime clock" indicates that there is an automobile stolen every 20 seconds, a burglary committed every 11 seconds, a theft perpetrated every 4 seconds, a murder committed every 22 minutes, a rape reported every 5 minutes, and at least 1 robbery and 2 assaults occurring every minute of every day!

These figures suggest that the American criminal justice system is under siege, and there is no letup in sight. In fact, the 1990s may prove to be the most violent period in the nation's history. In the 10-year period 1983–1992, the numbers of persons arrested each year for committing a violent crime increased from 391,000 to 590,000, which translates to a 50.8 percent increase. Rather than winning the war against crime, America seems to be losing it on a grand scale.

Perhaps even more frustrating is the fact that the country's incarceration rate has increased at an even faster rate than the criminal activity it is intended to contain. More than three-quarters of a million individuals are behind bars; that is a population equal to the whole of Baltimore, Maryland, or Milwaukee, Wisconsin, and substantially greater than the population of Atlanta, Georgia, or Boston, Massachusetts. If we add together the prison population with those on probation and parole, our "city of criminals" would be equal to more than 4 million persons—the second largest city in the United States.

In spite of this burgeoning prison population, Edwin W. Zedlewski argues that the U.S. prison system is woefully inadequate. For him an efficient determination of how many criminals should be sent to prison is predicated on equating the marginal social costs with the marginal social benefits. This cost-benefit analysis would compare the costs associated with incarceration with the economic value of the benefits society would enjoy if these individuals were no longer free. In a cost-benefit analysis, as long as the value of the benefits of one more prison bed is equal to or greater than the costs society must pay for this bed, society should increase its prison capacity.

The two readings that follow take up the challenge of determining the associated benefits and costs of increased incarceration. This is not a simple summation of easily identifiable expenditures and costs. We caution you to read with great care the assumptions made by Zedlewski and by David F. Greenberg.

YES

Edwin W. Zedlewski

WHEN HAVE WE PUNISHED ENOUGH?

Today's criminal justice system is in a state of crisis over prison crowding. Even though national prison capacity has expanded, it has not kept pace with demands.... National attention has focused on prison crowding. But the common cry among corrections professionals is not a need for more prisons but a need for alternatives to incarceration.

The search for alternatives to prison is curious inasmuch as public sentiment calls for more punishment. Recent legislative changes to penal codes in the form of mandatory prison terms for drunk drivers and for gun crimes, plus calls for the abolition of parole boards, argue for more prison space. Yet many professionals resist, arguing that prison construction is too expensive and does little for the reduction of crime.[1]

Do we need more prisons or more alternatives to prison construction? Before such questions can be answered, we need more information on both the costs and benefits of punishment. Since so many elements of the sentencing decision, such as victim harm, justice, and public fear, defy quantification, any picture will be necessarily incomplete. Nonetheless, the data assembled here quantify many of the missing benefits of prison capacity and thereby contribute to debate over prison crowding and alternative sentencing.

Significantly, even discarding the emotional and psychological costs mentioned, the data strongly support the need for more prison capacity. Subsequent sections of this paper apply the social cost-benefit framework to alternate uses of scarce prison space and the choice of alternatives to incarceration. These sections are less prescriptive because research findings are less definitive. They are sufficient, however, to offer at least some recommendations for policy makers.

THE SOCIAL COST OF CRIME

Gary Becker first sketched an analytic framework for deciding upon optimal expenditure for crime control.[2] By advancing the notion that the criminal justice system ought to minimize the "net social harm" of crime, Becker recognized that while expenditures to reduce crime drained resources, crime imposed other costs upon a community. There is nothing mystical about these so-called social costs. Home and business security systems, victim losses, and prematurely abandoned buildings are as much expenditures on crime as prisons and police salaries.

Three kinds of costs are involved: harm to victims, combating or preventing crime, and punishing offenders. Their sum represents the social cost of crime. These elements are interdependent in that an increase in punishment can simultaneously increase punishment costs and decrease victim and prevention expenditures. The trick is to find the balance among the elements that minimizes the total crime bill.

Available data cannot determine with precise accuracy what criminal justice expenditures ought to be to minimize net social costs. However, the logic of spending no more on a problem than one can realize in return is useful in examining sentencing decisions. There is now, moreover, sufficient data available to enable us to assess the direction—more or less prison—toward which sentencing should move.

Estimates of the social costs relevant to imprisonment decisions are generated using the notion of balancing the harm from crime against the costs of incarceration. Admittedly, this exercise is artificial in that defendants are imprisoned for a variety of reasons—retribution, rehabilitation, just deserts among them. Minimizing social harm may not even be among the reasons articulated by policy makers. Yet, judges and policy makers do in some sense weigh the safety of the community against the costs of punishment in their decisions and in that sense they are performing a social cost-benefit balancing.

Through their balancing, judges and corrections officials decide whether society will be better off if certain defendants are set free. They are concerned with the future: whether defendants will produce useful social products through jobs; whether the correctional system should expend several thousands of dollars to confine them; and whether society will be spared damage from future criminal acts. Two "costs," at least implicitly, are compared, the costs of imprisonment and the costs to society of setting a defendant free.

What Is a Year in Prison Worth?

What is the social cost of a year in prison? That figure can be obtained with reasonable accuracy. Custodial costs for a year in prison are about $15,000 according to the American Correctional Association. Construction and financing costs, if viewed improperly, can make building seem overwhelmingly expensive.[3] But construction financing costs are in fact like mortgage costs facing homebuyers who quickly find the relevant comparisons. To assess annual capital costs, one simply discounts future repayments into current dollars (to obtain the discounted present value of the investment) and then prorates total costs over the projected life of the facility. More simply, one can multiply the current interest rate times the value of the construction. Construction costs for new prisons average about $50,000 per bed space according to a recent General Accounting Office report.[4] Using a 10 percent interest rate on state bonds as the rental cost of capital, a prison space, with its share of the rest of the prison structure, costs about $5,000 per year.

Lost social output from the defendant is somewhat more difficult to value.

If a prisoner had been unique in his gainful employment, there would indeed be a loss. But, if imprisonment means that some unemployed person replaces him in the work force, then there might actually be a social gain. Added into these social dynamics are the net transfers of dependents, if there are any, into and out of other welfare support programs. A net social loss of $5,000 per year should generously account for lost social output.[5] Decisions to imprison, therefore, imply system costs of roughly $20,000 and total social costs of about $25,000. Subsequent development of this analysis shows that results are not sensitive to substantial errors in any one cost figure.

Letting Them Go Free, Is Not

The social cost of an imprisonment decision, about $25,000 per year, must be weighed against the social cost incurred by the release decision. That cost can be approximated, albeit crudely, by estimating the number of crimes per year an offender is likely to commit if left free and multiplying that number by an estimate of the average social cost of a crime. We develop estimates of these two figures here, realizing in advance the substantial imprecision of the results. It is virtually meaningless to say that "the average criminal in the United States commits q crimes per year" or that "the average American crime costs X dollars." The numbers help focus attention on important issues, however. The number of crimes averted by imprisonment and the social costs attendant with crime are critical determinants of how much prison space we should have. The results here suggest the direction that sentencing policy should take, even if they do not suggest the magnitude of change.

Given that prison space is limited, judges try to reserve it for the most active criminals.[6] For expository purposes, we can envision omniscient judges trying to gauge a defendant's criminality in terms of past and future offenses per year. If he were to focus on crime control, the judge would send to prison those with the greatest annual offense rates, q. Since prison space is limited, he would eventually set free all those with offense rates greater than some q. The question is whether the q crimes saved is greater than the expenditure to save them.

Judges are neither omniscient nor do they sentence offenders to prison solely on the basis of criminality. The average criminality of currently imprisoned offenders is, therefore, less than it would be under a pure and omniscient crime control sentencing policy. Still, knowing something about the criminality of current inmates at least helps us assess the benefits attained from current prison capacity.

In order to approximate the numbers of crimes likely to be committed by freed offenders, we used information about annual crime rates obtained from inmate interviews. Inmate characteristics should resemble those of marginal releasees— defendants that judges decided were almost but not quite deserving of a prison term. It is this group of borderline cases that would have been imprisoned if additional space were available and their crimes that would have been averted. Because of the severe limitations in predicting which defendants are most criminal, there is good reason to believe that inmate offense rates approximate those of borderline releasees.[7]

The estimates of annual offense rates here are taken from a survey by the Rand Corporation of 2,190 inmates who were housed in jails and prisons in California, Michigan, and Texas.[8] The average number of crimes per inmate serves well to assess the crime savings attained under current abilities to predict criminality.

... Rates varied from 1 to 1,000 offenses per year, and individual offenders specialized to varying degrees (a burglar for instance, may have been involved in few other kinds of theft).... Inmates averaged somewhere between 187 and 278 property crimes of various kinds per year, excluding drug deals. Those who said they had committed no property offenses —some 18 percent of the sample—have been excluded in order to sidestep difficulties in valuing violent crimes.

The Victim's Bill

A final estimate is the value of a crime to society. It is the most troubling element in the exercise, partly because of the statistical errors, and partly because of the conceptual difficulties in defining social value. Rather than exhaust the reader with a long digression on the relationship between social value and market costs or between average expenditure on crime versus expected savings, we shall simply state our procedure. We counted every published expenditure on crime we could find and updated them to reach $99.8 billion (1983). We counted every victimization we could estimate for 1983 and obtained 43.4 million crimes. We divided dollars by crimes to get expenditures of $2,300 per crime....

Admitting the inaccuracies involved in the estimation, does $2,300 per crime seem plausible, nonetheless? Expenditures have some merit as measures of value because people do not spend more for services than the value they de-

rive from them. Because the figure is a gross average, it probably overvalues petty larcenies and undervalues rapes or vicious beatings. Some overestimation occurs because not all criminal justice expenditures are crime-related. On the other hand, many household and urban expenditures are uncounted. At any rate, even fairly large errors will not alter the conclusions reached.

The estimates indicate that if judges were to sentence 1,000 more offenders (similar to current inmates) to prison, they would obligate the correctional system to roughly $25 million per year. About 187,000 felonies would be averted through incapacitation of these offenders. These crimes would represent about $430 million in social costs. The conclusion is insensitive to rather large errors in estimates. If we were to double the annual cost of confinement, halve the average crimes per offender, and halve the average cost per crime, we would still conclude that $50 million in confinement investments would account for $107 million in social costs.

Since estimates of social costs were based on money spent, not costs avoided, what actual savings would be realized is open to speculation. One can, however, envision several kinds of savings from declining crime rates. If householders and businessmen are objective in their expenditures, they would divert some money from protection of goods to the purchase of more goods. Fewer buildings would be abandoned because of crime risks. Inner city businesses would enjoy lower operating expenses due to reduced incidences of thefts. Mass transportation would be safer and more popular. The potential savings seem large.[9]

The Fat Half of the Wishbone

Our cost comparisons were based on an implicit assumption that incapacitation of offenders was the only source of crime savings. An extensive literature[10] argues that in fact the majority of crime savings are attributable to deterrence. General deterrence is the crime savings accrued because potential offenders take into account the risks of punishment (as measured by the fraction of crimes that result in punishment) in their crime commission decisions. As the risk of punishment increases, the number of people willing to commit crimes decreases.

Estimates of the savings attributable to punishment risk vary with the data used and the crimes and sanctions studied. Ehrlich,[11] using state-aggregated data from 1960, estimated that a 1 percent increase in imprisonment risk (prisoners per crime) would produce a 1 percent decrease in crimes per capita. Wolpin,[12] using a national-aggregate time series of England and Wales, estimated that a 1 percent increase in imprisonment produced a four-fifths (0.839) percent decrease in crime rates. Wolpin also separated the deterrence savings from incapacitation or imprisonment savings and estimated that slightly more than half the savings were due to deterrence for both property and violent crimes.

Other studies suggest that the deterrent component is even larger. Cohen's[13] review of incapacitation research uncovered a range of 2 to 25 percent estimated for incapacitation's share. Nagin and Blumstein[14] estimated that if sentencing policies in effect in 1970 had been changed from a 25 percent chance of prison upon conviction of a serious crime to 100 percent and if prison terms had been reduced from 2.6 years on average to 1, crime rates would have been reduced by 25 percent while prison populations would have risen by 25,000 inmates. Focusing on the appealing concept of preventing crime through imprisonment misses most of the benefits of the punishment.

Deterrence estimates of crime savings help corroborate our findings. A 1 percent increase in 1983 state prison populations would amount to 4,390 more prisoners, or about $110 million in expenditures. Using Wolpin's estimate of a 0.839 percent reduction in crime rates means that 364,000 crimes would have been averted at an assumed value of about $837 million.

Not surprisingly, the cost-benefit ratio has fallen from about 17:1 to 7:1 as we moved from using inmate-based estimates of crimes averted to general population estimates; inmates are likely to contain a disproportionate number of high-rate offenders. So long as incoming prisoners resemble current inmates, the higher benefit ratio is pertinent. If incarcerations increased to the point that additional inmates more nearly represented the general population's propensities for crime, cost-benefit ratios would move toward the lower figure. Society is likely to receive a substantial rate of return on prison investments in either case.[15]

SELECTIVE INCAPACITATION

Some opponents of prison expansion have argued that improved identification of high-rate offenders coupled with a policy of "selective incapacitation" might obviate the need for additional capacity. Selective incapacitation emphasizes future criminality as a cornerstone of sentencing decisions. It argues that long terms for high-rate offenders and short terms or non-prison sanctions for lesser criminals can increase crime savings without construction. It is in contrast to what many perceive current policies to be; namely, a balance between the offense committed and the offender committing.

The potential for selective incapacitation can be seen... from the Rand survey data.[16] Nearly half the sample admitted to fewer than 10 crimes per year. At the other extreme, some 20 percent admitted to more than 200 crimes per year. Imprisoning more high-rate offenders for longer periods would increase the incapacitation benefits of prisons.

Enhanced prediction of criminality would be desirable even if current policies were maintained. Unfortunately, the near-term prospects for improvements are severely clouded.

Greenwood and Abrahamse[17] scored prison inmates on a scale of 0 to 7 on bases such as prior record, drug use, and employment history and then predicted which among a sample from the 781 robbers and burglars from the Chaiken and Chaiken survey were likely to be high-, medium-, and low-rate offenders. They compared their predictions to inmate reports and concluded that they had predicted with fair accuracy. Unfortunately, this conclusion is sensitive to how their predictions are aggregated.

... The hypothetical policy under consideration gives long prison terms to high rate offenders and very short terms or probation to lesser offenders. This is consistent with a policy of targeting prison space for high-rate offenders. Using the study's classification scheme, judges would err by nearly 50 percent in both directions: every high-rate offender sentenced to a long term (15 percent) would be accompanied by a misclassified lesser offender (14 percent), and large numbers of high-rate offenders (13 out of 28 percent) would receive minor sentences.[18] One would expect classification errors to be even greater in any operational setting because a new set of offenders would differ from the study sample in terms of prediction characteristics.

Subsequent research in a decision-making environment reinforced pessimism over near-term prospects for identifying habitual offenders. Petersilia et al.[19] found that even comprehensive sentence investigations, which documented employment history, family structure, and criminal records, were poor predictors of the recidivists among a convicted population. Felons recommended for probation and felons recommended for prison but not incarcerated were back into the court system in nearly equal proportions. Only 3 percent of their sample of incoming prison inmates were predicted to be good probation risks.

Other problems requiring attention are the ethical questions raised for the nation's judiciary. Among them are the proportionality of punishment to the offense and the need to provide some sense of justice to victims. How should a judge decide between a first-time murderer and a career thief? Between imprisoning one habitual offender for 10 years and five lesser offenders for 2 years each? Such questions, largely resolved under current policies, must be reconsidered for selective incapacitation.

A final consideration is whether public sentiment would support long-term incarceration of juveniles. Youths under 18 accounted for over 30 percent of arrests for serious crimes in 1983; youths under 21 accounted for over 47 percent.[20] Thus, youths must figure into any crime savings calculated. Either current juvenile punishment policy, which minimizes the use of confinement, would have to be discarded or the hypothetical crime savings estimated from selective incapacitation would have to be revised.

The implications of this section are that selective incapacitation has many obstacles to overcome before it can be advanced as a viable policy. Besides the ethical issues of punishment structure and the social concerns over treatment of juvenile offenders, there is the distinct possibility that predicted crime savings are mythical. Increasing sentence lengths for some offenders means that bed spaces are taken away from other offenders. Reductions in punishment certainty are reductions in the deterrence power of sanctioning. Crimes saved through increased incapacitation may be fewer than those lost through reduced deterrence. Also, our current abilities to identify high-rate offenders from official statistics seem so limited that half the offenders sentenced to lengthy terms would likely be lesser criminals.

IF NOT PRISON, WHAT?

The same statistics that earlier argued for additional prison capacity support the notion that some offenders are not worth imprisoning. Indeed, most convicted offenders serve no prison time. Few who do serve prison time serve their full term. In 1983 American correctional systems were supervising 2.4 million persons. Some 73 percent of these persons were in the community, 252,000 as parolees from their prison terms and 1,502,000 probationers who had not been sent to prison. Jails, which house both convicted and some pretrial persons, held 224,000 and prisons held 439,000 inmates.[21] Persons who received only fines or suspended sentences are not counted in these figures because they receive no supervision. Incarceration is the extreme, not the standard, punishment for a crime.

The criminal justice system operates under a punitive philosophy nonetheless, and 20th century penologists have designed many alternatives to incarceration. Fines, restitution, forfeitures, community service, supervised and unsupervised probation, and suspended sentences are among the current alternatives. But despite the flexibility implied by the range of possibilities, alternatives to prison use either of two mechanisms: expropriation of assets (or work equivalent of assets) or monitoring of subsequent behavior in the community.

The World of Fines

Becker argued that fines were socially efficient because they punished offenders without draining significant amounts of resources for their administration. While correct in theory, the argument is eroded somewhat by two related considerations: a convict's ability to pay and the state's ability to enforce its fine policies. In *Tate v. Short*,[22] the Supreme Court ruled that fines could not be set beyond a defendant's ability to pay and then converted to imprisonment. This decision was buttressed by *Bearden v. Georgia*[23] in 1983 where the court ruled that unpaid fines could not be converted to imprisonment unless the state determined that the defendant had not made a *bona fide* effort to pay.

These decisions do not reflect disfavor of fines by the Supreme Court. In *Bearden*, the court explicitly recognized the enforcement of fines by imprisonment. What the court called attention to was the need for a rational and equitable fine structure. Amounts levied must be subjected to some sort of means test and enforcement must be tempered by subsequent considerations of ability to pay.

These restrictions do not appear to have severely restricted the use of fines. Hillsman *et al.*[24] found that fines were the predominant sanction for non-traffic violations in courts of limited jurisdiction (misdemeanors and lesser felonies) which handled 90 percent of all criminal cases brought and were also used in general jurisdiction felony courts. Only 2 of the 24 felony courts surveyed said they never imposed fines. The fraction of fine amounts actually collected, as much as 90 percent of the amounts levied, depended on the interest and persistence of the courts in collecting them.

Credible enforcement of fines requires the establishment and monitoring of payment schedules if the amounts set are anything but nominal. Setting fair but punitive fines requires information on the legitimate incomes of convicts. The equity problem has been solved in part in Sweden and West Germany by implementation of "day fines." Fines in these countries are levied in units of work days of the defendant. Defendant income is used to estimate the value of his work day and transform the days fined into a payable fine amount. Swedish and German courts enjoy easy access to a defendant's salary information, but it is not clear that easy access is an important ingredient of success. Simply asking the defendant his salary may be sufficient, particularly if the alternative to a fine is a jail term.

A popular American variation of the fine is restitution. Although the defendant is in essence fined, the fine amount is determined by the harm done to his victim and is paid to the victim, either in cash or labor. By combining punishment and compensation, restitution offers a strong sense of redress. But, only victims lucky enough to have a convicted assailant can receive compensation through restitution sentences. The large majority will have to look to other mechanisms. Victim compensation funds financed through fines and forfeitures, as established by the Victims of Crime Act of 1984, can offer more efficient and equitable restoration of damages.

Probation and Public Safety

While fines are popular in misdemeanor cases, the courts sentence the majority of felons and serious misdemeanants to probation.... [T]he relative use of probation and imprisonment has remained fairly stable despite perceptions of a large-scale shift toward imprisonment. What has changed is the absolute use of both sanctions and their use relative to the number of serious crimes.

As practiced in the early 1970s, probation was a cornerstone of rehabilitation. Probation officers operated in part as social workers. They either gave referrals for job and family counseling, drug and alcohol treatment, and vocational training, or provided these services personally. As disappointment over the prospects for rehabilitation grew in the late 1970s, probation officers gradually took on more of a watchman's role even though many social services were still provided.

Whatever the underlying rationale, probation has been perceived to be a minor sanction. Polling college students, Sebba[25] found that they ranked one year's probation just below a 12-month suspended sentence and above a $250 fine in terms of severity. Surveying prosecutors, Jacoby and Ratledge[26] found that one year's unsupervised probation ranked between fines of $10 and $100; a year's supervised probation ranked on a par with a 30-day suspension of a driver's license.

Concern over the severity of punishment implied by probation and the threat to community safety has caused several states, among them Delaware, New Jersey, Georgia, and Washington, to implement special probation programs that have increased oversight and restricted freedom in varying degrees.[27] Perhaps typical, Georgia's Intensive Probation Supervision (IPS) is designed for prison-bound cases. IPS probationers must either hold a full-time job or be a full-time student, perform community service, and pay part of their supervisory costs. They average 16 contacts per month with their supervisors.

State officials regard the program as successful. Although IPS probationers have been more expensive to monitor than regular probationers ($1,595 versus $275 per year), they are still less expensive than confinement at $10,814 per year. Earnings and taxes paid by IPS probationers are offsets to program costs and their higher revocation rates—25.5 percent versus 16.7 percent for a matched group given regular probation—suggests that the increased supervision increases community safety.[28]

Many costs are not captured in this assessment, however. Among the missing are victim losses, repeated criminal justice costs for apprehensions and court procedures, and confinement costs for some of those revoked. Thus the efficacy of the program is unclear in a more complete cost environment.

Haynes and Larsen[29] made similar comparisons among correctional treatments under fuller accounting of costs.

They estimated the social costs incurred from a cohort of Arizona burglars in three supervisory settings: confinement in prison or jail; community supervision under probation, parole, and halfway houses; and, unsupervised release, possibly after one of the aforementioned treatments. They captured a substantial number of the relevant cost components: corrections supervision, welfare and other social support, crime prevention, victim losses, and subsequent apprehensions. Costs were estimated for a variety of crimes and were applied to information on crimes committed obtained from interviews with the burglars. No attempt was made to estimate deterrence savings.

They found that incarceration was considerably less expensive than community supervision when identified crimes and costs were accounted for—$11,640 versus $26,868 per year. As previous studies found, small numbers of offenders (10 percent) committed most of the crimes (90 percent).[30] Haynes and Larsen also found that recurring system costs were substantial: $2,640 for arrest and prosecution of a burglary and $701 or a simple shoplifting, exclusive of general crime prevention and victim losses.

Twisting Punishment to Fit Crimes

Given that large numbers of convicted offenders are going to be released, how should one choose among alternatives to incarceration? Should a minor offense by a habitual offender receive the same sentence as a more serious offense by a first offender? Should equal offenses be treated the same if the defendants differ in criminal record?

If the answer to the last question is no, then there must be combinations of offender characteristics and crime seriousness that deserve equal amounts of punishment. This does not mean that identical punishments should be handed down to dissimilar convicts. We suggest that differences in propensities to commit future crimes, perhaps as evidenced by prior record, argue for different forms of punishment. Extending the cost-benefit reasoning presented at the outset, it is suggested that defendants with low propensities to commit future crimes should be punished as inexpensively as possible. As perceived future danger increases, the punishment should provide an opportunity to curtail future social costs. This logic suggests fines for first offenders and appropriately supervised probation for repeat offenders....

Absent evidence of habitual involvement in crime, the system should try to punish efficiently; that is, exact the penalty consuming the least resources. Properly set, fines can be made painful. If properly administered, nearly full payment can be extracted at low cost. Thus, fines produce economical deterrence. Evidence of future criminality, on the other hand, suggests that society may suffer additional crimes. The data presented here indicate that these costs are likely to exceed any reasonable costs of monitoring several times over. Supervised probation has a potential for detecting and limiting crimes.

Sanctions need not be administered separately. Judges can combined probation with a fine or with other forms of punishment. The important principle is that the punishment selected should minimize social costs while maintaining punishment equity.

CONCLUSION

The objective of this paper was to present research findings pertinent to the questions of how much offenders should be punished. Rather than rely on traditional but difficult to quantify *desiderata* [desired needs] of punishment such as retribution and justice, a cost-benefit perspective was used to investigate whether society spends more money punishing than it gains from punishment. Existing data are adequate only for a crude answer to that question. Yet, the results overwhelmingly support the case for more prison capacity. The case for current use of probation and fines is less clear because there is less data on the application of these sanctions. It appears, nonetheless, that social costs would be reduced if more probationers were given either prison terms or fines. Incapacitating borderline offenders now crowded out by today's space constraints would likely cost communities less in crime expenditure than they now pay in social damages and prevention. Punitive fines for first offenders would deter others and reduce system expenditures on supervision while producing revenues and perhaps compensating victims.

NOTES

1. See, for example, *Prison Crowding—A Crisis in Corrections*, a Report of the Task Force on Criminal Justice issues of the Policy Committee of the Center for Metropolitan Planning and Research (Baltimore: Johns Hopkins University Press, December 1984), p. 6.

2. Gary S. Becker, "Crime and Punishment: An Economic Approach," *Journal of Political Economy*, vol. 76 (March 1968), pp. 169–217.

3. See, for example, Gail S. Funke, *Who's Buried in Grant's Tomb?* (Alexandria, Va.: Institute for Economic and Policy Studies, Inc., 1982).

4. *Federal, District of Columbia, and State Future Prison and Correctional Institution Populations and*

Capacities, GAO/GOD-84-56 (Washington, D.C.: U.S. General Accounting Office, February 27, 1984), p. 30.

5. Clark R. Larsen estimated tax losses per prisoner at $408 per year and average welfare payments at $84 per year in *Costs of Incarceration and Alternatives* (Phoenix: Arizona State University Center for the Study of Justice, May 1983). The reason for such low average costs was that few of the inmates were employed in legitimate occupations or married at the time of imprisonment.

6. Some weight is undoubtedly given to a need for punishment of major criminal events rather than personalities. Justice demands that spouse killers be punished, for instance, even though repetition of the crime is unlikely.

7. Prior convictions alone have been found to be a weak predictor of underlying criminal activity. See Barbara Boland, *Age, Crime, and Punishment* (Washington, D.C.: The Urban Institute, 1978).

8. Jan Chaiken and Marcia Chaiken, *Varieties of Criminal Behavior*, R-2814-NIJ (Santa Monica, Calif.: Rand Corporation, 1982).

9. See William W. Greer, "What Is the Cost of Rising Crime?" *New York Affairs* (January 1984), pp. 6–16 or a comprehensive enumeration of social costs due to crime.

10. See A. Blumstein, J. Cohen, and D. Nagin (eds.), *Deterrence and Incapacitation: Estimating the Effects of Criminal Sanctions and Crime Rates* (Washington, D.C.: National Academy of Sciences, 1978) for an extensive review and assessment of the deterrence literature and evidence.

11. Isaac Ehrlich, "Participation in Illegitimate Activities: A Theoretical and Empirical Investigation," *Journal of Political Economy*, vol. 81 (May/June 1973), pp. 531–567.

12. Kenneth L. Wolpin, "An Economic Analysis of Crime and Punishment in England and Wales, 1894–1967," *Journal of Political Economy*, vol. 86 (October 1978), pp, 815–839.

13. Jacqueline Cohen, "The Incapacitative Effect of Imprisonment: A Critical Review of the Literature," in Blumstein, Cohen, and Nagin (eds.), *op. cit.*, pp. 187–243.

14. Daniel Nagin and Alfred Blumstein, "On the Optimum Use of Incarceration for Crime Control," *Operations Research*, vol. 26 (May 1978), pp. 381–405.

15. One cannot safely extrapolate too far from observed values of the data. A 50 percent increase in prison populations may generate more or fewer crime savings depending on how much deterrence is created by sizable increases in prison risks.

16. Table A.15 in Chaiken and Chaiken, *op. cit.*

17. Peter Greenwood and Allan Abrahamse, *Selective Incapacitation*, R2815-NIJ (Santa Monica, Calif.: Rand Corporation, 1982).

18. From Table 4.8, *ibid.*, all robbers and burglars in the study. Definition of low, medium, and high rates of criminal activity differed with each state and crime in the sample.

19. J. Petersilia, S. Turner, J. Kahan, and J. Peterson, *Granting Felons Probation*, R-3186-NIJ (Santa Monica, Calif.: Rand Corporation, 1985).

20. Federal Bureau of Investigation, *Crime in the United States: Uniform Crime Reports* (Washington, D.C.: U.S. Government Printing Office, 1984).

21. Bureau of Justice Statistics, *Probation and Parole 1983*, September 1984; *The 1983 Jail Census*, November 1984; and *Prisoners in 1983*, April 1984.

22. *Tate v. Short*, 401 U.S. 395 (1971).

23. *Bearden v. Georgia*, 461 U.S. 660 (1983).

24. S. Hillsman, J. Sichel, and B. Mahoney, *Fines in Sentencing: A Study of the Use of the Fine as a Criminal Sanction* (Washington, D.C.: National Institute of Justice, 1984).

25. Leslie Sebba, "Some Explorations in the Scaling of Penalties," *Journal of Research in Crime and Delinquency*, vol. 15 (July 1978), pp. 247–265.

26. Joan Jacoby and Edward Ratledge, *Measuring the Severity of Criminal Penalties: Provisional Results* (Washington, D.C.: Jefferson Institute of Justice Studies, 1982).

27. The Delaware program is part of a comprehensive revision of its criminal sanctions. See former Governor Pierre S. duPont's *Expanding Sentencing Options: A Governor's Perspective, Research in Brief* (Washington, D.C.: National Institute of Justice, 1985).

28. Billie S. Erwin, *Evaluation of Intensive Probation Supervision in Georgia* (Atlanta: Georgia Department of Offender Rehabilitation, 1984).

29. P. Haynes and C. Larsen, "Financial Consequences of Incarceration and Alternatives," *Crime and Delinquency*, vol. 30 (October 1984), pp. 529–550.

30. See for comparison J. Petersilia, P. Greenwood, and M. Lavin, *Criminal Careers of Habitual Felons*, R-2144-DOJ (Santa Monica, Calif.: Rand Corporation, 1977).

NO

David F. Greenberg

THE COST-BENEFIT ANALYSIS OF IMPRISONMENT

INTRODUCTION

For more than a decade, U.S. prison populations have grown at an historically unprecedented rate. In 1974 there were 218,466 sentenced prisoners in state and federal institutions; by the end of June 1989, there were 673,565. The annual growth rate in this period was approximately 8%, much larger than the 2.8% overall growth rate for the six decades between 1925 and 1985. Jail populations have also grown—from 141,588 in 1972, to more than 300,000 at the end of 1989. So far there have been no signs of leveling off.

Critics of this expansion have long argued that the expansion of the incarcerated population is a terribly inefficient way of reducing crime rates. Pointing to the high cost of building and operating new facilities, these critics have called for shorter sentences and/or greater use of alternatives to incarceration for many persons who are now sent to prison (President's Commission, 1967: 38; AFSC Working Party, 1971; Keller and Alper, 1970; Citizen's Study Committee, 1972: 1; Board of Directors, 1973; Mitford, 1973; National Advisory Commission, 1973; Killinger and Cromwell, 1974; Hahn, 1975; Perlstein and Phelps, 1975; Fox, 1977; Dodge, 1979; Irwin and Austin, 1987). Greater use of these alternatives would reduce the prison population, or at least prevent further increases. The anti-expansionist critics have recently been challenged by Edwin Zedlewski, a staff economist at the National Institute of Justice. In a journal article, and in a summary of his research issued by the National Institute of Justice, Zedlewski (1985, 1987) concludes that prisons are a highly cost-effective method of reducing crime, one whose use should be greatly expanded. During the summer of 1988, newspapers gave his findings and recommendations wide publicity.

Zedlewski's recommendations come in the wake of public campaigns in which politicians and mass media editorialists have both attacked judges for being too lenient and advocated putting more people in prison. President George Bush has proposed adding one billion dollars to the federal budget to pay for the addition of 24,000 beds to the federal prison system—a 77% increase in capacity—and the recent director of federal drug policy, William J. Bennett, called for even larger increases (Berke, 1989).

Zedlewski's cost-benefit analysis provides a seemingly scientific rationale for these proposals. Under this circumstance, his analysis must be subjected to especially close scrutiny. When this is done, it quickly becomes apparent that his computations are badly flawed. Once these flaws are corrected, Zedlewski's conclusions no longer follow.

In the pages below, I review Zedlewski's procedures and then show that they are invalid. I conclude with a broader discussion of the use of cost-benefit analyses in criminal justice policy-formation.

ZEDLEWSKI'S COST-BENEFIT ANALYSIS

The fundamental premise of a cost-benefit analysis of crime is that the resources a society deploys in preventing or coping with crime could, in the absence of crime, be used in other ways. It follows that a policy designed to minimize the costs of crime must consider not merely injuries to persons and the destruction of property, but also the "opportunity costs" of preventing crime—the costs of paying for police, courts, prisons, watchdogs, locks, private security forces, taxi fares, etc. (Votey and Phillips, 1973; Cook, 1983).

It is assumed that increases in prevention costs will reduce crime, but if total costs are to be minimized, prevention costs should be increased only to the point where an extra dollar spent on prevention yields a dollar's worth of prevented crime. Thus Hellman (1980: 59–60) remarks:

> The optimum amount of crime prevention for society to produce can now be defined; society should produce units of crime prevention up to the point at which the marginal benefit of the last unit of crime prevention equals the marginal costs of producing it. The marginal benefit of preventing one more crime is the harm avoided. The marginal cost is the additional cost of producing one more unit of prevention.

Eventually a point of diminishing returns will be reached, beyond which further spending on prevention will not produce commensurate benefits in lower crime rates. It is an empirical question to determine just what that point is.

To determine whether the benefits gained by putting people in prison to prevent crime are commensurate with the costs of incarceration, Zedlewski estimates both the costs and the benefits of doing so.

The Costs of Imprisonment

To compute the costs of putting more people in prison, Zedlewski quotes from a 1984 report of the General Accounting Office the figure of $50,000 construction costs per bed, which, assuming a 10% interest rate for borrowed money, leads to an annualized construction cost of $5,000 per prisoner. This figure will obviously rise and fall with the interest rate. To this he adds an annual maintenance cost of $15,000 for a medium-security prison, and $5,000 per prisoner/year in social costs (loss of economic production, taxes, and welfare payments to families of inmates), for a total of about $25,000 a year.

The Benefits of Imprisonment

Zedlewski restricts his consideration of the benefits of imprisonment to crime prevention. He estimates the number of crimes prevented by locking people up, taking into account both the incapacitative (restraining) function of imprisonment and its deterrent effect.

To estimate the incapacitative effect of imprisonment, Zedlewski draws on a survey sponsored by the National Institute of Justice and conducted by the Rand Corporation of 2,190 inmates of prisons and jails in California, Michigan, and Texas. The inmates told interviewers that they had, on the average, committed between 187 and 287 property crimes per year, not counting drug dealing. To be on the safe side, Zedlewski uses the smaller of these figures in his computations.

Because Zedlewski wants to examine the implications of expanding the prison population by sending to prison "borderline offenders—those . . . who would have gone to prison had space been available" (1987: 3)—(rather than by extending the sentences of those who are now incarcerated), he proceeds on the assumption that this figure can be applied to persons who are now not imprisoned, but are instead placed on probation or fined. If that assumption is correct, he reasons, then the imprisonment of a convicted defendant—who under present sentencing policies is not imprisoned—would prevent at least 187 felonies a year.

Further crime reduction, above and beyond what is achieved through incapacitation, can be achieved by deterring potential offenders. Zedlewski cites several studies on the magnitude of this effect, which found crime rates to be fairly sensitive to the size of the prison population. Interpreted causally, these findings suggest that the crime rate could be lowered by increasing the chances that a person who commits a crime will be imprisoned for it.

Translating an estimate for the number of crimes a given policy prevents into dollars is always a problem in cost-benefit analyses. The standard procedure is to value stolen property at its cost, to set the cost of injuries at medical costs and lost income, and loss of life on the basis of lost earnings for a person the victim's age, or at an arbitrary large figure such as $1 million.

This procedure is highly problematic. Victims are probably less likely to report a crime to the police when their loss is small; consequently, police records of losses are likely to be biased upward. Victims may also inflate their losses for insurance purposes. The psychic costs of crime, which often greatly exceed financial losses, are difficult to quantify meaningfully, but for many victims, they undoubtedly exceed the monetary value of lost property or the cost of medical care.

Zedlewski's highly original approach to the quantification of victims' costs is to abandon any attempt to establish an "objective" value for the cost of a crime. His alternate approach is based on the assumption that criminal justice policy can be regarded as if it were formulated by a rational actor. In the restricted sense that the term is conventionally used in economics, a rational person will try to minimize the total cost of crime and crime prevention by spending money to prevent crime only so long as the marginal cost of preventing a crime is smaller than the marginal cost of the crime prevented. Counting every conceivable cost of the criminal justice system, as well as private expenditures to prevent crime (and victim losses),

Zedlewski arrives at a figure of $99.8 billion per year as the total cost of crime in 1983 Victimization surveys suggest that there were 43.4 million crimes against victims committed in 1983. Dividing one figure by the other yields a cost per crime of $2,300.

Zedlewski reasons that imprisoning a thousand additional offenders comparable to those in the survey would cost an extra $25 million each year, and leading to 187,000 fewer crimes, worth an aggregate of $430,000,000. With benefits exceeding costs by a factor of 17, the conclusion that benefits substantially exceed costs remains valid even if there are some errors in the computation:

> Doubling the annual cost of confinement, halving the average cost per offender, and halving the average cost per crime would indicate that $50 million in confinement investments would avert $107 million in social costs (Zedlewski, 1987: 4).

How Large an Expansion?

Zedlewski does not say by how much prison populations should be expanded. The critical question is the size of the population of offenders that is committing crimes at very high rates without being imprisoned. Presumably Zedlewski believes this population to be substantial; otherwise there would be little point to his advocacy. But how large is it?

Some research suggests that the proportion of offenders who are not in prison at any given moment is high. Greene and Stollmack (1981) used arrest records to estimate the number of criminals actively committing index crimes in the District of Columbia. Their estimate for the years 1974–1975 was about 30,000. In those years, the average total jail and prison population for the District was

2,187, about 7.3% of the total. The ratio of prison population to the number of reported index crimes is roughly twice as high in the District of Columbia as in the rest of the United States. Consequently, the percentage of the U.S. criminal population that was incarcerated in those years was probably somewhat lower than 7.3% (U.S. Department of Justice, 1977: 16–21).

In a model of the Canadian criminal justice system devised and estimated by Blumstein, Cohen, and Nagin (1976), the ratio of prisoners to active criminals was found to be about 0.05 in equilibrium. Of course, the Canadian prison population is far smaller than that of the U.S. But so is its population, and the magnitude of its crime problem. Cross-national comparisons of crime rates are always a bit fuzzy, but if one takes index crimes as a rough measure of the volume of crime, then the ratio of prison population to crime volume is only slightly higher in the United States than in Canada. This does not suggest that a much higher proportion of criminals is behind bars in the U.S.

If the estimate that only one criminal in 20 is incarcerated at any given time, then there are approximately 19 million offenders at large who are potential candidates for incarceration. This could imply a call for prison construction that would truly gladden the hearts of construction contractors. For reasons that will be discussed below, however, the figure of 19 million is quite misleading.

A CRITIQUE OF ZEDLEWSKI'S COMPUTATIONS

The Cost Computations

The procedure Zedlewski uses to estimate the costs of more imprisonment is, as far as it goes, unexceptional. He simply adds up government expenditures and loss of revenue to arrive at $25,000 per year for each additional prisoner. These figures will undoubtedly vary from state to state because of regional differences in the costs of construction, standards of living considered appropriate for prisoners, etc.

However, as an overall figure, Zedlewski's number is unobjectionable. Yet, there are some costs of imprisonment not included in Zedlewski's estimation.

... [A] problem posed by Zedlewski's analysis is his assumption that the judicial processing of offenders will be unaffected by a tougher sentencing policy. There is every indication that this assumption is mistaken. Because most defendants want to avoid being put in prison, a sentencing policy that would incarcerate large numbers of persons who are not now incarcerated would entail additional court processing costs. Many defendants who now plead guilty on the promise of being sentenced to probation or to "time served" in jail awaiting trial would surely contest their charges if threatened with a substantial prison sentence. The proportion of cases that go to trial would undoubtedly increase. Defendants would be paying more for private attorneys, and governments would have to pay more for prosecutors, judges, subsidized defense lawyers, court reporters, and miscellaneous support staff.

Another consequence has been higher acquittal rates. In Massachusetts, a 1974 law required a one-year prison sentence without parole for illegal possession of a gun. Faced with this mandatory sentence, more defendants declined to plead guilty, went to trial, and were *acquitted*. Indeed, the acquittal rate rose from about 50% to about 80%. The net effect was to reduce the number of people going to prison on gun charges (Carlson, 1982; Currie, 1985: 63–64).

We can obtain a rough estimate of the magnitude of these costs by noting that in 1985, the total cost to federal, state, and local governments of judicial and legal services was $10.07 billion (Jamieson and Flanagan, 1987: 2). In 1984 there were 180,418 new court commitments to state and federal institutions. If judicial costs were allocated entirely to those cases that result in a commitment, the court costs per commitment come to $55,800.

Of course, a substantial fraction of these costs must be allocated to the prosecution of cases that do not result in such commitments. Judges and attorneys must still be paid for cases that are dismissed, or where sentences involving fines, probations, or short jail sentences are imposed. Numerically, those cases considerably exceed those that result in a prison sentence. On the other hand, the cases where prison sentences are imposed tend to be the more serious ones. They take more of the court's time, and they involve greater prosecutorial and defense efforts. It would be arbitrary to assign any given fraction of $55,800 to the prosecution of these cases, but the fraction may be large enough to add appreciably to Zedlewski's estimate of the cost of expanded imprisonment.

A further cost of imprisoning people is imposed on those who now benefit from the crimes prevented. Most of these crimes involve theft. Most of these thefts materially benefit someone, either the offenders themselves, or customers who purchase stolen goods at a discounted price. The savings to low-income consumers who live on the margins of subsistence may have substantially larger marginal utility to them than the marginal costs to middle- and upper-income victims of the loss of their property. The aggregate benefit to low-income communities of cheaper goods is probably quite large. Some of these benefits are documented in such ethnographic studies as Ianni (1974) and Walsh (1977). In the absence of such benefits, social welfare costs, which are ultimately borne by taxpayers, might rise appreciably.

These benefits of theft can be ignored only if one decides *a priori* that, as a matter of policy, benefits arising from illegal acts should not be counted. Such a procedure, however, skews an analysis in favor of the legal and economic *status quo*. Insofar as a cost-benefit analysis seeks to assess the implications of different policies or procedures, such an *a prior* decision should not be made without explicit justification.

The Benefit Computations

Zedlewski's use of the Rand survey to determine the benefits of expanded incarceration is, for a number of reasons, extremely problematic. First, the figure of 187 crimes per person per year pertains only to that fraction of the subject population that reported committing the particular felonies under consideration. Yet, 53.3% of the prison inmates said that they had not committed *any* of those crimes (these inmates had committed crimes that were not among those listed, e.g., drug offenses or kidnapping) (Chaiken and Chaiken, 1979: 6, 210). For this reason, the appropriate mean offense rate for the prison sample is not 187 offenses per year but (187)(.467) = 87.3 property offenses per year. This error alone leads Zedlewski to overestimate the benefits of imprisonment by a factor of two.

Second, the survey was conducted in three states—Texas, California, and Michigan—whose crime rates are all higher than the national average. These higher rates could stem from a higher proportion of the population engaging in crime, with the average offense rate per criminal being the same as in other parts of the country; or the proportion of the population that engages in crime could be about the same as elsewhere, but with active criminals violating the law more often. If the latter case holds, Zedlewski's procedure overestimates the national benefits of incarceration, because the incapacitation of offenders in other states will not yield as great a reduction in crime as in Texas, California, and Michigan. To take this possibility into account, Zedlewski's estimate of the crimes that might be prevented nationally should be reduced by about 20%.

In addition, the population that is now sentenced to prison is likely to be unrepresentative of the population that is now convicted but not incarcerated. There are several reasons why this is so. First, among those who violate the law, the frequency of violation is highly skewed. Recall Zedlewski's estimate that 43.4 million crimes are committed each year. Dividing that figure by the roughly 19 million offenders we estimated to be active every year, we find the average number of crimes committed by each offender to be only 2.28, far smaller than the 187 crimes per offender posited by Zedlewski.

The discrepancy is easily resolved: the offender population at large is extremely heterogeneous. What research has shown to be true of prison inmates is no doubt true of offenders outside prison as well—a small proportion commits many crimes, while a much larger proportion commits few. Surely this is true of probationers as well. Some may be committing crime at rates comparable to the high-frequency offenders in the Rand study. How many of them are doing so is unknown, as the shape of the distribution of offenses across offenders is not yet well known.

Selection from this heterogeneous population of offenders is unlikely to be totally random. Other things being equal, the more often people violate the law, the greater the likelihood that they will be arrested for at least one of the violations. Thus, the apprehended population is likely in the aggregate to commit crimes at higher frequencies than the offender population at large.

After conviction, further selection occurs. A study of federal sentencing in San Francisco found that probationers differed from those sent to prison in many ways—educational attainment, marital status, stability of residence and employment, dishonorable discharge from military status, pre-arrest income, participation in church activities, and length of prior criminal record—that are expected to be associated with lower rates of criminality (Robison et al., 1969). Indeed, many studies of the determinants of sentencing have found that length of prior record is a major influence on a judge's decision to imprison or release a convicted defendant (Vera Institute of Justice, 1977; Greenwood, 1980; Hagan and Bumiller, 1983; Panel on Sentencing Research, 1983). Within the Rand inmate sample, there is a positive relationship between self-reported offending rates and having a previous official record (Chaiken and Chaiken, 1979: 85–124).

These expectations are confirmed by studies comparing the recidivism of probationers and ex-prisoners. In the San Francisco study, 19.4% of the probationers recidivated, as did 35.4% of those sentenced to prison and then released. Wisconsin felony offenders placed on probation recidivated less often than parolees (29.4% vs. 39.4%), though the difference was largely confined to those without a prior record (Babst and Mannering, 1965). Adults placed on probation by the Superior Court in California's largest counties avoided rearrest more often than those who had been jailed (65.8% versus 48.6% after one year) (Beattie and Bridges, 1970). In a recent study of offenders from urban Los Angeles and Alameda counties, 63% of probationers and 72% of parolees were rearrested on new charges within two years (Petersilia and Turner, 1986). And in two other studies, the rate of recidivism was 22% lower for probationers than for released prisoners (Vito, 1987a; 1987b). Naturally enough, the magnitude of the differences varies with the jurisdiction, as do the absolute levels of recidivism; but the direction of the differences is consistent.

These findings have extremely important implications. The use of self-reports from existing prison inmates to determine how much crime would be prevented by incarcerating persons now placed on probation depends critically on the assumption that the distribution of offense rates in the target population is similar to the distribution of offense rates in the study sample. For the reasons just rehearsed, that assumption is most unlikely to be true. The target population is likely to be less criminally active than the study sample, and less seriously criminal.

Had we a reliable method for identifying the high-frequency offenders, it might matter little for a policy designed to achieve marginal effects that many offenders violate the law at low frequencies. Yet, the accuracy of prediction methods is notoriously poor. While one can select high-frequency offenders with a precision that exceeds random guessing, the improvement is usually modest. This means that any selection scheme is likely to miss some high-frequency offenders, and incarcerate many low-frequency offenders, a process that reduces the volume of crime prevented (AFSC Working Party, 1971; Von Hirsch, 1972, 1985: 105–114; Greenberg, 1975; Monahan, 1981; Blackmore and Welsh, 1983). Moreover, some predictors that could be used for predictive purposes are presumably already available to judges and play a role in the decision to grant or deny probation now. This makes it seem unlikely that there is a substantial body of identifiable high-crime probationers who are not being imprisoned already....

It is also possible that incarcerating convicted criminals leads them to commit more crimes. Incarceration can do this by stigmatizing convicts, weakening their ties to others who are not engaged in crime (family members, fellow workers, and community members), placing them in a milieu that facilitates affiliation with other criminals, generating feelings of bitterness toward "the law" or "respectable" people, attenuating their work skills, etc. These processes could lengthen crime careers or increase rates of return to crime by released prisoners.

It is not altogether easy to determine whether this happens, and if so, to what extent. A naive comparison of recidivism rates of probationers and ex-prisoners falters because the selection procedures that determine who is sent to prison serve as a filter that tends to keep those with low rates of involvement in crime out of prison. So the two populations are not entirely comparable; that is, they may differ in ways that account for differences in recidivism, independently of the criminal justice disposition they receive. However, one recent study that attempted to take account of such differences statistically found that imprisonment tended to *enhance* rates of return to crime (Petersilia and Turner, 1986).

If criminal careers are on the average long, even modest enhancements of this sort could negate much of the crime reduction that incapacitation achieves. Moreover, they will increase imprisonment costs, because recidivist criminals will return to the courts more often, and be imprisoned in the future for parole violations and new convictions.

A check of Zedlewski's high estimates for the amount of crime more imprisonment would prevent can be obtained by noting that changes over time in prison populations create "natural experiments" whose consequences for the crime rate can be readily assessed. If it is true that large increases in prison populations produce large reductions in crime rates, then the large increases in prison populations seen in recent years should already have produced large reductions in crime. A few simple "back of the envelope" calculations provide telling evidence that this has not occurred.

Between 1980 and 1985, for example, U.S. prison populations grew by 165,642, while index crimes reported to the police fell by 978,300. This comes to 5.91 index crimes per prisoner. This figure, unlike Zedlewski's, is comparable in magnitude to empirical estimates others have obtained (Greenberg, 1975; Cohen, 1978, 1983; Moore et al., 1984). Assuming a causal relationship, it follows that an increase in the prison population of 100,000 (an increase of 31.6%) would have reduced the number of index crimes committed by 591,000—a reduction of approximately 4%. This very modest reduction, corresponding to an elasticity of about −.123, suggests that imprisonment is a relatively inefficient way to reduce crime.

Our conclusion that rates of crime are relatively insensitive to the size of the prison population is confirmed by a study of imprisonment and crime rates in Illinois, where a program designed to relieve prison overcrowding reduced the size of the prison population by about 10% from the level to which it would otherwise have grown. Austin (1986) estimates that this reduction increased the crime rate by less than 1% (corresponding to an elasticity of approximately −.10).

Had Zedlewski's estimate of 187 felonies been valid, the number of index crimes (assuming for the sake of simplicity that all those felonies were index crimes) committed in the United States would have fallen by 30,975,054. Since there were 13,408,300 index crimes reported to the police in 1980, the index crime rate would have fallen to zero by 1985 (even if we take crimes not reported to the police into account) had Zedlewski's estimate been valid.

Alternately, we can look at victimization surveys. Between 1980 and 1985, victimizations (as estimated by household surveys) declined from 40,252,000 to 34,864,000. If this reduction is attributed entirely to the growth in prison population, the imprisonment of a single offender prevents 32.65 victimizations per year. Had the Zedlewski estimate of 187 victimizations been valid, victimizations would have fallen to 9,276,946, less than one-third their actual level. Further growth in prison populations after 1985 would have brought the victimization rate down to zero. Nothing of the kind has happened.

It must be stressed that these estimates are not to be taken too literally. My choice of years was arbitrary. Had I chosen a different set of years my estimates would have been somewhat different. For example, a comparison of index crime rates in 1981 and 1985 leads to the conclusion that the average prisoner commits 8.13 crimes while at large. With 1982 as a base year, the figure would have been 5.60. Comparing 1985 with 1979, one would conclude that the growth in the prison population did not prevent any crimes at all (the crime rate was higher in 1985 than in 1979 even though the prison population had grown).

It could be objected that other factors, which tend to increase the crime rate, may have been at work in these years. In the absence of the rapid expansion of prison populations that occurred, perhaps the crime rate would have risen more dramatically. There is, no doubt, some validity to this argument. The population was growing, and cultural and life-style changes contributing to the growth in crime may also have been taking place. Yet the upheavals of the 1960s were over. Though social change was continuing, it was not of such a large magnitude that it could conceivably have nullified the crime-prevention effects of such a large increase in the prison population, if Zedlewski's figures bear any resemblance to reality. The more plausible conclusion is that they do not.

This conclusion is strengthened when demographic changes occurring during this period are taken into account. Between 1980 and 1985, the age composition of the U.S. population shifted. In 1985 there were fewer people in the youthful high-crime-rate age brackets than there were in 1980. This demographic shift undoubtedly contributed to the observed decline in crime rates (Blumstein, 1985; Cohen, 1985; Blumstein, Cohen, and Rosenfeld, 1986; Steffensmeier and Harer, 1987). Taking this demographic shift into account would *reduce* one's estimates of the crime reduction that might be accomplished through an expansion of the prison population.

Before proceeding to the final step in Zedlewski's analysis—attaching a monetary value to each crime prevented, we may pause to point out the implications for the comparison of costs and benefits to the scaling down of the average rate of crimes per marginal candidate for incarceration. Taking without question Zedlewski's estimate of the dollar value of preventing a crime to be $2,300, the value of the crimes prevented by locking up a marginal offender who commits 10 crimes a year is $23,000 per year, slightly *less* than the cost of a year's incarceration.

But can the figure of $2,300 be trusted? There are several reasons it cannot. First, a substantial fraction of the amount of money spent on crime prevention and control goes for traffic offenses, and crimes that are not victimizing at all, such as narcotics violations and prostitution. Taxpayers do not pick and choose the kinds of crimes the criminal justice system prosecutes; given that choice, some of us might opt for a very different allocation of resources than the present one. As Zimring and Hawkins (1988) note, the figure of $2,300 is an average over all kinds of offenses, some of which would no doubt be costed at much more than $2,300, others at less. Under these circumstances, an average figure may not mean much.

Second, budgeting procedures for public goods can create a "fiscal illusion" that makes it difficult for taxpayers to know the full costs of providing those services publicly. This difficulty biases the provision of public goods toward overspending (Buchanan, 1967: Chapter 10).

Third, Zedlewski forgets that if public spending were increased exogenously, individuals might simply reduce their own private spending on crime prevention (Clotfelder, 1977). Depending on whether private or public expenditures are more efficient in preventing crime, a change in the mix of private and public expenditures might raise or lower crime rates.

Fourth, the procedure by which Zedlewski derives his figure for the amount individuals are willing to pay to prevent crime is entirely mistaken. Recall that Zedlewski derived this figure by adding victim losses of $35.4 billion to miscellaneous private and public expenditures for the prevention and punishment of crime ($61.4 billion). Though this may be the total cost of crime, it is not the appropriate figure to use for the amount that the public is willing to spend to reduce crime.

Within the cost-benefit framework, $61.4 billion is the amount being spent to reduce crime to its present level from the higher levels of crime that would presumably prevail in the absence of any spending for crime prevention and control. It is anyone's guess just what that level would be. It could conceivably be extremely large, far higher than present levels.

If one were to include only material losses in the cost-benefit calculus, it would be irrational to spend more money to prevent victim losses than the $35.4 billion those losses cost. If, as seems likely, it would cost more than that to prevent all those crimes, it would be cheaper to compensate victims.

Of course, people may be willing to pay to avoid the psychological costs associated with victimization as well. Yet Zedlewski's computation is still not the correct way of taking that willingness into account. The subjective value of a *marginal* reduction in crime below its present level depends on how much *additional* spending *beyond current expenditures* individuals would be willing to accept to achieve that reduction. This, too, is unknown. However, a recent survey of 400 Alabama residents suggests that it might not be high. Although 69% of the sample said that Alabama needed more prisons, only 19% favored paying for them with more taxes. Cutting back on state spending in other areas, such as education or health care, to pay for more prisons, was even less popular—only 3% supported that option (Doble and Klein, 1989: 22, 27).

In the abstract, then, the public may favor greater use of imprisonment, but it does not appear to be willing to pay for it. In any event, because Zedlewski uses an irrelevant figure for the number of crimes (those not prevented, rather than those prevented by present policy) and an incorrect dollar figure (total costs of crime rather than costs of crime prevention), his procedure cannot be taken as offering even a rough estimate of the marginal value of preventing a crime.

In sum, even when his caveats and qualifications are taken into account, Zedlewski grossly overestimates the potential benefits of expanded prison construction, and greatly underestimates the costs. Unfortunately, it is not easy to offer superior estimates of some factors that figure in his analysis because the empirical base for improved estimation is lacking.

To say that Zedlewsi's conclusions cannot be supported by the line of reasoning he advances is not to say that they cannot be supported in other ways. The question of how many people should be in prison is a difficult one that the present essay does not even attempt to address. The question of alternate sentences is equally outside the scope of the present discussion.

COST-BENEFIT ANALYSIS RECONSIDERED

Apart from the details of his computations, the terms in which Zedlewski develops his argument can themselves be criticized on a number of counts. First, by restricting the policy analysis to whether more prisons should be constructed, he fails to consider whether other alternatives might not be more cost effective than prisons. Even if all his calculations had been valid, it would still not follow that prison construction would be rational; after all, other alternate strategies might be even more efficient. Note that this is not an argument against cost-benefit analyses, only an insistence that the range of policy options needs to be broadened before such analyses are used to decide in favor of a given policy.

Second, governments have only a limited amount of funds to spend. Crime control is only one of many claims competing for the public purse. Even if further funding for crime control would in itself be desirable, it may not be desirable to take funds away from education, pollution abatement, or public health. Of course, by raising taxes or borrowing, funding or crime control can be increased without taking funds away from other public programs. However, there is a limit beyond which governments cannot tax or borrow. The reluctance of today's politicians to propose higher taxes to reduce the federal deficit suggests some of the political problems raising taxes can entail....

In a culture where utilitarian considerations are a widely accepted basis for legitimating policy decisions, it is inevitable that cost-benefit analyses will continue to be produced and disseminated to justify penal policy innovations. In itself, this is not a bad thing; at times, such analyses can illuminate policy choices. In other circumstances, such as the present one, cost-benefit analyses will be inconclusive because they will not be able to produce reasonable estimates of costs and benefits, or will not be able to cope with interpersonal comparisons of costs and benefits. On such occasions, social scientists, who may be called upon by policymakers to formulate and justify administrative initiatives, have a special responsibility not to suspend their critical sensibilities. When a policy cannot be justified, we should say so.

POSTSCRIPT

Are More Prisons and Prison Beds the Answer to America's Rising Crime Rate?

Crime prevention, like most other economic activities, faces marginal costs that increase and marginal benefits that decrease as more and more criminals are apprehended, tried, and incarcerated. As more and more individuals are imprisoned, the costs associated with jailing the least threatening offenders outweigh the associated benefits of removing these individuals from society. Thus, in terms of economics, we must resign ourselves to the presence of some criminals roaming freely on the streets.

The difficulty, however, is to calculate accurately the associated benefits and costs of increased incarceration. When we can correctly assess these costs and benefits, we can determine how aggressively we should try to rid the streets of criminals and place these individuals in prison. As the discussions in the two selections suggest, this determination is based on the assumptions made by the investigator. Zedlewski's study, as well as another report issued two years later, *Making Confinement Decisions* (Department of Justice, National Institute of Justice, 1987), represents one polar position. Zedlewski's analysis leads to public policy that would dramatically increase America's prison population. Although the Zedlewski study is now 10 years old, it continues to be a "lightning rod." Zedlewski is also not alone in his views. Several other respected researchers have come to the same conclusion and supported his views. See, for example, Morgan O. Reynolds, "Crime Pays, But So Does Imprisonment," *Journal of Social, Political, and Economic Studies* (Fall 1990), and Richard B. Abell, "Beyond Willie Horton," *Policy Review* (Winter 1989).

However, Zedlewski's work and the policy prescription delivered with his investigation have not gone unchallenged. Many have taken exception to his conclusions. See, for example, John Irwin and James Austin, *It's About Time: Solving America's Prison Crowding Crisis* (NCCD, 1987). Still other researchers have concluded that punishing harder will not reduce the crime rate as much as making punishment more effective will. This view comes clear in John J. DiIulio's paper "Punishing Smarter," *The Brookings Review* (Summer 1989). Yet another position is taken by Jeffery Grogger in a technical paper entitled "Certainty vs. Severity of Punishment," *Economic Inquiry* (April 1991), in which he argues that there is a "larger deterrent effect... [from] certainty of punishment... [and] insignificant effects... [from] increased severity of punishment."

ISSUE 8

Is Choice a Panacea for the Ills of Public Education?

YES: John E. Chubb and Terry M. Moe, from "America's Public Schools: Choice *Is* a Panacea," *The Brookings Review* (Summer 1990)

NO: Bill Honig, from "Why Privatizing Public Education Is a Bad Idea," *The Brookings Review* (Winter 1990/1991)

ISSUE SUMMARY

YES: Political scientists John E. Chubb and Terry M. Moe believe that the United States must free public schools from "political and bureaucratic control" and instead rely upon "markets and parental choice" in the quest for quality education.

NO: Public school superintendent Bill Honig replies that privatizing public schools through a system of choice is both unnecessary, given the school reforms of the 1980s, and dangerous, in light of the expected market consequences.

Before we embark upon a discussion of the benefits and costs of privatizing public schools, we should recognize that the provision of education, whether it is elementary, secondary, or higher education, can be undertaken by either the private sector or the public sector. That is, education can be marketed. If the United States wanted an unfettered market to operate in the education industry, it could. Without public education, however, those individuals who could afford education and wanted it would purchase it from private vendors; but those who wanted it but could not afford it would be excluded from the classroom.

It is only in recent years that a large percentage of the population has reaped the benefits of education. In 1940, about 14 percent of the adult population had less than six years of formal education. Now all but 2.4 percent have at least six years of schooling. Since 1940, the number of adults with four or more years of high school has grown from less than 25 percent of those 25 years or older to more than 76 percent, and those with four or more years of college has grown from 1 in 20 to more than 1 in 5.

The consequences of this educational attainment are far-reaching. Not only are individuals better off—there is a high positive correlation between education and income—but society is better off. That is, there are externalities or spillover effects associated with the consumption of education. Individuals who are educated are more likely to make better political decisions. Those who are educated and earn higher incomes are less likely to engage in criminal activity or become dependent on welfare. As the average level of education increases in a community, economic productivity is enhanced, and this in turn results in a higher rate of economic growth. Even if these third-party effects were not present, the public sector probably would continue to underwrite the cost of education. Educational opportunity is too closely bound up with American notions of equal opportunity to be ignored by lawmakers.

This does not mean, however, that the provision of public education has come without a cost. Quite the contrary, public education has been massively expensive. In 1987, state and local governments spent approximately $226.7 billion on education, while the federal government spent an additional $14 billion. This represents more than 5 percent of U.S. gross national product. These dollar expenditures are only part of the cost, however. Public schools, at least at the elementary and secondary level, exert a significant monopoly influence in the education marketplace.

Some argue that this public monopoly stifles creativity and has led to inferior education. These individuals cite the large number of school dropouts and the decline in Scholastic Aptitude Test (SAT) scores as evidence of the flagging effectiveness of the public school system. (They note that SAT scores drifted downward from the mid-1960s to the early 1980s. For the past 10 years they have remained in the lower ranges of the 25-year experience with this examination.)

During the 1980s corrective steps were taken by many state governments: Spending was increased, standards were raised, rigorous testing was introduced, and teacher certification and training requirements were augmented. Whether these actions are sufficient or whether there is a need to introduce market competitors into the education system is debated in the pages that follow. The ultimate resolution of this clash of educational philosophies could dramatically reshape schools.

YES

John E. Chubb and
Terry M. Moe

AMERICA'S PUBLIC SCHOOLS: CHOICE *IS* A PANACEA

For America's public schools, the last decade has been the worst of times and the best of times. Never before have the public schools been subjected to such savage criticism for failing to meet the nation's educational needs—yet never before have governments been so aggressively dedicated to studying the schools' problems and finding the resources for solving them.

The signs of poor performance were there for all to see during the 1970s. Test scores headed downward year after year. Large numbers of teenagers continued to drop out of school. Drugs and violence poisoned the learning environment. In math and science, two areas crucial to the nation's success in the world economy, American students fell far behind their counterparts in virtually every other industrialized country. Something was clearly wrong.

During the 1980s a growing sense of crisis fueled a powerful movement for educational change, and the nation's political institutions responded with aggressive reforms. State after state increased spending on schools, imposed tougher requirements, introduced more rigorous testing, and strengthened teacher certification and training. And, as the decade came to an end, creative experiments of various forms—from school-based management to magnet schools—were being launched around the nation.

We think these reforms are destined to fail. They simply do not get to the root of the problem. The fundamental causes of poor academic performance are not to be found in the schools, but rather in the institutions by which the schools have traditionally been governed. Reformers fail by automatically relying on these institutions to solve the problem—when the institutions are the problem.

The key to better schools, therefore, is institutional reform. What we propose is a new system of public education that eliminates most political and bureaucratic control over the schools and relies instead on indirect control through markets and parental choice. These new institutions naturally function to promote and nurture the kinds of effective schools that reformers have wanted all along.

SCHOOLS AND INSTITUTIONS

Three basic questions lie at the heart of our analysis. What is the relationship between school organization and student achievement? What are the conditions that promote or inhibit desirable forms of organization? And how are these conditions affected by their institutional settings?

Our perspective on school organization and student achievement is in agreement with the most basic claims and findings of the "effective schools" literature, which served as the analytical base of the education reform movement throughout the 1980s. We believe, as most others do, that how much students learn is not determined simply by their aptitude or family background—although, as we show, these are certainly influential—but also by how effectively schools are organized. By our estimates, the typical high school student tends to learn considerably more, comparable to at least an extra year's worth of study, when he or she attends a high school that is effectively organized rather than one that is not.

Generally speaking, effective schools—be they public or private—have the kinds of organizational characteristics that the mainstream literature would lead one to expect: strong leadership, clear and ambitious goals, strong academic programs, teacher professionalism, shared influence, and staff harmony, among other things. These are best understood as integral parts of a coherent syndrome of organization. When this syndrome is viewed as a functioning whole, moreover, it seems to capture the essential features of what people normally mean by a team—principals and teachers working together, cooperatively and informally, in pursuit of a common mission.

How do these kinds of schools develop and take root? Here again, our own perspective dovetails with a central theme of educational analysis and criticism: the dysfunctions of bureaucracy, the value of autonomy, and the inherent tension between the two in American public education. Bureaucracy vitiates the most basic requirements of effective organization. It imposes goals, structures, and requirements that tell principals and teachers what to do and how to do it—denying them not only the discretion they need to exercise their expertise and professional judgment but also the flexibility they need to develop and operate as teams. The key to effective education rests with unleashing the productive potential already present in the schools and their personnel. It rests with granting them the autonomy to do what they do best. As our study of American high schools documents, the freer schools are from external control the more likely they are to have effective organizations.

Only at this late stage of the game do we begin to part company with the mainstream. While most observers can agree that the public schools have become too bureaucratic and would benefit from substantial grants of autonomy, it is also the standard view that this transformation can be achieved within the prevailing framework of democratic control. The implicit assumption is that, although political institutions have acted in the past to bureaucratize, they can now be counted upon to reverse course, grant the schools autonomy, and support and nurture this new population of autonomous schools. Such an assumption, however, is not based on a systematic understanding of how these institutions operate and what their consequences are for schools.

POLITICAL INSTITUTIONS

Democratic governance of the schools is built around the imposition of higher-order values through public authority. As long as that authority exists and is available for use, public officials will come under intense pressure from social groups of all political stripes to use it. And when they do use it, they cannot blithely assume that their favored policies will be faithfully implemented by the heterogeneous population of principals and teachers below—whose own values and professional views may be quite different from those being imposed. Public officials have little choice but to rely on formal rules and regulations that tell these people what to do and hold them accountable for doing it.

These pressures for bureaucracy are so substantial in themselves that real school autonomy has little chance to take root throughout the system. But they are not the only pressures for bureaucracy. They are compounded by the political uncertainty inherent in all democratic politics: those who exercise public authority know that other actors with different interests may gain authority in the future and subvert the policies they worked so hard to put in place. This knowledge gives them additional incentive to embed their policies in protective bureaucratic arrangements—arrangements that reduce the discretion of schools and formally insulate them from the dangers of politics.

These pressures, arising from the basic properties of democratic control, are compounded yet again by another special feature of the public sector. Its institutions provide a regulated, politically sensitive setting conducive to the power of unions, and unions protect the interests of their members through formal constraints on the governance and operation of schools—constraints that strike directly at the schools' capacity to build well-functioning teams based on informal cooperation.

The major participants in democratic governance—including the unions—complain that the schools are too bureaucratic. And they mean what they say. But they are the ones who bureaucratized the schools in the past, and they will continue to do so, even as they tout the great advantages of autonomy and professionalism. The incentives to bureaucratize the schools are built into the system.

MARKET INSTITUTIONS

This kind of behavior is not something that Americans simply have to accept, like death and taxes. People who make decisions about education would behave differently if their institutions were different. The most relevant and telling comparison is to markets, since it is through democratic control and markets that American society makes most of its choices on matters of public importance, including education. Public schools are subject to direct control through politics. But not all schools are controlled in this way. Private schools—representing about a fourth of all schools—are subject to indirect control through markets.

What difference does it make? Our analysis suggests that the difference is considerable and that it arises from the most fundamental properties that distinguish the two systems. A market system is not built to enable the imposition of higher-order values on the schools, nor is it driven by a democratic struggle to exercise public authority. Instead, the authority to make educational choices is radically decentralized to those most immediately involved. Schools compete for the support of parents and students, and parents and students are free to choose among schools. The system is built on decentralization, competition, and choice.

Although schools operating under a market system are free to organize any way they want, bureaucratization tends to be an unattractive way to go. Part of the reason is that virtually everything about good education—from the knowledge and talents necessary to produce it, to what it looks like when it is produced—defies formal measurement through the standardized categories of bureaucracy.

The more basic point, however, is that bureaucratic control and its clumsy efforts to measure the unmeasurable are simply *unnecessary* for schools whose primary concern is to please their clients. To do this, they need to perform as effectively as possible, which leads them, given the bottom-heavy technology of education, to favor decentralized forms of organization that take full advantage of strong leadership, teacher professionalism, discretionary judgment, informal cooperation, and teams. They also need to ensure that they provide the kinds of services parents and students want and that they have the capacity to cater and adjust to their clients' specialized needs and interests, which this same syndrome of effective organization allows them to do exceedingly well.

Schools that operate in an environment of competition and choice thus have strong incentives to move toward the kinds of "effective-school" organizations that academics and reformers would like to impose on the public schools. Of course, not all schools in the market will respond equally well to these incentives. But those that falter will find it more difficult to attract support, and they will tend to be weeded out in favor of schools that are better organized. This process of natural selection complements the incentives of the marketplace in propelling and supporting a population of autonomous, effectively organized schools....

EDUCATIONAL CHOICE

It is fashionable these days to say that choice is "not a panacea." Taken literally, that is obviously true. There are no panaceas in social policy. But the message this aphorism really means to get across is that choice is just one of many reforms with something to contribute. School-based management is another. So are teacher empowerment and professionalism, better training programs, stricter accountability, and bigger budgets. These and other types of reforms all bolster school effectiveness in their own distinctive ways—so the reasoning goes—and the best, most aggressive, most comprehensive approach to transforming the public school system is therefore one that wisely combines them into a multifaceted reformist package.

Without being too literal about it, we think reformers would do well to entertain the notion that choice *is* a panacea. Of all the sundry education reforms that attract attention, only choice has the capacity to address the basic institutional problem plaguing America's schools. The other reforms are all system-preserving. The schools remain subordinates in the structure of public authority—and they remain bureaucratic.

In principle, choice offers a clear, sharp break from the institutional past. In practice, however, it has been forced into the same mold with all the other reforms. It has been embraced half-heartedly and in bits and pieces—for example, through magnet schools and limited open enrollment plans. It has served as a means of granting parents and students a few additional options or of giving schools modest incentives to compete. These are popular moves that can be accomplished without changing the existing system in any fundamental way. But by treating choice like other system-preserving reforms that presumably make democratic control work better, reformers completely miss what choice is all about.

Choice is not like the other reforms and should not be combined with them. Choice is a self-contained reform with its own rationale and justification. It has the capacity *all by itself* to bring about the kind of transformation that reformers have been seeking to engineer for years in myriad other ways. Indeed, if choice is to work to greatest advantage, it must be adopted *without* these other reforms, since they are predicated on democratic control and are implemented by bureaucratic means. The whole point of a thoroughgoing system of choice is to free the schools from these disabling constraints by sweeping away the old institutions and replacing them with new ones. Taken seriously, choice is not a system-preserving reform. It is a revolutionary reform that introduces a new system of public education.

A PROPOSAL FOR REAL REFORM

The following outline describes a choice system that we think is equipped to do the job. Offering our own proposal allows us to illustrate in some detail what a full-blown choice system might look like, as well as to note some of the policy decisions that must be made in building one. More important, it allows us to suggest what our institutional theory of schools actually entails for educational reform.

Our guiding principle in the design of a choice system is this: public authority must be put to use in creating a system that is almost entirely beyond the reach of public authority. Because states have primary responsibility for American public education, we think the best way to achieve significant, enduring reform is for states to take the initiative in withdrawing authority from existing institutions and vesting it directly in the schools, parents, and students. This restructuring cannot be construed as an exercise in delegation. As long as authority remains "available" at higher levels within state government, it will eventually be used to control the schools. As far as possible, all higher-level authority must be eliminated.

What we propose, more specifically, is that state leaders create a new system of public education with the following properties.

The Supply of Schools

The state will be responsible for setting criteria that define what constitutes a "public school" under the new system. These criteria should be minimal, roughly corresponding to the criteria many states now use in accrediting private schools—graduation requirements, health and safety requirements, and teacher certification requirements. Any educational group or organization that applies to the state and meets these minimal criteria must then be chartered as a public school and granted the right to accept students and receive public money.

Existing private schools will be among those eligible to participate. Their participation should be encouraged, because they constitute a supply of already effective schools. Our own preference would be to include religious schools too, as long as their sectarian functions can be kept clearly separate from their educational functions. Private schools that do participate will thereby become public schools, as such schools are defined under the new choice system.

School districts can continue running their present schools, assuming those schools meet state criteria. But districts will have authority over only their own schools and not over any of the others that may be chartered by the state.

Funding

The state will set up a Choice Office in each district, which, among other things, will maintain a record of all school-age children and the level of funding—the "scholarship" amounts—associated with each child. This office will directly compensate schools based on the specific children they enroll. Public money will flow from funding sources (federal, state, and district governments) to the Choice Office and then to schools. At no point will it go to parents or students.

The state must pay to support its own Choice Office in each district. Districts may retain as much of their current governing apparatus as they wish—superintendents, school boards, central offices, and all their staff. But they have to pay for them entirely out of the revenue they derive from the scholarships of those children who voluntarily choose to attend district-run schools. Aside from the governance of these schools, which no one need attend, districts will be little more than taxing jurisdictions

that allow citizens to make a collective determination about how large their children's scholarships will be.

As it does now, the state will have the right to specify how much, or by what formula, each district must contribute for each child. Our preference is for an equalization approach that requires wealthier districts to contribute more per child than poor districts do and that guarantees an adequate financial foundation to students in all districts. The state's contribution can then be calibrated to bring total spending per child up to whatever dollar amount seems desirable; under an equalization scheme, that would mean a larger state contribution in poor districts than in wealthy ones.

While parents and students should be given as much flexibility as possible, we think it is unwise to allow them to supplement their scholarship amounts with personal funds. Such "add-ons" threaten to produce too many disparities and inequalities within the public system, and many citizens would regard them as unfair and burdensome.

Complete equalization, on the other hand, strikes us as too stifling and restrictive. A reasonable trade-off is to allow collective add-ons, much as the current system does. The citizens of each district can be given the freedom to decide whether they want to spend more per child than the state requires them to spend. They can then determine how important education is to them and how much they are willing to tax themselves for it. As a result, children from different districts may have different-sized scholarships.

Scholarships may also vary within any given district, and we strongly think that they should. Some students have very special educational needs—arising from economic deprivation, physical handicaps, language difficulties, emotional problems, and other disadvantages—that can be met effectively only through costly specialized programs. State and federal programs already appropriate public money to address these problems. Our suggestion is that these funds should take the form of add-ons to student scholarships. At-risk students would then be empowered with bigger scholarships than the others, making them attractive clients to all schools—and stimulating the emergence of new specialty schools.

Choice Among Schools

Each student will be free to attend any public school in the state, regardless of district, with the student's scholarship —consisting of federal, state, and local contributions—flowing to the school of choice. In practice most students will probably choose schools in reasonable proximity to their homes. But districts will have no claim on their own residents.

To the extent that tax revenues allow, every effort will be made to provide transportation for students who need it. This provision is important to help open up as many alternatives as possible to all students, especially the poor and those in rural areas.

To assist parents and students in choosing among schools, the state will provide a Parent Information Center within its local Choice Office. This center will collect comprehensive information on each school in the district, and its parent liaisons will meet personally with parents in helping them judge which schools best meet their children's needs. The emphasis here will be on personal contact and involvement. Parents will be required to visit the center at least once, and encouraged to do so often. Meetings will be arranged at all schools so that parents can see firsthand what their choices are.

The Parent Information Center will handle the applications process in a simple fashion. Once parents and students decide which schools they prefer, they will fill out applications to each, with parent liaisons available to give advice and assistance and to fill out the applications themselves (if necessary). All applications will be submitted to the Center, which in turn will send them out to the schools.

Schools will make their own admissions decisions, subject only to nondiscrimination requirements. This step is absolutely crucial. Schools must be able to define their own missions and build their own programs in their own ways, and they cannot do that if their student population is thrust on them by outsiders.

Schools must be free to admit as many or as few students as they want, based on whatever criteria they think relevant— intelligence, interest, motivation, special needs—and they must be free to exercise their own, informal judgments about individual applicants. Schools will set their own "tuitions." They may choose to do so explicitly, say, by publicly announcing the minimum scholarship they are willing to accept. They may also do it implicitly by allowing anyone to apply for admission and simply making selections, knowing in advance what each applicant's scholarship amount is. In either case, schools are free to admit students with different-sized scholarships, and they are free to keep the entire scholarship that accompanies each student they have admitted. That gives all schools incentives to attract students with special needs, since these children will have the largest scholarships. It also gives schools incentives to attract students from districts with high base-level scholarships. But no school need restrict itself to students with special needs, nor to students from a single district.

The application process must take place within a framework that guarantees each student a school, as well as a fair shot at getting into the school he or she most wants. That framework, however, should impose only the most minimal restrictions on the schools.

We suggest something like the following. The Parent Information Center will be responsible for seeing that parents and students are informed, that they have visited the schools that interest them, and that all applications are submitted by a given date. Schools will then be required to make their admissions decisions within a set time, and students who are accepted into more than one school will be required to select one as their final choice. Students who are not accepted anywhere, as well as schools that have yet to attract as many students as they want, will participate in a second round of applications, which will work the same way.

After this second round, some students may remain without schools. At this point, parent liaisons will take informal action to try to match up these students with appropriate schools. If any students still remain unassigned, a special safetynet procedure—a lottery, for example— will be invoked to ensure that each is assigned to a specific school.

As long as they are not "arbitrary and capricious," schools must also be free to expel students or deny them readmission when, based on their own experience and standards, they believe the situation warrants it. This authority is essential if schools are to define and control their own organizations, and it gives students a strong incentive to live up to their side of the educational "contract."

Governance and Organization

Each school must be granted sole authority to determine its own governing structure. A school may be run entirely by teachers or even a union. It may vest all power in a principal. It may be built around committees that guarantee representation to the principal, teachers, parents, students, and members of the community. Or it may do something completely different.

The state must refrain from imposing *any* structures or requirements that specify how authority is to be exercised within individual schools. This includes the district-run schools: the state must not impose any governing apparatus on them either. These schools, however, are subordinate units within district government—they are already embedded in a larger organization—and it is the district authorities, not the schools, that have the legal right to determine how they will be governed.

More generally, the state will do nothing to tell the schools how they must be internally organized to do their work. The state will not set requirements for career ladders, advisory committees, textbook selection, in-service training, preparation time, homework, or anything else. Each school will be organized and operated as it sees fit.

Statewide tenure laws will be eliminated, allowing each school to decide for itself whether or not to adopt a tenure policy and what the specifics of that policy will be. This change is essential if schools are to have the flexibility they need to build well-functioning teams. Some schools may not offer tenure at all, relying on pay and working conditions to attract the kinds of teachers they want, while others may offer tenure as a supplementary means of compensating and retaining their best teachers.

Teachers, meantime, may demand tenure in their negotiations (individual or collective) with schools. And, as in private colleges and universities, the best teachers are well positioned to get it, since their services will be valued by any number of other schools. School districts may continue to offer districtwide tenure, along with transfer rights, seniority preference, and whatever other personnel policies they have offered in the past. But these policies apply only to district-run schools and the teachers who work in them.

Teachers will continue to have a right to join unions and engage in collective bargaining, but the legally prescribed bargaining unit will be the individual school or, as in the case of the district government, the larger organization that runs the school. If teachers in a given school want to join a union or, having done so, want to exact financial or structural concessions, that is up to them. But they cannot commit teachers in other schools, unless they are in other district-run schools, to the same things, and they must suffer the consequences if their victories put them at a competitive disadvantage in supplying quality education.

The state will continue to certify teachers, but requirements will be minimal, corresponding to those that many states have historically applied to private schools. In our view, individuals should be certified to teach if they have a bachelor's degree and if their personal history reveals no obvious problems. Whether they are truly good teachers will be determined in practice, as schools decide whom to hire, observe their own teachers in action over an extended period of time, and make decisions regarding merit, promotion, and dismissal.

The schools may, as a matter of strategy, choose to pay attention to certain formal indicators of past or future performance, among them: a master's degree, completion of a voluntary teacher certification program at an education school, or voluntary certification by a national board. Some schools may choose to require one or more of these, or perhaps to reward them in various ways. But that is up to the schools, which will be able to look anywhere for good teachers in a now much larger and more dynamic market.

The state will hold the schools accountable for meeting certain procedural requirements. It will ensure that schools continue to meet the criteria set out in their charters, that they adhere to nondiscrimination laws in admissions and other matters, and that they collect and make available to the public, through the Parent Information Center, information on their mission, their staff and course offerings, standardized test scores (which we would make optional), parent and student satisfaction, staff opinions, and anything else that would promote informed choice among parents and students.

The state will not hold the schools accountable for student achievement or other dimensions that call for assessments of the quality of school performance. When it comes to performance, schools will be held accountable from below, by parents and students who directly experience their services and are free to choose. The state will play a crucial supporting role here in monitoring the full and honest disclosure of information by the schools—but it will be only a supporting role.

CHOICE AS A PUBLIC SYSTEM

This proposal calls for fundamental changes in the structure of American public education. Stereotypes aside, however, these changes have nothing to do with "privatizing" the nation's schools. The choice system we outline would be a truly public system—and a democratic one.

We are proposing that the state put its democratic authority to use in creating a new institutional framework. The design and legitimation of this framework would be a democratic act of the most basic sort. It would be a social decision, made through the usual processes of democratic governance, by which the people and their representatives specify the structure of a new system of public education.

This framework, as we set it out, is quite flexible and admits of substantial variation on important issues, all of them matters of public policy to be decided by representative government. Public officials and their constituents would be free to take their own approaches to taxation, equalization, treatment of religious schools, additional funding for disadvantaged students, parent add-ons, and other controversial issues of public concern, thus designing choice systems to reflect the unique conditions, preferences, and political forces of their own states.

Once this structural framework is democratically determined, moreover, governments would continue to play important roles within it. State officials and agencies would remain pivotal to the success of public education and to

its ongoing operation. They would provide funding, approve applications for new schools, orchestrate and oversee the choice process, elicit full information about schools, provide transportation to students, monitor schools for adherence to the law, and (if they want) design and administer tests of student performance. School districts, meantime, would continue as local taxing jurisdictions, and they would have the option of continuing to operate their own system of schools.

The crucial difference is that direct democratic control of the schools—the very *capacity* for control, not simply its exercise—would essentially be eliminated. Most of those who previously held authority over the schools would have their authority permanently withdrawn, and that authority would be vested in schools, parents, and students. Schools would be legally autonomous: free to govern themselves as they want, specify their own goals and programs and methods, design their own organizations, select their own student bodies, and make their own personnel decisions. Parents and students would be legally empowered to choose among alternative schools, aided by institutions designed to promote active involvement, well-informed decisions, and fair treatment.

DEMOCRACY AND EDUCATIONAL PROGRESS

We do not expect everyone to accept the argument we have made here. In fact, we expect most of those who speak with authority on educational matters, leaders and academics within the educational community, to reject it. But we will regard our effort as a success if it directs attention to America's institutions of democratic control and provokes serious debate about their consequences for the nation's public schools. Whether or not our own conclusions are right, the fact is that these issues are truly basic to an understanding of schools, and they have so far played no part in the national debate. If educational reform is to have any chance at all of succeeding, that has to change.

In the meantime, we can only believe that the current "revolution" in public education will prove a disappointment. It might have succeeded had it actually been a revolution, but it was not and was never intended to be, despite the lofty rhetoric. Revolutions replace old institutions with new ones. The 1980s reform movement never seriously thought about the old institutions and certainly never considered them part of the problem. They were, as they had always been, part of the solution—and, for that matter, part of the definition of what democracy and public education are all about.

This identification has never been valid. Nothing in the concept of democracy requires that schools be subject to direct control by school boards, superintendents, central offices, departments of education, and other arms of government. Nor does anything in the concept of public education require that schools be governed in this way. There are many paths to democracy and public education. The path America has been trodding for the past half-century is exacting a heavy price—one the nation and its children can ill afford to bear, and need not. It is time, we think, to get to the root of the problem.

NO

Bill Honig

WHY PRIVATIZING PUBLIC EDUCATION IS A BAD IDEA

One of the loudest salvos in the ongoing battle over "choice" in public schools came this year from theoreticians John E. Chubb and Terry M. Moe in *The Brookings Review* ("America's Public Schools: Choice *Is* a Panacea," summer issue). Chubb and Moe propose to transform our public schools from democratically regulated to market-driven institutions. They argue that the past decade has seen the most ambitious period of school reform in the nation's history, but that gains in test scores or graduation rates are nil. Their explanation: government, with its politics and bureaucracy, so hampers schools' ability to focus on academic achievement that improvement efforts are doomed.

Using data from the early eighties, Chubb and Moe contend that freeing schools from democratic control boosts performance a full grade level. Thus, they would give students scholarships for any public, private, or newly formed school; prohibit states or school districts from establishing organizational or effective curricular standards or assessing school performance; and allow schools to restrict student entry. They assert that parent choice alone will assure quality.

What's wrong with this proposal to combine vouchers with radical deregulation? Everything.

In the first place, Chubb and Moe's basic charge that current reform efforts have not succeeded is dead wrong and, consequently, the need for risky and radical change unjustified. While their data say something useful about the dangers of rigid bureaucracy and the overpoliticization of education, their findings cannot be used to judge the reform effort, since the students in their study were tested before reforms began. Evidence gathered more recently points to substantial gains.

For example, in 1983 California began refocusing on academic excellence, reducing bureaucracy, enhancing professional autonomy, and moving away from a rule-based to a performance-driven system. We raised standards; strengthened curriculum and assessment; invested in teacher and principal training; established accountability, including performance targets and incentives for good results and penalties for bad; provided funds for team building at the school; pushed for better textbooks; and forged alliances with parents, higher education, and the business community.

The result of this comprehensive approach has been real progress. In 1989, in reading and math, California high school seniors scored *one year* ahead of seniors in 1983, the exact improvement that Chubb and Moe say their proposal would achieve and just what they argue could not be accomplished within the existing system.

Since 1986, California eighth grade scores have risen 25 percent, the pool of dropouts has decreased 18 percent, and the number of high school graduates meeting the University of California entrance requirements has risen 20 percent. Since 1983, the number of seniors scoring about 450 in the verbal section of the Scholastic Aptitude Test has grown 19 percent, the number scoring above 500 has increased 28 percent, and the rate of seniors passing Advanced placement tests has jumped 114 percent—to more than 50,000 students a year.

California educators achieved these results even though the number of students in poverty doubled, the number of those who do not speak English doubled to one out of five, and California's student population grew explosively.

Impressive gains were also made nationally during the 1980s. The dropout pool shrunk by a third; the number of graduates attending college grew 18 percent; and on the National Assessment of Educational Progress, the number of 17-year-olds able to solve moderately complex problems increased 22 percent in mathematics, and 18 percent in science. Reading and writing scores, however, grew less.

Further evidence of improvement in the performance of college-bound American youngsters is that Advanced Placement courses taken have nearly doubled since 1982. The number of students taking the more demanding curriculum, suggested by *A Nation at Risk*, of four years of English; three years of social studies, science, and math; and two years of foreign languages more than doubled between 1982 and 1987, from 13 percent to 29 percent of high school graduates. In science, the number of graduates taking chemistry grew 45 percent to nearly one of every two students, and the number taking physics expanded 44 percent to one of every five students.

Certainly, these gains are not sufficient to prepare American youngsters for the changing job market, to reach their potential, to participate in our democracy, or to keep up with international competition. We still have a long way to go. But that is not the issue. Educators are being challenged on whether we have a strategy that can produce results. We do, and this nation should be discussing how best to build on this record and accelerate the pace of reform—not how to dismantle public education.

* * *

It is no exaggeration to say that Chubb and Moe's ideas for change would jeopardize our youngsters and this democracy. Any one of the following objections should be enough to sink their plan.

First, the proposal risks creating elite academies for the few and second-rate schools for the many. It allows schools to exclude students who do not meet their standards—almost guaranteeing exacerbation of existing income and racial stratification. We had such a two-tiered system in the 19th century before mass public education helped make this country prosperous and free. We should not go back 100 years in search of the future.

Second, cult schools will result. Nearly 90 percent of American youngsters attend public schools, which are the major institutions involved in transmitting our democratic values. By prohibiting common standards, Chubb and Moe enshrine the rights of parents over the needs of children and society and encourage tribalism. Is it good public policy to use public funds to support schools that teach astrology or creationism instead of science, inculcate antiminority or antiwhite attitudes, or prevent students from reading *The Diary of Anne Frank* or *The Adventures of Huckleberry Finn?* Absent democratic controls, such schools will multiply.

Third, their plan violates the constitutional prohibition against aiding religious schools.

Fourth, the lack of accountability and the naivete of relying on the market to protect children is alarming. In the 19th century the slogan was "let the buyer beware," and meat packers sold tainted meat to consumers. In the 20th century deregulation produced the savings and loan debacle. Nobody seriously proposes rescinding environmental safeguards—why should our children not be similarly protected? Look at private trade schools. Regulation is weak, and scholarships are available. The results: widespread fraud and misrepresentation. Similar problems occurred when New York decentralized its school system. Corruption and patronage surfaced in its local boards of education. All across the nation there are calls for *more* accountability from our schools, not less.

Fifth, the plan would be tremendously chaotic. Vast numbers of new schools would have to be created for this plan to succeed; yet most new enterprises fail. Many youngsters will suffer during the transition period, and with no accountability we will not even know if the experiment was successful.

Sixth, taxpayers will have to pay more. Chubb and Moe maintain that competition will produce savings, but they offer no proof. A potent counter-example: colleges compete, yet costs are skyrocketing. Furthermore, if this plan is adopted nationwide, a substantial portion of the cost of private school students—about $17 billion a year—currently paid for by their parents will be picked up by taxpayers (unless public school expenditures are reduced 10 percent, which would make the plan doubly disastrous). In addition, the proposal includes expensive transportation components and the creation of a new level of bureaucracy—Choice Offices. These offices will include Parent Information Centers, where liaisons will meet with parents and students to advise them on what schools to choose. But how many employees will be necessary for this process if parents are to receive the information they need in a timely manner?

* * *

If this country is willing to spend billions to improve education, there are much better investments with proven returns than Chubb and Moe's fanciful idea. One is providing funds to bring teachers up to speed in math, science, and history. Investing in team-building efforts, technology, improving assessment, Headstart programs, or prenatal care also offers proven returns for the dollar spent.

Chubb and Moe misread the evidence on choice and claim it is the only answer. We *should* give public school parents more choice, either through magnet schools or through open-enrollment plans. Choice builds commitment of parents and students and keeps the system honest. But limits are necessary to prevent skimming of the academic or athletically talented or furthering racial segregation. More important, where choice has been successful, such as in East Harlem, it has been one component of a broader investment in quality.

This country has an incredible opportunity to build a world-class school system. Public schools have turned the corner, educators have developed an effective game plan for the nineties, and promising ideas to encourage further flexibility within a context of vision and accountability are being implemented. If our leaders support that plan instead of chasing will-o'-the-wisp panaceas, come the year 2000, America's children will enjoy the schools they deserve.

POSTSCRIPT

Is Choice a Panacea for the Ills of Public Education?

Those of us who have attended public schools know firsthand the strengths and weaknesses of that part of the public education system we have experienced. Others of us are the products of private schools and likewise may hold strong beliefs as to the strengths and weaknesses of the system to which we have been exposed. Care must be taken, however, in generalizing from personal experience. One person's school experience may not be reflective of the system at large, and knowledge of the alternative system may not be complete. Good social science demands that we examine the broader experience with public and private schools.

In their examination of the broader experience, Chubb and Moe conclude that bureaucratic control of public schools is the "fundamental [cause] of poor academic performance." They maintain that the monopoly position of these bureaucrats should be challenged and that allocation decisions should be returned to individuals who can make their choices known through the operation of a market mechanism.

Honig thinks this is a bad idea. He believes that Chubb and Moe's proposals would have devastating effects, ranging from the creation of schools for elites to chaos in the remaining portions of the system. What he finds most damaging to Chubb and Moe's argument is that they employed data gathered before the impact of the reforms could possibly be felt. His data suggest that test scores are rising and dropout rates are falling, in spite of the increase in the number of students who live in poverty and in the number of students whose first language is not English.

Thus, we are again confronted with authors who provide conflicting evidence. It is our responsibility to analyze this evidence carefully and to read other studies that discuss this issue. Since privatizing education is an extremely popular proposal among market-oriented policymakers, there is much written about the benefits of "choice" in editorials of business newspapers such as the *Wall Street Journal* and in the publications of conservative-leaning think tanks such as the Cato Institute, the American Enterprise Foundation, or the Hoover Institute. We suggest that you begin, however, by reading the 1983 report, *A Nation at Risk*, by the National Commission on Excellence in Education, which details the failures of the system. You might then turn to a collected set of essays on this topic such as William Lowe Boyd and Herbert Walberg, eds., *Choice in Education: Potential and Problems* (McCutchan, 1990), and end with Deborah W. Meier, "Choice Can Save Public Education," *The Nation* (March 4, 1991).

PART 2

Macroeconomic Issues

Government policy and economics are tightly intertwined. Fiscal policy and monetary policy have dramatic input on the economy as a whole, and the state of the economy can often determine policy actions. Decisions regarding welfare payments or tax rates must be made in the context of broad macroeconomic goals, and the debates on these issues are more than theoretical discussions. Each has a significant impact on our economic lives.

- Will the North American Free Trade Agreement Help the Macroeconomy?

- Does the United States Need to Save More?

- Is a Consumption Tax a Good Substitute for the Income Tax?

- Do Federal Budget Deficits Matter?

- Should the Federal Reserve Target Zero Inflation?

- Does the United States Have an Income Distribution Problem?

- Can We End Welfare as We Know It?

ISSUE 9

Will the North American Free Trade Agreement Help the Macroeconomy?

YES: Gary Clyde Hufbauer and Jeffrey J. Schott, from "Prescription for Growth," *Foreign Policy* (Winter 1993/1994)

NO: Jeff Faux, from "The NAFTA Illusion," *Challenge* (July/August 1993)

ISSUE SUMMARY

YES: Gary Clyde Hufbauer and Jeffrey J. Schott, senior fellows at the Institute for International Economics, argue that the North American Free Trade Agreement (NAFTA) will lead to increased trade with Mexico and boost U.S. employment. They also maintain that NAFTA's most important effect will be to stimulate U.S. productivity and efficiency.

NO: Jeff Faux, president of the Economic Policy Institute, argues that there is no evidence that NAFTA will be a net job creator for Americans. More generally, he maintains that NAFTA does not support the goals of justice and sustainable development.

The effects of the international sector on the macroeconomy are both direct and indirect, both simple and complex, and they operate on both aggregate demand and aggregate supply. Take, for example, the direct, aggregate-demand effect of net exports of goods and services (NEGS). NEGS is normally treated as one of four major components of aggregate demand, along with personal consumption expenditures, gross private domestic investment, and government purchases of goods and services. If NEGS increases, then —according to standard macroeconomic analysis—aggregate demand will increase along with a subsequent increase in total production and overall employment. An example of an indirect, complex aggregate-supply effect involves interest rates, exchange rates, and the costs of production. A decrease in U.S. interest rates may lead to depreciation of the dollar in foreign exchange markets. Dollar depreciation will raise the costs of inputs that U.S. business firms buy from abroad. When business firms experience an increase in their costs, they can be expected to increase the prices they charge their customers. This is normally treated as a decrease in aggregate supply and can be expected to lead to a decrease in both overall production and employment.

Because it is easier for persons to understand direct and simple effects, the news media typically focuses on NEGS. In 1993 the United States bought about $77 billion more goods and services from abroad than it sold abroad;

that is, NEGS was negative. In the simple, direct macroeconomic perspective just mentioned, the negative value of NEGS means that aggregate demand was less than it could have been and that, therefore, there was less overall production and employment. This became an important point in the debate on the North American Free Trade Agreement (NAFTA), which took place during the summer and fall of 1993. Opponents of NAFTA argued that "free trade" with Mexico would increase U.S. imports and reduce U.S. exports: NAFTA would mean a reduction in aggregate demand, and this would mean a reduction in U.S. production and employment.

Although the basic agreement was negotiated by the Republican Bush administration, the Democratic Clinton administration took up the challenge of convincing Congress and the American people that NAFTA would work to the benefit of the United States as well as Mexico. At one point, President Bill Clinton resorted to dramatic means to press the case for NAFTA. He had all the former, then–living U.S. presidents (Bush, Reagan, Carter, Ford, and Nixon) speak out in support of NAFTA. The public debate probably reached its zenith with a face-to-face confrontation between Ross Perot, probably the most visible and most outspoken opponent of NAFTA, and Vice President Al Gore on the *Larry King Live* show. The vote on NAFTA in the House of Representatives reflects the sharpness of the debate: it passed by only a slim margin.

The two selections that follow were both written before NAFTA was enacted. Even though NAFTA has now become law, there are at least two reasons to review the arguments raised on this piece of legislation. First, NAFTA highlights the connections between international economic considerations and the macroeconomy: trade can have important impacts on overall production, employment, and economic growth. Second, NAFTA provides a good example of an issue that cuts across political lines, with some liberals and conservatives supporting NAFTA and other liberals and conservatives standing in opposition. The arguments offered by Gary Clyde Hufbauer and Jeffrey J. Schott are typical of the arguments presented by those who supported the passage of NAFTA. Jeff Faux presents economic arguments against NAFTA, but he also raises considerations of justice and sustainable development in his attack on the agreement.

YES

**Gary Clyde Hufbauer
and Jeffrey J. Schott**

PRESCRIPTION FOR GROWTH

The North American Free Trade Agreement (NAFTA) is an important commercial agreement; too bad so few people are actually talking about it. Instead, the U.S. debate about free trade with Mexico and Canada has devolved into an introspective on problems confronting the American economy. Indeed, the United States seems to have caught a Canadian disease: "emporiophobia"—literally, fear of trade. After the entry into force of the Canada–United States Free Trade Agreement in 1989, the Canadian public blamed an amazing variety of economic ills on the free trade virus.

The Canadian disease is psychosomatic, but nonetheless dangerous to the American body politic. A dose of economic statistics should provide an antidote, if not a cure. The objective is twofold: to debunk the myths most prominently propounded by Ross Perot and his congressional and labor allies, and to demonstrate that NAFTA provides small but positive benefits to America in economics and foreign policy.

To be sure, NAFTA's critics cite important problems confronting U.S. industry and labor. The NAFTA debate has been dominated by concerns both about the erosion of the country's manufacturing base and the consequent loss of well-paid blue collar jobs, and about the degradation of the environment, particularly in the U.S.-Mexican border region. Those concerns, however, predate NAFTA, will not be significantly affected for better or worse by it, and will persist whether or not the U.S. Congress ratifies it.

Perhaps because of emporiophobia, the American public debate over NAFTA suffers from two major delusions: that NAFTA will depress U.S. employment and wages, and that it will shift large sums of investment capital from the United States to Mexico. Both fears have spawned an isolationist response from the extreme wings of the political spectrum, uniting the back-to-the-1920s nationalism of Pat Buchanan with the back-to-the-1930s protectionism of labor leaders and Ross Perot.

The NAFTA critics have grossly exaggerated the impact of the trade agreement on the giant $6 trillion American economy, especially since the pact would require little change in existing U.S. policies. To put NAFTA into perspective, consider the statistics on jobs, wages, and investment.

From Gary Clyde Hufbauer and Jeffrey J. Schott, "Prescription for Growth," *Foreign Policy* (Winter 1993/1994). Copyright © 1993 by The Institute for International Economics. All rights reserved. Reprinted by permission.

The "jobs debate" has been marked by hyperbole on both sides. The trade pact is not primarily about increasing U.S. employment, as a few overly enthusiastic proponents claim, but neither does it pose a threat to American workers, as the critics assert.

Increased trade with Mexico will continue to boost U.S. trade and employment, but the overall impact will be very small as a portion of total U.S. trade and total U.S. labor force. That result should not be surprising, given the disparities in size and development of the two economies: Mexican gross domestic product is less than 5 per cent of that of the United States, and trade with Mexico accounts for only 7 per cent of total U.S. trade.

We project that NAFTA will modestly improve the U.S. jobs picture. From a base year of 1990, the agreement (in conjunction with the continuation of Mexico's domestic economic reforms) should, over five years, *create* approximately 320,000 new jobs in the United States and *displace* about 150,000 workers, resulting in about 170,000 *net* new U.S. jobs. The latest U.S.-Mexican bilateral trade statistics suggest that those projections are on track, especially when allowance is made for the current downturn in Mexican growth resulting from tough anti-inflation policies.

Under NAFTA, the volume of trade in both directions will rise dramatically, and that will cause employment to shift within and among American industries. Those changes will affect the composition of U.S. jobs and thus heighten the anxieties of many American workers. Yet the magnitude of both job gains and losses will be small relative to the overall economy and the total U.S. labor force of more than 125 million people. Compared to the 9 million workers displaced from

their jobs from 1985 to 1990, NAFTA-related job losses represent fewer than 2 per cent of the total job dislocations that normally occur in the U.S. economy over a five-year period.

The major cause of job dislocation in America is technological innovation, not trade liberalization. Industries constantly need to develop new or improved products and adapt to changing tastes —and the pace of innovation is now reaching deep into the ranks of white collar employees and middle managers. When the car was born, the buggy business went flat. In the computer age, typewriters and bank tellers are becoming passé. In short, NAFTA is but a small part of a revolution in the U.S. labor force—a revolution that will destroy and create tens of millions of jobs in the decades ahead.

Better American macroeconomic policies are essential to prevent that revolution from creating a new movement of Luddite industrial policies and "social" protection against imports. In particular, the Federal Reserve Board may need to engineer a long period of low or even negative real interest rates to ensure a buoyant job market.

MAQUILADORA MARKETS

A key criticism of NAFTA is that, with new capital investment and on-the-job training, Mexican labor productivity will fast approach U.S. levels. Opponents of NAFTA further argue that Mexican wages will remain low, suppressed by oligarchic collusion between the Mexican government and private companies; the result will be Perot's "giant sucking sound" as U.S.-based plants pack off to Mexico. As proof, the critics point to the rapid growth of *maquiladora* operations, from 151,000 Mexican workers in 1983 to 505,000 in 1992. Yet the evidence contradicts their line of criticism.

First, Mexican manufacturing workers are not underpaid relative to their productivity. In 1991, the hourly compensation of an American production worker ($15.60) was eight times greater than that of a Mexican ($1.95). But U.S. manufacturing productivity measured by value added per employee ($72,740) was also more than eight times that of Mexico's *maquiladora* operations ($8,813). Set side by side, the two ratios (8.0 and 8.2) undermine the claim that, on average, labor costs per unit of output are much lower in Mexico.

Of course, there are some notable exceptions. At Ford's assembly plant in Hermosillo, productivity has reached world-class levels. But if Hermosillo were the norm and not the exception, Mexico would be the economic equal of Germany —and Mexican hourly compensation would be closer to $20 than to $2.

Second, while productivity at *maquiladora* operations in Mexico is increasing, the *maquiladoras* are not showing South Korean-style double-digit productivity growth. Between 1982 and 1992, real Mexican productivity in *maquiladora* operations grew only 17 per cent, or by less than 2 per cent per year.

Third, the "sucking sound" argument completely ignores the stimulative effect of larger Mexican payrolls and greater capital spending on U.S. exports. About 75 per cent of all Mexican merchandise imports come from the United States. Mexico is one of the world's best markets for American goods and services. The rapidly expanding *maquiladora* workforce, for example, provides a ready-made market for a range of U.S. consumer goods. The same cannot be said of newly employed industrial workers in Bangkok or Sao Paulo.

Investment is another issue being distorted by NAFTA's critics. The accord is *not* going to significantly affect a company's decision to invest in Mexico. Foreign direct investment in Mexico has grown not because of NAFTA, but because 10 years of domestic economic reform have dramatically improved the investment climate. Growth prospects are up, regulation is less onerous, and corruption is less pervasive. NAFTA reinforces those reforms, but it has cross-cutting effects on the private choices about whether to invest in Mexico or to export to Mexico.

On the one hand, Mexican tariff cuts will eliminate the barriers to that market that caused some companies to open plants in Mexico. On the other hand, NAFTA's investment chapter provides an "insurance policy" that reduces the hazards of doing business in Mexico. That will encourage more firms to open facilities in Mexico to serve markets there as well as in the United States and elsewhere. Many factors influence the decision to invest abroad, but trade agreements are generally less important than the economic conditions in the host country.

Moreover, growth in foreign direct investment coincided with the resumption of growth in real wages in Mexico—debunking the charge that U.S. investment in Mexico hurts both Mexican and American workers. Mexican wages plummeted between the boom year 1981 and the bust year 1986 as a consequence of the debt crisis and tumbling oil prices. However, since foreign investment began to reappear in the Mexican economy in 1987, that country's manufacturing wages have risen sharply, outstripping its average productivity growth.

Since 1986, direct investment in Mexico by U.S. firms has more than doubled to $23.1 billion; and more than 60 per cent of the $37.5 billion in foreign direct investment in Mexico at the end of 1992 is American. The stock of direct investment is significant for a country the size of Mexico, but it represents only a small share of the plant and equipment investment of U.S. firms. We optimistically estimate that NAFTA will enlarge the Mexican capital stock by about $60 billion over several years, a tiny fraction of the total U.S. capital stock committed to industrial plant and equipment. Contrary to the claims of Perot and others, Mexico has not and will not attract a "flood" of investment from the United States.

NAFTA is not a magic elixir that will cure the ills of the Mexican and U.S. economies. But it is good medicine, especially when taken in conjunction with domestic economic reforms.

Over the long term, NAFTA's most important consequence will not be a gain or loss of jobs but rather a spur to America's economic efficiency and productivity. That will translate into higher incomes for Americans. Conservatively calculated, NAFTA's annual "efficiency" gains in the United States, Mexico, and Canada could reach $15 billion. We believe those gains are equivalent to adding at least $75 billion to the capital stock of the United States and Mexico. As the most protected and regulated of the three NAFTA economies, Mexico would benefit the most from the pact's reforms; but U.S. gains would likely reach $2 to $3 billion annually, and could be considerably higher.

Moreover, by widening both the market and the range of available labor skills, NAFTA will enable North American firms and workers to compete more effectively against foreign producers. The resulting U.S. trade gains with Europe and Asia could, over time, outweigh the more immediate increase in regional trade. Indeed, North America could become the world's low-cost producer of cars and trucks as well as a major exporter of them, ultimately surpassing Japan and South Korea.

In the mercantilist jargon of trade negotiations, NAFTA is one-sided and unbalanced. The 2,000-odd pages of text primarily spell out Mexico's obligations in joining the Canadian-U.S. free-trade club. Much of the accord details Mexican commitments to open its protected market to U.S. and Canadian firms and to radically reform its intellectual property, investment, and services laws and regulations.

By contrast, NAFTA requires only minor changes in existing U.S. laws, regulations, and trade policies. American concessions are modest: The average U.S. tariff on dutiable imports from Mexico is less than 4 per cent. Moreover, Mexico already enjoys relatively unfettered access to the American market because of special tariff provisions and the expansion of U.S. quotas on Mexican imports of clothing, steel, and textiles in the late 1980s. Carla Hills, the former Bush administration trade representative, correctly notes that a virtual one-way free-trade zone already exists through Mexican access to the U.S. market. NAFTA actually levels the North American playing field, to America's advantage.

With few exceptions (notably in fruits and vegetables), NAFTA reforms should not impose substantial additional adjustment burdens on the United States. NAFTA essentially turns unilateral preferences the United States already accords to Mexico into contractual obligations. In other words, NAFTA does not open the U.S. market to Mexican suppliers; it keeps it open.

What NAFTA opponents are really attacking is the existing openness. What they really want is new protection against producers in Mexico (and other developing countries). Perot makes the point brazenly, advocating that the United States "impose a 'social tariff' at a level that is equal to the difference between the wage paid in the developing nation and the wage paid in the United States for comparable work." The Perot prescription would call for tariff rates of 100 per cent and higher on U.S. imports from Mexico, the rest of Latin America, and most of Asia. Perot would thus raise the average U.S. tariff to a rate more than double the infamous Smoot-Hawley tariff that contributed to the Great Depression.

Several other features of NAFTA also deserve mention. First, NAFTA will eliminate Mexican tariffs, which are much higher than those applied by the United States. The average Mexican tariff is now about 11 per cent, but some important products like autos and heavy trucks face the maximum rate of 20 per cent. In brief, NAFTA makes it as easy for U.S. companies to export to Mexico as it already is for Mexican companies to ship to the United States.

Second, NAFTA opens the Mexican market to U.S. banks, insurance companies, and brokerage firms, which will be able to serve the Mexican market through either Mexican offices or cross-border transactions. That means more white-collar jobs in U.S. financial centers such as New York, Chicago, and Atlanta. Meanwhile, the pact requires little change in U.S. policies toward the financial services industry.

NAFTA will also require the United States to permit Mexican transport firms and truck drivers to operate within the United States, and vice versa. NAFTA critics claim that this concession will enable ill-equipped Mexican trucks and ill-trained Mexican drivers to terrorize the national highways. Such criticisms are unfounded. U.S. highway safety regulations are not affected by NAFTA; if abuses arise, the answer is better enforcement. That problem already exists with U.S. truckers and the states should handle it themselves.

Third, NAFTA establishes path-breaking rights and obligations with regard to investment and intellectual property. Those NAFTA chapters do not demand significant changes in existing U.S. policies. Rather, they require Mexico to align its policies to U.S. and Canadian norms and entail major reform of Mexico's investment policies. Under NAFTA, Mexico will have to ensure that American and Canadian investors are treated as well as Mexican firms operating in their own country. Over 10 years, the agreement will phase out all Mexican requirements relating to export performance, domestic content, domestic sourcing, trade balancing, product mandating, and technology transfer. In addition, Mexico agrees to permit private investors to seek binding arbitration rulings against the host government in an international forum, effectively repudiating the long-espoused and contentious Calvo Doctrine, which asserted that disputes between foreign investors and the Mexican government could only be settled in a Mexican court.

Further, the intellectual property chapter provides protection for U.S. firms against the piracy or misappropriation of important assets—patents, copyrights, trademarks, and trade secrets. It should raise U.S. service exports, bringing in higher royalties and fees from the use of intellectual property within Mexico.

Fourth, NAFTA improves the dispute procedures established in the Canadian-U.S. free-trade area and extends the benefits to Mexico *provided* that Mexico overhauls its antidumping laws and regulations to more closely mirror U.S. and Canadian practice. Here the U.S. concession is more pronounced because it gives Mexico rights to contest national antidumping and countervailing duty decisions in NAFTA arbitration panels. In return, however, Mexico agrees to undertake significant legal and judicial reforms to guarantee due process and ensure effective judicial review for disputing parties.

Finally, NAFTA establishes unprecedented rights and obligations on environmental and labor issues. NAFTA's text took an important step toward addressing the nexus of trade and trade-related environmental and labor issues. The NAFTA side agreements on labor and the environment go further and establish commitments to the aggressive enforcement of national laws and regulations, monitoring of labor markets and environmental conditions by new North American commissions, and dispute settlement to encourage compliance. In most cases, the glare of publicity should be sufficient to promote compliance. If subsequent government talks prove inadequate, however, fines or trade sanctions can be authorized, under carefully circumscribed conditions. As a result of NAFTA, labor and environmental issues will be an integral component of the U.S. agenda in future bilateral, regional, and multilateral trade negotiations.

THE "BETTER NAFTA" DODGE

Critics such as House majority Leader Richard Gephardt (D-Missouri) take care to separate themselves from the strident denunciations of Perot and Buchanan. In effect, more moderate opponents say: "Renegotiate NAFTA, follow the European model, and perhaps we can support the new deal." In other words, "not this NAFTA, but a better NAFTA."

At worst, that advise is disingenuous. At best, it reflects the old saying, "the best is the enemy of the good." Those cautious critics need to be reminded of four basic points:

- The European Community (EC) of 1993 did not emerge "full blown from the head of Zeus." It was foreshadowed by the Benelux Economic Union (1944), the European Coal and Steel Community (1951), the Treaty of Rome (1957), regional assistance funding during the EC's enlargement from six to twelve members (1973–1986), and the far-reaching Europe 1992 program (1986 to present). Even today, an EC social charter setting common minimum labor and environmental standards is an aspiration, not a reality.

- The EC pools significant elements of the sovereignty of member states. Neither Mexico, nor Canada, nor the United States is prepared now or in the foreseeable future to do likewise.

- The EC is built on the free mobility of labor, but individual members maintain substantial immigration controls. Legalized free labor mobility in North America is not a realistic prospect given existing U.S. concerns about illegal immigration from Mexico (more than 1 million people annually, most of whom are temporary sojourners in the United States).

- Mexico is not asking for, and the United States and Canada are not offering, large sums to upgrade the Mexican infrastructure, like the roughly $20 billion annually in fiscal transfers from the richer to the poorer EC members.

"This NAFTA" is not perfect, but it is a start. It could lead to a wider agenda as the North American partners grow more comfortable with one another. A more ambitious EC-style NAFTA is not conceivable now, if ever. Critics who argue "not this NAFTA" are really seeking to delay free trade and investment with Mexico until that distant time when Mexican living standards approximate U.S. levels. In their formulation, free trade and investment are not part of the answer to easing Mexican poverty, but are obtained only once Mexico has solved all its economic problems by itself.

Almost forgotten in the clamor about job losses, runaway plants, and the "deficiencies" of NAFTA compared with the EC are the important U.S. foreign policy interests advanced by NAFTA. The debate blithely assumes that Mexican economic and political reforms are irreversible. But Mexico's economic liberalization is still vulnerable to political and financial shocks, and democratic reforms are still in their infancy. Three U.S. foreign policy interests should be highlighted.

First, Latin America's experience over the past decade demonstrates that economic liberalization promotes political pluralism. NAFTA reinforces the very economic reforms in Mexico that have put that country on the path of political reform.

While U.S. efforts to promote democracy abroad deserve a high priority, some holier-than-thou opponents of NAFTA forget their American history. Our southern states maintained one-party rule for generations after Reconstruction, and residents of Washington, D.C., are still denied voting representation in Congress. Obviously, serious abuses plague Mexican politics, but political reforms are under way. The United States should encourage the process, not stand on the sidelines.

The second critical American interest is seeing that the Mexican model of economic reform is emulated throughout the hemisphere. Mexico is a bridge between the United States and Central and South America. If NAFTA is voted down, emporiophobia may grow more virulent, undermining U.S. efforts to negotiate trade pacts with other developing countries. If exaggerated fears of low-wage Mexican suppliers topple NAFTA, the United States is likely to avoid serious dialogue with countries whose wages are even lower and whose labor practices are worse. Fledgling democracies that have staked their future on market-oriented reforms and increased trade with America will be left high and dry, and vulnerable to policy reversals.

Finally, NAFTA is complementary to U.S. efforts to strengthen the multilateral trading system. With NAFTA's ratification, a successful conclusion of the General Agreement on Tariffs and Trade (GATT) talks will become both more likely and more important. NAFTA will improve the competitiveness of North American firms, making them better able to seize new trade opportunities from an expanded GATT agreement. Directly and indirectly, NAFTA will help spur the creation of American jobs and income, not destroy them.

NO

Jeff Faux

THE NAFTA ILLUSION

This article is based on remarks made before a congressional briefing on NAFTA on March 25, 1993.

Asking an economist to be part of the opening of a conference on the NAFTA proposal is like asking Neal Bush to address a conference on savings and loan deregulation; there is a lot of damage to explain.

Indeed, if NAFTA goes through as presently negotiated, and with side agreements only designed to paper over its fundamental weaknesses, there will be a lot of damage to explain. It is acknowledged widely, even by supporters of NAFTA, that in the United States, jobs will be lost, community tax revenue will shrink, wages will be reduced, and environmental standards will be undercut. It is admitted also by supporters that the damage to incomes and jobs will be concentrated on those who are least able to adjust—workers in the bottom two-thirds of the family income distribution. Although the vulnerable population includes many more people than those more traditionally thought of as disadvantaged, NAFTA will reduce especially employment in our troubled cities and areas of rural poverty. In a society that professes to believe that "the best anti-poverty program is a job," a policy that will further shrink jobs for low-income people must be examined very, very carefully.

IF IT AIN'T BROKE, DON'T FIX IT

Knowledgeable people provide detailed analysis of the economic, environmental, and social costs of NAFTA, but I want to focus here on the potential *benefits*. Given the grudging admission by NAFTA supporters that there will be substantial human and economic costs, the case for the Agreement now rests entirely on the proposition that the costs are compensated for by the long-run economic benefits to the United States. We have all read the editorials that repeat the conventional wisdom: "Many working families and communities may be hard-hit, but in the long run, most people will be better off." Among many Democrats, there is the feeling that the problem is simply that George Bush was insensitive to the "short-term" problems of workers and the environment. So, if we can ease just the short-term pain, the

Agreement will be a long-term boon for Americans. I want to challenge that assumption.

First, a comment about the debate itself. There is a curious notion implicit in the inside-the-beltway discussion over NAFTA that it is up to the critics to prove that NAFTA is a bad deal. This is curious because, in the natural order of public debate, the burden of proof is on the advocates of a proposal. As the old saying goes: "If it ain't broke, don't fix it." So, I think we should set straight the terms of the debate. Given the certainty that NAFTA will cause economic and environmental loss to a significant number of Americans, the burden of proof is on those who advocate this proposal. They must tell us what is broke, and how NAFTA will fix it.

On neither count have the supporters of NAFTA made their case. They made many claims during the "fast-track" debates of two years ago. Today, after sifting through the evidence for long-term economic gain, one simply cannot come up with a credible economic argument that the benefits are worth the costs and the risks. And, believe me, if the benefits were there, the supporters would have found it. For at least two years, the economic and statistical resources of the U.S. Government, the Business Roundtable, and the largest, most generously supported think-tanks and economics departments of universities in America have devoted time, energy, and money to find all the identifiable benefits of NAFTA to the United States. The rewards of their efforts are embarrassingly trivial. I believe that there are few benefits to the people of Mexico and Canada as well, but it is not my place to address their situation. Representatives of both nations are analyzing their respective situations, and they can speak for themselves.

THE BENEFITS OF NAFTA?

Over the last two years, I have debated and discussed NAFTA with academicians, members of Congress, business and labor leaders, and numerous lobbyists in the pay of the Mexican Government. These are the major assertions they have made. And I will spell out why those assertions do not hold up.

First, there is the assertion that NAFTA, in the long run, will create many more jobs than it will destroy. The evidence does not support this claim. The U.S. International Trade Commission, after making several attempts to come up with estimates of big job gains, and after combing through all the economic models on this point, found that the highest estimate of a potential NAFTA contribution to employment in the United States was—are you ready?—eight one-hundredths of one percent!

The Hufbauer-Schott study, regarded as the definitive case for NAFTA, guesses that 316,000 jobs will be gained and 145,000 lost in the first five years—for a net increase of about 170,000 jobs. There are two things you should know about this study. First, it turns out that most of this job gain has already occurred because of the opening up of Mexico's market. NAFTA itself adds only about 25,000 more jobs. Hufbauer and Schott also assumed that, although foreign investment to Mexico would grow substantially, none of it would be diverted from the United States—a fact which few people find credible. But the most interesting thing about this study was what was *not* in it. As Thea Lee of the Economic Policy Institute discovered, the

NO Jeff Faux / 179

published version of the report omitted a table from an earlier manuscript that showed a job *loss* over the long term from NAFTA. One of the authors later said they dropped the table from the book because there wasn't enough room.

Note that I am focusing on the estimates of job gains by public advocates of NAFTA. Other reputable scholars have estimated job losses of 500,000 to almost one million.

The reason even the supporters can't find long-run job benefits for the United States in this Agreement is that the current trade surplus with Mexico cannot last. The current surplus is a result of the fact that Mexican producers—many of them American-based firms—are now importing machinery and equipment and other capital goods. They are installing these capital goods in their new factories, which are being built in order to produce more consumer goods for export to the United States. Currently, the United States has a trade deficit with Mexico in practically every major category of consumer goods. Moreover, the Mexican peso is now overvalued; and that is now making U.S. exports cheaper. To some degree, this reflects the Mexican Government's desire to keep luxury imports inexpensive for the influential upper classes. After the next election, the peso will be devalued; that will help Mexican exports and hurt ours.

Second, there is the assertion that free trade will create higher-wage jobs for U.S. workers because Mexican workers will take jobs at the lower end of the skill ladder while U.S. workers will move up the ladder to higher-wage jobs. Again, there is no evidence for this claim. Historically, U.S. workers who lose jobs due to imports fall down the ladder, or off the ladder. Neither the ITC studies nor the

Hufbauer-Schott report can substantiate this assertion. The latter flatly concludes that there will be no net change in the composition of wages one way or another. And Professor Ed Leamer of the University of California, a well-known advocate of free trade, concludes from his research that the effect of NAFTA will be an average wage loss of $1,000 per worker for seventy percent of the labor force.

This history of the NAFTA debate about wages is interesting. At the time of the fast-track vote, NAFTA advocates were dismissing concern over the large gap between U.S. and Mexican wages. Economic theory, they insisted, says that low wages reflect low productivity. From this, they argued that firms were not moving to Mexico for low wages, but to take advantage of the tiny Mexican consumer market. But evidence from the real world now clearly shows that while the gap between U.S. and Mexican wages is enormous, the gap in productivity is much smaller. Moreover, in a growing number of industries, labor productivity in Mexico is equal to or, in some cases, higher than labor productivity in the United States. The work of Professor Harley Shaiken at the University of California at San Diego and an EPI study by Walter Russell Mead have been particularly useful in dispelling this myth. I would also recommend the several recent articles on this question by *New York Times* reporter Louis Uchitelle.

A few weeks ago, I accompanied Majority Leader Richard Gephardt and some other members of Congress on a trip to the Maquila area in Tijuana, Mexico, which is south of San Diego. Unannounced, we went to a Sanyo plant that makes television parts and assembles television sets for shipment to the United States. We asked the manager of that plant, who is also an international vice-president of Sanyo, how labor productivity in this plant compared with that in the sister Sanyo plant in the United States. He replied that, after four and one-half years, productivity in the Mexican facility was one hundred percent of that of the U.S. plant.

Next question: "What is the ratio of entry wages in your plant versus entry wages in the United States plant?" Without blinking an eye, he said, "One to ten." This was no theoretical economist making that statement. This is the guy who runs the plant in Tijuana and signs the checks.

This point alone undermines much of the economic case for NAFTA. When confronted by the facts, economists who support NAFTA have no real answer. "It's a mystery." one economist said to me the other day. Another said weakly, "Well, it sort of happens like that under capitalism, I guess."

Third, there is the assertion that NAFTA will slow immigration. The same claim was made thirty-years ago when the Maquila agreement with Mexico was made. The Maquiladora program actually increased immigration. It drew workers to the border areas (where most of Mexico's growth will continue to occur because of its close location to U.S. markets). Once there, workers got jobs at wages kept low as a result of collusion among an authoritarian government, captive labor unions, and business associations. Not being able to raise a family on the wages paid, workers soon quit, climbed the fences, and crossed the rivers to the United States. The lesson is clear: If you stimulate low-wage employment in industries that export to the U.S. market under current conditions in Mexico, you will stimulate immigration.

Moreover, NAFTA is likely to result in the massive unemployment of poor farmers in the Mexican countryside; they will not be able to compete with U.S. grain exporters. The result is likely to be more social disruption and more immigration. There is no longer any credible argument that NAFTA will reduce (much less stop) illegal immigration from Mexico.

Fourth, there is the assertion that these jobs will eventually be lost anyway, and so it's better to lose jobs to Mexico than to Asia. It's probably true that some jobs probably would be lost to Asia anyway, but many would not. Asia is, after all, a very long way off. And after two years, the supporters have come up with not a shred of evidence on this question. Moreover, it is just as likely that NAFTA will divert to Mexico the Asian investment that otherwise would have come into the United States and created jobs here. In any event, saying that some jobs would eventually be lost anyway is no argument for accelerating that loss with NAFTA.

Fifth, having lost the argument on the facts, NAFTA supporters will often retreat to the generalizations of abstract theory. "Well, everyone knows," goes the typical claim, "that free trade always creates benefits for both sides and that protectionism is bound to fail."

Any time someone begins an argument with a phrase like "everyone knows" or "most economists agree," watch out. It is an attempt to win an argument by bluster —calling on some vague authority without actually having to prove anything.

FREE TRADE VERSUS PROTECTIONISM?

Here's how to think about this assertion. First, the NAFTA debate is not about free trade versus protectionism. This two-thousand-page document is an investment agreement designed to protect American investors. Second, the assertion that history vindicates free trade is wrong. At best, history is ambivalent on this point. In some cases, and under certain controlled conditions (such as the integration of Western Europe), free trade has been beneficial. But in more cases than not, the major industrial nations of the world developed their economies behind high walls of protection. This not only includes Japan, Korea, and Taiwan in our own century, but the United States of America (a thoroughly protectionist nation for over a hundred years prior to the end of World War II) as well. Third, in order for the free-trade case to work, you need some very rigid conditions, even in theory. If the following conditions are not met, you simply cannot tell what the effect of free trade will be. One condition is full employment on both sides of the border. I leave it to you to decide whether or not we have that condition fulfilled in Mexico, the United States, or Canada. Another condition is no mobility of capital between the countries. Again, it is obvious that this condition is not met.

But what if we give the proponents the benefit of all the doubt about free trade and NAFTA? In other words, what would the net benefits be to the United States if, for the sake of argument, we accepted their unrealistic assumptions?

Here is where it gets interesting. Economic theory tells us that the benefits of free trade will show up in lower prices to the consumer. This is a result of assuming that larger markets increase the economies of scale and increase competition.

Now, if I were to ask everyone in this room, in this city, or in this country to list on a piece of paper the ten major problems with the U.S. economy, where would they place the problem of the U.S. consumer market not being big enough? To ask the question is to answer it. We have, by far, the largest consumer market in the world, and foreigners who come here marvel at the high level of retail competition in the United States. If ever there was a trivial economic issue, this is it. Indeed, NAFTA is a solution in search of a problem.

Again, let's accept all the assumptions of the proponents and ask what is their estimate of the benefits to the American consumer. According to Hufbauer and Schott, the total "efficiency" benefit to American consumers comes to $2 billion. This is $2 billion in a $6 trillion economy. It works out to $8 a year for the average American (or two cents per day)—a number that is so small that you cannot find it in the economic data. It is smaller than the statistical margin of error in the Gross Domestic Product. Statistically speaking, it is *nothing*.

In the end, therefore, the best economic case they can make for NAFTA is that, if you accept all the assumptions of its supporters, you may get two-cents-a-day's worth of lower prices to the average consumer. This is the fabled long-term benefit that we are told justifies the risks of unemployment, community dislocation, environmental degradation, increased social disruption in Mexico, and the expanded immigration that will inevitably result.

But, there is one final desperate argument for NAFTA. It is not an economic argument; it is a political one. It is reflected in a discussion I had with a member of Congress who, after acknowledging that the economic case was weak, said, "But we have to do something for

[Mexican president] Salinas, don't we?" The sensible response to that question is to ask, "Why?"

DO IT FOR SALINAS

They reply that Salinas is a "good guy." He is a reformer. The people around him are young and smart, and are dedicated to the free market. The lobbyists in Washington virtually swoon over these "best and brightest" of all Mexicans. As one Washington lobbyist who works for the Mexican Government said to me about Salinas, "He's one of us. He went to Harvard!"

I suppose for some people that is enough of a credential to justify almost anything. But before you buy it, take a closer look. For example, read what the London *Economist* (a solid supporter of free trade) says about Salinas and his associates: "The ugly truth is that Mr. Salinas and his band of bright technocrats, adored though they are by the great and good on the international-conference circuit, wield power courtesy of PRI-fixers and worse in the countryside." It adds that, "Mexican politics is not without its violent side," and it refers to claims that 164 members of the opposition PRD party have been murdered since 1988.

I cannot judge these charges, nor do I know the truth about what goes on in Mexican politics behind the public-relations imagery. I am also certain that the members of Congress who are so solicitous about the welfare of Mr. Salinas similarly are ignorant of the murky details. But no one disputes that Mexico is a one-party dictatorship, and that it lacks free trade unions, an autonomous environmental movement, and an independent judiciary. It is also obvious that Salinas and the PRI are depending on NAFTA to secure their power for decades to come. So, the idea that, somehow we might influence democratic reforms after we have rewarded the dictatorship with permanent economic benefits that, in practical terms, we can never take back, flies in the face of everything we know about human nature and politics. You don't change behavior by rewarding it.

NAFTA supporters gravely warn that Mexico will have an economic crisis if Salinas suffers a defeat. But Mexico is going to have a crisis with or without Salinas, and with or without NAFTA. The peso is overvalued, and real-estate markets and financial markets are going through speculative excess. These bubbles will burst as soon as the NAFTA issue is resolved. And what is the catastrophe if they do? Except for Americans who have bet on Salinas, it won't cause a ripple in the real economy of the United States, and investment will continue to flow to Mexico because labor will remain cheap. Salinas and the PRI may lose face; but how much pain and suffering is it worth to the bottom two-thirds of the U.S. labor force to keep a Harvard man and his cronies in political power in Mexico? And the notion, as some have asserted, that if we reject NAFTA, the United States won't be trusted in the world any more, is absurd. Indeed, it's not a bad lesson for other nations to learn that the last word on treaties and agreements lies with Congress, and that it is unwise to become partisan in U.S. politics—as Salinas' government did in the last election.

THE SIDE AGREEMENTS

Finally, can we fix NAFTA with side agreements? I am skeptical, but the President wants to try. At the very minimum, fixing it is going to require tough enforcement standards on labor and the environment—including a path to harmonization of minimum wages in the export sectors. It's also going to require an independent trinational commission to enforce those standards. And it's going to require us to pay for the costs of labor adjustment and environmental repair and upgrading out of taxes and tariffs on the increase of trade.

But supporters say that such demands will violate national sovereignty. Sorry, but with this Agreement as written, we have already crossed that bridge. Mexico's sovereignty has been violated by detailed requirements as to how American investors in Mexico are to be protected. U.S. state sovereignty (we are, after all, a nation of sovereign states) has also been violated by this Agreement that overrides state authority on issues from transportation to environmental regulation. U.S. national sovereignty has also been impaired. For example, the United States cannot have an industrial policy [with NAFTA] because the treaty prohibits policies that favor and subsidize domestic industries.

Let me leave you with the following thought: Rejecting NAFTA does not relieve us of the responsibilities for developing North America in concert with our neighbors to the North and to the South. I favor North American economic integration, but, in the words of Reverend Campbell whose wise words preceded me this morning, one that aims for "justice and sustainable development." This Agreement accomplishes neither goal. Any objective analysis will show that the benefits simply do not justify the costs.

POSTSCRIPT

Will the North American Free Trade Agreement Help the Macroeconomy?

Personal circumstances can explain some of the differences that emerge on this issue. If a person has a secure job, that person might be predisposed to accept the arguments advanced by Hufbauer and Schott. If, instead, a person works in one of those industries that will suffer because of NAFTA, then that person will be persuaded by the case made by Faux. Even politicians, in deciding whether or not to vote for NAFTA, have been influenced by personal political circumstances. If their election or reelection depends on strong support from organized labor, they are likely to have been anti-NAFTA. If the area they represent stands to gain jobs from NAFTA, would it be surprising to find those politicians voting for NAFTA?

Sometimes the controversy on trade is expressed in terms of positive-sum, zero-sum, and negative-sum games. This approach becomes more complex when it is recognized that the games can be played at the regional, national, and global levels. For example, suppose NAFTA involves a loss of 100,000 jobs in a particular geographic area of the United States but a gain of 200,000 jobs in another area. This would be a negative-sum game for the first geographic area and a positive-sum game for the second area, as well as for the two areas combined. Suppose that NAFTA leaves U.S. employment unchanged but that it increases employment in Mexico. This would be a zero-sum game for the United States, a positive-sum gain for Mexico, and a positive-sum game for the world. Analysis and evaluation become even more complex when the gains and losses are measured across different dimensions—factoring gains and losses in employment, efficiency, productivity, and "justice" into the benefits and costs.

In making the case for NAFTA, Hufbauer and Schott start with employment. They indicate that the United States as a whole will gain jobs because of NAFTA. As for efficiency and productivity, they state that NAFTA is a positive-sum game for both the United States and Mexico. Considering environmental and labor elements, they believe that NAFTA will bring Mexico's standards closer to those that already exist in the United States, which represents a positive-sum game for the two countries combined.

In his opposition to NAFTA, Faux begins with the assertion that there is no credible argument that the benefits are worth the costs; that is, NAFTA is a negative-sum game. On employment, Faux states that "reputable scholars" have projected job losses in the United States of between 500,000 and 1,000,000. He also disputes the presumed gains in efficiency and productivity. Although Faux declares his support for North American economic integration, he states that NAFTA is not the most effective means of accomplishing that objective.

Hufbauer and Schott present a more complete analysis in their book *NAFTA: An Assessment*, rev. ed. (Institute for International Economics, 1993). For other pro-NAFTA arguments, see "Grasping the Benefits of NAFTA," by Peter Morici, *Current History* (February 1993), and "The North American Free-Trade Agreement," in the *Economic Report of the President 1993*. For views consistent with the position taken by Faux, see "The High Cost of NAFTA," by Timothy Koechlin and Mehrene Larudee, *Challenge* (September–October 1992).

ISSUE 10

Does the United States Need to Save More?

YES: William D. Nordhaus, from "What's Wrong With a Declining National Saving Rate?" *Challenge* (January/February 1990)

NO: Fred Block and Robert Heilbroner, from "The Myth of a Savings Shortage," *The American Prospect* (Spring 1992)

ISSUE SUMMARY

YES: Economics professor William D. Nordhaus believes that increased amounts of saving and investment are necessary if the United States is to avoid a substantial decrease in its standard of living.

NO: Sociology professor Fred Block and economics professor Robert Heilbroner argue that when the personal saving rate is calculated appropriately, "the much touted decline in the saving rate disappears." They conclude that the problem is not how much the country is saving but that there is a lack of political leadership and economic sense.

When Ben Franklin said "A penny saved is a penny earned," he was extolling the virtues of individual thrift. To spend less than is earned—to save—means that a person can have funds available for future spending. If those savings can be lent to someone else and interest is earned on the amount lent, then future consumption can be even greater than the amount saved. However, once the benefits of saving are recognized, there is another question that is still unresolved: How much money should be saved?

When the discussion shifts from the individual perspective to the national economy, much the same argument can be made concerning the benefits of saving. In the case of the national economy, saving becomes investment, and investment means that the nation's capital stock is increasing. This means that the nation's ability to produce goods and services—its production possibilities—increases, and more future production and consumption are possible.

This analysis suggests that it is always better to save more, but there is an opposite side to the saving coin. Because saving does not automatically become investment, it is possible that increased saving may decrease total spending in the economy. This reduction in total spending, or aggregate demand, may mean a decrease in current production and an increase in unemployment. It is possible for saving to be too great (generating a recession) or too small (impeding investment and future production and consumption).

During the 1930s economists feared that saving was too great. More recently, concern has arisen that saving has been too small.

Before deciding whether saving is too high or too low, it must be measured. This is no easy task for several reasons. First, saving is an activity undertaken by various sectors of the economy. For example, a business firm wishing to invest in a new factory can borrow the funds from the savings of four different sectors. It can borrow or use the savings of persons (personal savings), of other business firms (business savings), of the federal, state, and local governments (government savings), or the savings of foreigners (foreign savings). A second complicating factor is that there are different ways of measuring the amount of savings available from the four sectors, particularly personal savings.

The conventional approach defines personal savings as the difference between disposable income and personal outlays. The overall saving rate is the ratio of total saving to some measure of aggregate income, such as net national product. In the first of the following selections, William D. Nordhaus relies on this approach to argue that the United States saves too little, and he suggests that action should be taken to raise the saving rate.

Sometimes the saving rate is calculated at the personal level as the ratio of personal savings to personal income. Fred Block and Robert Heilbroner, focusing on the personal savings rate, argue that the conventional approach used in this calculation is too crude. They assert that adjustments need to be made to bring the data in "closer touch with economic realities." Proper measurement, according to Block and Heilbroner, reveals that the saving rate has not really declined.

YES

William D. Nordhaus

WHAT'S WRONG WITH A DECLINING NATIONAL SAVING RATE?

The 1980s was the "Cheerful Decade," a period of restored faith in America, of rapid economic growth, of robust consumption. During the euphoric Reagan expansion of 1982–1988, unemployment fell by half, and real per capita personal consumption expenditures grew 3 percent annually. America was enjoying a perpetual Christmas, and believing, as President Reagan stated in his valedictory *Economic Report,* that "America is brimming with self-confidence and a model for other countries to emulate."

Amid this bonhomie, however, the world's economists and central bankers, like a chorus of nagging Scrooges, kept repeating that "we are living on borrowed time and borrowed money." The United States has been saving less and less for the future, and the bill for our Cheerful Decade eventually will be rendered in the form of reduced growth, even a decline in living standards for the future.

TRENDS IN U.S. SAVING

... The recent history of the saving rate (see Table 1) reveals the extent of the problem. Net private national saving and investment as a percent of net national product [NNP] ("the net national saving rate") averaged around 8 percent for three decades after 1950. Then, in the early 1980s, the net national saving rate began to fall, reaching a postwar low of 2.4 percent in the past two years.

Three components of decline in national saving stand out, including a decline in government saving, a decline in the personal saving rate, and a decline in business saving. The decline in government saving constitutes the sharpest change during the 1980s. The net saving position of all levels of government was roughly zero over most of the period from 1950 to 1980. Since that time, however, the federal budget swung sharply toward deficit, while the surpluses of state and local governments changed but little. Although economists continue to dispute the source of the rising federal deficit, it

From William D. Nordhaus, "What's Wrong With a Declining National Saving Rate?" *Challenge,* vol. 33, no. 1 (January/February 1990). Copyright © 1990 by M. E. Sharpe, Inc., 80 Business Park Drive, Armonk, NY 10504. Reprinted by permission.

seems clear that Lafferism and unrealistic hopes for expenditure cuts helped launch the deficit-bound fiscal experiment of the 1980s.

Although the decline in the personal saving rate is well known, causes are elusive. After averaging around 7 percent of personal disposable income for the period 1950–1980, the personal saving rate headed downhill, troughing at 3.2 percent in 1987. Barry P. Bosworth suggests that part of the decline in personal saving is due to the inclusion of corporate pension contributions in household saving, while consumer spending may have been buoyed by the phenomenal rise in the stock market after 1982. But even after allowing for these influences, personal saving declined more than expected over the last decade.

A little-remarked component of our sinking saving is the fall in business saving. Business saving is conventionally measured in the national accounts by retained earnings of corporations. As a percent of GNP, this fell from around 4.5 percent in the mid-1960s to 2.75 percent in the late 1970s, and to 1 percent of GNP in the last two years. An alternative measure of corporate saving constructed by the Federal Reserve (which includes stock dividends and nondividend cash payments) indicates that corporate saving actually turned *negative* in the last two years with the rash of LBOs and stock repurchases.

What was the impact of these changes on saving and investment patterns? In the past decade, the gross national saving rate declined by 5.2 percent of GNP. By elementary accounting, this must correspond to an equal decline in gross investment. As it turned out, more than half of the decline in investment surfaced as a drop in net foreign investment. Another

Table 1

The Net Savings Rate, 1950–88

Period	Net national savings rate (national saving as percent of NNP)
1950–59	8.4 percent
1960–69	8.4
1970–79	7.8
1980–86	3.8
1987–88	2.4

Source: National saving equals net private domestic investment plus net foreign investment. Data from Department of Commerce, National Income and Product Accounts.

large decline occurred in business investment, while a small decline occurred in the share of residential housing.

WHAT IS AT STAKE?

To understand the dilemmas posed by lower saving, we need to understand the stakes. Lower saving lowers future living standards in two steps. First, declining national saving reduces our investment for the future. Second, lower investment reduces the growth of output, wages, and living standards. Present pleasures are, in essence, at the expense of future consumption.

Investment in durable productive goods is in the long run determined by the nation's willingness to save. Both investment and saving should be broadly interpreted to include all channels of saving (personal, government, and corporate) and all forms of investment (plant, equipment, R & D, education, and the environment, in the public as well as the private sector). As the nation effectively increases its saving rate, investment in different areas will rise and the stock of tangible, human, and informational capital will increase.

At the same time, we must recognize a loose coupling between attempts to save and higher investment. Keynes argued, in his famous paradox of thrift, that increased saving would reduce aggregate demand, depress the economy, and increase unemployment rather than investment. Keynes's concern may be justified in the short run or in particular historical circumstances. But today, with the Federal Reserve in essence targeting output and inflation, a potentially contractionary higher saving rate will quickly be offset by the Federal Reserve actions so that interest-sensitive components of aggregate demand will rise to take up the slack left by lower consumption.

An additional concern arises, however, because the higher saving will not necessarily be channeled to the most desirable form of investment. Table 2 presents estimates of the impact of a policy shift that reduces the federal deficit while monetary policy maintains the same level of real GNP and unemployment. This result indicates that every dollar of deficit reduction will produce about 90 cents of higher national saving. Most of the higher saving comes in a reduced trade deficit, with but a modest increase in business investment.

These results should give us pause because, while many people emphasize the importance of increasing business investment, Table 2 shows that higher saving is likely to flow primarily into housing and foreign investment. This observation emphasizes the need to buttress saving policies with investment policies, so that the increased saving is channeled into the most productive sectors.

The second link from saving to economic growth is the impact of higher

Table 2

Impact of Changing Fiscal-Monetary Policies on National Savings and Consumption

Sector	Change in output (billions of dollars) (1989 prices)
Investment sectors	$45
Gross private domestic investment	$20
Housing	10
Business fixed investment	7
Net exports	25
Consumption sectors	−45
Government purchases of goods and services	−19
Personal consumption expenditures	−26
Memorandum:	
Change in real GNP	0
Change in federal deficit	−50

Source: Simulation of the DRI model in which federal deficit is cut by $50 billion through higher personal taxes and lower federal nondefense expenditures; monetary policy loosened to keep real GNP at the same level. Simulation examines second and third years of the experiment.

investment on productivity growth. As capital is accumulated, the nation will enjoy rising output, real wages, and living standards. How large is this impact?

The impact of higher investment on living standards is difficult to measure exactly, but the "growth-accounting" technique of Solow and Denison gives an approximate quantitative answer. Assume that during the 1980s, the national saving rate (defined as net national saving divided by NNP) had been 7.5 percent instead of 3.5 percent of NNP. Under conventional assumptions, GNP at decade's end would be 3 percent higher, this amounting to around $150 billion in today's prices....

HOW TO INCREASE NATIONAL SAVING

How should the nation increase its saving rate? How should the increased saving be channeled into the most productive purposes?

First, the nation must take steps to reduce the level of full-employment consumption. Second, we should ensure that the increased potential flow of saving is channeled into high-priority investments. Third, we should balance the needs for intangible and public investment with the value of tangible capital.

There is little dissent today about the need to increase national saving. There are two general sets of policies to promote saving: "income-affecting" policies and "price-affecting" policies. The former include increases in taxation or decreases in government transfers and consumption spending. The latter comprise policies that leave incomes untouched but change relative input or product prices.

Conventional wisdom before the 1980s held that saving is insensitive to the return on saving. The 1980s constituted a grand experiment in the use of "price-affecting" policies to bolster saving. These included higher real interest rates, lower tax rates on income, and special incentives for saving. One measure of the impact of these policies was that the real post-tax return (measured by the real return on tax-free bonds) rose from *minus* 2.5 percent in 1979 to *plus* 3 percent in 1988. Yet personal saving declined. This experiment, along with the volumes of corroborating sophisticated econometric work, should give pause to those who desire to use price-affecting policies to raise our saving rate.

By contrast, conventional wisdom a decade ago held that "income-affecting" measures are an effective tool in changing saving. Such measures would include either direct taxation (e.g., increases in personal taxation) or indirect taxation (e.g., tax increases on consumption). Notwithstanding elegant contrary theoretical arguments, the conventional wisdom has been largely confirmed by the fiscal experiments of the 1980s. It is difficult to find a $2.4 trillion nest egg that individuals have set aside to pay back their share of the federal debt accumulated since 1980.

What "income-affecting" measures would be most effective and efficient in increasing national saving? While some expenditure increases may be possible, the swiftest, simplest, and fairest route to reducing consumption is through higher taxes, particularly taxes on personal income or consumption. I would particularly endorse a stiff tax on gasoline and other forms of energy use, excises on alcohol and tobacco, environmental taxes, and, for fairness, increases in the top rate on individuals and increases in inheritance taxes.

"READ MY LIPS"

To a first approximation, a penny taxed is a penny saved. So what President Bush's lips really are saying is, "No new saving."

But a policy to increase national saving is not enough. We must consider where that saving should go. By coordinating our monetary and fiscal policies we can channel saving into the most productive investments.

I would submit that the priorities for conventional investment should be in two areas: increasing investment in the corporate sector, and reducing our foreign disinvestment. The priority on corporate investment arises from the high private rate of return on those investments, the importance of the corporate sector to international trade, and the potential for social returns that exceed private returns. The priority of the second area is based on the fundamental immorality of the world's richest country draining the world's saving pool, along with the practical proposition that we cannot forever continue to borrow at current levels.

With respect to corporate investment, it is ironic that the Tax Reform Act of 1986, which was designed to level the economic playing field, instead *aggravated* the tax burden on corporate investments. Because of repeal of the Investment Tax Credit and tightening depreciation allowances, the tax rate on corporate investments now approaches historical highs.

I believe that the basic approach to business taxation followed in 1986 was a mistake. In order to channel investment into the corporate sector, we should go back to the drawing boards and redesign an investment tax credit. The new credit should be refundable (to promote start-ups and unprofitable industries), should apply to net investment only, and should include all capital, not just equipment. Such an expanded investment tax credit would ensure that our increased national saving is channeled into high-return investments.

Popular discussion today concentrates on changes in private investment in plant, equipment, and housing. But the economic welfare of a nation depends equally upon the public capital stock, intangible investments in R & D and education, and environmental investments.

This area deserves greater study, but I will mention only two areas of concern: public capital and R & D. During the Reagan years, real gross federal physical investment was near constant; within this total, military spending rose while civilian investment fell. Curbing productive public investments at a time when the nation is concerned about its declining savings rate represents an accounting fallacy that only measured investment contributes to economic growth. To let roads, bridges, dams, nuclear facilities, and the environment deteriorate in order to cut the deficit, with some fraction of the lower deficit flowing to private investment, is misguided economic management. Moreover, unlike most other forms of investment, public investment is under the direct control of economic policy. There is no slip 'twixt the cup and the lip when expenditures are devoted to public investments.

The most critical investment program for economic growth lies in the area of research and development. Total federal R & D rose from $37.4 billion to $45.8 billion from 1980 to 1986 (all figures here are in constant 1982 prices). Within this, however, military R & D rose from 49.1 percent to 67.8 percent. Civilian federal research fell 23 percent. The largest decreases were in energy, space, and environmental R & D.

The increasing militarization of the federal R & D effort is one of the most pernicious sides of the Reagan military buildup. Half of our national R & D effort is now devoted to military and space. While some claim that military R & D will have beneficial spillovers to the civilian sector, it is challenging to imagine the civilian benefits from projects like enhanced radiation nuclear weapons, space surveillance and target acquisition, and Trident II enhancements. Perhaps a Soviet delegation could tutor us on the desirability of a "dual economy" in which the premier scientific talent is siphoned off into increasingly esoteric projects for enhanced destruction.

Who, then, will pay the bills for the Cheerful Decade? In the end, American consumers will. But the choice to be faced is: Should the payment be made in slow consumption growth over the long run, with mounting foreign debt, stagnant technology, and a crumbling capital stock? Or should the nation take bold steps to curb its consumption now and devote the higher saving to cutting foreign indebtedness, bolstering informational and business capital, and setting in motion renewed long-term growth? The latter path will require the leadership to take painful steps and the judgment to choose wise policies, but it is the only course that will provide a sound economic foundation for America's next century.

NO

**Fred Block and
Robert Heilbroner**

THE MYTH OF A SAVINGS SHORTAGE

The United States is being held hostage by a dubious statistic and a serious misapprehension. The statistic shows that household saving in the U.S. economy dropped precipitously during the 1980s. The serious misapprehension is that this drop has impaired economic growth and that the economy cannot revive until the savings rate increases. In the standard view, without savings there can be no investment, and without investment, no growth—whence comes the deceptively simple but misleading idea that the path to recovery lies in a revival of household savings.

The drop in household saving over the past decade reported by the Commerce Department is certainly dramatic. From 7.5 percent of disposable personal income in 1981, saving fell to only 2.9 percent in 1987, the lowest ever recorded. Since then the rate has moved up to just over 4 percent.

Household saving by no means comprises total national saving. It is dwarfed by corporate saving (profits plus depreciation), which is some five times as large. Corporate saving shows no downward trend; it amounted to 12.8 percent of gross national product (GNP) in 1981 and 12.4 percent in 1988.

The savings rate is also often said, mistakenly, to be affected by the "drain" of government deficits on private savings. However, the failure of government accounting to differentiate government investment from government consumption makes it impossible to know whether public deficits are using private savings to finance consumption or investment. Other advanced nations manage to combine public-sector deficits of 3 or 4 percent of GNP with ample private savings rates. Thus, with corporate saving steady, the real debate over saving rates in the U.S. goes back to whether household saving is down.

Household savings has also received special attention because its reported decline is taken as evidence that Americans are failing in their personal responsibility for prosperity. Indeed, the drop from 7.5 percent to 2.9 percent of disposable personal income does suggest an alarming decline in our collective provision for the future.

But is this decline to be believed? The answer depends entirely on how we calculate it. The Department of Commerce, which prepares the National

Income and Product Accounts that are the official books of the economy, does not directly measure how much the nation saves. Instead, it calculates saving in two steps. First, it measures "disposable personal income," which is total household income minus tax payments. Then it subtracts "personal outlays," a measure of household spending on consumption that includes all personal goods and services, except houses, which are counted as investment. The difference between disposable personal income and personal outlays is, in this approach, what households save. For the second half of 1991, for example, disposable personal income ran at an annual rate of $4.068 trillion and personal outlays at $3.898 trillion. Personal saving was the difference, or $170 billion. This figure divided by disposable income, yields our "personal" saving rate of 4.2 percent.

While there is nothing inherently wrong with measuring saving this way, it has one serious drawback. Because saving is the rather small difference between two large numbers, small proportional changes in the larger numbers greatly affect the result. For example, if total income for 1991 was underestimated by 4 percent, while estimates of consumption spending were accurate, savings would jump from $170 billion to $332 billion, and the saving rate from 4.2 percent to 7.8 percent, right up there in the big leagues. In our view, this is exactly what happened in the 1980s; indeed, the Commerce Department underestimated income by much more than 4 percent. When we take that error into account, the much touted decline in the saving rate disappears.

THE CAPITAL OMISSION

We need to make three adjustments to the Commerce Department figures to bring them in closer touch with economic realities. The first is a proper accounting of capital gains.

Disposable personal income, as the Commerce Department measures it, currently does not include the capital gains that come to individuals when they sell stocks or other assets. There has been a long debate as to whether or not these gains are properly considered income, since they do not reflect any earnings from additional output but only changes in prices. We do not need to challenge the Commerce Department's definitions, which seek to portray the real changes in the economy. But in calculating the financial surplus available for investment, it is clearly a mistake to omit capital gains. Not only are capital gains a source of much business financing; during the 1980s, they reached unprecedented levels.

A look back to 1970 makes the point. Capital gains that year amounted to $21.3 billion, or 3 percent of disposable income. In the 1980s, they grew explosively, from $70.8 billion in 1980 to a peak of $295.8 billion, or 9.8 percent of disposable income, in 1986. The 1986 level was exceptionally high because the tax reforms adopted that year led investors to take capital gains while they still enjoyed lower tax rates. Yet even the 1987 and 1988 levels of capital gains were high by historical standards.

No plausible measure of the national saving rate should ignore this immense addition to the financial investment power of household, or more accurately, of those households at the apex of the income pyramid. Moreover, these figures are conservative because they omit another $60 billion to $80 billion a year of capital gains income that did not have to be reported to the Internal Revenue Service, including most gains on sales of owner-occupied homes.

For some economists, the idea of including realized capital gains in household income is heretical. However, dollars earned by households from asset sales do not disappear just because the national income accounts exclude them from income. Moreover, the accounts do treat as income all capital gains earned on assets held for less than six months, while omitting gains on assets held longer. This exclusion becomes a problem in the measurement of savings when long-term capital gains increase as a proportion of personal income—and when the statistics fail to reflect the change.

MISSING PENSION FUNDS

A second problem arises in the treatment of net household contributions to pension funds—that is, any excess of contributions (or earnings on past contributions) over what pension funds pay out. Pension plans are a critical part of the saving story. For all but the richest 20 percent of households, most financial saving occurs through pension plans. Only the highest-income households save significant amounts by accumulating stocks, bonds, and bank accounts. And since pension assets grew rapidly during the 1980s, there is no basis for the view that spendthrift middle-income Americans caused a savings shortfall.

In the National Income and Product Accounts, net contributions to private pension funds are counted as part of household income and therefore are figured into household saving. But when the net contributions go to state and local government pension funds or to the Social Security Trust Fund, they are not counted that way. These accounting decisions, like the classification of capital gains, do have a rationale. But, again, accounting procedures need to reflect changes in the real world. In 1975 household net contributions to state and local government pension plans amounted to only $7 billion; they reached $69 billion in 1988 and are still growing. A similar shift took place in Social Security contributions. Prior to 1984, net household contributions were negative; families were taking more out of the Social Security funds than they were putting into them. But in 1984, as a result of changes adopted by Congress, the flow was reversed. In 1988 a net flow of $53 billion went from household incomes into the Treasury bonds in which Social Security Trust Funds are invested.

Should we count these very large net contributions as saving? The Department of Commerce ignores contributions to public pension funds on the grounds that they are spent to finance "deficits," not "investments," as are private pension funds. One reason why the Commerce Department makes this determination is that it fails to divide the government deficit into consumption and capital accounts. Since it does not officially recognize a category of public investment against which it could credit government pension contributions, the Commerce Department finds no alternative but to consider them as financing mere consumption, and therefore not deserving the accolade of saving.

Of course, state and local pension funds invest in the capital markets, and Social Security purchases of Treasury bonds go into the same pool as capital from private buyers that also purchase those bonds. Yet, coming from government, these funds are counted as consumption; coming from private sources, they count as investment.

Once more the data should not ignore a remarkable change in the pool of funds for financing investment. Taken together, public net pension flows amounted to less than 1 percent of disposable income in 1980. By 1988 they had more than tripled; in that year household contributions increased government pension reserves by $122 billions. Since we treat contributions to private pension funds as saving, it seems illogical to exclude contributions to public pension funds, especially because they increased so markedly during the years when the saving rate underwent its mysterious decline.

THE EFFECT OF HOUSING INFLATION

The final source of the great saving decline arises from the official treatment of owner-occupied housing. Here the Commerce Department's division of personal outlays into consumption and investment enters into the saving controversy.

The Commerce Department calculates the amount that households allow for wear-and-tear on their housing, the personal equivalent of the set-aside that businesses take as the depreciation on their plant. This expense is then subtracted from the income that these owner-occupants enjoy as "free rent." Of course, no one we know, including our economist friends, figures annual income that way. But, as before, the important point is the effect of accounting procedures on the official measure of saving.

During the 1980s, real estate was rapidly inflating. As a result, the depreciation calculated by the Commerce Department also increased sharply. As this depreciation "expense" grew, the presumed income of these households diminished, whether or not they were aware of it.

The impact of this accounting illusion was substantial. If the imaginary depreciation charge had not been levied against household income, savings in 1988 would have been measured at $222 billion, rather than $145 billion, raising the saving rate from 4.2 to 6.2 percent.

ADDING UP THE ERRORS

It remains only to sum up. The bars in Figure 1 show the estimates for personal saving from the Commerce Department's National Income and Product Accounts (identified as "NIPA"), along with the dollar adjustments from adding to householders' incomes the net proceeds of their capital gains ("Cap Gains"), contributions to government pension funds ("Pensions"), and depreciation expenses on their housing ("Housing")....

One major conclusion leaps out. It is the complete disappearance of any fall in our saving performance, once allowance is made for changes in the real economy whose effects did not show up in the statistics. The most important of these changes, by far, was the Wall Street frenzy that generated the surge of capital gains, which financed perhaps half to two-thirds of all household surplus during the decade. Higher capital gains, together with the statistical side-effects of real estate inflation and growing public pension plans, created a serious gap between the measurement of saving in the national income accounts and the real-world capacity to finance investment. The official index showed a serious decline in house-

Figure 1

Adjustments to the Commerce Department's Saving Data

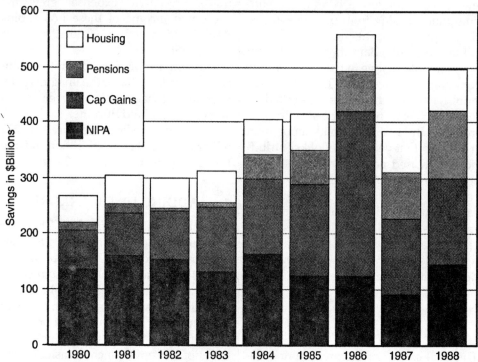

Source: *Economic Report of the President, 1991; Statistics of Income Bulletin* (IRS); *Survey of Current Business,* and other Department of Commerce data.

hold saving. A properly adjusted measure shows none.

CORROBORATION FROM THE FED

Another reason to prefer our adjusted measure of saving is the testimony of an entirely separate source—data compiled by the Federal Reserve Board. Unlike the Department of Commerce, the Federal Reserve measures saving not as income minus consumption, but as additions to household financial net worth, such as household bank deposits, stock and bond portfolios, insurance policies, and the like. This approach permits us to measure net saving by the change in

household net worth from year to year. (We make two adjustments: subtracting paper profits, that is, unrealized capital gains, from the value of stockholdings, and adding in assets omitted in Federal Reserve data, namely, Social Security net contributions and increases in the stock of owner-occupied housing.)...

That saving did not fall should really be unsurprising, because the evidence was there all along, before our eyes. The purported fall in savings ill accords with trends of the last decade. As Kevin Phillips points out in *The Politics of Rich and Poor,* the top 5 percent of households, who account for a disproportionate share of saving, saw their real income increase by 23.4 percent from 1977 to 1988. The boom in stock market prices that began in the early 1980s hardly suggests a period of financial stringency. Neither does the past decade's massive wave of office-building indicate any shortage of credit. The downward trend of interest rates—the return on a three-month Treasury bill dropped from 14 percent in 1981 to under 7 percent in 1988—does not agree with the conventional answer to the question: "What will happen to interest rates if saving dries up?"

The skeptical economist may object that rates would have risen had it not been for Japanese inflows of capital. Perhaps. But that simply changes the question from calculating the trend in saving to estimating its consequences. The availability of Japanese and other foreign capital suggests that even if there had been a fall in household saving, it would not have hurt investment because access to credit is today worldwide.

There remains one last, and perhaps most important, point. It concerns the serious misapprehension mentioned at the outset that only an increase in savings will revive the economy. This is a view of saving presumably banished by John Maynard Keynes when he published his epoch-marking *General Theory of Employment, Interest, and Money* in 1936.

Before Keynes, economists believed that savings were a hoard, like a cache of gold coins, which determined the ability of a nation to finance its capital-building operations. After Keynes, we have come to see saving in a different light—not as a hoard, but as a flow that rises and falls with the level of economic activity. This flow of saving does limit our ability to create new capital when our economy is running at full blast, for we cannot then pry loose the labor needed for additional investment unless we can release it from its current employments. We do that by saving more, which means cutting back consumption to free up resources for investment projects. Hence, saving in a fully employed economy limits what we can invest, unless we are willing to unleash an inflationary contest among enterprises to attract, or retain, their labor.

* * *

But none of this, Keynes stressed, applied to an economy that was at less than "full" employment. Throughout the 1980s, we faced no such need to constrict consumption, because a fifth of our labor force was unemployed or only partially employed, and the same portion of our manufacturing capacity was standing idle. In underemployed times, the capacity to finance additions to plant and equipment is not limited by the release of otherwise fully occupied workers, but by the willingness and ability of banks to lend. That ability, in turn, is solely determined by the Federal Reserve Board of Governors.

Thus even if the saving rate had fallen, the lending capacity of the banking system or the expandability of the system would not have been significantly impaired. But that is not what the public has heard during recent years. Economists from both sides of the political fence have sounded the alarm in words that leave no room for uncertainty.

"It is widely recognized," said Lawrence Summers, then an economic adviser to Michael Dukakis, "that low national saving is the most serious problem facing the U.S. economy." Similarly, Alan Greenspan told us that "inadequate domestic savings is impairing our economic prospects for the long run. By choosing to consume more now and save less, we are limiting our ability to expand and upgrade our stock of capital." *The New York Times,* usually no friend of President Bush, editorialized, "Give him credit for focusing on the problem: Savings are needed for investment, and thus growth."

The lamentations would have been more to the point had they warned that our savings was as high as it was only because of capital gains and Wall Street shenanigans. But the economists and editorialists who predicted diminished growth from the disease of undersaving were saying, in effect, that our six to eight million unemployed were without jobs because households were spending too much. Recently, while wringing his hands over our failure to save enough, President Bush called on Americans to buy more cars and to take advantage of falling mortgage rates to acquire homes. This is more than a serious misapprehension. It is an absence of comprehension.

A capitalist economy in the doldrums can save as much as it wishes, but those savings, in and of themselves, will not generate the momentum that is wanting. In our view, the quickest, simplest, and most dependable way to revitalize a stagnating economy is to start up the engine of public investment, fueled with private savings. This not only uses saving for the very purpose that presumably justifies it—financing growth—but also creates more saving as the nation's households find their real income beginning to rise again. What is scarce in America is not saving, but political leadership and economic sense.

POSTSCRIPT

Does the United States Need to Save More?

Nordhaus begins by examining the national saving rate (national saving as a percent of net national product using the national income and product accounts) for various time periods since 1950. It has fallen from 8.4 percent during the 1950–59 period, to 3.8 percent during the 1980–86 period, to 2.4 percent during the 1987–88 period. The decline in the saving rate means a decrease in future living standards in a two-step process: first, a falling saving rate reduces investment for the future, and in turn, lower investment decreases the growth of output, wages, and living standards. To prevent this, Nordhaus argues, actions must be taken to increase the national saving rate and to ensure that the additional saving is "channeled into the most productive purposes." Although this means less consumption today, he concludes, "it is the only course that will provide a sound economic foundation for America's next century."

Block and Heilbroner argue that to calculate the saving rate accurately, income and consumption need to be measured accurately. They believe that while consumption is measured accurately, income is underestimated and, therefore, the saving rate is underestimated. They identify what they consider to be three errors that lead to the underestimation of income, or at least the underestimation of savings, by the Department of Commerce: the omission of capital gains; the treatment of the net household contributions to pension funds; and the treatment of owner-occupied housing. According to the authors, correcting the Department of Commerce calculations for these three errors indicates that there was no decline in either the personal or the national saving rate. Block and Heilbroner say that the appropriateness of their corrections receives support from estimates of saving from the Federal Reserve.

Fred Block has presented a more detailed argument in his article "Bad Data Drive Out Good: The Decline of Personal Savings Reexamined," *Journal of Post Keynesian Economics* (Fall 1990). For readings supporting the view that the United States saves too little see "The Saving Shortfall," by Lou Ferleger and Jay R. Mandle, *Challenge* (March–April 1989), and "U.S. Net Foreign Saving Has also Plunged," by Peter Hooper, *Challenge* (July–August 1989). For an altogether different perspective on this issue, see "What is the 'Right' Amount of Saving?" by Milton Friedman, *National Review* (June 16, 1989). The same issue of the *National Review* contains a number of conservative and liberal responses to Friedman's argument.

ISSUE 11

Is a Consumption Tax a Good Substitute for the Income Tax?

YES: Council of Economic Advisers, from *Economic Report of the President 1993* (Government Printing Office, 1993)

NO: Joseph A. Pechman, from "Why We Should Stick With the Income Tax," *The Brookings Review* (Spring 1990)

ISSUE SUMMARY

YES: The Bush administration's Council of Economic Advisers argues that consumption taxes would "distribute the tax burden more fairly than income taxes" and "lead to a more efficient allocation of the Nation's resources."

NO: The late Joseph A. Pechman, former president of the American Economic Association, argues that "income is a better indicator of ability to pay than consumption" and that the substitution of a consumption tax for an income tax is not justifiable.

Government undertakes a variety of activities. It provides national defense and fire protection. It provides for the education of young people. It tries to maintain and improve environmental quality. It builds and maintains roads and airports. It is responsible for the administration of justice through the provision of police, courts, and penal institutions. It redistributes income, giving financial assistance to the elderly, the unemployed, and the poor. In financing these various activities, government has three options: it can create money, it can borrow, and it can tax. In the United States, the first option is not used. Thus, the government utilizes the latter two strategies to finance its undertakings. For example, in fiscal year 1993, the federal government spent $1.4 trillion; this was financed with $1.15 trillion of taxes and $0.25 trillion (the deficit of $250 billion) of borrowing. The $1.15 trillion of revenues came from different sources, primarily taxes: $510 billion from the individual income tax, $118 billion from the corporate income tax, $428 billion from social insurance taxes and contributions, $48 billion from excise taxes, $13 billion from estate and gift taxes, $19 billion from customs duties, and $19 billion from miscellaneous receipts. Thus, the individual or personal income tax was the major source of revenue for the federal government.

There is one thing that can be said with a fair amount of certainty about taxes: no one likes to pay them. People's displeasure with taxes, however, can be tempered if the tax system meets certain criteria. The first general criterion is that the tax be equitable or fair. Fairness—from an economic perspective—involves both horizontal equity and vertical equity. The former suggests that persons in identical economic circumstances pay identical amounts in taxes while the latter holds that persons in more favorable economic circumstances pay more in taxes than those in less favorable economic circumstances. But what does it mean to "pay more"? Does this mean more in dollar terms or more in percentage terms?

Besides being equitable, a tax system needs to satisfy a second general criterion: it should not interfere significantly with the efficient operation of the economy. Consider, for example, a tax that takes all of a person's income. Such a tax would be inefficient, for it would destroy all work incentives. Why work if the government takes all of your pay? Or consider the case where the government imposes a lower tax rate on property income than on labor income. The preferential treatment of property income would cause a distortion in economic behavior. People would be less willing to invest in human capital—for example, to spend money on their education—and more willing to invest in commodities such as commercial real estate.

The moral of the story is that taxes are necessary, and the best taxes are those that are equitable and do not interfere with the efficient operation of the economy. In pursuit of these objectives, there have been significant changes in taxes over time. During the 1980s, for example, the federal government made two dramatic changes in the individual or personal income tax with the passage of the Economic Recovery Tax Act of 1981 and the Tax Reform Act of 1986. Both pieces of legislation were justified by the government in terms of equity and efficiency. In spite of these changes, the Bush administration argued in 1993 for even more change, proposing a partial or complete replacement of the income tax with a consumption tax. The proposal was also justified in terms of both equity and efficiency. This view is presented in the first of the following selections. However, there are those who believe that the income tax promotes equity and efficiency more effectively than a consumption tax. This argument is presented by economist Joseph A. Pechman in the second selection.

Before reading the two selections, you should understand that a consumption tax is one form of an expenditure tax; that is, there can be taxes on various forms of expenditure with consumption representing just one form or category of expenditure. However, because consumption represents the largest of the several expenditure categories, the terms *expenditure tax* and *consumption tax* are most often used interchangeably. This is the case in the two selections that follow.

YES

Council of Economic Advisers

CONSUMPTION TAXES

In recent years, consumption taxes have been discussed as a partial or total replacement for the income tax. The recent Treasury proposal, for example, would partially replace the current income tax with a type of consumption tax. Consumption taxes can take various forms. Under some, tax liability is tied directly to a person's level of consumption. Under others, tax liability may be assessed only on wage, salary, and business income. Despite differences in form, these taxes share one common principle: either they tax income only when it is consumed, so that the tax on income saved is deferred, or they impose no tax on the return to saving. Proponents argue that consumption taxes distribute the tax burden more fairly than income taxes, that they permit vast simplification of tax rules, and that, partly as a result of this simplification, they would lead to a much more efficient allocation of the Nation's resources.

PERSONAL CONSUMPTION TAXES

Income taxes in the United States are generally thought to be progressive, while consumption taxes commonly employed, such as State sales taxes and the value-added taxes used by many foreign countries, may not be. *However, consumption taxes can be designed to achieve any desired level of progressivity.*

The individual income tax is progressive because it ties the tax rate to income: The more a person earns, the higher the tax rate. In the same way, a consumption tax is progressive if it is based, at least in part, on total household consumption. A consumption tax of this form is frequently called a personal consumption tax.

One type of personal consumption tax, the consumed income tax, permits taxpayers to deduct net saving from taxable income. In its pure form, this tax would extend the present income tax treatment of pension saving and deductible individual retirement accounts (IRAs) to all forms of saving, with no restrictions on the amount that can be saved and no requirement that the money be used only for retirement. Since the difference between income and saving is consumption, this method effectively taxes households on total annual consumption. The pure form of the consumed income tax would not

From Executive Office of the President, Council of Economic Advisers, *Economic Report of the President, Transmitted to the Congress, January 1993* (Government Printing Office, 1993).

tax businesses (including corporations) directly, although employers would typically be required to withhold taxes in the same way as they do now.

Unlike sales and value-added taxes that tax consumption proportionately, the consumed income tax can tax high levels of consumption at higher rates, achieving any desired level of progressivity. The double tax on saving under the income tax is eliminated, because income saved is taxed only once—in the year it is consumed. A consumed income tax in its pure form would treat borrowed funds in the same way it would a withdrawal from an IRA and subject the amount to tax. Subsequent repayment of interest and principal would be considered saving and would therefore be deductible. Some versions of consumed income taxes allow the taxpayer to exclude from the tax calculation both the initial borrowing and subsequent repayment.

An alternative method of addressing progressivity through a consumption tax is a two-tiered cash-flow tax that levies taxes at both the individual and the business level. At the individual level, only wages and other compensation are taxed according to a progressive rate schedule. At the business level, both corporate and noncorporate enterprises are taxed at a flat rate on their gross receipts after deducting costs such as materials, capital goods, and labor. Borrowing, lending, and interest paid and received are entirely omitted from the tax calculation at both the business and individual level— a major simplification. By not subjecting business income to a second tax at the individual level, the double taxation of corporate income under the current tax system is eliminated; the business level tax is in place of a direct tax on the owners.

IMPROVED ECONOMIC EFFICIENCY UNDER CONSUMPTION TAXES

Advocates of consumption taxes believe that they result in a more efficient allocation of resources than income taxes. With consumption taxes, the government essentially becomes a silent partner in every business, sharing in the costs of the business in the same proportion to which it shares in the earnings. Thus, consumption taxes do not distort relative incentives among alternative investment projects. The market can ensure that investments with the highest expected returns are undertaken, the same as would occur in the absence of taxes.

In contrast, under an income tax, the government shares in the returns of investment projects, but not in the costs of the funds invested. As a result, the income tax creates a bias against investment, favoring current consumption over future consumption.

In addition to the distortion an income tax creates in favor of consumption at the expense of investment, any income tax that is reasonable to administer also is likely to affect the allocation of investment across diverse assets. This occurs when the income tax fails to provide depreciation deductions that accurately correspond to the actual decline in the value of assets. Investment patterns are distorted as investors seek out projects that receive relatively favorable tax treatment and avoid those receiving less favorable treatment. Projects may be attractive only because of the favorable depreciation deductions offered. Other projects that offer higher pretax but lower after-tax returns may be passed over. Because the pretax return measures a project's entire yield, including both the return the investor keeps after taxes are paid and the tax revenues the government collects, projects with the highest pretax returns offer the greatest benefit to the economy as a whole. *Allowing investment to move to its most productive use generates the maximum economic output.* A consumption tax can help allocate investment more efficiently across different activities. A consumption tax also treats debt and equity equally, avoiding the distortions the income tax creates in the choice of the source of financing.

Both forms of consumption taxes provide capital gains income with more favorable treatment than it receives under the current income tax. Under the consumed income tax, income earned on savings is taxed only when it is actually used for consumption, permitting the tax-free rollover of reinvested capital gains. The two-tiered cash-flow tax does not tax capital gains at all at the personal level; at the business level, the government shares in all earnings of the business to the same degree that it shares in the costs of the business.

The income tax affects saving behavior in two ways: It reduces the reward to saving (a substitution effect), which can be thought of as reducing the incentive to save; the tax also reduces lifetime income, and this loss in income can also affect saving (an income effect).

In many cases, however, consumption taxes result in higher rates of saving than an income tax. A consumption tax that generates the same revenue as an income tax can have a similar income effect to that of the income tax, but without the *saving-reducing* substitution effect. It is possible, in theory, for this positive saving response not to occur if labor supply declines under the consumption tax and by enough to offset the substitution ef-

fect. Although some people incorrectly believe that the labor supply must fall under a consumption tax, there is no reason to expect such an effect. While the tax rate on income consumed presently may have to be higher than it is under the income tax, those choosing between working more and working less face two tradeoffs: the amount of *present* consumption affordable by working more *and* the amount of *future* consumption affordable by working more. The first tradeoff is likely to be worsened under a consumption tax, but the second tradeoff is improved. The net effect on labor incentives is ambiguous.

The efficiency effects of consumption taxation can be summarized as promoting the efficient allocation of assets in production and reducing the distortion in favor of present consumption relative to future consumption, while its effects on work incentives are ambiguous. Under a range of parameters, researchers find that a consumption tax generates net efficiency gains compared with the present tax system. The advantages of a consumption tax could, of course, be weakened in practice, depending on the extent to which it was complicated by special exemptions and deductions added through the political process.

IMPROVED FAIRNESS AND SIMPLICITY

Fairness is inherently difficult to define, but a personal consumption tax can be considered fairer than the income tax for several reasons. First, it does not treat people differently on the basis of when they choose to consume the income they earn. In addition, consumption may be a better measure of people's living standards than current income. When making decisions on major purchases, families may try to estimate their likely earnings and expenses at least several years in advance. As a result, consumption reflects, in part, expected income over an extended period. Consumption may thus provide a more accurate measure of the family's "permanent income" than annual income, which often fluctuates from year to year, depending on personal circumstances. Others believe consumption taxes are fairer because they base tax liability on what people take out of the economy rather than on what they produce. To the extent that it is desirable to have those who consume more pay higher rates of tax, consumption taxes can be made progressive.

Finally, the consumption taxes outlined here could potentially be much simpler than the current income tax. Tax filing under the two-tiered cash-flow tax could be particularlyeasy for individuals. Tax liability could be determined by subtracting personal exemptions and a standard deduction from compensation and applying the rate structure. Business returns too could be very simple under this form of taxation. Multiyear accounts for depreciation would be eliminated, since all investments are deducted the year they are made. Because tax considerations would be removed from the investment process, business investments could be evaluated more simply.

The abundance of exclusions, adjustments, deductions, and credits under the current income tax creates complexity, increases paperwork, and interferes with economic decisions. One estimate suggests that Americans spend $75 billion annually in direct costs and lost time associated with complying with the U.S. tax system. Reducing the needless complexity of the current tax system can only help the economy.

NO
Joseph A. Pechman

WHY WE SHOULD STICK WITH THE INCOME TAX

The federal income tax has been under attack by economists for more than a decade. The attack comes from two directions: supply-siders, who believe that progressive income taxation impairs economic incentives, and more traditional economists, who would substitute a progressive expenditure tax for the income tax. Support for the expenditure tax was once confined to a few members of the profession, including such distinguished names as John Stuart Mill, Irving Fisher, Nicholas Kaldor, and James Meade. Today, it is fair to say that many, if not most, economists favor the expenditure tax or a flat rate income tax. This group has joined the opponents of progressive taxation in the attack on the income tax....

ANSWERING THE INCOME TAX CRITICS

Most people support tax progressivity on the ground that taxes should be levied in accordance with ability to pay, which is assumed to rise more than proportionately with income. Economists have long had trouble with the "ability to pay" concept. In recent years they have revived the old notion that consumption measures ability to pay better than income does. I believe that the person in the street is right and that we should continue to rely on the income tax to raise revenue in an equitable manner.

Ability to Pay

In the latter half of the 19th century, progressive income taxation was justified by "sacrifice" theories that emerged from discussions of ability to pay. Under this doctrine, ability to pay is assumed to rise as incomes rise, and the objective is to impose taxes on a basis that would involve "equal sacrifice" in some sense. If the marginal utility of income declines more rapidly than income increases and the relation between income and utility is the same for all taxpayers, equal sacrifice leads to progression. Whether or not one believes in sacrifice theory, the concept of ability to pay has been a powerful force in

From Joseph A. Pechman, "Why We Should Stick With the Income Tax," *The Brookings Review* (Spring 1990). Copyright © 1990 by The Brookings Institution. Reprinted by permission.

history and has undoubtedly contributed to the widespread acceptance of progressive taxation....

Economic Incentives

The effects of the progressive income tax on incentives to work and to save are hard to measure. As is well known, the substitution and income effects of taxation work against each other, and the net result cannot be predicted....

The strongest conclusion one can draw from the available evidence is that the incentive effects of taxation have been relatively small. Yet the supply-siders were convinced that the incentive effects are large enough to increase revenues when tax rates are reduced. U.S. tax rates were cut sharply in 1981 and 1986, but these cuts had little effect on labor supply and no effect on saving. Under the circumstances, so long as tax rates are not pushed to punitive levels, incentive considerations do not justify neglect of the distributional objective of tax policy.

Income vs. Expenditure Tax

The revival of interest in the expenditure tax can be traced to the difficulties of taxing income from capital under the income tax. However, economists and tax lawyers have also found efficiency reasons to prefer the expenditure tax, and these need to be addressed.

A basic difference between the income and expenditure taxes is in the time perspective of the two taxes. The perspective of the income tax is relatively short run—a year or several years to allow for short-run income fluctuations. Consumption is more stable than income and is alleged, therefore, to be a better measure of long-term well-being. In fact, under certain simplifying assumptions, the *bases* of taxes on the discounted present value of income and expenditure are the same over a lifetime. Assuming perfect capital markets, constant discount rates that apply equally to all people under all circumstances, tax rates that are constant and proportional, and no gifts and bequests, the present values of lifetime expenditures of people with the same (discounted) lifetime incomes are the same regardless of when the incomes are consumed.

Advocates of the expenditure tax regard the lifetime perspective as a major advantage because it permits them to pretend that taxing consumption is equivalent to taxing personal endowments. A tax on endowments, if they could be measured, would avoid the distortionary effects of either an income tax or an expenditure tax. If it is assumed that lifetime consumption approximates endowment, then taxing consumption at flat and constant rates treats equally all taxpayers with the same endowment. This logic seems to lie behind the strong support of the expenditure tax by many economists, even though the unrealistic assumptions involved in this line of reasoning strain credulity.

The lifetime perspective has little merit even without the endowment rationale. In my view, it is difficult enough to measure economic circumstances over relatively short periods. Taxation of lifetime consumption (or income) hardly seems appropriate in a world of changing tax rates, substantial family instability, economic and political change, and uncertainty. Except for the attractiveness of the arithmetic, lifetime economic circumstances as measured by discounted lifetime incomes or consumption cannot be regarded as satisfactory indexes of ability to pay. Moreover, taxation of annual consumption expenditures at graduated rates would destroy the identity of lifetime taxes of taxpayers with the same (discounted) lifetime incomes.

The expenditure tax is alleged to be superior to the income tax on the additional ground that the income tax reduces the return on saving and therefore encourages current rather than future consumption. Even if saving remained unchanged, the distortion generates a welfare loss for consumers. It has been pointed out by many economists that this effect must be balanced against the welfare cost of further distorting the choice between labor and leisure. There is no theoretical basis for judging whether the welfare gain from eliminating the intertemporal distortion of consumption would exceed the welfare loss from increasing the intratemporal distortion of the labor-leisure choice.

A tax that omits saving from the tax base can be shown to be the same as a tax applying only to labor income and exempting all property income. Several expenditure tax advocates have, in fact, proposed a tax on labor income on grounds of simplicity and administrative feasibility. Most people would be appalled by a proposal to substitute a wage tax for income tax, yet that is essentially what expenditure tax proponents are advocating.

Many economists are attracted to the expenditure tax because it would not tax income from capital and would thus eliminate all the income tax problems arising from the use of the realization principle for calculating capital gains and losses and the accounting conventions for inventories, depreciation, and depletion in arriving at net business profits. There would also be no need to adjust the tax base for inflation as consumption would be measured appropriately in current dollars. These are serious problems

for income taxation and I shall deal with them later, but it would be unfortunate to abandon the income tax for administrative and compliance reasons alone.

The transition from the income tax to an expenditure tax would be troublesome. The retired elderly would draw down assets, some of which had been previously taxed under the income tax, to finance current consumption that would be taxed yet again. To avoid this double tax, some method would need to be devised to identify consumption from previously taxed accumulations. Grandfathering all assets at the time an expenditure tax is initiated would leave a big loophole for people with large amounts of untaxed accrued capital gains. But I have not seen any practical method of making the distinctions necessary to prevent wholesale tax avoidance and to achieve equity.

Under an expenditure tax, those taxpayers who save could accumulate large amounts of wealth over a lifetime. Many, but by no means all, expenditure tax advocates support wealth or estate and gift taxes to prevent excessive concentrations of wealth. But the history of transfer taxation here and abroad provides little assurance that effective death and gift taxes would be levied to supplement an expenditure tax.

Proponents of expenditure taxation often compare the merits of a comprehensive expenditure tax with the income tax as it has developed. It is hard to believe that an expenditure tax would be enacted without numerous exemptions and exclusions. In fact, most of the eroding features of the income tax (for example, the preferences for housing, fringe benefits, child care, and state and local borrowing) might be carried over to the expenditure tax. Thus, an expenditure tax is no less immune to erosion than the income tax, and in such circumstances, it loses much of its attractiveness.

I conclude that income is a better indicator of ability to pay than consumption and that the major upheaval of substituting an expenditure tax for an income tax cannot be justified on theoretical or practical grounds.

POSTSCRIPT

Is a Consumption Tax a Good Substitute for the Income Tax?

President Bush's Council of Economic Advisers (BCEA) begins by defining consumption taxes. According to the council, these taxes all have one common principle: "They tax income only when it is consumed." The BCEA expresses this common principle in a different way: "They impose no tax on the return to saving." The BCEA then takes up the issue of progressivity and a consumption tax. *Progressivity* refers to the percentage of income that various income groups pay in taxes. A tax is progressive if higher income persons pay a higher percentage of their income in the form of taxes than lower income persons, and the greater the differences in the percentages, the more progressive the tax. The BCEA argues that a consumption tax can be structured to achieve any desired level of progressivity, even the level presently attained by the income tax. A consumption tax can improve economic efficiency by stimulating investment, allowing investment to move to uses in which its returns are greatest. The BCEA offers two additional reasons for substituting a consumption tax for the income tax: fairness and simplicity. It is fairer, in part, because "consumption may be a better measure of people's living standards than current income." And it potentially provides greater simplicity because the present array of "exclusions, adjustments, deductions, and credits under the current income tax" could be eliminated.

Pechman states that the attack on the income tax comes from both supply-siders, who believe that the progressivity of the income tax reduces economic incentives, and more traditional economists, who favor a consumption tax or a flat-rate income tax. He defends progressive taxation, stating that the concepts of ability to pay and sacrifice have "undoubtedly contributed to the widespread acceptance of progressive taxation." As for the effects of taxation on incentives to work and save, Pechman maintains that the empirical evidence shows these effects to be "relatively small." Moving specifically to the debate on an expenditure tax as compared to an income tax, Pechman takes on three arguments that the supporters of the consumption tax use to justify their position. First, there is the argument that consumption is subject to less variation than income over time, implying that consumption is a better measure of economic well-being and a better basis for taxation. Second, there is the argument that the income tax reduces the return on saving and, therefore, promotes current consumption at the expense of current investment and economic growth. Third, there is the argument that all sorts of technical problems make the determination of capital income difficult and that the switch to an expenditure tax would eliminate these problems. Pechman counters each of these arguments. With respect to the first argument, Pechman asserts that, over time, an economic unit experiences a number of changes so that neither lifetime income nor lifetime consumption represents an adequate basis for taxation. He goes on to say that those who justify a consumption tax by using the second argument are essentially advocating the substitution of a wage tax for an income tax, a prospect most people would find appalling. On the last argument, Pechman simply asserts that "it would be unfortunate to abandon the income tax for administrative and compliance reasons alone." Thus, he concludes, the substitution of "an expenditure tax for an income tax cannot be justified on theoretical or practical grounds."

Every proposed tax change seems to generate much controversy. It might be instructive to review the controversy that arose with the passage of the 1981 and 1986 tax legislation, as well as other proposed changes. Additional perspectives on the issue can be found by reading the suggestions for reforming the income tax offered by Pechman in the full version of his selection and the section entitled "Improving the Income Tax" in the BCEA's *Economic Report of the President 1993*.

ISSUE 12

Do Federal Budget Deficits Matter?

YES: Alan Greenspan, from "Deficits Do Matter," *Challenge* (January/February 1989)

NO: Robert Eisner, from "Our Real Deficits," *Journal of the American Planning Association* (Spring 1991)

ISSUE SUMMARY

YES: Federal Reserve chairman Alan Greenspan believes that federal government budget deficits, in the long run, hurt the economy. The deficits crowd out or reduce net private domestic investment. This means a reduction in the rate of growth in the nation's capital stock. This, in turn, means less capital per worker and a reduction in labor productivity. If workers are less productive, then the output of goods and services is smaller and individuals are worse off.

NO: Economics professor Robert Eisner believes that if the budget position of the government is measured appropriately, then in "a fundamental, long-run sense... the total budget is now in balance." The real problems of the U.S. economy, he argues, are not budget deficits but a lack of expenditures on "human capital and in public investment."

The Full Employment and Balanced Growth Act of 1978 lists a number of economic goals for the federal government. Besides the familiar objectives of full employment, price stability, and increased real income, the act specifically mentions the goal of a balanced federal budget. This means that the government is to collect in taxes an amount equal to its expenditures. Despite this legislative call to action, the federal government has failed to balance its budget, and recent deficits have been of record proportions. For example, between the years 1940 and 1975 there were only two instances when the deficit was in excess of $50 billion. For the years 1980 through 1990, the federal government deficit averaged about $140 billion. In spite of legislative efforts to reduce budget deficits in 1990 and 1993, deficits are projected to continue at least through fiscal year 1998. In its 1994 *Economic Report of the President*, the Clinton administration predicts a budget deficit of $187 billion in fiscal year 1998.

When the federal government runs a deficit it sells securities: treasury bills, notes, and bonds. In this respect the government is just like a business firm that sells securities to raise funds. The total of outstanding government securities is called the public or national debt. Thus, when the federal government runs a deficit the public debt increases by the amount of the deficit. Thus, the public debt at any point in time is a summary of all prior deficits (offset by the retirement of securities if the government chooses to repurchase its securities when it has a budget surplus). By September 1993 the gross federal debt was approximately $4.4 trillion. The debt is owned by, meaning it has been purchased by, different groups, including individuals, commercial banks, pension funds, life insurance companies, federal government agencies, state and local governments, and corporations. Some securities are also sold to foreign individuals, businesses, and governments.

There are three major questions regarding federal government budget deficits and debt. The first concerns measurement. For example, to adjust for the impact of the business cycle on the government's budget, economists have developed the concept of the cyclically adjusted budget. There are other adjustments that economists have suggested are in order to obtain a correct measure of the government's fiscal position.

The second question concerns the causes of the deficit. One possibility is that the government spends more than it collects in revenues because it does not exercise fiscal restraint: it may be easy for politicians to spend money, but it is difficult for them to increase taxes to fund additional spending. The budget position of the government is also influenced by the state of the economy. The deficit is likely to increase if the economy enters a recession. A downturn in economic activity will decrease tax revenues (lower incomes mean less tax revenue) and will increase government spending (more expenditures for programs such as unemployment compensation). Because a deficit can arise for different reasons, it is important to understand exactly what forces create a deficit.

A third major question about deficits concerns the economic consequences of deficits. Some persons perceive the deficits as harmful. With a deficit, the government borrows funds that otherwise would have been available to business firms who might have built new factories or purchased new machinery with the borrowed funds. This is referred to as *crowding out*, since government borrowing to finance deficits presumably reduces the funds available for private investment. The reduction in investment slows the growth of productivity, and this means that the ability of the economy to produce goods and services is also reduced.

In reading these opposing views, it is important to keep these three questions in mind. Alan Greenspan accepts the conventional definition of the deficit while Robert Eisner does not. Greenspan believes that deficits must be reduced because they are harming the economy. Eisner believes that there is no real deficit problem and that all the talk about deficit reduction is diverting attention away from the true economic problems of a lack of expenditures on human capital and in public investment. Even though the views of Greenspan and Eisner were expressed before the legislative actions of 1990 and 1993 to reduce the deficit, concern on this issue remains.

YES

Alan Greenspan

DEFICITS DO MATTER

There is a significant view being expressed lately, fortunately to date a minority opinion, that federal government deficits do not matter much. Or in any event, there is no urgency in coming to grips with them. In fact, deficits do matter. Over the long term, they have a corrosive effect on the economy, and it is from this perspective that the case for bringing down the deficit is compelling. More important, the long run is rapidly turning into the short run. If we do not act promptly, the imbalances in the economy are such that the effects of the deficit will be increasingly felt and with some immediacy.

It is beguiling to contemplate the strong economy of recent years in the context of very large deficits and to conclude that the concerns about the adverse effects of the deficit on the economy have been misplaced. But this argument is fanciful. The deficit already had begun to eat away at the foundations of our economic strength. And the need to deal with it is becoming ever more urgent. To the extent that some of the negative effects of deficits have not as yet been felt, they have been merely postponed, not avoided. Moreover, the scope for further such avoidance is shrinking.

To some degree, the effects of the federal budget deficits over the past several years have been muted by two circumstances, both of which are currently changing rapidly. One was the rather large degree of slack in the economy in the early years of the current expansion. This slack meant that the economy could accommodate growing demands from both the private and public sectors. In addition, to the extent that these demands could not be accommodated from U.S. resources, we went abroad and imported them. This can be seen in our large trade and current-account deficits.

By now, however, the slack in the U.S. economy has contracted substantially. And, it has become increasingly clear that reliance on foreign sources of funds is not possible or desirable over extended periods. As these sources are reduced along with our trade deficit, other sources must be found, or demands for saving curtailed. The choices are limited; as will become clear, the best option for the American people is a further reduction in the federal budget deficit, and the need for such reduction is becoming more pressing.

Owing to significant efforts by the administration and the Congress, coupled with strong economic growth, the deficit has shrunk from 5 to 6 percent of gross national product a few years ago to about 3 percent of GNP today. Such a deficit, nevertheless, is still very large by historical standards. Since World War II, the actual budget deficit has exceeded 3 percent of GNP only in the 1975 recession period and in the recent deficit experience beginning in 1982. On a cyclically adjusted or structural basis, the deficit has exceeded 3 percent of potential GNP only in the period since 1983.

THE SAVING FACTOR

Government deficits, however, place pressure on resources and credit markets, only if they are not offset by saving elsewhere in the economy. If the pool of private saving is small, federal deficits and private investment will be in keen competition for funds, and private investment will lose.

The U.S. deficits of recent years are threatening precisely because they have been occurring in the context of private saving that is low by both historical and international standards. Historically, net personal plus business saving in the United States in the 1980s is about 3 percentage points lower relative to GNP than its average in the preceding three decades.

Internationally, government deficits have been quite common among the major industrial countries in the 1980s, but private saving rates in most of these countries have exceeded the deficits by very comfortable margins. In Japan, for example, less than 20 percent of private saving has been absorbed by government deficits, even though the Japanese

general government has been borrowing almost 3 percent of its gross domestic product in the 1980s. In contrast, over half of private U.S. saving in the 1980s has been absorbed by the combined deficits of the federal and state and local sectors.

Under these circumstances, such large and persistent deficits are slowly but inexorably damaging the economy. The damage occurs because deficits tend to pull resources away from net private investment. And a reduction in net investment has reduced the rate of growth of the nation's capital stock. This in turn has meant less capital per worker than would otherwise have been the case, and this will surely engender a shortfall in labor productivity growth and, with it, a shortfall in growth of the standard of living.

POWER OF GOVERNMENT

The process by which government deficits divert resources from net private investment is part of the broader process of redirecting the allocation of real resources that inevitably accompanies the activities of the federal government. The federal government can preempt resources from the private sector or direct their usage by a number of different means. The most important are: 1) deficit spending, on- or off-budget; 2) tax-financed spending; 3) regulation mandating private activities such as pollution control or safety equipment installation, which are financed by industry through the issuance of debt instruments; and 4) government guarantees of private borrowing.

What deficit spending and regulatory measures have in common is that the extent to which resources are preempted by government actions, directly or indirectly, is not sensitive to the rate of interest. The federal government, for example, will finance its budget deficit in full, irrespective of the interest rate it must pay to raise the funds. Similarly, a government-mandated private activity will almost always be financed irrespective of the interest rate that exists. Borrowing with government-guaranteed debt may be only partly interest-sensitive, but the guarantees have the effect of preempting resources from those without access to riskless credit. Government spending fully financed by taxation does, of course, preempt real resources from the private sector, but the process works through channels other than real interest rates.

Purely private activities, on the other hand, are, to a greater or lesser extent, responsive to interest rates. The demand for mortgages, for example, falls off dramatically as mortgage interest rates rise. Inventory demand is clearly a function of short-term interest rates, and the level of interest rates, as they are reflected in the cost of capital, is a key element in the decision on whether to expand or modernize productive capacity. Hence, to the extent that there are more resources demanded in an economy than are available to be financed, interest rates will rise until sufficient excess demand is finally crowded out.

The crowded-out demand cannot, of course, be that of the federal government, directly or indirectly, since government demand does not respond to rising interest rates. Rather, real interest rates will rise to the point that private borrowing is reduced sufficiently to allow the entire requirements of the federal on- and off-budget deficit, and all its collateral guarantees and mandated activities, to be met.

A FISCAL FACT

In real terms, there is no alternative to a diversion of real resources from the private to the public sector. In the short run, interest rates can be held down if the Federal Reserve accommodates the excess demand for funds through a more expansionary monetary policy. But this will only engender an acceleration of inflation and, ultimately, will have little if any effect on the allocation of real resources between the private and public sectors.

The Treasury has been a large and growing customer in financial markets in recent years. It has acquired, on average, roughly 25 percent of the total funds borrowed in domestic credit markets over the last four years, up from less than 15 percent in the 1970s. For the Treasury to raise its share of total credit flows in this fashion, it must push other borrowers aside.

The more interest-responsive are the total demands of these other, private borrowers, the less will the equilibrium interest rate be pushed up by the increase in Treasury borrowing. That is, the greater the decline in the quantity of funds demanded, and the associated spending to be financed, for a given rise in interest rates, the lower will be the rate. In contrast, if private borrowing and spending are resistant, interest rates will have to rise more before enough private spending gives way. In either case, private investment is crowded out by higher real interest rates.

Even if private investment were not as interest-elastic as it appears to be, crowding out of private spending by the budget deficit would occur dollar-for-dollar if the total supply of saving were fixed. To the extent that the supply of saving is induced to increase, both the equilibrium rise in interest rates and the amount of crowding out will be less. However, even if more saving can be induced in the short run, it will be permanently lowered in the long run to the extent that real income growth is curtailed by reduced capital formation.

SHORT-TERM MENTALITY

But aggregate investment is only part of the process through which the structure of production is affected by high real interest rates. Higher real interest rates also induce both consumers and business to concentrate their purchases disproportionately on immediately consumable goods and, of course, services. When real interest rates are high, purchasers and producers of long-lived assets, such as real estate and capital equipment, pull back. They cannot afford the debt-carrying costs at high interest rates, or if financed with available cash, the forgone interest income resulting from this expenditure of the cash. Under such conditions, one would expect the GNP to be disproportionately composed of shorter-lived goods, such as food, clothing, services, etc.

Indeed, statistical analysis demonstrates such a relationship—that is, a recent decline in the average service life of all consumption and investment goods and a systematic tendency for this average to move inversely with real rates of interest. In other words, the higher real interest rates, the heavier the concentration on short-lived assets. Parenthetically, the resulting shift toward shorter-lived investment goods means that more *gross* investment is required to provide for replacement of the existing capital stock, as well as for the *net* investment necessary to

raise tomorrow's living standards. Thus, the current relatively high ratio of gross investment to GNP in this country is a deceptive indicator of the additions to our capital stock.

Not surprisingly, we have already experienced a disturbing decline in the level of net investment as a share of GNP. Net investment has fallen to 4.7 percent of GNP in the 1980s from an average level of 6.7 percent in the 1970s, and even higher in the 1960s. Moreover, it is low, not only by our own historical standards, but by international standards as well.

International comparisons of net investment should be viewed with some caution because of differences in the measurement of depreciation and in other technical details. Nevertheless, the existing data do indicate that total net private and public investment, as a share of gross domestic product over the period between 1980 and 1986, was lower in the United States than in any of the other major industrial countries except the United Kingdom.

TEMPORARY REPRIEVES

It is important to recognize, as I indicated earlier, that the negative effects of federal deficits on growth in the capital stock may be attenuated for a while by several forces in the private sector. One is a significant period of output growth in excess of potential GNP growth—such as occurred over much of the past six years —which undoubtedly boosts sales and profit expectations and, hence, business investment. Such rates of output growth, of course, cannot persist, making this factor inherently temporary in nature.

Another factor tending to limit the decline in investment spending would be any tendency for saving to respond positively to the higher interest rates that deficits would bring. The supply of domestic private saving has some interest elasticity, as people put off spending when borrowing costs are high and returns from their financial assets are favorable. But most analysts find that this elasticity is not sufficiently large to matter much.

Finally, net inflows of foreign saving can be, as recent years have demonstrated, an important addition to saving. In the 1980s, foreign saving has kept the decline in the gross investment-GNP ratio, on average, to only moderate dimensions (slightly more than one-half percentage point) compared with the 1970s, while the federal deficit rose by about 2 1/2 percentage points relative to GNP. Net inflows of foreign saving have amounted, on average, to almost 2 percent of GNP, an unprecedented level.

Opinions differ about the relative importance of high U.S. interest rates, changes in the after-tax return to investment in the United States, and changes in perception of the relative risks of investment in various countries and currencies in bringing about the foreign capital inflow. Whatever its source, had we not experienced this addition to our saving, our interest rates would have been even higher and domestic investment lower. Indeed, since 1985, when the appetite of private investors for dollar assets seems to have waned, the downtrend in real long-term rates has become erratic, tending to stall with the level still historically high.

Looking ahead, the continuation of foreign saving at current levels is questionable. Evidence for the United States and for most other major industrial nations over the last 100 years indicates that such sizable foreign net capital inflows have not persisted and, hence, may not be a reliable substitute for domestic saving on a long-term basis. In other words, domestic investment tends to be supported by domestic saving alone in the long run.

Clearly, the presumption that the deficit is benign is false. It is partly responsible for the decline in the net investment ratio in the 1980s to a suboptimal level. Allowing the deficit to persist courts a dangerous corrosion of our economy. Fortunately, we have it in our power to reverse this process, thereby avoiding potentially significant reductions in our standard of living.

NO
Robert Eisner

OUR REAL DEFICITS

Budget deficits of $300 billion! A federal debt over $3 trillion! Repeated trade deficits that have made the United States "The World's Greatest Debtor Nation!" A savings and loan bailout to "cost the taxpayer" $500 billion! What are we to make of these astronomical numbers and apocalyptic proclamations? They are dear to politicians, press, and assorted pundits, but what is their substance? Is the overweening attention they attract obscuring the real issues facing our nation and its economy? And is it preventing vital policy planning and decisions?

This is not going to be an article of gloom and doom. As I write, we have apparently slipped into a recession that costs more than 200,000 jobs in one month, and promises to get worse—no one can honestly say how much worse—before it gets better. Justified concern has been expressed both about where we are now and whether we are providing properly for our future. We also slipped into a brief but fairly expensive war, with initial "off-budget" funding requests running over $60 billion and uncounted billions more anticipated to replenish military stockpiles and compensate for at least some of the war's destruction and political consequences. Paradoxically, war expenditures serve generally to combat recessions, but they also drain resources from investment in the future.

Still the United States remains the globe's greatest economic power. We are the nation with the greatest total wealth and the highest average standard of living—whatever that means—with the exception of any surviving oil sheikdoms and possibly Sweden and Switzerland. We are the envy of much of the world. We are the (probably misunderstood) model for many of our former antagonists in the old communist empire, as their efforts at a transition from Stalinist command socialism to a market (and capitalist?) economy make matters worse before, it is hoped, they get better.

Our economy, though, is far from perfect. There is trouble now, and there is trouble ahead. To find a cure for our troubles we shall have to disabuse

From Robert Eisner, "Our Real Deficits," *Journal of the American Planning Association,* vol. 57, no. 2 (Spring 1991). Copyright © 1991 by The American Planning Association. Reprinted by permission.

ourselves of some very widespread myths and face up to some ignored realities.

FAULTY CONCEPTS AND FAULTY MEASURES

It is hard to know where to start on the myths of deficits and debt. Many people talk about them; few know, literally, what they are talking about. First, the numbers and statements in our opening paragraph, however closely they reflect widespread assertions, are false on their face. Even without basic revisions to give them real economic content, the official deficit should be put not at $300 billion but at $162 billion. The relevant measure of the federal debt is not the total gross public debt of $3.2 trillion but the debt held by the public, a more modest $2.5 trillion, from which might well be subtracted some $235 billion of Treasury securities held by the Federal Reserve.

The figures purporting to make the United States the world's greatest debtor nation have little to do with debt. They are calculated as the difference between the value of foreign investments in the United States and investment by Americans in the rest of the world. These values have been so inappropriately and inconsistently calculated that the source of the figures, the Bureau of Economic Analysis of the U.S. Department of Commerce, has ceased publishing their totals pending a review and revision of the underlying methodology. The savings and loan bailout figure of $500 billion is put forth on the basis of double-counting—the original capital amount plus accruing interest. By that measure the federal debt, if it is not paid off, is infinite, because interest payments will keep accumulating forever.

The Deficit and the Real Change in Debt

Many observers, including countless TV newspeople and newspaper headline writers, do not even seem able to distinguish between the federal deficit and the national debt. The deficit, of course, is in principle the change in debt. If an individual starts with a debt of $100,000 and spends $40,000 when his income is $30,000 he must borrow $10,000 to finance the shortfall (or sell off assets) and his (net) debt goes to $110,000.

So it is too, or would be if we measured right, for the federal government. With a current debt held by the public, that is, outside of the government itself, of close to $2,500 billion and a deficit of, say, $200 billion over the year, the debt at the end of fiscal 1991 would go to $2,700 billion. And here we stumble on one of the critical failures of official measures of the deficit; they do not adjust the value of the debt for inflation.

To understand the necessity and nature of the needed inflation correction, we have to recognize first that the central significance of the federal government's net debt is not to the government itself but to the holders of that debt, essentially the American people and their businesses, banks, insurance companies, and pension funds; contrary once more to popular mythology, the proportion of that debt held by foreigners remains little more than 15 percent, less than it was a decade ago. The greater the federal debt, therefore, the wealthier, in holdings of Treasury securities, are the American people.

A federal deficit of $200 billion in effect showers the United States with close to $200 billion in *assets* in the form of Treasury bills, notes, and bonds or, if the securities end up owned by Federal

Reserve banks, the money that they back. The effect of this increase in perceived wealth (except for the unlikely incidence of worry that taxes will be higher in the future as a consequence of the increase in debt) is to make us less inclined to save and more inclined to spend. It is in this way that deficits generally prove stimulative to the economy. By giving us greater wealth in the form of Treasury securities they increase our purchases and keep business humming.

Thus, deficits frequently, in fact much more often than not, prove good for us. Properly measured deficits over the past four decades have been positively correlated with subsequent increases in GNP and *decreases* in unemployment.[1] The one way deficits can be bad is if they are *too* large. But for them to be too large they must be bringing about a demand to purchase more than can be produced. The consequence then is rising prices and inflation. Measures to combat the inflation, such as tight money and higher real estate rates, may then "crowd out" desirable investment.

If deficits are to be seen as significant because they increase debt, it must be the real debt that increases, that is, that debt after adjustment for inflation. Clearly the person who had $100,000 at the beginning of the year and $101,000 at the end of the year will not long see herself as richer if she has to reckon that prices have risen 4 percent. In real terms her $100,000 is now worth only about $97,000 compared to a year ago. That person will spend less, not more.

And what is true for the individual will be true for the economy as a whole. A deficit will increase spending to the extent that public holdings of Treasury securities have risen more than inflation. To gauge how much those holdings have

gone up in real terms, and hence how large the *real* deficit is, we must adjust for inflation. With inflation running at about 4 percent and the debt held by the public at about $2,500 billion, this is an adjustment of some $100 billion, more or less than half, depending on how it is measured, of the anticipated deficit over this year.

Peculiar Accounting

There are further corrections to be made to official measures. For one thing, private business and state and local governments keep separate capital budgets. The business income or profit-and-loss statement includes only "current" expenses, not the outlays for new machinery or the building of factories; it counts only the depreciation on those assets as a current cost. If the federal accounts were to be kept in similar fashion and we were to substitute depreciation for current outlays labeled by the Office of Management and Budget as "investment," we would knock another $70 billion or so off our measure of the deficit.

And if we were to note that some $130 billion of federal outlays are grants-in-aid to state and local governments, we might see it as all the more appropriate to balance federal deficits by at least the $40 billion or so of state and local government surpluses. Adding in this correction would finally move our total government budget to surplus.

Another way of looking at this is to note the ratio of debt to income. For individuals, businesses, or government, since debt is increasing (if only because of inflation but also along with general growth), an appropriate question is whether it is increasing faster than income. For the nation, the relevant income is national income, or gross national product. To keep the ratio of debt to GNP constant, debt must grow at the same rate as GNP. For our recent 7-percent growth of GNP, the deficit that, again, is the increase in debt, would come to $175 billion currently, pretty close to the deficit we are actually running and, since the debt-GNP ratio is now three-sevenths, 3 percent of a growing GNP in the future.[2]

There is plenty of room for the debt-income ratio to rise if we see any reason for that. True, it was considerably less—about 25 percent before the large deficits of the 1980s—but it was well over 100 percent at the end of World War II, which ushered in a period of substantial prosperity and growth. In spite of all the hullabaloo to the contrary, the deficit now is not too large. And reducing it now, as the economy plunges into recession, can only further reduce purchases of the nation's output and aggravate that recession.

Phony New Gramm-Rudman Numbers
The pressure to reduce the deficit is fueled in part by other strange games of accounting. Indeed, the new budget deal, the "Budget Enforcement Act of 1990," compounds existing peculiarities so that, in the face of a "unified budget" deficit of $220 billion for fiscal year 1990, it can raise the old Gramm-Rudman 1991 target from $64 billion to $327 billion and claim a $35-billion deficit reduction.

A major reason for the jump in the Gramm-Rudman numbers is the new edict requiring that these numbers not reflect the unified budget total, but rather be measured exclusive of the net inflow of tax revenues into the social security trust funds. The combined trust fund surplus came to $58 billion in 1990 and is projected in the new budget at $60 billion in 1991. Removing these positive components from the total makes the "deficit," restricted arbitrarily to the rest of the budget, that much higher. Political rhetoric about protecting the sanctity of social security aside, this requirement does not make economic sense, any more than would excluding defense expenditures of $300 billion from a unified budget reportedly in deficit by $220 billion and then asserting that the budget is truly in surplus by $80 billion. The deficit's impact on the economy relates to the difference between total expenditures and total tax revenues, regardless of where the Congress or the administration chose to deposit them. Hence it relates to the increase in the debt held by the public, not to the accounting entries of debt "held" in trust funds.

Another reason for the spurt in the deficit numbers is the improper inclusion of the "costs" of the S&L bailout. Those came to $58 billion in fiscal 1990 and have been projected at $112 billion for 1991. These amounts, however, are merely financial transactions signifying no new government expenditures or commands on the nation's economic resources. They entail putting on different kinds of paper a debt that the government already has to S&L depositors as a consequence of insurance of those deposits. They do not add to the net wealth of the public, although by preventing S&L depositors from losing their money they do preserve that wealth. They are not properly part of the budget deficit and, despite all the contrary rhetoric, they have nothing to do with "the taxpayer." They are no proper excuse for raising taxes or demanding cuts in government expenditures.

Including social security and excluding the S&L bailout, as is recommended by the Congressional Budget Office,[3] puts both the 1990 deficit and the pre–recession-projected 1991 deficit at $162 billion. Under the criterion of preventing an increase in the debt-GNP ratio, these figures are within the bounds. The war against Iraq, of course, brought a significant increase in the deficit but, unless it leads to more subsequent military spending, that impact may be viewed as a temporary aberration. Stability of the debt-GNP ratio is further disturbed by the recession, which has driven the growth of GNP well below its recent 7-percent per year, and has already contributed to the larger, 1991 figure of $207 billion projected by the administration in its 1992 budget document. A severe recession, though, is just the time when we should allow the debt-GNP ratio, along with the deficit, to grow.

In a fundamental, long-run sense, then, the total budget is now in balance; there is no real deficit. Projections for the years ahead, if legislated expenditure ceilings are observed, in fact indicate a real surplus. And that, as we shall explain, is a matter more for concern than for cheers.

REAL DEFICITS

In a still more fundamental sense, our economy—and our society—are not in balance. The real issues are not mismeasured financial magnitudes. They are rather the distribution of income and product and well-being among our current population. They are the composition of our output as between public and private goods and among public goods. They are the decisions that we make now that will affect life well into the next century.

On the level of the budget, the critical problem is not the amount of spending or how it is financed. It is its composition. Some two-thirds of federal expenditures for goods and services go for "national defense." The great bulk of those expenditures, aside from their function in preserving "the offensive option" for crises in the Persian Gulf or elsewhere, are shown more than ever, with the inability to curtail them sharply with the end of the cold war, to be related at least as much to preserving jobs and profits as national security.

In the past decade, the inequality of distribution of the national income has increased sharply. The rich have gotten richer, the poor poorer, and those in the middle have been squeezed. Tax changes in the first half of the decade, with huge cuts for upper income groups and investment "incentives" that increased capital gains while the rate at which they were taxed was cut aggravated the inequality, as did the lowering of "safety nets" and the starving of uplift programs. The tax reform of 1986 improved horizontal equity, reducing some of the glaring loopholes, but did little if anything on balance to level the playing field as between traditional winners and losers.

The False Issues of National Saving and Investment

The budget deficits of the eighties did actually contribute significantly to bringing the economy out of its deep recession of 1982–83. Unemployment, which had reached a post–World-War-II high of 10.7 percent, was cut in half before beginning to inch up again in 1990. A widespread lament, however, was that these deficits were bringing on a consumption binge and "crowding out" private domestic investment. To the argument that in fact gross private domestic investment as a percent of GNP remained at or close to its previous highs (16 and 17 percent), the retort was that it was being financed by foreigners. Our net foreign investment had turned negative and, further, depreciation or capital consumption had increased so that national saving, the sum of net private domestic investment and net foreign investment, had declined. We were hence not providing enough for future productivity, and a considerable part of the fruits of that productivity would be going to foreign owners of American stocks, bonds, and real assets.

This argument too, though, is out of focus. As long as we maintain a prosperous, growing economy, without restrictive fiscal or monetary policy, private investment in a reasonably free market economy can and should be expected to take care of itself. Business can be expected to invest in what is productive and therefore profitable. And if foreigners choose to invest here they can do so to a greater extent than we invest abroad only so far as we import more than we export. That jointly determined outcome may, unfortunately, stem from restrictive monetary policy that raises real interest rates and hence the value, and cost, of the dollar, thus making U.S. goods unduly expensive to foreigners and foreign goods unduly cheap for Americans. But if that is not the cause, there is nothing to fear here either.

In contradiction to the statements about our "debtor" status, receipts on U.S. assets abroad in the third quarter of 1990 still exceeded payments on foreign assets in the United States, by 8 percent— $33.08 billion to $30.63 billion, or about a $10-billion surplus at annual rates. Even if the current account deficit—negative net foreign investment—continued at its swollen Gulf-crisis rate of $100 billion

a year for five years it would bring only a trivial move to net payments of capital income to foreigners. At a 4-percent real rate of return, the cumulated net acquisition of $500 billion of U.S. assets would entail new net payments to foreigners of only $20 billion per year, which would be well under three-tenths of one percent of our GNP. Given the surplus we are still enjoying, we would then have a net deficit on capital income of not much more than one-tenth of 1 percent of GNP, a level that would hardly justify any of the alarm so often expressed. And indeed, with the dollar allowed to fall, our trade balance would improve and the value of our foreign-currency denominated assets as well as the income from them would grow in relevant, dollar terms, so that even this minimal swing to deficit in our capital income accounts might not eventuate— particularly if we could learn to cut our military expenditures abroad.

The Real Issues

Having put in their proper place, cut down to size, or dismissed most of the deficits that receive so much misguided attention, I must point now to the real and important deficits. . . . Private tangible investment in a free market economy, once government has played its part with nonrestrictive and sufficiently stimulative fiscal and monetary policy, can safely and properly be left to find its own level. The real rub is in intangible investment, including investment in human capital, and in public investment—everything that is not automatically pulled along by the actuality or the lure of private profits.

We can begin to see the wastage and failure to develop human capital in the figures for unemployment. In January 1991, it was counted at over 7,715,000, or 6.1 percent of the total labor force. Unemployment was little over 3 percent during the height of the Vietnam War and close to 1 percent during World War II. We should not require wars to reach minimum unemployment levels.

Yet those contrasting numbers present only a small part of the problem. The widely cited unemployment numbers include only those people not working at all who are either looking for work or not looking because they are awaiting recall by their employers. Workers reduced to part-time employment "for economic reasons," even to an afternoon a week in a car-wash, constitute 5,510,000 more, not included in the total. Also excluded are "discouraged workers," 941,000 of them in the fourth quarter of 1990, who have despaired of finding another job and hence have stopped looking. And most important, uncounted millions in inner cities as well as outlying ghettos remain outside the labor force, outside the mainstream of the economy, poorly educated if at all, a deadweight loss to society as well as to themselves.

Elimination of this human waste requires public policy and public investment. A private firm cannot take into account social costs when it lays off workers. If a tight government budget or tight money deprive a firm's customers of the purchasing power necessary to buy its products, the firm cuts production and employment. Efforts to reduce the budget deficit as an economy slips into recession, whether by cutting government payments or expenditures or by increasing taxes, only aggravate the deficit in purchases, deepen the recession, and add to unemployment.

Further, since we do not have a slave economy, private employers lack adequate incentive to offer basic educational skills to workers. If they do take a chance on an underprivileged youth, and the investment in his employment is successful, they retain only part of the fruits of that investment. Some of it is retained by the worker and much of the rest goes to his next employer.

There is a similar problem with investment in basic research that will over the long run keep us at an advancing, technological frontier. By its nature, and all the more so in a free society, basic research involves the free and open interchange of ideas. Since the people who undertake it are thus unable to keep its benefits to themselves, it is likely to prove inadequate without public support.

In the way of public investment, the needs are more and more evident in our decaying highway system, in crumbling bridges, in skies crowded with planes waiting to land at overcrowded airports, in staggering problems of waste disposal, in the lack of resources devoted to protecting and improving our environment of land, water, and air. One set of estimates suggests the need to double, from $13 billion to $26 billion annually, the expenditures to attain and maintain minimum standards on existing highways. These estimates also suggest $50 billion needed to repair or replace 240,000 bridges, $1 billion a year more just to maintain existing flying conditions, $11 billion to clean up nuclear and non-nuclear military waste, $3 billion for non-military hazardous waste, and $2.4 billion to comply with the Clean Water Act.

And then there are $2 billion in unmet needs for Head Start and early education, $5 billion for education for "at-risk" youth, $7 billion to support long-term health insurance, $4 billion to repair existing public housing. One estimate has set at least $130 billion annually as the shortfall in the nation's investments to tackle some of these most grievous problems.[4]

The United States, the only developed country without a comprehensive system of health insurance, ranks with the worst in infant mortality. In standardized tests in math and science for 13-year-olds, given in a number of advanced countries in Asia, Europe, and North America, United States students came out dead last. Where will that stand us in international economic competition in the twenty-first century? George Bush declared that he intended to be the "education president." But new resources to put into education are declared not available or, in perhaps a convenient rationalization, unnecessary.

Our so painfully arranged and much ballyhooed Budget Enforcement Act of 1990, pretty much a successor to Gramm-Rudman-Hollings, promised to reduce what it denotes as budget deficits by an average of close to $100 billion annually over five years. It would accomplish this very considerably by sharply limiting increases in the aggregate of real "discretionary" domestic expenditures. Any of the hoped-for "peace dividend" that might remain after the Gulf War and its aftermath can be used only to reduce the deficit. The nonmilitary, domestic expenditures would not even grow with the population or total product, let alone meet any of the needs just indicated.[5] One may doubt whether, with a slowing economy, this law will even reduce the "deficits" to which it refers. It can only stand in the way of reduction of the real deficits faced by our nation and its economy.

NOTES

1. See Robert Eisner and Paul J. Pieper, "A New View of the Federal Debt and Budget Deficits," *American Economic Review*, March 1984: 11–29; Robert Eisner, *How Real Is the Federal Deficit?* (New York: The Free Press, 1986); and, for an update, Robert Eisner, "Deficits and Us and Our Grandchildren," in *The Debt and the Twin Deficits Debate*, ed. James Rock (Mountain View, CA: Bristletone Books/Mayfield, 1991).

2. Noting that the deficit, D, equals the change in the debt, ΔB, and that for a constant ratio of debt to GNP the ratio of the change in debt to the change in GNP must equal that debt-GNP ratio, we can write:

$$\Delta B/GNP = (\Delta B/\Delta GNP)*(\Delta GNP/GNP),$$

whence we have d = b*g,

where d = D/GNP, the constant ratio of deficit to GNP, b = B/GNP, the constant ratio of debt to GNP, and g = ΔGNP/GNP, the rate of growth of GNP. With B = $3/7$ and g = 0.7, we then have d = .03.

3. See the statement of Robert D. Reischauer, director of the Congressional Budget Office, before the Committee on the Budget, U.S. House of Representatives, December 6, 1990, and "CBO Papers—The 1990 Budget Agreement: An Interim Assessment," December 1980, released with the statement.

4. This last figure is from the center for Community Change, as cited in Tom Wicker, "America's Real Deficit," *New York Times*, Op. Ed. page, November 7, 1990, the secondary source for the numbers offered above. The original figures are variously attributed to a number of public and private agencies: the Congressional Budget Office, the General Accounting Office, the Department of Energy, the Environmental Protection Agency, the Department of Housing, the Federal Aviation Administration, the Ford Foundation, and the W. T. Grant Foundation.

5. A quirk in the law, noted only after its passage, apparently putting certain necessarily rising expenditures within the "discretionary" domestic total, may (in order to keep within the legislated aggregate ceiling) actually force vital public investment to decline.

POSTSCRIPT

Do Federal Budget Deficits Matter?

Greenspan argues that the fundamental problem with current deficits is that they have not been "offset by saving elsewhere in the economy," which has led to higher real interest rates. As a consequence, net investment as a percentage of gross national product has fallen from 6.7 percent during the 1970s to 4.7 percent during the 1980s. This decline in investment means that workers will have less capital to work with and productivity will grow less rapidly. The long-term implication, Greenspan concludes, is that the ability of the economy to produce goods and services will be reduced and the standard of living of Americans will be less than it could have been.

Eisner believes that in order to obtain an economically correct assessment of the fiscal position of the government, it is necessary to make several adjustments to the published data. If these adjustments are made and "other strange games of accounting" are ignored, he argues, then there is no real deficit nor are there any debt problems. Rather, the real problems for the U.S. economy are a shortage of human capital and public investment. Eisner suggests that efforts to reduce the unadjusted financial deficit block the efforts to solve these real problems.

Several years have passed since Greenspan and Eisner presented their views, and two major efforts have been undertaken to reduce the deficit. One effort was undertaken under the Bush administration (the Omnibus Budget Reconciliation Act of 1990) and one under the Clinton administration (the Omnibus Budget Reconciliation Act of 1993). In spite of these two actions, the federal government's budget remains in the red—although the sizes of the deficits have been, and are expected to be, lower than they would have been without the two deficit-reduction efforts.

For more on the budget deficit, see the annual series entitled *The Guide to the Federal Budget* by Stanley E. Collender (The Urban Institute Press). Other interesting books include *The Deficit Dilemma* by Gregory B. Mills and John L. Palmer (The Urban Institute, 1983); *Federal Budget Deficits* by Paul N. Courant and Edward M. Gramlich (Prentice Hall, 1986); and *The Debt and the Deficit* by Robert Heilbroner and Peter Berstein (W. W. Norton, 1989). Interesting articles on the deficit include "Is the Deficit Really So Bad?" by Jonathan Rauch, *Atlantic Monthly* (February 1989); "America's Budget Deficits: They Don't Crowd Out; They Redistribute Income to the Rich," by Richard C. Koo, *The International Economy* (May/June 1991); and "Budget Ties That Bind," by Daniel Hage, *U.S. News & World Report* (September 9, 1991).

ISSUE 13

Should the Federal Reserve Target Zero Inflation?

YES: W. Lee Hoskins, from "The Case for Price Stability," *Economic Comentary* (March 15, 1990)

NO: Michael Meeropol, from "Zero Inflation: Prescription for Recession," *Challenge* (January/February 1990)

ISSUE SUMMARY

YES: Former Cleveland Federal Reserve Bank president W. Lee Hoskins supports House Joint Resolution 409, which calls for the Federal Reserve to pursue policies to eliminate inflation. Hoskins believes zero inflation would "help markets avoid distortions and imbalances, stabilize the business cycle, and promote the highest sustainable growth in our economy."

NO: Economics professor Michael Meeropol opposes House Joint Resolution 409. He believes that a move to zero inflation will not reduce unemployment and reduce the risk of inflation, it will not produce a higher possible rate of saving and investment, and it may increase income inequality by redistributing income to high-income people from low-income people.

In December 1913 the Federal Reserve Act became law. It created the Federal Reserve System (Fed), which began operations early in 1914. The Fed was designed as an institution that would counter the periodic financial panics that had plagued the U.S. economy. Indeed, the financial panic of 1907 led Congress to establish the National Monetary Commission. Following the Commission's studies, several proposals were advanced and, after extensive debate, the Fed was born.

As originally designed, the Fed had three purposes: "to give the country an elastic currency, provide facilities for discounting commercial credits, and improve the supervision of the banking system." Over time there have been many changes in the Fed. For example, the structure of the Board of Governors of the Fed, whose prime function is the formulation of monetary policy, was changed during the 1930s. Perhaps more important than changes in structure have been the changes in its goals. From the original three purposes, the Fed has extended its purview to include "stability and growth of the economy, a high level of employment, stability in the purchasing power of the dollar, and reasonable balance in transactions with foreign countries." In moving from narrow financial goals to broader macroeconomic goals, the Fed has responded to legislative demands, primarily the Employment Act of 1946 and the Full Employment and Balanced Growth Act of 1978. While the Fed is usually described as an independent agency of the federal government, its structure, goals, operations, and, indeed, its very existence are determined by Congress and the president.

The conventional interpretation of the Fed is that it uses its tools—open market operations, discount rate changes, and changes in legal reserve requirements—to engage in countercyclical monetary policy. Thus, the Fed will purchase government securities, lower the discount rate, and/or lower legal reserve requirements in an effort to increase the money supply and lower interest rates in order to stimulate an economy operating at less than full employment. But this conventional interpretation has been under attack for some time. Conservatives, led by monetarists such as Milton Friedman and Anna Schwartz, have argued that the Fed has hurt rather than helped the cause of economic stability. The monetarists point to a number of instances in U.S. economic history where the Fed has made things worse and not better. The moral of U.S. economic history, according to the monetarists, is that the economy would be more stable if the Fed did not engage in countercyclical monetary policy.

House Joint Resolution 409 (HJR 409) can be seen as a logical extension of the monetarist position. Instead of a multiplicity of goals, HJR 409 mandates the Fed to pursue the single goal of eliminating inflation. Once inflation has been eliminated, the Fed is to maintain price stability. In the context of a simple monetarist framework, this would mean that the Fed would increase the money supply at approximately the same rate as the increase in the economy's ability to produce goods and services. In this way, the arguments presented in favor of HJR 409 by W. Lee Hoskins can be viewed as the conservative monetarist position regarding the proper role for the Fed, while the position taken by Michael Meeropol can be interpreted as the conventional liberal view for an activist Fed.

Although the specific focus of this debate has diminished, the general thrust has not. During the first half of 1994, the Fed moved to increase interest rates in order to prevent an increase in inflation. That is, even though HJR 409 did not become law, the Fed has been acting as if it did. Some economists, taking the position advanced by Meeropol, have argued that by its actions during 1994, the Fed has sacrificed economic growth and employment in a single-minded pursuit of price stability. The Fed and its supporters have defended its actions during 1994 using many of the arguments presented by Hoskins. Thus, the arguments of Hoskins and Meeropol are as timely today as they were in 1990.

YES
W. Lee Hoskins

THE CASE FOR PRICE STABILITY

Mr. Chairman, I am pleased to appear before this Subcommittee to testify on House Joint Resolution 409. I strongly support your resolution directing the Federal Reserve System to make price stability the main goal of monetary policy. Ultimately, the price level is determined by monetary policy. While economic growth and the level of employment depend on our resources and the efficiency with which they are used, the aggregate price level is determined uniquely by the Federal Reserve.

Efficient utilization of our nation's resources requires a sound and predictable monetary policy. H.J. Res. 409 wisely directs the Federal Reserve to place price stability above other economic goals because price stability is the most important contribution the Federal Reserve can make to achieve full employment and maximum sustainable growth.

THE BENEFITS OF PRICE STABILITY

Price Stability Leads to Economic Stability
An important benefit of price stability is that it would stabilize the economy. High and variable inflation has always been one of the prime causes of financial crises and economic recessions. Certainly U.S. experience since World War II reaffirms the notion that inflation is a leading cause of recessions. Every recession in our recent history has been preceded by an outburst of cost and price pressures and the associated imbalances and distortions.

A monetary policy that strives for price stability, or zero inflation, as mandated by H.J. Res. 409 would help markets avoid distortions and imbalances, stabilize the business cycle, and promote the highest sustainable growth in our economy.

Price Stability Maximizes Economic Efficiency and Output
A market economy achieves maximum production and growth by allowing market prices to allocate resources. Money helps make markets work more efficiently by reducing information and transactions costs, allowing for better decisions and improved productivity in resource use. Stabilizing the price

From W. Lee Hoskins, "The Case for Price Stability," *Economic Commentary*, Federal Reserve Bank of Cleveland (March 15, 1990). Copyright © 1990 by The Federal Reserve Bank of Cleveland. Reprinted by permission.

level would make the monetary system operate more efficiently and would result in a higher standard of living for all Americans. Money is a standard of value. Much of our wealth is held either in the form of money or in claims denominated in and payable in money. Money represents a claim on a share of society's output. Stabilizing the price level protects the value of that claim, while inflation reduces it.

When we borrow, we promise to pay back the same amount with interest. When we allow unpredictable inflation, we arbitrarily take from the lender and give to the borrower. When this condition persists, we create an environment in which interest rates rise once to accommodate expected inflation and again to accommodate the increased risk involved in dealing with an uncertain inflation. When inflation rises and becomes uncertain, people are forced to develop elaborate, complicated, and expensive mechanisms to protect their wealth and income, such as new accounting systems, markets for trading financial futures and options, and cash managers who spend all their time trying to keep cash balances at zero. It would be inefficient to allow the length of a yardstick to vary over time, and it is inefficient to allow inflation to change the yardstick for economic value.

While the evidence that price stability maximizes production and employment is not as direct or as extensive as I would like, it is persuasive to me. One source of evidence can be found in the comparison of inflation and real growth across countries. A number of studies find that higher inflation or higher uncertainty about inflation is associated with lower real growth.

Inflation adds risk to decision-making and retards long-term investments. Infla-

tion causes people to invest scarce resources in activities that have the sole purpose of hedging against inflation. Inflation interacts with the tax structure to stifle investment incentives.

More evidence comes from the extreme cases, the cases of hyperinflation. There we see that economic performance clearly deteriorates with high inflation. Both specialization and trade decline as small firms go bankrupt and people return to home production for a larger share of goods and services.

Even a relatively predictable and moderate rate of inflation can be quite harmful. During the seven years of our economic expansion since 1982, inflation has averaged between 3 and 4 percent. While that is low by the standards of the 1970s, the purchasing power of the dollar has been reduced by about 25 percent. Interest rates continue to include a premium for expected inflation and a premium for uncertainty about inflation.

Research at the Federal Reserve Bank of Cleveland indicates that a fully anticipated inflation, with no uncertainty about future inflation, would reduce the capital stock through taxes on capital income. Using 1985 as a benchmark and using conservative assumptions, we have estimated that the interaction of an expected 4 percent inflation rate with the tax on capital income leads to a present value income loss in the American economy of $600 billion or more. This is an amount much greater than the output loss typically associated with recessions. This estimate is from a policy of a perfectly anticipated 4 percent inflation and includes only the welfare loss associated with the failure to fully index taxes on capital income. It ignores the greater damage done to market efficiency by making our monetary yardstick variable.[1]

Even beyond these costs, I believe that inflation diminishes productivity growth. Because the worldwide slowdown in productivity growth occurred simultaneously with the acceleration in inflation and the oil price shocks, the evidence is very difficult to sort out satisfactorily. But if I am correct in believing that inflation inhibits productivity growth, the present value of lost output from even a very small reduction in the trend of productivity growth would far exceed the adjustment costs associated with the transition to price stability.

THE LIMITATIONS OF MONETARY POLICY

A Fallacious Trade-Off: Inflation for Prosperity

Unfortunately, over the years we have come to believe that we can prolong expansion, or avoid recession, with more inflation. A look at recent history reminds us that there is no trade-off between inflation and recession. Although we don't understand recessions completely, we have seen that they can be caused by monetary policy actions as well as by nonmonetary factors.

In the early 1980s we had recessions caused by monetary policy mistakes.

The policy mistake was the excessive monetary growth of the 1970s, which allowed accelerating inflation and rising interest rates and ultimately led to the need for disinflationary monetary policies. The disinflationary policies were necessary to get our economy back to an acceptable level of real activity. Yet even today, we are apt to blame the recessions on policies that reduced inflation instead of blaming the policies that created the inflation to begin with. While recessions will occur even under an ideal monetary policy, they will not be as frequent or as severe. With price stability, we would not have recessions induced by inflation and the subsequent need to eliminate it.

Even if we thought that eliminating the business cycle was a desirable and healthy long-term goal, I believe it is impossible to do so. There are several reasons that prevent us from using monetary policy to offset nonmonetary surprises. First, we cannot predict recessions. Second, monetary policy does not work immediately or predictably; it works with a lag, and the lag is variable and poorly understood.

The Crystal Ball Syndrome

The limitations of economic forecasting are well-known. Analysis of forecast errors has shown that we often don't know that a recession has begun until it is well under way. At any point in time, the range of uncertainty around economic forecasts of business activity for one quarter in the future is wide enough that both expansion and recession are plausible outcomes.

The people who make forecasts and those who use them often get a false sense of confidence because forecast errors are not distributed evenly over the business cycle. When the economy is doing well, forecasts that prosperity will continue are usually correct. And when the economy is performing poorly, forecasts that the slump will continue are also usually correct. The problem lies in predicting the turning points. However, the turning points are the things we must forecast to prevent recessions.

Monetary Policy's Long and Variable Lags

We don't know exactly how a particular policy action will affect the economy. Macroeconomic ideas about monetary policy and its effect on real output have changed profoundly in the last decade as we have recognized that the effect of monetary policy depends importantly on how economic agents form and alter expectations about policy.

Even if we could predict recessions and wanted to vary monetary policy to alleviate them, we still face an almost insurmountable problem—monetary policy operates with a lag. Moreover, the length of the lag varies over time, depending on conditions in the economy and on public perception of the policy process. The effect of today's monetary policy actions will probably not be felt for at least six to nine months, with the main influence perhaps two to three years in the future. The act of trying to prevent a recession may not only fail, but may also create a future recession—via an inflation —where otherwise there would not have been one.

Economic agents, businessmen and consumers alike, do not act in a vacuum. The political forces operating on a central bank make inflation always a possibility. Uncertainty about future inflation adds risk to future investments. Uncertainty about future inflation will raise real interest rates, drive investors away from long-term markets, and delay the very adjustments needed to end the recession. The more certain people are about the stability of future monetary policy, the more easily and quickly inflation can be reduced and the economy can recover.

Lessons We Should Have Learned

If we have learned anything about economic policymaking in the last 20 years, we ought to have learned to think about policy as a dynamic process. To claim that "in order to reduce inflation, we must have a recession," is a wrongheaded notion that completely ignores the ability of humans to adapt their expectations as the environment changes.

People do their best to forecast economic policies when they make decisions. If the central bank has a record of expanding the money supply in attempts to prevent recessions, people will come to anticipate the policy, setting off an acceleration of inflation and misallocation of resources that will lead to a recession.

An economy often goes into recession following an unexpected burst of inflation because people have made decisions that were based on an incorrect view of the future course of asset prices and economic activity. The central bank can help prevent the need for such adjustments by providing a stable price environment. Moreover, price stability will be the optimal setting for adjustments in business inventories and bad debts, should such adjustments be necessary.

THE IMPORTANCE OF ADOPTING HOUSE JOINT RESOLUTION 409

Sound Policies Minimize Uncertainty

Economic policies must have clear objectives, verifiable outcomes, and rules that are consistently adhered to in order to minimize uncertainty. Predictable, verifiable policies ensure that long-term planning and resource allocation decisions will be efficient. Sound policy thus requires a resolute focus on the long term and resistance to policies that, while expedient in the short run, introduce more uncertainty into an already unpredictable world. If enacted, H.J. Res. 409 would make a valuable contribution to this important objective. In the long run, inflation is the one economic variable for which monetary policy is unambiguously responsible. The zero inflation policy called for in H.J. Res. 409 satisfies the key requirements of sound policy: it is clear, it is verifiable, and it has consistent rules. Unlike other rates of inflation, zero inflation is a policy goal that will be understood by everyone.

Responding to Multiple Goals
The Federal Reserve Reform Act of 1977 amended the Federal Reserve Act so that it now requires the Federal Reserve "... to promote effectively the goals of maximum employment, stable prices, and moderate long-term interest rates." However, it is the Federal Reserve's responsibility to decide how best to pursue those goals.

Because of the multiplicity of goals established by Congress for the Federal Reserve, the Federal Reserve can choose which goal it emphasizes at any moment. Such discretion increases the likelihood that political and special-interest groups could try to influence the Federal Reserve to pursue the policy that is currently important to that group.

In this respect, the Federal Reserve's situation is different from that of West Germany's central bank, which is also independent. More than one goal is specified by law for that bank, but West German law states that the goal of price stability is to be given highest priority whenever another goal might conflict with maintaining price stability. This is a major reason why West Germany's price level only doubled between 1950 and 1988, while the U.S. price level quadrupled.

Since current law requires the Federal Reserve to promote maximum employment, stable prices, and moderate long-term interest rates, the Federal Reserve must choose a viable strategy to accomplish this mission. Two approaches seem plausible.

One approach would be for the central bank to try to achieve a balance among its three Congressionally mandated objectives. The Federal Reserve could use its own judgment about what balance among the objectives to pursue, and could change that balance from time to time, depending on its view of how the economy works and what course is broadly acceptable to the public. In essence, this is the practice that the Federal Reserve has followed. It has strived to balance desirable economic conditions such as full employment, economic growth, and low long-term interest rates with low rates of inflation. But the major drawback to this approach is its feasibility. To strike a balance among the mandated goals requires that they be reliably linked to one another. Furthermore, monetary policy would need to be capable of influencing simultaneously all these economic dimensions in the desired directions and quantities.

While monetary policy is capable of influencing the economy in the short to intermediate run, over long periods of time monetary policy can only affect the rate of inflation. The rate of inflation, in turn, affects all dimensions of economic performance, including output, employment, and interest rates. Maximum production and employment and low interest rates can be achieved only with price stability.

By its very nature, a balancing act among complex economic goals causes substantial confusion about the Federal Reserve's intentions. Such confusion could be avoided to a large degree if Congress or the Federal Reserve assigned priorities to the goals.

A more promising approach is to select one objective—the only one that the Federal Reserve can influence directly. Under the provisions of H.J. Res. 409, the Federal Reserve would seek to maintain a stable price level over time. Price stability is defined as an inflation rate so small that it does not systematically affect economic decisions. The definition may appear less specific than some would like, but I believe that the decisions of economic agents will be very important in monitoring success in achieving price stability.

In practice, the size of the inflation premium estimated to be found in long-term interest rates, surveys of the public's inflation expectations, and other market-generated measures of inflation expectations can be very useful. If policy is credible, both the inflation component and the inflation uncertainty risk premium would be eliminated from interest rates. Temporary and unforeseen factors will cause the price level to deviate from the desired course. It would be a mistake to try to keep some inflation index on target each and every quarter, or even each and every year.

Price stability can be achieved by holding the money supply (as measured by M2) on or close to a path which is consistent with price stability over long periods. The relationship between money and the price level over long periods of time is stable and strong. However, the link between money and the economy over periods perhaps as short as a year is loose enough to afford the Federal Reserve considerable leeway in responding to problems and crises —as long as economic agents believe that the future value of money will be stable. Clearly, this resolution would not prevent the Federal Reserve from providing liquidity in times of financial crises, such as the stock market crash in 1987.

Announcing a Commitment to Price Stability

Announcement of a commitment to price stability, as embodied in H.J. Res. 409, would enhance the ability of Congress to hold the Federal Reserve accountable for achieving the goal. Central-bank accountability is appropriate in a democracy and, in fact, Congress has the ultimate authority to change the Federal Reserve's goal.

A legislative commitment to price stability would also enhance the Federal Reserve's independence from political pressures as it pursued that goal. A commitment by Congress to price stability would reduce the effectiveness of political pressure to deviate from that goal. Thus, a distinction can be made between a central bank that is accountable for long-run performance and a central bank that can be influenced to pursue short-run goals that might be incompatible with desirable long-term economic performance.

The commitment to price stability supported by a legislative mandate would foster the credibility of the Federal Reserve. Improving the Federal Reserve's credibility would strengthen the expectation that prices will be stable, and would contribute to price and wage decisions that would make price stability easier to achieve and maintain.

ARGUMENTS AGAINST ADOPTING HOUSE JOINT RESOLUTION 409 ARE WEAK

What About the Transition Costs?

A commitment by Congress and the Federal Reserve to achieve price stability would entail adjustment costs. Adjustment costs would arise from two sources: contractual obligations and the credibility problem, or uncertainty about whether price stability would be achieved and maintained. The contractual costs can be alleviated with an appropriate adjustment period. H.J. Res. 409 recognizes that abrupt policy changes can be disruptive and provides a phase-in period to help reduce adjustment costs.

Much of our day-to-day economic activity is conducted under contracts and commitments that extend over longer periods of time and that embody the expectations of a continuing moderate inflation rate. Most of these contracts will expire in the next few years. The disruption to business and the arbitrary wealth redistribution of an abrupt adjustment to price stability would be greatly reduced by an appropriate phase-in period. H.J. Res. 409 gives us five years to get to price stability —a period long enough to reduce substantially the transition costs.

The second set of adjustment costs emanates from the expectations of economic agents. As the Congressional Budget Office points out in its recent *Economic and Budget Outlook*, if everyone believed that inflation would be reduced to zero, and planned accordingly, these costs would be very low. The Federal Reserve has stated that it intends to reduce inflation to zero or to low levels, but it has not committed to a specific timetable for eliminating inflation, or to a plan for doing so. The result is that the public in general and the markets in particular wonder just how serious we are in those intentions, or whether we will switch our priorities to some other goal, as we have in the past.

Large-Scale Econometric Model Estimates of the Transition Cost

Economists have not made much progress in estimating the transition costs of eliminating inflation. Frequently, econometric models that embody a large number of complex relationships and variables are used to estimate the adjustment costs.

For manageability, econometric models are built with many simplifying assumptions, one of which is the presumption that economic agents are backward-looking in the way they form and change expectations. In these models, expectations, which in effect determine adjustment costs, are formed from past experience, and are changed only slowly as the future unfolds.

The presumption that expectations change only slowly inevitably generates estimates of high transition costs. The real question about a change in policy as specified by H.J. Res. 409 is how forward-looking economic agents would behave under a fully credible and fully understood policy change. Backward-looking models are relatively useless in answering this question.

In almost every case, such models are constructed to display the effects that are consistent with the model builder's theories and biases. Almost all of the large models are based on the dual notion that the only way to eliminate inflation is to raise the unemployment rate. Naturally, these models will find that eliminating inflation is very costly. These exercises have been conducted many times in the past, and they have consistently overestimated the costs of eliminating inflation and ignored the benefits of doing so. I might also observe that those who really believe the analytical structures contained in these models logically should advocate an acceleration of inflation because the models would predict great benefits from doing so.

One member of the Council of Economic Advisers, an expert on such matters, has developed large econometric models with sluggish resource adjustment induced by labor contracts. Even in these models, there is almost no short-run cost to eliminating inflation with a credible policy change. The reason is simply that, in these models, people are assumed to change their behavior in response to the policy change.

As the CBO study states, "... inflation could be reduced relatively painlessly by lowering inflationary expectations." A commitment by the Congress and the Federal Reserve would enhance credibility and convince economic agents to begin to base decisions on gradual elimination of inflation over a five-year period. The transitional costs presented elsewhere in the CBO study then would be grossly overestimated.

A consistent commitment to a long-run policy goal of price stability is important. One of the worst things we could do is to eliminate inflation for a while and then return to high inflation later. H.J. Res. 409 would contribute to an important change in the policy process, focusing it toward consistent long-run goals and away from reactions to each new report of economic activity. Each policy action would become part of a policy process that is consistent with long-run price stability.

Fiscal Policy Is No Obstacle to Price Stability

Federal budget deficits should not compromise either the Federal Reserve's goal of price stability or the adoption of a specific timetable to achieve it. I do not mean to suggest or imply that current fiscal policy is ideal, appropriate, or the result of bad monetary policy. Savings are too low, at least partly because of budget deficits, and measures to address our savings shortfall must include measures to reduce the deficit. However, while we strive for better fiscal policy, we should recognize that monetary policy cannot offset whatever harm may result from fiscal policy; indeed, it can only add to those costs.

We are all familiar with the argument that large federal budget deficits cause high interest rates, forcing the Fed to ease monetary policy in order to keep interest rates at levels consistent with full employment. This argument ignores the fact that both the federal budget deficit and, more important, government spending, at least measured relative to the economy, have been falling for the past several years and should continue to do so.

There is, of course, legitimate concern that the progress in deficit and expenditure reduction might cease or even be reversed, for any number of reasons. How should such a reversal influence monetary policy? Even if fiscal policy choices were to put upward pressure on interest rates, and there is little consensus among economists that this is the case, it is far from clear that the Federal Reserve can do anything to alleviate the economic consequences of that problem. Ultimately, it is real interest rates that affect the consumption and production decisions of individuals and businesses and the allocation of resources over time. Real rates of return are based on the productivity of labor, capital, and other real assets in a society, and have very little, if any, connection with monetary policy.

In an inflationary environment, nominal rates of return include an inflation premium to compensate lenders for being repaid in money of reduced purchasing power. The correlation between monetary policy and nominal interest rates that dominates discussion in the financial press tells us next to nothing about the relationship between monetary policy and the real interest rates that govern the allocation of resources over time. Every movement in the federal funds rate does not produce equivalent changes in real interest rates, in the productivity of our capital stock, or in any of the other important real variables that affect economic activity. The fact that monetary policy exerts relatively direct control over the federal funds rate does not imply that real interest rates can, similarly, be controlled by monetary policy.

It is unnecessary and undesirable for sound monetary policy choices to await sound fiscal policy choices. Sound fiscal policy decisions, like sound private economic decisions, require the stable inflation environment that H.J. Res. 409 would direct the Federal Reserve to provide. The tax-related distortions and economic complexities associated with even stable, positive rates of inflation argue strongly for price stability.

CONCLUSION

If H.J. Res. 409 is enacted and the Federal Reserve commits to an explicit plan for price stability, the transition period will soon be over, and any costs that arise because of this policy change will be outweighed by the benefits. These benefits will be large and permanent, and will far outweigh the costs of getting there.

H.J. Res. 409, if enacted, would be a milestone in economic policy legislation because it would shift the focus of monetary policy away from short-term fine-tuning to the long term, where it belongs. It would enforce accountability for the one vital objective that the Federal Reserve can achieve. It would officially sanction those sometimes unpopular short-run policy actions that most certainly are in our nation's long-term interest. It would make clear that the Federal Reserve cannot achieve maximum output and employment without achieving price stability. I fully support House Joint Resolution 409.

NOTES

1. David Altig and Charles T. Carlstrom. "Expected Inflation and the Welfare Losses from Taxes on Capital Income," manuscript, Federal Reserve Bank of Cleveland, February 1990.

NO

Michael Meeropol

ZERO INFLATION: PRESCRIPTION FOR RECESSION

I recently received a letter that was sent out to many economists (and perhaps other professionals) from Representative Stephen L. Neal (D-NC) asking for our opinions about a proposed congressional resolution (H.J.R. 409) that would order the Federal Reserve System to make zero inflation the "primary and dominant objective of monetary policy." The *Wall Street Journal* also has taken up the call, noting that Fed Chairman Alan Greenspan "testified in support of Mr. Neal's resolution and said its goal—zero inflation within five years—was attainable."

I submit that virtually every one of the several assertions justifying the resolution is based on an erroneous reading of recent history. Most importantly, they fail to demonstrate any understanding of the difference between real and nominal interest rates.

The preamble of the proposed resolution claims that zero inflation will:

- reduce interest rates to—and maintain them at—their lowest possible levels;
- promote the highest possible sustainable level of employment;
- generate the maximum sustainable rate of economic growth;
- encourage the highest possible rate of saving and investment, thereby boosting productivity and enhancing our standard of living; and
- help stabilize the economy, thereby minimizing risk and uncertainty in economic decision-making and abolishing the need to devote resources, time, and energy to predicting and coping with the consequences of inflation.

As for the first point, it is not true that moving to a zero inflation rate will lower interest rates. If the experience of the 1980s is any indication, there will be a period of rising real interest rates followed by a period of higher than usual real rates. A simple comparison of changes in the consumer price index and the prime lending rate shows us the last nineteen years of real interest rates (see Table 1).

A substantial rise in real interest rates as a result of Fed tightening even more intensely than in the last two years will undoubtedly reinforce the

From Michael Meeropol, "Zero Inflation: Prescription for Recession," *Challenge*, vol. 33, no. 1 (January/February 1990). Copyright © 1990 by M. E. Sharpe, Inc., 80 Business Park Drive, Armonk, NY 10504. Reprinted by permission.

squeeze on heavily indebted small businesses (especially in agriculture) that has been the hallmark of this recovery.

The business failure rate, which usually falls during recoveries, actually rose to unprecedented levels in the 1983–86 period before declining slightly in 1987. We can expect more of the same if a move toward zero inflation raises the real interest rate.

Zero inflation will not reduce unemployment and minimize the risk of recession. Unemployment averaged 6.17 percent in the inflationary 1970s and 7.49 percent in the low inflation 1980s. Even if we omit the years 1980–82, unemployment averages 7.16 percent in 1983–88. This is true despite the fact that there were more quarters of recession in the 1970s than in the 1980s. The only way we have ever been able to lower inflation in this country is by increasing unemployment.

Claiming that zero inflation will create the highest *sustainable* level of employment is a tidy way of avoiding the evidence, because one can always say that previous low levels of unemployment were "not sustainable." It is important to note that I am not asserting a long-run stable trade-off between inflation and unemployment, only that there are successive short-run trade-offs, each within a historical context. I predict that a move by the Fed toward zero inflation will subject the economy to a short-run trade-off similar to that experienced in the period of the post-1979 Volcker anti-inflation strategy.

LOW INFLATION = SLOWER GROWTH

Meantime, the low inflation 1980s has seen only a marginally faster rate of productivity growth than the high inflation 1970s, a slower rate of real GNP growth, and a slower growth in real wages. Real GNP in 1979 was 31.7 percent higher than in 1969. Real GNP in 1988 was 26 percent higher than in 1979. That averaged out to 3.17 percent per year in the '70s and 2.89 percent in the '80s.

Real wages rose an average of only 0.26 percent in the 1970s, but actually fell an average of 0.44 percent in 1980–87. Even if we omit 1980 from the calculation of the 1980s, we observe an average growth rate of 0.07 percent for the years 1981–87. Productivity growth averaged 1.29 percent in the 1970s and 1.38 percent in the period 1980–87.

Some may object to a comparison between the 1980s and the 1970s since inflation remained quite high for the first two years of the '80s, but we must remember that the Fed's anti-inflationary policy had been in place since November 1979. Even though it took two years for the policy to begin to work on the rate of inflation, the rise in unemployment was already apparent in 1980 and the rise in both unemployment and real interest rates was very clear in 1981. It is the *policy* of attempting to reach zero inflation that I am attacking, and my evidence is based on our experience with a tight anti-inflationary monetary policy that lasted for the entire decade of the 1980s.

It is also a mistake to suggest that zero inflation will encourage the highest possible rate of saving and investment. The 1970s had higher rates of saving and investment than the 1980s. Comparing saving rates is probably unnecessary, given the widespread publicity of the spectacular failure of supply-side economics to raise the personal saving rate, but investment as a percentage of GNP averaged 16.41 percent in the 1970s and 15.8 percent in the 1980s.

Table 1

Nineteen Years of Real Interest Rates

Year	Column 1 Nominal Interest Rate (prime rate)	Column 2 Inflation Rate (CPI)	Column 3 Real Interest Rate (col. 1–col. 2)	Column 4 Unemployment Rate (all workers)
1970	7.91	5.7	2.21	4.8
1971	5.72	4.4	1.32	5.8
1972	5.25	3.2	2.05	5.5
1973	8.03	6.2	1.83	4.8
1974	10.81	11.0	1.81	5.6
1975	7.86	9.1	1.24	8.5
1976	6.84	5.8	1.04	7.7
1977	6.83	6.5	.33	7.1
1978	9.06	7.6	1.46	6.1
1979	12.67	11.3	1.37	5.8
1980	15.27	13.5	1.77	7.1
1981	18.87	10.3	8.57	7.6
1982	14.86	6.2	8.46	9.7
1983	10.79	3.2	7.59	9.6
1984	12.04	4.3	7.74	7.5
1985	9.93	3.6	6.33	7.2
1986	8.33	1.9	6.43	7.0
1987	8.22	3.6	4.62	6.2
1988	9.32	4.0	5.32	5.5

Sources: Column 1, *Economic Report of the President*, 1989, p. 390; Column 2, *Ibid*, p. 378. Column 4, *Ibid*, p. 532. 1988 data from *Survey of Current Business*, Vol. 69, No. 3 (March 1989), col. 1, p. S-10, col. 2, p. S-5, col. 4, p. S-14.

Investment decisions depend on expected rates of return that depend in large part on the current and most recent rate of growth of demand. If the effort to achieve zero inflation raises real interest rates dramatically, it will slow down the growth of demand and thus be associated with lower rates of investment.

The argument that a zero rate of inflation will stabilize the economy would only be true *after* real interest rates fall. So far in the 1980s, they have yet to fall to their historical levels. Until they do, the effort to reach zero inflation will be associated with continued instability. We must remember that consistently achieving any *anticipated* rate of inflation will promote stability. Conversely, when the rate of inflation (whatever it is) is unanticipated, that is destabilizing.

Even if it were to become the policy of the Fed to reach zero inflation, that does not mean business can immediately stop devoting resources to predicting inflation. Even after the unlikely event of the Fed achieving zero inflation, each separate business will still have to devote resources to predicting how their *particular* costs (specific input prices and their labor costs) and their *specific* products' prices *deviate* from the general rate of inflation, whatever that rate might be.

DON'T GET ME WRONG

In making these arguments, I do not wish to be misunderstood. Obviously, volatile swings in the rate of inflation can produce tremendous uncertainties and hurt real economic performance. Also, because of the differing ability of individuals to insulate themselves from the effects of inflation by indexing their incomes, it would probably be a good thing if we could wave a magic wand and get zero inflation with a lock-step drop in nominal interest rates to prevent a rise in real interest rates.

It was one of the predictions of the rational expectations school that a credible anti-inflation policy would produce such an immediate fall in nominal interest rates. As soon as the Fed's anti-inflation policy was deemed "credible" by the financial community, borrowers would refuse to pay inflation premia on their loans, and lenders would cease insisting on them because they would correctly anticipate the success of the Fed's policy.

The fact that this did not happen in the early 1980s and the persistence of high real interest rates to the end of the decade—even after the Fed put the economy through the wringer of 1981–82—is evidence that the rational expectations approach is incorrect. This experience should be a strong warning to those who support H.J. Res. 409 because they expect an immediate response to the Fed's efforts.

It is also important to note that I am not asserting that the rate of inflation is always negatively correlated with the real interest rate. I am merely suggesting that the inflation premia built into any interest rates are more likely correlated with the recent past than with the predictions of "rational economic theory" about the "credibility" of the Fed's declared policy.

Thus, should Congress adopt the resolution, nominal interest rates will not

fall as fast as the rate of inflation, if they fall at all. In fact, they will undoubtedly rise in the short-run until the recession becomes apparent. This is particularly true given the continued expansiveness of Federal fiscal policy.

NEAL'S ARGUMENT

Congressman Neal included in his questionnaire a speech he made on the House floor on August 1, 1989. In it, he attempted to anticipate some of the criticisms I have mentioned. He noted that many "... fear that the cost in terms of recession and slow growth would be intolerable." He then argued that inflationary surges are followed by big increases in unemployment.

Neal then correctly anticipated the counter that this unemployment is caused by draconian anti-inflationary policies rather than the inflation itself. His only argument to that was "the public in developed economies will sooner or later turn against governments that tolerate rising inflation, and elect leaders willing to rein it in, even at the cost of recession."

But, in the United States, the voters never turned against rising inflation *in support of* what turned out to be the Volcker-Carter-Reagan policy. No one elected Paul Volcker to be head of the Fed and to put the economy through the cold shower anti-inflation treatment of 1979–83. Jimmy Carter was defeated in large part because of his role in permitting the *recession* of 1980, not the inflation of the previous year.

Ronald Reagan was elected on a promise to cut taxes, cut inflation, cut unemployment, restart our productivity engines, stimulate investment, increase saving, and ultimately balance the budget by

1984. He was not elected to preside over the worst recession since the 1930s. The utter failure of Reaganomics on its own terms has been obscured by the length of the recovery from the 1981–82 recession, but even that long recovery has not made the '80s a better decade than the 1970s in terms of economic growth, investment, and unemployment.

Recipients of interest income have benefited most from the reduction in inflation. (Net interest as a percentage of personal income reached a maximum of 10.9 percent in 1979, jumped to 12 percent in 1980, to 13.3 percent in 1981, and peaked at 14.3 percent in 1985 and 1986. In 1988, it was still at 14 percent.) Debtors who contracted their debt during the years of high nominal interest rates (1978 to 1984) have been particularly hard hit by that reduction. Included in this group, of course, has been the biggest debtor in the country, the federal government.

As Robert Eisner showed in *How Real Is the Federal Deficit?* (Free Press, 1986), inflation reduces the real burden of the federal debt on the taxpayers. The reduction of inflation has raised that real burden in the 1980s. A zero inflation rate will end the automatic erosion in the real burden of the debt, increasing again the advantages of interest recipients while raising the interest burden on the average taxpayer.

It is not a very popular point to make, but inflation in the 1970s actually benefited the majority of people in the country because the majority of people in the country were (and still are) net debtors. Inflation made property owners with low interest mortgages wealthy by reducing their real interest rates (in some instances to negative values) while the values of their homes rose faster than inflation. It also eased the

burden of debt on small businesses, permitting a relatively rapid expansion of activity. This is why investment as a percentage of GNP was actually higher in the inflationary 1970s than in the low inflation 1980s.

Obviously, a stated policy of moderate inflation would not produce this same result once inflation premia had been built into interest rates. Here, however, an easy money policy by the Fed can actually force nominal interest rates down or at least slow their rise, permitting that moderate inflation to once again produce a relatively painless redistribution of income back from the rentiers to the rest of us.

Given a real choice between the slow erosion of the real burden of debt associated with moderate inflation and the unprecedented real interest rates and the accompanying high levels of unemployment we have experienced for the last decade, perhaps American voters might surprise Mr. Neal. However, given what passes for economic discourse by our politicians, it is most unlikely our voters will ever be given such a clear choice.

Finally, it is essential that we recognize that associated with a move toward zero inflation would be an increased redistribution of income away from low income people toward high income people. Low and moderate income people are net debtors. Net creditors are generally high income people and heavily capitalized financial institutions, like insurance companies. Though the poor are not able to carry much debt because they usually do not qualify, they are harmed by the unemployment associated with the anti-inflationary struggle.

The 1980s has seen a significant drift toward greater inequality in the distribution of income and in the quality of life for our low income citizens. A rising percentage of American children live in poverty. Traditional income redistribution programs for the poor have been cut in real terms, even in the era of lower inflation. The poor kept pace with the rest of society during the inflationary 1970s in terms of health, nutrition, housing, and income support. The percentage of the population living in poverty did not rise dramatically despite the inflation of the 1970s, yet it did rise despite the reduction of inflation in the 1980s.

I hope the majority of my colleagues in the profession will let their member of Congress know that the move to zero inflation would be exactly the wrong kind of medicine for the economy. It appears that the economy will enter a recession some time in 1990 or at least experience very sluggish growth. This is not the time to compound that sluggishness with a big run-up in real interest rates.

We are still waiting for the end of the "short-run" transition from high inflationary expectations in the early '80s to the low inflationary expectations of the late '80s. Meanwhile, real interest rates have remained above their historic averages for the entire decade. Do we have to, indeed, wait for death before the "long-run" and low real interest rates arrive?

POSTSCRIPT

Should the Federal Reserve Target Zero Inflation?

Hoskins begins his statement of support for House Joint Resolution 409 (HJR 409) by asserting that the behavior of the aggregate price level, the rate of inflation, is uniquely determined by the Federal Reserve. He further asserts that "the most important contribution the Federal Reserve can make to achieve full employment and maximum sustainable growth" is to achieve price stability. Price stability or zero inflation promotes these ends by "helping markets avoid distortions and imbalances." Hoskins cites three reasons for adopting HJR 409: It specifies a policy that minimizes uncertainty, eliminates multiple goals and posits instead a single goal that the Federal Reserve can achieve, and enhances Federal Reserve accountability to Congress. Hoskins admits that there may be some transition costs but these are minimized by HJR 409, for it provides for a five-year transition to zero inflation.

Meeropol argues that the claims made on behalf of HJR 409 are not supported by recent economic history. He also argues that low or zero inflation will do little to increase saving and investment and stabilize the economy. These conclusions are both based on a comparison of the high-inflation 1970s and the low-inflation 1980s. Finally, Meeropol argues that inflation tends to benefit debtors at the expense of creditors and, given that low-income persons are net debtors, the elimination of inflation will work to the benefit of high-income creditors. This increase in economic inequality will be made worse if the reduction of inflation generates a recession, for it will be low-income persons who will experience unemployment.

For a complete discussion of the Federal Reserve System, see *The Federal Reserve System: Its Purposes and Functions* (AMS Press, 1984). For a critical evaluation of the Federal Reserve, see *Secrets of the Temple: How the Federal Reserve Runs the Country,* by William Greider (Simon & Schuster, 1987). HJR 409 is reprinted on page 56 of the January/February 1990 issue of *Challenge.* For additional arguments by Hoskins in support of HJR 409 and zero inflation, see "Defending Zero Inflation: All For Naught," *Economic Commentary,* Federal Reserve Bank of Cleveland (April 1, 1991) and "Some Observations on Central Bank Accountability," *Economic Commentary,* Federal Reserve Bank of Cleveland (April 15, 1991). For further arguments against HJR 409 and zero inflation, see S. Roo, "Response to a Defense of Zero Inflation," *Quarterly Review,* Federal Reserve Bank of Minneapolis (Spring 1991).

ISSUE 14

Does the United States Have an Income Distribution Problem?

YES: Greg J. Duncan, Timothy M. Smeeding, and Willard Rodgers, from "The Incredible Shrinking Middle Class," *American Demographics* (May 1992)

NO: Council of Economic Advisers, from *Economic Report of the President 1992* (Government Printing Office, 1992)

ISSUE SUMMARY

YES: University researchers Greg J. Duncan, Timothy M. Smeeding, and Willard Rodgers argue that a growing inequality in the distribution of income is causing a significant decline in the share of adults who can be considered middle class.

NO: The Bush administration's Council of Economic Advisers concludes that median levels of family and household money income have increased since the mid-1960s, that improvement in the economic condition of the lowest income groups is understated, and that long-term income is distributed more equally than annual income.

An economic system represents the structures that a society puts in place to answer three fundamental questions: What goods and services should be produced? How should the goods and services be produced? Who will get the goods and services that are produced? In judging how well an economic system resolves these questions, two criteria are used.

The first criterion is efficiency, and it involves several perspectives. Is the society producing the goods and services that people want? Given scarce inputs and available technology, is the output of desired goods and services at a maximum? The efficiency criterion is a positive concept. That is, it can be judged, more or less, by an analysis of facts. Clearly, if there are people who want jobs but are unable to obtain them, there is unemployment, which signifies that the economy is operating inefficiently. If a company is producing a good that people do not want, then its inventories will be increasing, which also represents inefficiency. Market economies, as opposed to command economies or traditional economies, are usually given high marks for their efficiency. The self-correcting operation of prices in competitive markets generates the efficiency.

The second criterion for judging an economic system is equity, or fairness, and it also involves several perspectives. Does the economic system take care of persons who are unable, for reasons beyond their control, to provide for themselves? Are the rewards that people get for their participation in economic activity commensurate with the contributions they have made? The equity criterion is usually viewed as a normative concept. That is, the evaluation of the degree of equity in an economic system depends on the values of the person making the judgment. This does not mean that facts don't play a part in judging equity. However, the point remains that in the normative domain, different persons can interpret a particular set of facts differently.

The most common procedure for judging the equity or fairness of an economic system involves an examination of the distribution of income and the changes in that distribution over time. People exhibit concern with equity when they ask, Are the poor getting poorer and the rich getting richer? Market economics, by their very nature, generate inequalities in the distribution of income, and these inequalities are accepted as equitable. For example, if two persons have identical jobs but one chooses to work more hours, then that individual should receive a larger income. If a particular job requires more training and education, as in the preparation necessary to become a medical doctor, then the persons who undergo the training and education should receive additional compensation. Certain differences in income are justifiable—fair and equitable.

The present issue considers income distribution. Unfortunately, there are a number of questions that need to be answered in completing the analysis. Exactly what constitutes income? Which is more important, the dollar value of income an economic unit receives or its share of total income? Is the long-run perspective more important than the short run? After answering these questions, there remains the values through which the analyst filters the data. Different values allow one person to give an optimistic interpretation to a given set of numbers and another to give a pessimistic interpretation. The issue of income distribution is an equity issue, a normative issue. All of these considerations feed into the opposite conclusions reached by Greg J. Duncan and his colleagues, on the one hand, and the Bush administration's Council of Economic Advisers, on the other.

YES

Greg J. Duncan, Timothy M. Smeeding, and Willard Rodgers

THE INCREDIBLE SHRINKING MIDDLE CLASS

For more than a quarter century, researchers have watched an uneven but unmistakable decline in the size of America's middle class. The overall distribution of wages and earnings has become more unequal. The share of total household income derived from earnings has fallen, while the share derived from capital investments has grown.

Social researchers usually rely on cross-sectional surveys—snapshots of household conditions at certain points in time—to study the economic conditions of Americans. But this method can only reveal net changes in income distribution. It cannot show another important aspect of the issue, which is the movement of families into and out of the middle class.

To study the economic migration of Americans, we looked at 22 years of data (1968–89) from the Survey Research Center's Panel Study of Income Dynamics (PSID). This study attempts to follow all members of its nationally representative sample through time, so it provides a unique historical record of a family's financial ups and downs.

The data show that the 1980s were simultaneously a time of enhanced upward mobility and more frequent downward mobility.

THE SHRINKING MIDDLE

The public debate on the middle class focuses on prime-age adults: those who are old enough to be independent of their parents, but too young to be candidates for retirement. Accordingly, we limited the sample to adults aged 25 to 55.

There is no standard definition for the term "middle class," even among researchers who attempt to measure "class" by measuring household income. Some studies adjust incomes for household size, while others do not. Some analyses use after-tax income to chart economic fortunes, but most use pretax money income. And some researchers define affluence in terms of an absolute dollar figure, while others measure it relative to a distribution.

From Greg J. Duncan, Timothy M. Smeeding, and Willard Rodgers, "The Incredible Shrinking Middle Class," *American Demographics* (May 1992). Copyright © 1992 by *American Demographics*. Reprinted by permission.

We developed two measures of economic status, one of which adjusts a household's income for household size. Both measures are based on after-tax household income, and both set the boundaries of middle income between the 20th and 90th percentile of the sample. Since food stamps are arguably equivalent to cash, we include their dollar value as a component of household income.

Our unadjusted measure places the boundaries of the middle class between $18,500 and $55,000 in 1987 dollars. The second measure, which adjusts for household size, is characterized by an income-to-needs index based on the official poverty threshold. The index equals 1.0 when a household's income is equal to the poverty threshold.[1] Using this measure, the boundaries of the middle class fall between the index values of 2.0 and 6.0, or two to six times the poverty line.

Both of our measures reveal similar economic pictures. And when our PSID data are compared with the Census Bureau's Current Population Survey, both indicate similar declines in the proportion of middle-income households.

Our PSID analysis also reveals the story behind the overall census numbers. Using the household-size adjusted income index, we found that smaller households helped to increase the proportion of prime-aged adults in the middle class during most of the 1970s, but failed to prevent a dramatic decline in the size of the middle class in the 1980s.

Seventy-five percent of 25-to-55-year-olds were middle income in the early 1970s. This share fell in the mid-1970s, and again reached 75 percent in the late 1970s. Then it plummeted to 65 percent in 1983, and it had recovered only slightly (to 67 percent) in 1985–86.

The income-to-needs index shows even steeper declines. Only about 65 percent of prime-aged adults in 1985 were middle class according to this measure.

A growing number of upper-income households drew people out of the middle class in the late 1970s and throughout the 1980s. Between 1979–80 and 1985–86, the proportion of high-income households grew from 8 percent to over 13 percent. The income-to-needs measure shows that the share increased from 10 percent to over 16 percent.

The erosion of the middle class becomes even more pronounced if you account for household size. While a substantial percentage of middle-class adults have moved into upper-income brackets, an even greater fraction are joining America's poor. This raises two important questions: what kinds of people cross these economic boundaries, and what life events determine their income losses or gains?

THE ECONOMIC MIGRANTS

Over a typical five-year period during the 1970s and 1980s, nearly 7 percent of adults with initial after-tax household incomes of between $18,500 and $55,000 ended the period by making more than $55,000 a year. A much larger share of initially high-income adults—more than 29 percent—dropped into the middle class. In addition, one-third of low-income adults succeeded in making the transition to a middle-class life, while 7 percent of middle-income adults fell below the lower-income limit. The smaller share of people in the upper- and lower-income groups means that the actual numbers of people making these transitions were more nearly equal than these proportions suggest.

Figure 1

The Disappearing Middle

Percent of middle-income adults aged 25 to 55, by two different measures,* 1968–86.

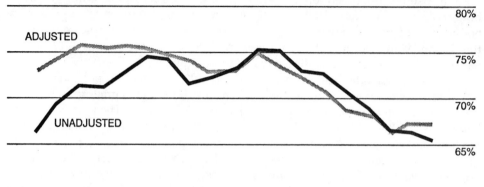

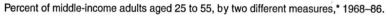

The share of adults who are middle class declined from 75 percent in 1978 to 67 percent in 1986.
*The unadjusted measure is the share of all adults aged 25 to 55 with after-tax incomes between $18,500 and $55,000 in 1987 dollars, including food stamps. The adjusted measure is the share of all adults aged 25 to 55 with an income-to-needs index between 2 and 6. An income-to-needs index of 1 indicates that a family is at the poverty threshold.

Source: Authors' calculations based on the Survey Research Center's Panel Study of Income Dynamics

Married couples dominate the group that successfully makes the transition from a lower to a higher income. This was especially true before 1980, when married couples accounted for 90 percent of all transitions into high-income status. But they also accounted for 79 percent of transitions from high- to middle-income status.

The probability that a female head of household would move into the upper-income group improved after 1980. Most of the upwardly mobile women were highly educated, young, and childless. Their good fortune was due to real earnings growth.

In the late 1960s and in the 1970s, the transitions into and out of the middle class roughly canceled each other out. But in the 1980s, all four transition streams tended to sap the middle class. A higher percentage of individuals climbed into high-income status, while a smaller share fell out. A lower proportion of low-income individuals moved into the middle class, while a larger share dropped down.

LIFE'S UPS AND DOWNS

A college education is the single most important factor in facilitating favorable economic transitions and avoiding unfavorable ones. Also, transitions into high-income status are more common among older adults than younger adults. Being under age 35 or black hinders one's upward mobility. Both before and after 1980, blacks were only half as likely as others to move into high-income status, even after adjusting for differences in schooling, household composition, age, and income.

After 1980, it became more difficult for Americans to move out of the low-income

Figure 2
Fewer Moving In

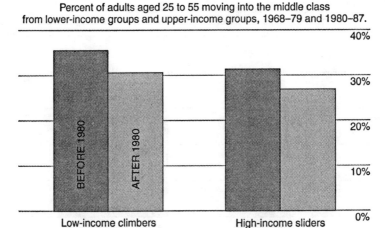

Percent of adults aged 25 to 55 moving into the middle class
from lower-income groups and upper-income groups, 1968–79 and 1980–87.

Rich or poor, fewer people moved into the middle class after 1980.
Source: Panel Study of Income Dynamics

group. Only college-educated adults had a significantly higher-than-average chance of rising into the middle class. Blacks and women heads of household continued to have difficulties breaking out of the lower-income group. And being young gave an edge to economic climbers in the 1970s, but not in the 1980s.

Overall, a smaller share of adults dropped out of the upper class after 1980. But the probability of falling from middle-income to lower-income status increased significantly after 1980. Women heads of households and blacks maintained their already higher-than-average risk of downward mobility. The risk was much lower than average for people with at least a high school education.

EARNINGS INEQUALITY

Our study found that the biggest single factor behind the withering of the middle class is the growing inequality in the distribution of men's earnings. Women's earnings are becoming more and more important to family finances, but men's earnings play the dominant role in most economic transitions. This is true both before and after 1980. For both men and women, the economic rewards of a college degree increased dramatically, while less-educated adults often saw the real value of their earnings decline.

Higher rates of pay, rather than overtime or second jobs, account for most of the favorable transitions driven by men's earnings. But upward mobility associated with women's earnings was evenly split between pay increases and longer hours. Downward transitions for men were usually associated with job loss. For women, changes in both wages and hours accounted for negative changes in earnings.

The withering of the middle class is marked by two major forces. First, there has been upward movement among

Figure 3

More Moving Out

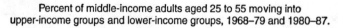

Percent of middle-income adults aged 25 to 55 moving into
upper-income groups and lower-income groups, 1968–79 and 1980–87.

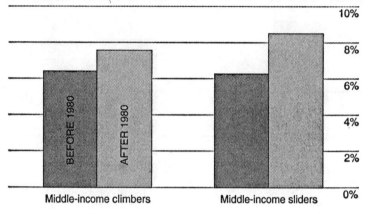

In the 1980s, middle-income people found it easier to achieve wealth and harder to avoid poverty.

Source: Panel Study of Income Dynamics

prime-age men and women who managed to get and maintain large gains in their earning power. At the same time, lower-income households saw a stagnation of real earnings. In other words, the rich got richer and the poor got poorer.

The middle-class decline documented in our study may well continue into the 1990s. The recession of 1990–92 should further retard upward mobility for lower-income adults, while causing many borderline cases to fall into poverty.

The good news is that late 20th-century America has offered abundant opportunity for the upper-middle class. The bad news is that at the same time, it has reduced upward mobility among the working class and produced persistently high poverty rates for families with children. These two opposing forces are draining America's middle class.

NOTES

1. In 1991, the poverty threshold for a family of four was about $13,500.

GOVERNMENT AND THE LEVEL AND DISTRIBUTION OF INCOME

THE LEVEL AND DISTRIBUTION OF INCOME

The most commonly used measure of income, and the one used in this section, is "money income" as defined by the Bureau of the Census. This measure includes all periodic earned and unearned monetary income except capital gains. Money income includes government cash transfers but does not count noncash government transfers, such as medicaid and food stamps, or fringe benefits, such as employer-provided health insurance, and it does not deduct taxes paid.

While wages are earned by individuals, income is typically shared among members of a family or household. Thus, analyses of income typically focus on these groups rather than on individuals. The Census Bureau defines a family as a group of two or more people related by birth, marriage, or adoption who live together. A household is defined as all related family members and all unrelated people living in a given housing unit. A family, a person living alone, or a group of unrelated people living together in a single housing unit each counts as a single household.

To measure the evolution of income over time, adjustments need to be made for the changing cost of living. Estimates of the cost of living are measured in the consumer price index (CPI) published by the Bureau of Labor Statistics. ... [T]he CPI was modified in 1983 to incorporate an improved measure of the cost of shelter for homeowners. The modified price index used below, the CPI-U-X1, incorporates the improved measure of costs on a consistent basis back to 1967. Most analysts believe this index is the more appropriate measure of changes in the cost of living.

Level of Income

Median income adjusted for inflation is used to track the history of typical families and households. The median represents the midpoint of the income distribution; there are as many families (or households) with income above the median as there are with income below.

From Executive Office of the President, Council of Economic Advisers, *Economic Report of the President, Transmitted to the Congress, February 1992* (Government Printing Office, 1992).

Figure 1 traces the evolution of real median family and household income since 1967. *Although the year-to-year changes are sometimes small, median family income grew by a substantial amount, from $28,563 in 1967 to $35,353 in 1990.* This represents an increase of about $6,800 or 23.8 percent. Median household income was $29,943 in 1990, an increase of about $4,200, or 16.4 percent, since 1967. Medians of both family and household income reached all-time highs in 1989.

Effects of the Level of Economic Activity
Fluctuations and trends in aggregate economic activity produce similar fluctuations and trends in median family and household income. Long economic expansions in the 1960s and the 1980s led to strong advances in income. Inflation and three recessions between 1973 and 1982 resulted in fluctuating levels of income.

Figure 1 shows that real median family income rose sharply in 1967–69, was stagnant in the 1969–70 recession, and then rose during the expansion in 1971–73. After falling in 1974–75 in the recession following the first oil crisis, income rose again until 1979. However, the high inflation of the late 1970s and the subsequent back-to-back recessions in 1980 and in 1981–82 brought real wages and income down sharply. Real median family income in 1982 was lower than it was in 1973. From 1982 to 1990, median family income increased by about $3,300, or 10.4 percent. Since 1973, an earlier business cycle peak, median family income has increased by about $2,000, or 5.9 percent.

Similar cyclical patterns occurred for median household income and for black, Hispanic, and white families and households. *These patterns indicate that the most effective and durable way to raise the income of typical families and households has been through sustained, long-term economic growth.*

The Role of Demographics

Substantial income growth between 1967 and 1990 is particularly noteworthy in light of several long-term demographic trends. During this period, average family size fell by 14 percent, and average household size fell by 19 percent. Income growth rates for families and households thus understate the growth rate of income per person. *Between 1967 and 1990, average, or mean, real money income rose by 62 percent per person,* as opposed to 35 percent per family.

Large shifts in the composition of the households have also influenced income growth. Between 1969 and 1989, the proportion of household heads living alone or with unrelated individuals rose from 18.5 percent to 29.1 percent, and the proportion of families with children that have a female householder rose from 11.3 percent to 21.7 percent. In 1990, more than two-thirds of household heads living alone or with unrelated individuals and one-third of female heads of families were under 35 years old. At this age, many workers are still acquiring skills and training and may also have had short job tenure or little overall labor market experience. Female heads of families also often face child care responsibilities that make full-time participation in the labor force difficult. The means-tested transfer system creates incentives for some women to reduce or eliminate work outside the home. For these and other reasons, female-headed families and people living alone or with unrelated individuals have median incomes well below the overall median. One study found that in the absence of

Figure 1
Real Median Income
1990 dollars

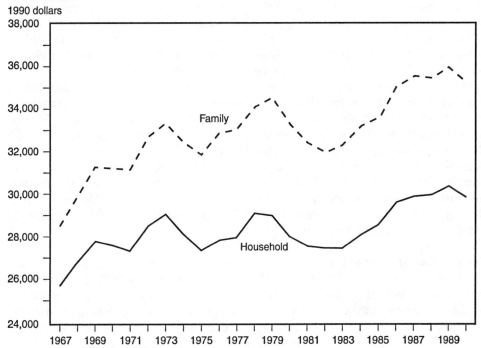

Real median income of families and households has grown substantially since 1967.
Note: CPI-U-X1 used as deflator.
Source: Department of Commerce and Department of Labor.

these demographic trends, real median household income between 1969 and 1989 would have grown another $3,200, more than doubling its actual rate of growth.

Two-Earner Families

A related issue is the extent to which sustained income growth is due to the increased proportion of married women that work outside the home. In 1970, 39 percent of married women worked outside the home. That figure rose to 50 percent in 1980 and 58 percent in 1990. The number of working married women rose more in absolute and percentage terms in the 1970s than in the 1980s.

Determining the effect of this trend on *median* income is difficult. Determining the contribution of new second earners to overall income growth is much more straightforward. Average income for married couple families rose by $4,232 (in 1990 dollars) between 1970 and 1980, and $6,035 between 1980 and 1990. The role of the increased number of second earners can be calculated using data on the number and average income of married couple families and second earners. *The increased number of married women in the labor force accounts for only about 18 percent of the real increase in income of married couple families between 1980 and 1990. The corresponding figure for the 1970s is 19* percent. For all families, about 14 percent of the increase in income in the 1980s and 16 percent in the 1970s is due to the increase in two-earner families.

The small role of the rising number of two-earner families in income growth can be attributed to two factors. First, average earnings of second earners are lower than average earnings for all earners, in part because a high proportion of second earners work part-time. Second, the recent *increase* in two-earner families is small relative to the total number of families. From 1980 to 1990, the number of married women in the labor force rose by 5.5 million; the total number of families in 1990 was 66.3 million.

Distribution of Annual Income

The long-term and cyclical factors that affect income levels also affect the distribution of income. Incomes in any year can differ across households for many reasons. Because the primary source of income for most people is labor earnings, the determinants of the wage distribution..., including workers' education and changes in labor supply and demand, also help determine the distribution of annual income. Because families and households in the United States experience a significant amount of mobility across income classes, the distribution of *long-term* income differs from the distribution of annual income.

The distribution of income and its evolution over time can be measured in several ways. Perhaps the simplest approach is to choose particular income thresholds and examine what percentage of families exceed these thresholds. Although there is no official definition of the middle class, the range of $15,000 to $50,000 (in 1990 dollars) in money

income is used in Figure 2 to demarcate middle-income families. The chart shows the often-noted declining proportion of families in the middle-income range. The proportion of families with middle incomes fell from 64.8 percent in 1967 to 52.7 percent in 1990.

Many middle-income families have moved into higher income categories; the proportion of families with real income above $50,000 showed a sustained increase, from 14.9 percent in 1967 to an all-time high of 31.6 percent in 1989, before it declined slightly in 1990. The proportion of families with real money income below $15,000 fell from 20.3 percent in 1967 to 16.9 percent in 1990.

Using alternative definitions of middle income (for example, $25,000 to $75,000, or $25,000 to $50,000) preserves the basic results that the proportion of high-income families has increased and the proportion of low-income families has fallen. Similar patterns hold for households as well. *These trends indicate that substantial numbers of families and households have moved into higher income categories over time.*

Income Growth by Quintile

Figure 3 displays mean, or average, money income for the highest, middle, and lowest fifth, or quintile, for households from 1967 to 1990, as a percentage of 1967 income. (The major points below also hold for families.) *Average money income in each quintile has increased since 1967.* Thus, long-term trends have raised money income in each part of the income distribution.

Changes in average money income in every quintile reflect changes in the level of macroeconomic activity, just as the measures of median income did. The real money incomes of households along

Figure 2

Distribution of Families by Income Class

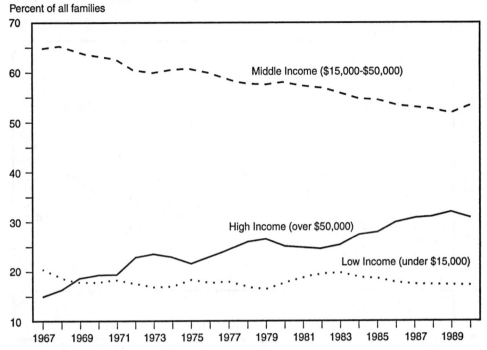

Percent of all families

The proportion of high-income families has more than doubled since 1967, while the proportion of low- and middle-income families has fallen.

Note: All income is in 1990 dollars; CPI-U-X1 used as deflator.

Source: Department of Commerce and Department of Labor.

all parts of the income distribution have improved the most during periods of economic growth. In particular, *the economic expansion between 1982 and 1989 produced strong growth in each quintile.*

Money income grew faster in the highest quintile than in the other quintiles. From 1967 to 1990, real money income grew by 35 percent in the highest quintile, 25 percent in the lowest quintile, and 17 percent in the middle quintile. The relative magnitudes of growth rates for the highest and lowest quintiles shifted between 1979 and 1982. This shift coincided with a shift in real wage patterns: wages for high-wage workers

were roughly the same level in 1979 and 1982, while wages for low-wage workers fell.

Figure 3 understates the improvement in income for the lowest group because, among other reasons, money income omits noncash transfers. Real Federal and State spending on means-tested medical assistance, the vast majority of which is medicaid, grew by $67 billion (in 1990 dollars) from 1967 to 1990, while spending on other means-tested noncash transfers grew by $46 billion. Real payments for medicare, which is not means-tested, grew by $96 billion. In 1990, households in the lowest

Figure 3

Real Household Income Relative to 1967 Income for Selected Quintiles

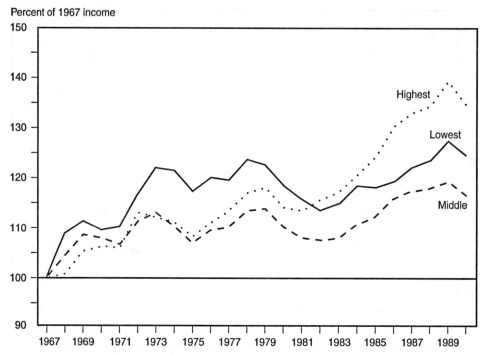

Real income of low-, middle-, and high-income households generally rose from 1967 to 1979, fell from 1979 to 1982, and rose after 1982.
Note: CPI-U-X1 used as deflator.

Source: Department of Commerce and Department of Labor.

income quintile received about 10 percent of medicare payments, 17 percent of medicaid payments, and 59 percent of other means-tested noncash transfers. Maintaining these allocations over time and using the Census Bureau's best estimates of the value of these transfers to recipients provides estimates of noncash transfers per household. *For households in the lowest quintile, money income plus the estimated value of noncash transfers, adjusted for inflation, increased by 48 percent between 1967 and 1990, nearly double the 25-percent growth rate for money income alone....*

The Distribution of Long-Term Income and Wealth

Families and households display a substantial amount of mobility across income classes in the United States. For this reason, *analyses of income distribution that focus only on annual income tend to overstate the degree of income inequality.*

One reason annual income data are misleading is that earnings of individual workers tend to rise as they acquire training and experience and then to fall when they retire. A 20-year-old worker just starting out and a 45-year-old worker who is in his or her peak earning years could have equal incomes over their careers, but very different wages in the same calendar year.

Data on annual income can also prove misleading because of transitory income, that is, income gains or losses that are thought to be temporary. A person who owns a small business, for example, may face greater year-to-year fluctuations in income than someone who works at a steady wage.

There is substantial mobility across income classes from year to year. One study found that in the mid-1980s, *about one-third of all families were in a different income quintile than they had been in the previous year.* In each of the lowest quintiles, about 18 percent of the families moved to a higher quintile the following year. In each of the highest three quintiles, more than 20 percent of the families moved to lower quintiles the following year. Another study found that more than half of families in the highest quintile in 1971 had fallen into lower quintiles by 1978. Similarly, almost half of those in the lowest quintile had risen to a higher quintile.

Over longer periods, the extent of mobility increases. One study, using data from the 1970s and 1980s, found that *more than 75 percent of households are in a different decile when ranked by lifetime income than when ranked by current income.* A decile includes one-tenth of the households. About 44 percent had current income two or more deciles away from their lifetime income. More than half of households in each of the lowest three deciles for annual income had lifetime income in a higher decile. More than half of households in the top three deciles for annual income had lifetime income in a lower decile....

These findings underscore the importance of income mobility for a large number of families. Nevertheless, even after removing temporary income changes and the effects of the life-cycle on income, part of the population still faces very low long-term income prospects.

Because the distribution of long-term income is less dispersed than are annual incomes, trends in the distribution of annual income may not accurately reflect trends in the distribution of long-term income. For example, an increase in income mobility or in the importance of transitory income can increase inequality of annual income but have no effect on the distribution of long-term income. Nevertheless, one study found that, like annual incomes, incomes averaged over 4- and 7-year periods became more dispersed between 1967–73 and 1979–85.

A related issue is the distribution of wealth. A family's wealth holdings consist of financial assets, such as saving accounts; property, such as a house or family business; pensions and future Social Security benefits; and human capital, the value of future labor earnings. For most households, housing, public and private pensions, and human capital constitute the vast bulk of wealth. One study found that between 1983 and 1989 the median value of households' real financial net worth and property rose 11 percent and that holdings of these assets became more concentrated.

Summary

- Median levels of family and household money income have shown sustained long-term growth since the mid-1960s. Median income is influenced by cyclical and long-term economic activity and demographic patterns.
- Since the mid-1960s and in particular since the early 1980s, income growth

has occurred in all quintiles and the distribution of annual money income has become more dispersed in the United States. Earnings distributions have also become more dispersed in several other countries in recent years.

- Because money income omits in-kind transfers, data on money income understate both the level of and improvement in income for the lowest income groups.

- Families and households display significant mobility across income classes. The distribution of long-term income is more equal than the distribution of annual income.

POSTSCRIPT

Does the United States Have an Income Distribution Problem?

Duncan, Smeeding, and Rodgers evaluate the income of prime-age adults, persons ranging in age from 25 to 55 years. Using data from the Survey Research Center at the University of Michigan over the 1968–86 period, they define the middle class in two ways: unadjusted—the lower and upper limits of middle class are set at after-tax household incomes of $18,500 and $55,000, respectively, in 1987 dollars; and adjusted—ratios of household incomes to the poverty thresholds between two and six. Both definitions of the middle class yield similar results for Duncan et al.: the share of prime-age adults who were middle class in 1986 was lower than the share of prime-age adults who were middle class in 1978. This finding indicates an income distribution problem to the authors, who state that "the biggest single factor behind the withering of the middle class is the growing inequality in the distribution of men's earnings."

Bush's Council of Economic Advisers (BCEA) examines the distribution of annual income to make several points. First, if the middle class is defined as incomes between $15,000 to $50,000 in 1990 dollars, then the percentage of families in the middle class fell from 64.8 percent in 1968 to 52.7 percent in 1990. However, the proportion of families with incomes above $50,000 increased while the proportion of families with incomes less than $15,000 fell. Second, when income distribution is assessed by quintiles, the BCEA finds that the real money incomes grew strongly in each quintile. In particular, for households in the lowest quintile, real household income adjusted for the estimated value of noncash transfers increased by 48 percent between 1967 and 1990. As for the distribution of long-term income and wealth, the BCEA finds that there is a substantial amount of mobility between income classes and, therefore, annual-income data overstate the degree of income inequality.

Articles that support the position reported by Duncan et al. include "The Disappearance of the Middle Class," by Lester Thurow, *The New York Times* (February 2, 1984), and "Untouched by the Rising Tide," by David M. Cutter and Lawrence F. Katz, *The Brookings Review* (Winter 1992). Also see *Dollars and Dreams: The Changing American Income Distribution* by Frank Levy (Basic Books, 1987). For views consistent with the position taken by the BCEA, see "Decade of Greed?" by Ed Rubenstein, *National Review* (December 31, 1990); "The Middle Class Boom of the 1980s," by Alan Reynolds, *The Wall Street Journal* (March 12, 1992); and "The 'Fortunate Fifth' Fallacy" by Richard McKenzie, *The Wall Street Journal* (January 28, 1992).

ISSUE 15

Can We End Welfare as We Know It?

YES: Donna E. Shalala, from Statement Before the Committee on Education and Labor, U.S. House of Representatives (August 2, 1994)

NO: Robert Rector, from "How Clinton's Bill Extends Welfare As We Know It," *Issue Bulletin* (August 1, 1994)

ISSUE SUMMARY

YES: Donna E. Shalala, secretary of health and human services, argues that the welfare system in the United States is a major problem that requires dramatic changes. She maintains that the Clinton welfare reform proposal is a "bold, balanced plan that will really make a difference."

NO: Robert Rector, senior policy analyst with the Heritage Foundation, finds little true reform in the Clinton welfare reform proposal, and he argues that there is not much hope of curtailing the expanding welfare system.

Given American society's traditional commitment to a market system and its fundamental belief in self-determination, Americans are generally uncomfortable enacting social welfare legislation that appears to give someone "something for nothing," even if that individual is clearly in need. Thus, when we trace the roots of the existing U.S. social welfare system back to its origins in the New Deal legislation of President Franklin D. Roosevelt during the Great Depression of the 1930s, we see that many of the earliest programs linked jobs to public assistance. One exception was Aid to Families with Dependent Children (AFDC), which was established as part of the 1935 Social Security Act. This program provides money to families in which there are children but no breadwinner. In 1935, and for many years thereafter, this program was not particularly controversial. Two reasons explain this acceptance of AFDC: the number of beneficiaries was relatively small, and the popular image of an AFDC family was that of a white woman with several young children whose husband had died as the result of an illness or an industrial accident.

In the early 1960s, as the U.S. economy prospered, poverty—and what to do about it—captured the attention of the nation. The Kennedy and Johnson administrations focused their social welfare programs on poor individuals: a minority of the population, especially—but not exclusively—a black minority, left behind as the general economy reached record levels of income and employment. Their policies were designed to address the needs of those who were trapped in "pockets of poverty," a description popularized in the early 1960s in the writings of Michael Harrington (1929–1989), a political theorist and prominent socialist. Between 1964 and 1969 the number of AFDC recipients increased by more than 60 percent and the costs of the program more than doubled. The number of AFDC families continued to grow throughout the 1970s and the 1980s, and the program became increasingly controversial.

The controversy grew for several reasons: the increase in the number of recipients, the increase in costs, and a change in perceptions. A welfare mother was now perceived as a woman in a big-city public housing project whose children had been deserted by their father, or as an unmarried woman who bore more children only to get more financial assistance through welfare. By the late 1980s and early 1990s, AFDC had become one of the most controversial social welfare programs.

In the 1980s social critics began to attack AFDC. One prominent voice was that of Charles Murray. He charged AFDC with encouraging welfare dependency, teenage pregnancies, the dissolution of the traditional family, and an erosion of the basic American work ethic. Such criticisms set the stage for the first major reforms in AFDC in 25 years. In 1988 the Family Support Act was passed. The intent of this legislation was to develop state-run programs that would help individuals who receive welfare assistance to break away from their dependency on the benefits through work, training, and education. Fundamental change, however, did not follow.

Welfare reform became a prominent issue in the 1992 presidential campaign. During this campaign, candidate Bill Clinton promised, if elected, to "end welfare as we know it." Even though the broad outline of welfare reform was known during the first two years of the Clinton presidency, actual legislation was not sent to Congress until the summer of 1994. President Clinton's welfare reform program is officially entitled the Work and Responsibility Act of 1994. The issue is: will the changes in the welfare system, as proposed in this piece of legislation, end welfare as we know it?

YES

Donna E. Shalala

STATEMENT OF DONNA E. SHALALA

Welfare as we know it has become a national tragedy. More than 14 million Americans depend on monthly AFDC [Aid to Families with Dependent Children] checks that now cost taxpayers more than $22 billion dollars each year. In the last five years alone, well over 3 million recipients have been added to the AFDC rolls. Almost 30 percent of all births are to unmarried mothers. And nearly one in four children currently lives in poverty. Too many children grow up in households where none of the adults are working.

President Clinton, and many of us—both inside and outside of his Administration—have worked long and hard to put together this legislation [to reform welfare]. And we are proud of the result.

The Work and Responsibility Act of 1994 will fundamentally change this country's approach to helping parents move from dependence to independence. And, equally important, it will improve the quality of life for millions of young children. America's children—increasingly our poorest citizens—deserve a chance to grow up to opportunity, not poverty and hopelessness.

If there is one thing that stands out the most from our nationwide hearings on this issue, it is that our current system doesn't work and that nobody likes it—least of all the people who depend most on it for help—welfare recipients themselves. So as Congress debates this issue, we know it won't be about whether or not we need welfare reform—we all agree on that. The question is how best to go about it. . . .

This issue has become even more urgent in light of some disturbing trends: more and more children today are born to teenage mothers and outside of marriage. Almost half of all single mothers receiving AFDC—about 42 percent—are or have been teenage mothers.

The welfare system will continue to be part of the problem rather than part of the solution unless dramatic changes are made. We believe we have put on the table a bold, balanced plan that will really make a difference.

Under our plan, by the year 2000, almost one million people will either be working or completely off welfare. Even using conservative assumptions, our projections show that more than 330,000 adults who would otherwise have been on welfare will have left the rolls by that time. About 222,000 adults

From U.S. House of Representatives. Committee on Education and Labor. Hearing, August 2, 1994. Washington, DC: Government Printing Office, 1994.

will be working part-time in unsubsidized jobs. And 394,000 adults will be in subsidized jobs in the WORK Program—up from 15,000 in work experience programs now. In addition, another 873,000 recipients in the year 2000 will be in time-limited education or training programs leading to employment. And by that time, federal child support collections will have more than doubled, from $9 billion to $20 billion.

Let me add that we hope to proceed on welfare reform in a bipartisan manner. In fact, there are many similarities between our bill and the major initiatives introduced in the House and the Senate. Several congressional proposals share the President's vision for reform, making public assistance a transitional program leading to mandatory work. They provide funding for education, training, child care, and job creation. And all the major proposals recognize that it will require an investment of time and money to move young mothers toward self-sufficiency.

Our welfare reform strategy has three overarching principles: work, responsibility, and reaching the next generation.

WORK

Under the President's welfare reform plan, welfare will be about a paycheck, not a welfare check. To reinforce and reward work, our approach is based on a simple compact. Support, job training, and child care will be provided to help people move from dependence to independence. But time limits will ensure that anyone who can work, must work —in an unsubsidized job if possible, in a temporary, subsidized job if necessary. These reforms will make welfare a transitional system leading to work.

As a crucial ingredient of reform, support will be provided to help people keep jobs once they get them. Tax credits, health care and child care will make it possible for everyone who works to be better off than they were on welfare, and for even workers in entry-level jobs to support their families.

The key to ensuring the success of this transition from welfare to work is expanding on the success of the Job Opportunities and Basic Skills or JOBS program, the cornerstone of the Family Support Act of 1988 (FSA).

FSA paved the way for our reforms by introducing the expectation that welfare should be a period of preparation for self-sufficiency, and by recognizing the need for investment in education, training, and employment services for welfare recipients.

However, the JOBS training program created by the FSA did not change the welfare system as much as was intended. Because of its broad exemption policy and relatively low participation rates, only a small portion of the AFDC caseload is actually required to participate in the JOBS program. Only 17 percent of mandatory participants engaged in work or training activities in fiscal year 1993....

The FSA has worked best where states have used it to change the culture of the welfare office to one focusing on moving people quickly toward work and independence. The Riverside County GAIN program, for example, has significantly increased recipients' hours of work and earnings. Successful JOBS programs also build effective partnerships with local employment services, other employment and training programs, schools, business communities, and labor organizations. For example, in Kenosha County, Wisconsin, the welfare agency relies upon the Kenosha County Job Center to serve its JOBS participants. This Center coordinates all employment and training activities in the community. It also houses both the income maintenance and JOBS services of the welfare agency. Through the Center, services of 15 public and private agencies are collocated and integrated. As a result, the JOBS program in Kenosha has succeeded in achieving very high participation levels (85 percent of participants receive services) and high job placement rates (60 percent above the State average). In successful programs, however, one agency retains clear accountability for ensuring that recipients participate and that they receive services.

The President's Work and Responsibility Act seeks to build on this by creating a new transitional assistance program that includes four key elements: a personal employability plan; training, education and placement assistance to move people from welfare to work; a two-year time limit; and work requirements. We also propose a significant narrowing of the participation exemptions contained in current law.

Making Welfare a Transition to Work: Building on the JOBS Program

Our philosophy is simple and fair: all parents who receive cash support must do something to help themselves. The JOBS program will be the centerpiece of the public assistance system.

From day one, the new system will focus on making young mothers self-sufficient. Each applicant will sign an agreement to move quickly toward independence in return for assistance. Working with a caseworker, each recipient will develop an employability plan—a work and training agreement—designed to move that person into an unsubsidized job as quickly as possible. Participants who are job-ready will immediately be engaged in job search and anyone offered a job will be required to take it. We expect that many recipients will be working well before they hit the two-year time limit.

Several mechanisms will integrate the JOBS program with other education and training programs to expand access to the system and reduce the administrative burden on states. The JOBS program will be part of any one-stop career centers that states operate. Our plan also will ensure that even those unable to participate in education, training or work still meet certain expectations.

It is important to note that our proposal defers only people with disabilities or those who need to care for disabled children; mothers with infants under one year old; and certain people living in remote areas. AFDC mothers who have additional children while on assistance will be deferred for only 12 weeks after the child's birth.

In contrast, current law allows much broader exemptions for women with any child under three, young mothers under 16, and women in their second trimester of pregnancy.

By the year 2000, these changes will move us from a situation in which almost three quarters (73 percent) of the target group are neither working nor expected to participate in training, to one in which more than three quarters (77 percent) of the phased-in group are either off welfare, working, or in a mandatory time-limited placement and training program.

In short, JOBS participation will be greatly expanded through increased participation rates, and JOBS participants will participate in more work experience, education, and training programs.

To achieve this, we have given states and localities flexibility in designing the exact mix of JOBS program services. Employability plans may be adjusted as a family's situation changes. But parents who refuse to stay in school, or look for work or attend job training programs will be sanctioned, generally by losing their share of the AFDC grant.

In addition, the Federal cap on JOBS spending will be increased from $1 billion to $1.75 billion in fiscal year 1996. Over the five-year period between 1996 and the year 2000, we will increase JOBS spending by $2.8 billion—a 56 percent increase over current spending. The capped entitlement for JOBS will rise further if the national unemployment rate reaches 7 percent or higher....

As you know, President Clinton was the first to propose national time limits on welfare benefits. The cumulative two-year time limit on benefits will give both recipients and caseworkers a framework for fulfilling the objectives of the employability plan and, ultimately, finding a job. We believe that only with time limits will recipients and caseworkers know without a doubt that welfare has changed forever. And only then will the focus really be on work and independence.

States will, however, be permitted to grant a limited number of extensions for completion of education or training programs, or for those who are learning-disabled, illiterate, or facing other serious obstacles to employment. And in order to encourage states to meet their responsibilities, we require them to grant extensions to persons who have reached the time limit but who have not been provided employment-related services specified in their employability plan. Extensions in all of these categories will be limited to 10 percent.

The WORK Program: Work Not Welfare After Two Years

If the time limit is reached, welfare ends and people are expected to work. We recognize that some recipients will reach the end of the two-year limit without having found jobs, despite their best efforts—and we are committed to providing them with the opportunity to support their families if they are willing to work. Each state will be required to operate a WORK program that makes paid work assignments available to recipients who have reached the time limit for cash assistance.

The WORK program is different from "workfare" (or CWEP) programs. It has a strong private sector focus. It is designed to help people move into, rather than serve as a substitute for, unsubsidized employment. Workers will receive paychecks based on the hours they actually work. They will not be guaranteed welfare checks and sent out to work sites. Those who do not show up for work will not get paid. This is a straight-forward and radical end to the status quo.

To move people into unsubsidized private sector jobs as quickly as possible, participants will be required to perform an extensive job search before entering the WORK program, and after each WORK assignment. No single WORK assignment will last more than 12 months and participants will typically be paid the minimum wage. States will be allowed to pursue any of a wide range of strategies to provide work for those who have reached the two-year limit, including subsidized private-sector jobs, public-sector positions, contracts with for-profit placement firms, agreements with non-profit agencies, and microenterprise and self-employment efforts. WORK participants will not displace any currently employed workers, nor be placed in a vacancy created by a layoff, strike or lockout.

To create a further incentive to find unsubsidized jobs, participants in subsidized WORK positions will not receive the Earned Income Tax Credit [EITC]. This ensures that any unsubsidized job will pay more than a subsidized work assignment. Anyone who turns down a private sector job will be removed from the rolls, as will people who refuse to make good faith efforts to obtain available jobs....

Supporting Working Families: The EITC, Health Care Reform, and Child Care

We recognize that a fundamental flaw in the current welfare system is that it does little to encourage work. Those who work often lose benefits dollar for dollar, face burdensome reporting requirements, and cannot save for the future because of asset limitations.

Moving people from welfare to work also means making work pay in this country—ending the perverse incentives that lead countless people to opt for welfare over work, even though they want to enter the workforce.

Today, 70 percent of those on welfare leave the system within 2 years—but the vast majority of them return, often because the low paying jobs they get do not come with essential benefits such as health care and child care. We need to concentrate on two key goals: moving people off welfare and helping them stay off.

To "make work pay," this Administration has focused on three critical components—providing tax credits for the working poor, ensuring access to health insurance, and making safe child care available....

As you know, Mr. Chairman, Congress has already passed the first crucial element of welfare reform by expanding the EITC [Earned Income Tax Credit], a key initiative of the Clinton Administration. The EITC is effectively a pay raise for the working poor. It will ensure that in 1996, a full-time job, with the help of food stamps, would keep a family with two children out of poverty.

We believe that low-income individuals could benefit from receiving the EITC throughout the year, instead of in a lump-sum payment at the end of the year. Our proposal will allow up to four states to conduct demonstrations promoting the use of the advance EITC payment option by shifting the outreach and administrative burden from employers to selected public agencies....

Some studies suggest that 7 to 15 percent of the current welfare caseload —at least one million adults and children —are on welfare to qualify for Medicaid. And a 1994 Urban Institute study found that over a 20-month period, only 8 percent of those who were on AFDC and went to work were able to find a job with health insurance.

We believe that people should not have to choose welfare over work just to get health coverage for their families. And when Congress passes health care reform, our hope is that this perverse incentive to stay on welfare will end.

The third ingredient in our strategy to make work pay is affordable, accessible, high quality child care for families on cash assistance and the working poor. As members of the Committee know from your years of leadership on child care issues, parents must have dependable child care in order to work or to prepare themselves for work. In addition to the Administration's requested increase in Child Care and Development Block Grant funding, our welfare reform proposal would significantly expand child care spending. People on welfare will continue to receive child care assistance while working or in education or training. We continue to guarantee one year of transitional child care for those who leave welfare for work, and will extend child care assistance to those participating in the new WORK program. Our proposal also will significantly expand the At-Risk Child Care program for the working poor from $300 million per year now to over $1 billion by the year 2000....

Together, these elements will help ensure that the millions of recipients who leave welfare within two years will not fall back into the system. And it will be clear that work and responsibility are at the core of our values and the heart of our policies.

RESPONSIBILITY

The second pillar of our plan is responsibility: the responsibility of parents for their children; the responsibility of the system to deliver performance, not process; and the responsibility of the government to provide accountability for taxpayers.

Parental Responsibility

We believe that mothers and fathers must be held responsible for the support of their children. Men and women must understand that parenthood brings serious obligations and that these obligations will be enforced.

While many improvements have been made to the current system, it still fails to ensure that children receive adequate support from both parents. The potential for child support collections is approximately $48 billion per year. Yet only $14 billion is actually paid, leading to an estimated collection gap of about $34 billion. We are proposing the toughest child support system ever to make sure fathers pay their child support. It is simply not acceptable for non-custodial parents to walk away from the children they helped bring into this world.

Establishing awards in every case is the first step toward ensuring that children receive financial support from non-custodial parents. Paternity must be established for every out-of-wedlock birth, regardless of welfare status. Our proposal would greatly expand outreach and public education programs that encourage voluntary paternity establishment, and build on existing hospital-based programs. The genetic testing process will be further streamlined for cases where paternity is contested.

In addition, mothers who apply for AFDC benefits must cooperate fully with paternity establishment procedures *prior* to receiving benefits. Except in rare circumstances in which paternity establishment is inappropriate, parents who refuse to cooperate will be sanctioned, generally by losing their share of AFDC benefits. We are proposing to systematically apply a new, stricter definition of cooperation in every AFDC case.

The child support agency—which has the most expertise and most at stake —will administer this new cooperation requirement within each state. When mothers have fully cooperated, the state must establish paternity and will be given one year to do so or risk losing a portion of its Federal match for AFDC benefits. Performance-based incentives will encourage states to improve their paternity establishment rates for all out-of-wedlock births, regardless of welfare status.

Fair awards also are crucial to getting support to children who need it. Periodic updating of awards will be required for both AFDC and non-AFDC cases, so that awards accurately reflect the parents' current income. In addition, a National Guidelines Commission will be established to assess the desirability of uniform national child support guidelines or national parameters for state guidelines.

Many enforcement tools will allow states to collect support more effectively. The state-based child support enforcement system will continue, but with changes to move it toward a more uniform, centralized, and service-oriented program. All states will maintain central registries and centralized collection and disbursement capabilities. The registry will maintain current records of all support orders and operate in conjunction with a centralized payment center for the collection and distribution of child support payments.

Centralized collection also will vastly simplify withholding for employers since they will have to send payments only to one source. In addition, this change will ensure accurate accounting and monitoring of payments.

The federal role will be expanded to ensure more efficient location of the noncustodial parent and enforcement of orders, particularly in interstate cases. In order to coordinate activity at the federal level and to track delinquent parents across state lines, a National Clearinghouse will be established. This Clearinghouse will consist of an expanded Federal Parent Locator Service, the National Child Support Registry, and the National Directory of New Hires. A stronger federal role in interstate enforcement will make interstate procedures more uniform throughout the country.

Enforcement measures will include revocation of professional, occupational and drivers' licenses to make delinquent parents pay child support; expanded wage withholding; improved use of income and asset information; expanded use of credit reporting; and authority to use the same wage garnishment procedures for federal and non-federal employees.

Our proposal also recognizes the problem absent parents sometimes face in getting work and their genuine desire to help support their children. We propose allowing states to allocate up to 10 percent of their JOBS and WORK funds for programs for non-custodial parents. States also will be allowed to require non-custodial parents with delinquent child support payments to work off what they owe....

Performance: Not Process
The Administration's plan demands greater responsibility from the welfare office itself. Unfortunately, the current system too often focuses on documenting eligibility and sending out welfare checks. Instead, the welfare office must become a place that is about helping people find work and earn paychecks as quickly as possible. Our plan offers several provisions designed to help agencies reduce paperwork and focus on results.

The legislation would allow the phase in of an outcome based system with funding incentives and penalties directly linked to the performance of states and caseworkers in service provision, job placement, and child support collection. In order to better coordinate and simplify program administration, we have also proposed several changes in program rules designed to simplify and standardize disparate Food Stamp and AFDC policy rules.

Accountability for Taxpayers

To eliminate fraud and ensure that every dollar is used productively, welfare reform will coordinate programs, automate files, and monitor recipients. We propose several new fraud control measures. States will be required to verify the income, identity, alien status, and Social Security numbers of new applicants. A national public assistance clearinghouse will follow individuals whenever and wherever they use welfare, monitoring compliance with time limits and work. A national "new hire" registry will monitor earnings to check AFDC eligibility and identify non-custodial parents who switch jobs or cross state lines to avoid paying child support. Anyone who refuses to follow the rules will face tough new sanctions, and anyone who turns down a job offer will be dropped from the rolls.

REACHING THE NEXT GENERATION

It is absolutely critical that our reforms send a strong message to the next generation. All young people must understand the importance of staying in school, living at home, preparing to work, and building a real future. And they must realize that having a child is an immense responsibility—not an easy route to independence.

Preventing Teen Pregnancy

We recognize that welfare dependency could be significantly reduced if more young people delayed childbearing until both parents were ready and able to assume the responsibility of raising children. And we are committed to doing everything we can to prevent teenage pregnancy in the first place.

I don't have to tell you how big a challenge that is. And it would be naive to suggest that government can do it alone. We are well aware that reducing the incidence of unmarried teen pregnancy will require the involvement of every sector of our society.

The link between unmarried teen births and poverty is clear: According to an Annie E. Casey Foundation study, approximately 80 percent of the children born to teen parents who dropped out of high school and did not marry are poor. In contrast, only 8 percent of children born to married high school graduates aged 20 or older are poor.

We are proposing a number of measures, including a national campaign against teen pregnancy designed to send a clear and unambiguous message to young people about delayed sexual activity and responsible parenting....

Phasing in Young People First

We have chosen to phase in the plan [to reduce teen pregnancy] by starting with young people: those born after 1971. We chose this strategy not because young single mothers are easiest to serve, but because they are so important to our future.

The younger generation of welfare recipients is our greatest concern. Younger recipients are likely to have the longest stays on welfare. They also are the group for which there is the greatest hope of making a profound difference. We strongly believe that the best way to end welfare as we know it is to reach the next generation; to devote energy and new resources to young people first, rather than spreading our efforts so thinly that little real help is provided to anyone.

This proposal represents a radical change in how we think about and administer welfare. But to get it right requires a solid and well-planned implementation strategy. Even if resources were plentiful, the lessons we learned from the Family Support Act, as well as from our site visits and discussions with state administrators, have convinced us that attempting to implement a time-limited transitional assistance program for the entire caseload at once would create enormous difficulties. We believe these difficulties could be avoided and the changes we envision successfully implemented by adopting this phase-in strategy.

Moreover, recent evidence from several programs serving teen mothers suggests that this population needs special attention and can be reached. By phasing in the plan with the youngest recipients first, we send a strong message of responsibility and opportunity to the next generation....

A Clear Message for Teen Parents
The proposal includes several incentives for young parents designed to promote responsible behavior. Minor parents will be required to live in their parents' households unless that environment is unsafe. Minor parents are still children themselves and they ought to live with adults who can offer supervision and guidance. The welfare system should not encourage young people who have babies to leave home, set up separate households and receive separate checks. In cases where there is a problem such as danger of abuse, states will be encouraged to find a responsible adult with whom the teen parent can live....

In the end, Mr. Chairman, this is not about dollars and data. It is about values. For too long, the welfare system has been sending all the wrong messages. The Work and Responsibility Act is designed to get the values straight. It translates our values about work, responsibility, family and opportunity into a framework for action. It places new expectations and responsibilities on recipients, and on federal and state governments alike.

That is the message that Congress started to send with the Family Support Act. It is time to fully realize that vision, and to build a bold new future based on the core values we all share.

We believe that this issue is critical—that welfare reform is about nothing less than our vision of what kind of country we are and want to be. Do we want to be a country that encourages work over dependency? Do we want to be a country that expects our young people to act responsibly? Do we want to be a country that rewards hard work and fair play and accepts nothing less? Do we want to be a country that helps provide a brighter future for our children?

The Work and Responsibility Act of 1994 answers those questions with a resounding YES. We believe this bill will truly strengthen America's families and communities.

NO

Robert Rector

HOW CLINTON'S BILL EXTENDS WELFARE AS WE KNOW IT

INTRODUCTION

Americans are alarmed by the growth and effects of welfare. They correctly perceive the current system to be an extraordinarily expensive debacle which destroys the lives of those it is intended to help. And by promoting illegitimacy and undermining the family, they see welfare as threatening the foundation of society.

Campaigning for President, Bill Clinton acknowledged that the War on Poverty had failed. He promised to "end welfare." Now, more than two years later, President Clinton has unveiled the details of his "end" to welfare. But far from reform, the President's plan, called the Work and Responsibility Act of 1994, is simply a public relations facade intended to forestall real criticism and change. When the masquerade of "reform" is removed, the plan represents little more than a continuing rapid expansion of the current destructive system.

The cosmetic nature of the Clinton plan should not come as a surprise. Periodic sham reform has become the lifeblood of the welfare system. With each such reform the system grows larger and more expensive. Just a few years ago, Congress declared it had "ended welfare" with the Family Support Act of 1988. This act was touted in the press as a dramatic change in the foundations of the welfare state. In describing the 1988 act, Senator Daniel Patrick Moynihan (D-NY), its chief sponsor, declared:

> We're going to turn the welfare program upside down. We're going to take a payments program with a minor emphasis on jobs, and create a jobs program in which the income supplement is assumed to be temporary.[1]

The next day he added:

> This is the first time ever we're going to take a [income] maintenance program with a slight work component and turn it around to be a job program with income supplements until you're on your own.[2]

And later he declared:

> For the first time in [welfare's] half-century existence, the U.S. Senate has moved to an entire redefinition and overhaul of what we've come to know as our welfare system ... [under the revised system] welfare will no longer be a permanent or extended condition.[3]

For good measure, Senator Howard Metzenbaum (D-OH) declared, "[t]his bill makes a dramatic step forward to encourage the stability of the family."[4]

At the time, conservatives said the act was a resounding lie, in that it did none of these things. They were right. The 1988 legislation did nothing to overhaul the welfare system. It did not introduce real work requirements: today, seven years after its passage, less than one percent of adult AFDC recipients are required to work. It did not curb growth of welfare spending: welfare rolls and costs have exploded at near-record rates. And it did not help to stabilize the low-income family: illegitimacy has soared.[5]

Nor was the welfare system starved for funds after 1988. In fact, aggregate welfare spending has increased at a near-record rate of 10 percent per year in the last five years. In the same period, Congress deliberately expanded eligibility for programs such as Medicaid. Few funds were provided for workfare, however, because the liberal Congress is privately opposed to it.

Carbon Copy. Clinton's present welfare plan is a carbon copy of the welfare reform fraud of 1988. The rhetoric and description of Clinton's proposal is virtually indistinguishable from the earlier "historic" legislation. As with the 1988 act, Clinton's proposal does not reform welfare but merely creates the appearance of reform, blunting public disaffection with welfare while permitting the continuous rapid expansion of the current system.

Deception is the core of Clinton's plan. The President claims his bill ends welfare after two years. It does not. It does not even require a significant number of recipients who have been on welfare for over two years to participate in government make-work jobs in exchange for future benefits....

While the bill's time limits and work requirements are a sham, even worse it does nothing about the two most important welfare reform issues: **exploding welfare costs** and **the crisis of illegitimacy.** Last year, federal and state governments spent over $320 billion on welfare; by 1998 welfare costs will rise to over $500 billion, costing on average nearly $5,000 for each taxpaying household. And today nearly one in three American children are born out of wedlock; President Clinton himself has warned the illegitimate birth rate will soon rise to fifty percent.

Yet the Clinton "reform" will do nothing to deal with mushrooming welfare costs or the soaring illegitimate birth rate. In fact, on both issues the Clinton plan will make the situation worse.

Why does the reality of the Clinton plan depart so much from the rhetoric surrounding it? No doubt in large part it is because many top officials in the Administration and Congress have long opposed work requirements. It is also because the professional social welfare organizations, which are so influential within the Administration and on Capitol Hill, want more spending on the services they provide rather than real reductions in the welfare caseload.

But if Congress really is to "end welfare as we know it," and thereby improve the lives of those in the system as well as reducing the burden on taxpayers, it must focus clearly on several key goals. Lawmakers must change the incentives in the current welfare system that encourage illegitimacy rather than curbing it. They must channel money now going directly to unwed mothers instead to other ways to improve the lives of affected children. Lawmakers must place a real cap in the growth of welfare spending. And they must introduce genuine work requirements, focusing on those recipients who are most employable—such as able-bodied males —not on single mothers with young children. Legislation to do these things has been introduced (S. 2134, H.R. 4566) by Senator Lauch Faircloth (R-NC) and Representative Jim Talent (R-MO), but is opposed by the White House.

The American people—the poor on welfare as well as the taxpayers who support them—have been promised an end to welfare many times before by congressional leaders and by Presidents. Each time the rhetoric was persuasive, and each time the result was more spending, more people on welfare, and higher rates of illegitimacy. The Clinton plan is merely the latest example. And like the others, it is a fraud.

PROVISIONS OF THE CLINTON BILL

To understand why the Clinton welfare plan will not deliver on its rhetoric, it is important to know a number of key facts about the legislation.

Fact #1: The Clinton Bill Does Not Establish Time Limits on Welfare.

Although President Clinton has claimed his welfare reform bill will "end cash assistance after two years," this is untrue.

Not one individual will have her cash aid terminated because she has received welfare benefits for over two years—or even for over twenty years. Instead a few individuals who have received AFDC for two years will be placed in a new welfare program misnamed WORK. These individuals will participate in government make-work jobs closely resembling the CETA "jobs" created by Jimmy Carter in the late 1970s. Individuals in the WORK program will continue to be on the welfare rolls and to receive welfare cash aid—but the cash aid will now be dubbed "wages."

Welfare recipients may remain in the WORK program indefinitely and may even be exempted from actual work assignments in the future and be recycled back into the main AFDC caseload. Welfare recipients (including those in the WORK program) may also receive Food Stamps, public housing aid, and medical aid indefinitely; the Clinton Administration opposes placing time limits or work requirements on these programs.

Fact #2: Virtually No Welfare Recipients Will Actually Be Required to Work.

When forced to acknowledge that the Clinton plan does not actually terminate welfare after two years of enrollment, defenders of the plan adopt a fallback position: they claim that the plan does at least require those who have received welfare for over two years to work in exchange for further benefits by participating in the WORK program. But this also is untrue. Under Clinton's plan virtually none of the parents who have received AFDC for over two years will be required to work, even in a government make-work job with wages paid by the welfare system.

The bottom line is clear. Among the nearly 5 million families receiving AFDC at any point in time almost half have received AFDC continuously for the last two years, and a far higher percentage have been enrolled for over two years when prior spells on the rolls are counted. Yet, under the Clinton plan, it turns out that only 7 percent of the adult AFDC caseload is required to work under the WORK program and even this requirement will not occur until 1999.

The reason only a tiny number of recipients will be required to work under the Clinton plan is because of the huge number of exemptions and limitations associated with the work obligation. The most glaring exemption is that parents born before 1972 will not be subject to any time limits or work requirements at all.[6] This alone exempts nearly 80 percent of the current AFDC caseload from the work requirement.

Fact #3: Most Welfare Recipients Born After 1972 Will Not Be Required to Work.

Many journalists and lawmakers, as well as other Americans, might assume that Clinton's rule of requiring work after two years will at least be applied rigorously to recipients born after 1972. But even this is not true. Further exemptions apply to this group as well.[7] Even five years from now, in 1999, only one-third of the AFDC parents who were born after 1972 and who have received AFDC for over two years would be required to work. The "two years and then work" rule is purely cosmetic. It is subject to so many limitations that, if enacted, it would have virtually no effect on the actual operation of the welfare system.

Fact #4: Under the Clinton Bill, Even the Small Number of Welfare Recipients Required to Work Must Do So for Only a Few Hours Per Week.

The small number of AFDC recipients who are actually required to work under the Clinton plan will have to perform very little labor. According to the bill, recipients who participate in the CETA-like WORK program will be required to work just 15 hours per week, mainly in public service positions created by local governments.[8] States may require more than 15 hours of labor, but experience from the 1988 Family Support Act, as well as earlier welfare reforms, suggests strongly that most state governments will adhere to the minimum standard. Fifteen hours of work thus will be the norm in all but a few jurisdictions.

Fact #5: WORK Participants Will Be Paid Well Above the Minimum Wage.

The Clinton Administration has claimed that participants in the WORK program will be paid the minimum wage. This is untrue. The plan actually states that all participants in the WORK program must be paid a wage plus an "earnings supplement," which together must be equal to at least the normal AFDC benefits received by the family.[9] The typical family on AFDC currently receives about $97 per week in benefits.[10] This typical recipient would thus receive a base rate of about $6.46 per hour for 15 hours of work under the WORK program, or almost 50 percent above the current minimum wage.

However, nearly all participants in the WORK program also will receive Food Stamps and Medicaid. The value of this total compensation (cash, food, and medical care) amounts to about $240 per week for the typical AFDC family.[11] With participants "working" for 15 hours per week, total compensation under the WORK program would average $16.00 per hour. (Even if the work standard were doubled to 30 hours per week, total compensation for the average participant would still equal $8.00 per hour.) In addition, WORK recipients will receive free day care. Finally, any state is free to provide any WORK participant with all or part of his or her normal AFDC benefits in addition to the wages paid by the WORK program.[12]

Yet even these above calculations still understate the actual wage rates mandated by the Clinton plan because they do not include an additional hidden wage provision in the bill. This provision stipulates that all WORK participants must be paid an hourly wage at least equal to the wage rates of normal employees within the employing organization performing similar work.[13] Under the plan, most WORK slots will be provided within municipal governments, many of which have unionized workforces. So in these localities, the bill requires that welfare recipients be paid union-scale wages. For example, if New York City wished to have a welfare recipient perform janitorial services in the public schools, the recipient would have to be paid about $20 per hour.[14]

Fact #6: Many WORK Participants Will Join Public Sector Unions.

Section 103 of the Clinton bill states that participants employed under the WORK program shall be provided with "working conditions and rights at the same level and to the same extent as the other employees of the same employer performing the same type of work" and having a similar length of employment.[15] This means that if the welfare recipient were placed in a unit of government which was unionized, the WORK participant would become part of the bargaining unit and would be represented by the union. If the municipality had a closed shop rule, the welfare recipient would become a union member and government funds would be used to pay the required union dues.

Fact #7: The Bill Limits Useful Work.

The Clinton plan makes it difficult for local governments to place WORK participants in useful work by creating strong barriers against jurisdictions wishing to fill normal job openings within the government with WORK participants. When a normal government job becomes vacant, WORK participants must be given the lowest priority in filling that job. WORK participants can fill normal job vacancies only after the government has attempted to fill the vacancy unsuccessfully through normal employment channels for at least 60 days.[16]

This provision will tend to push welfare recipients into pointless, makework positions reminiscent of CETA program in the 1970s, which provided "jobs" such as attending dance class and performing street theater. In the real world, it is also probable that a large number of the "jobs" provided under the WORK program will consist of para-political activity such as voter registration drives as well as advocacy activities under the auspices of the Legal Services Corporation and other "public interest" legal centers.

Fact #8: The Minimal Work Requirements Are Improperly Targeted.

The work requirements in the Clinton bill are poorly targeted and inefficient. Proper work requirements should be targeted on those welfare recipients who have the least justification for being out of the labor force: single able-bodied males, fathers in two-parent families, and single mothers with older children. But Clinton's plan focuses on the least employable welfare recipients: young single mothers with pre-school children. Clinton thus reverses the emphasis of current law by phasing out current work requirements on employable males while creating new (but modest) work requirements for single mothers with young children.

Current law properly focuses workfare on the most employable AFDC families. These are the 300,000-plus two-parent families in the Aid to Families with Dependent Children-Unemployed Parent (AFDC-UP) program. Under existing law one of the two parents in an AFDC-UP family will be required to work in community service (workfare) in exchange for the family's welfare benefits. This work requirement will cover up to 75 percent of AFDC-UP families in the mid and late 1990s.

Experience shows that firm work requirements on AFDC-UP families will cause an immediate drop in caseloads and large savings for the taxpayer. In 1983, Utah imposed a 40-hour-per-week work requirement on parents in their AFDC-UP program. The result was an immediate 90 percent reduction in that caseload.[17] Faced with having to perform serious work for their family's welfare benefits, most AFDC-UP fathers went out and obtained real jobs in the private sector. Utah's AFDC-UP population has remained at ten percent of the pre-workfare levels since 1983. Broadening and toughening the current nationwide work requirements on AFDC-UP families could save the taxpayers up to $15 billion in the next five years alone.[18]

But rather than toughening existing AFDC-UP work standards, the Clinton bill takes the unfathomable step of phasing them out by 1998.[19] The meager alternative work requirements in the bill would focus on exactly the wrong population: young single mothers, many with pre-school children. Because of the huge day care costs associated with trying to impose work requirements on this group, the result will be a great increase in welfare spending and barely a dent in the AFDC caseloads.

The inefficient nature of the Clinton work requirements perhaps should not come as a surprise. The Clinton Administration represents the interests of the professional welfare industry, which is naturally threatened by any reform which will significantly reduce welfare caseloads. By contrast, welfare bureaucrats are delighted by "reforms" which require them to provide an ever expanding array of services to their welfare clientele (such as lengthy negotiations of career goals and plenty of training and day care). Growing welfare caseloads mean full employment and plenty of career potential to welfare bureaucracies; shrinking caseloads mean the opposite. Therefore, despite pious rhetoric, most welfare bureaucracies quietly but strenuously oppose any workfare measures which will quickly cut caseloads. Instead, they relentlessly promote "investments" which increase costs but are claimed to reap savings at some ever-receding point in the future.

Fact #9: The Costs of Operating the Work Program Are Exorbitant.

Although the Clinton plan will require only a small percentage of welfare recipients to work, and those only for a few hours per week, the per recipient cost of operating the WORK program will be extremely high. The Clinton bill allocates $4,000 per year for each participant in WORK just to cover the administrative costs of the program (roughly $3,000 in federal funds and $1,000 in required state funding).

It should be emphasized that this $4,000 per year cost is not for training or education. It simply represents the extra cost of supervising an individual in a WORK slot. Day care and wage subsidies will add even further, large costs. Although the Clinton Administration has not provided clear figures, it is likely that maintaining a single individual in the WORK program will involve some $8,000 in extra expenses above the level of conventional welfare benefits.

In the typical state, the total taxpayer cost for a family of three participating in the WORK program for 15 hours per week is likely to be around $20,000 per year—a figure covering all wage subsidies, food stamps, medicaid, administrative costs and day care. Many participating families would receive even further benefits through other welfare programs such as public housing, WIC, school lunch, and energy aid. According to the rhetoric of the Clinton Administration, such a family is said to be "off welfare."

Fact #10: The Clinton Bill Is Not Deficit Neutral.

In addition to the high cost of operating the WORK program, the Clinton bill calls for a wide variety of other increases in welfare spending. It provides new funding for education, training, day care, and administration of the JOBS[20] program (for individuals who have been on AFDC for less than two years). Other spending items include increases in welfare benefits, expansions in welfare eligibility, and day care subsidies for single mothers who have found employment and left AFDC.

The Clinton Administration nevertheless claims its bill is deficit neutral. Officials say the new spending will not increase the deficit because it is paid for by spending cuts in other government programs. This claim is false. What the Administration does is take advantage of a loophole in federal budget law which requires that the financial impact of proposed legislation be estimated only for five years into the future. It turns out that much of the increased welfare spending in the Clinton plan is scheduled to occur in the sixth year and beyond—conveniently outside the period for which costs must be calculated. Clinton's proposed spending cuts, if enacted by Congress, may be sufficient to pay for the proposed spending increases over the next five years (from 1995 through 1999). But the plan does not even attempt to pay for the extra spending increases mandated to occur after 1999. These future welfare spending increases will be paid for either by higher deficits, higher taxes, or both.

Fact #11: The Clinton Plan Makes No Attempt to Control the Growth of Welfare Spending.

The federal government currently runs over 70 different welfare programs providing cash, food, housing, medical care, training, and social services to low-income Americans. Federal and state welfare spending combined amounted to over $320 billion in 1993.[21]

Even without any changes in law, welfare spending will rise to over $500 billion per annum by 1998. In that year, the cost of welfare will equal nearly $5,000 for each tax-paying household.

The U.S. then will spend two dollars on welfare for each dollar spent on national defense.

Clinton's response to this spending explosion is to call for even more spending. He attempts to defend his proposed spending increases by claiming that welfare increases are an investment which will yield long-run savings. This is a time-worn ploy. Proponents of nearly every welfare expansion in the last 30 years have justified new spending as an investment which will ultimately save money. Of course it never does. In launching the War on Poverty, for instance, Lyndon Johnson proclaimed that the war would be an "investment [which] will return its cost many-fold to our entire economy." Since Johnson's proclamation, annual welfare spending has increased nine-fold, after adjusting for inflation. As with past "reforms," Clinton's plan can be expected to increase welfare spending and caseloads.

Fact #12: The Clinton Bill Ignores the Illegitimacy Crisis.

The most serious fault in the Clinton reform plan is that it avoids the central problem of welfare almost completely: America's soaring illegitimate birth rate. In addition to all its other deficiencies, Clinton's proposal focuses almost exclusively on the superficial symptom of welfare dependence and ignores the underlying cause of this dependence—the sky-rocketing number of out-of-wedlock births. Last year, over one million children were born out of wedlock. Nearly one-third of all American children are now born to single women, up from around 8 percent when Lyndon Johnson launched the War on Poverty in 1965. The real goal of welfare reform should not be to put thousands of single mothers in government make-work jobs, while their children are raised in government day care centers. It must instead be to reduce dramatically the number of children born out of wedlock.

Clinton's rhetoric on the question of illegitimacy has been quite good. The President correctly states that illegitimacy is a key cause of crime in the United States. He also points out correctly that welfare plays a major role in promoting out-of-wedlock births. And in his State of the Union message this year, Clinton warned that unless something dramatic is done, half of all American children will soon be born out of wedlock

However, despite his laudable rhetoric, the President proposes no serious policies to combat the illegitimacy crisis. In fact, his reform plan would go in the opposite direction, establishing pilot programs to provide new cash welfare entitlements exclusively for unmarried mothers.[22] Even worse, by claiming to provide fundamental reform while changing virtually nothing, the Clinton plan, if enacted, will substantially relieve public pressure for change. Thus, it will effectively shut the door on desperately needed real reforms for the next five or ten years.

Fact #13: On Teen Abstinence, the Clinton Administration Uses Conservative Rhetoric to Camouflage Liberal Policies.

In an attempt to camouflage his Administration's policy vacuum on the crisis of illegitimacy, the President has included some small sex education programs in his bill. In describing this feature, like other provisions, the President uses bold, conservative rhetoric. In advertising the proposed education programs, Administration materials proclaim,

[W]e need to send a strong signal that it is essential for young people to delay sexual activity, as well as having children, until they are ready to accept the responsibilities and consequences of these actions. It is critical that we help all youth understand the rewards of.... deferring childbearing until they are married.[23]

But once again, conservative rhetoric conceals a contradictory liberal policy. In establishing the proposed education programs, the bill itself never mentions marriage, abstinence, or moral education to delay sexual activity. This should perhaps come as no surprise, since Health and Human Services Secretary Donna Shalala has spent most of the last year seeking to abolish the federal government's only abstinence education program. In its place, the Clinton bill will promote a stock set of tired policy failures: lavish condom distribution, "self-confidence" programs, values clarification, "life-skills training," and "decision-making skills training."[24]

If the Clinton Administration proposed a broad effort to promote moral-based abstinence education, this could be expected to cause a modest reduction in illegitimacy. Such programs have a demonstrated track record.

Example: Students who participated in the Title XX-sponsored program "Sex Respect: The Option of True Sexual Freedom" had considerably lower pregnancy rates one and two years after participation than the comparison group.[25]

Example: San Marcos Junior High School, San Marcos, California, has also used an abstinence-only program. The year before it was implemented 147 girls were reported pregnant. Two years after its initial implementation only 20 girls became pregnant.[26]

However, HHS Secretary Donna Shalala is vehement in her opposition to such programs. Commenting on her elimination of Title XX funds she said: "abstinence-only messages provide no hope of protection at all against the risks of pregnancy and disease."[27]

Thus, despite its conservative rhetoric, Clinton's bill does not propose to expand abstinence education. Instead, the proposed programs will be closely modeled on affect-based drug education programs. But, according to one of the principal originators of the techniques used in these programs, psychologist W. R. Coulson, such programs, featuring life-skills training, self-esteem building, and decision-making skills, have been shown scientifically to increase drug, alcohol, and tobacco use.[28] Similar counterproductive results can be expected from Clinton's education proposals.

TRUE REFORM

Even the simplest analysis of the White House proposal shows that Clinton's "time limits" and "work requirements" are a sham. Moreover, the President's "reforms" do not seriously address the more important issues of reducing illegitimacy and controlling welfare costs. True and comprehensive welfare reform is needed.

Only one piece of legislation before Congress provides real reform. This is The Welfare Reform Act of 1994 (S. 2134) introduced by Senators Lauch Faircloth (R-NC), Charles Grassley (R-IA), and Hank Brown (R-CO) with a companion bill (H.R. 4566) introduced by Representatives Jim Talent (R-MO), Tim

Hutchinson (R-AZ), and Charles Canady (R-FL).

This legislation embodies four basic reform principles:

1. It reduces illegitimacy in the future by eliminating those welfare benefits which subsidize and promote out-of-wedlock births.[29]
2. It provides an improved quality of life for those children who are born out of wedlock in the future. It does so by channeling those welfare funds which, under the current system, go directly to unwed mothers, into alternative and superior forms of care, such as adoption services and closely supervised group homes for young unmarried women and their children.
3. It controls the size of the welfare state by putting a cap on the future growth of aggregate federal welfare spending.
4. It establishes serious but sensible work requirements for welfare recipients. It does so by focusing those requirements on the most employable welfare recipients first (such as single able-bodied males and fathers in two-parent families), rather than on single mothers with infant children.

The authors of this legislation realize that the welfare system is waging a war of annihilation against the American family. In that war, welfare is winning and the family is losing. Welfare pays low-income Americans to adopt self-defeating courses of action. By encouraging young women to have children out of wedlock, welfare ruins the lives of the women and their children. The disintegration of the family promoted by welfare is, in turn, a major cause of most of America's other social problems includ-ing crime, poverty, school failure, and drug and alcohol abuse.[30]

CONCLUSION

Candidate Bill Clinton vigorously promoted his pledge to "end welfare" throughout the presidential election campaign. It is unlikely that voters listening to this thought that "ending welfare" meant that President Clinton now proposes: requiring just 7 percent of the AFDC caseload to work in public sector make-work jobs by the end of this century.

Administration officials argue that reform must be incremental and that changes take time. However, the true rationale of the Clinton plan can be better understood by examining the history and politics of the issue of work and welfare. The liberals who have dominated the U.S. Congress have adamantly opposed work requirements for welfare recipients for nearly a quarter century.[31] Many of the liberal professionals who staff key posts in the Clinton Administration share this view.[32] But since over 85 percent of the public now favor making welfare recipients work, most liberals no longer publicly oppose work requirements. Instead, they have adopted Fabian tactics, seeking quietly to minimize and delay work requirements as long as possible, while publicly claiming to support them. While public disaffection for welfare is assuaged through sham work requirements, liberals quietly move to expand welfare programs. This strategy of delay and obfuscation packaged as "bold reform" began with the Family Support Act of 1988 and will continue for the fore-seeable future.

Unlike Bill Clinton, Senator Faircloth and Congressman Talent realize that the War on Poverty has failed. The Faircloth-Talent bill delivers what Clinton promised: if not an end to welfare, at least the beginning of fundamental change.

NOTES

1. Martin Tolchin, "Welfare Revision: Moynihan Seeking to Stand System on Its Head," *The New York Times,* June 12, 1988.

2. Moynihan on the McNeil-Lehrer NewsHour June 13, 1988.

3. *St Petersburg Times,* September 30, 1988.

4. *The Congressional Record,* June 13, 1988, p. 7661.

5. The conventional explanation for the failure of the 1988 Family Support Act is that it did not receive enough funding. This is untrue. The 1988 act has operated exactly as designed by Congress. The crucial fact is that the act required virtually no welfare recipients to work, and only a tiny fraction even to search for work. Most states have executed the requirements of the 1988 act faithfully; but these requirements were designed to affect less than a tenth of the AFDC caseload. Furthermore, even the minimal JOBS participation requirements in the 1988 act were opposed by Senator Moynihan.

6. All citations to the Clinton bill refer to *Message from the President of the United States Transmitting A Draft of Proposed Legislation Entitled "Work and Responsibility Act of 1994,"* House Document #103-273 (U.S. Government Printing Office: Washington, D.C., June 21, 1994). This document is hereafter referred to as the "Clinton bill document." All cited page numbers will refer to the large page numbers at the top of each page in this document, which will differ from the page numbers on separate copies of the bill itself. The exemption for parents born before 1972 appears on page 2.

7. In addition to the many layers of exemptions from work, the Clinton bill contains a simple override mechanism which dictates that the number of participants in the WORK program will be determined by the amount of federal funding devoted to WORK divided by a fixed per capita participant amount. Since the WORK program is extraordinarily expensive to operate, this ensures that no more than a small fraction of AFDC recipients will ever be required to participate. See Clinton bill document pages 77 and 271.

8. The fifteen hour requirement appears on page 250.

9. Clinton bill document, p. 38.

10. AFDC benefits for a single mother with two children in 1992 averaged $4,785 per year. Assuming a total increase of 5 percent for inflation over the last two years benefits would average about $97 per week in 1994. See Ways and Means Committee, *Green Book: 1993,* p. 1240.

11. Estimated value of AFDC, Food Stamps, and Medicaid for a family of three in 1994 based on data from the Ways and Means Committee, *Green Book: 1993,* pp. 1644 and 1240.

12. Clinton bill document, pp. 250–251.

13. *Ibid.,* p. 233.

14. The beginning salary for a janitor in the New York public schools is $40,000 per year or roughly $20 per hour. Senior janitors receive up to $38 per hour. Charisse Jones, "Pact Breaks Grip of New York School Custodians," *The New York Times,* May 5, 1994, pp. A1 and B8.

15. Clinton bill document, p. 12.

16. Clinton bill document, p. 224.

17. See Robert Rector, "Welfare Reform, Dependency Reduction, and Labor Market Entry," *Journal of Labor Research,* Summer 1993, pp. 284–297.

18. The Faircloth-Talent welfare reform bill (S. 2134 and H.R. 4566) establishes work requirements modeled on the Utah plan on the entire nationwide AFDC-UP caseload starting in 1995.

19. The Clinton Administration has sought to abolish the current AFDC-UP work requirements since coming into office in early 1993. The original draft of the Clinton welfare bill circulated in late June of this year, when the President announced his plan, again sought to abolish the separate work requirements on AFDC-UP families. Stung by immediate criticism showing that this would result in a net reduction in the total number of welfare recipients who would be required to work for the next five years, the Clinton Administration hurriedly revised its bill. In the present draft the existing AFDC-UP work requirements are retained, but only through 1998; they are then eliminated.

20. JOBS is the acronym for the Job Opportunities and Basic Skills program, created by the 1988 Family Support Act. This is not a jobs program, despite the acronym, but instead mainly requires welfare recipients to look for employment through "job search" programs.

21. This figure covers means-tested programs for low-income individuals and communities. General spending programs for the middle class, such as Social Security and Medicare, are not included.

22. Clinton bill document, pp. 496–504.

23. "Work and Responsibility Act of 1994: a Detailed Summary," p. 32.

24. Clinton bill document, pp. 365, 351.

25. Project Respect, *Final Report; Office of Adolescent Pregnancy Programs.* Performance Summary Report, #000816, Title XX, 1985–1990.

26. Dinah Richard, "Has Sex Education Failed Our Teenagers; a Research Report" Focus on the Family, Pamona, California, 1990, pp. 56–60.

27. Cheryl Wetzstein, "Teen Abstinence funding deleted in Clinton Budget," *The Washington Times*, May 23, 1994, p. A-11.

28. W. R. Coulson, *Questianity: Why the War on Drugs Drags*, Research Council on Ethno-Psychology, Box 134, Comptche, California 95427. Dr. Coulson was a close associate of Dr. Carl Rogers and one of the originators of non-directive therapy and values clarification during the late 1960s and early 1970s. Coulson's techniques serve as the basis for most programs featuring decision-making and life skills training in the public schools. See also, William Kilpatrick, *Why Johnny Can't Tell Right from Wrong* (New York: Simon and Schuster, 1993).

29. One year after enactment, the bill would eliminate AFDC, Food Stamps, and Housing aid to women under age 21 who have children out of wedlock. Since the bill is intended to affect the future illegitimate birth rate, the cut-off would be prospective; it would not affect women who had children out-of-wedlock before the cut-off date. All savings from the elimination of direct welfare payments to unmarried women would be directed to alternative methods of caring for illegitimate children, including adoption and closely supervised group homes for unmarried mothers and their children.

30. See Patrick F. Fagan, "Rising Illegitimacy: America's Social Catastrophe," Heritage Foundation *FYI* No. 19, June 29, 1994.

31. Senator Russell Long first proposed the idea of workfare (requiring some AFDC recipients to work for benefits) in the early 1970s, but his ideas were blocked by liberals in Congress. During the late 1970s, the Carter Administration actually declared workfare illegal and expelled the state of Utah from the AFDC program for a number of years for attempting to make some recipients work for benefits. In 1981, President Reagan finally succeeded in making workfare legal, providing states with the option to operate very limited workfare programs. However, Reagan's repeated efforts to require even a small fraction of the AFDC caseload to actually participate in job search or workfare were rebuffed by Congress on a yearly basis during the mid-1980s. During the 1988 reforms, efforts to require even a small percentage of AFDC recipients to participate in job search or to work for benefits again were opposed by liberals led by Senator Moynihan. Conservatives led by then-Representative Hank Brown (R-CO) and Senator Bill Armstrong (R-CO) succeeded in establishing, over liberal opposition, actual work requirements for some AFDC-UP recipients to take effect in 1994. Thus due to persistent liberal opposition, nearly a quarter century passed between Russell Long's initial proposals for workfare and the time when the federal government actually required the first AFDC recipient to work for benefits. See Lawrence M. Mead, *Beyond Entitlement: The Social Obligations of Citizenship* (New York: The Free Press, 1986).

32. For example, HHS Secretary Shalala is a former member of the board of the Children's Defense Fund, an organization which historically has taken the lead in opposing even token work requirements for welfare recipients.

POSTSCRIPT

Can We End Welfare as We Know It?

Shalala provides a description of the Work and Responsibility Act of 1994, as well as a rationale for the proposed changes. She states that the proposal has "three overarching principles: work, responsibility, and reaching the next generation." To move people from the dependence of welfare to the independence of work involves financial support, job training, child care, and time limits for assistance. Responsibility, she feels, extends to parents, the system, and the government. Reaching the next generation, Shalala says, is critical for the success of any welfare reform, and to reduce welfare dependency, teen pregnancy must be prevented. Also, she notes that the plan will start with those persons born after 1971 because young mothers "are so important to our future."

Rector argues that the actual contents of the Work and Responsibility Act of 1994 are inconsistent with President Clinton's rhetoric regarding welfare reform. He believes that the proposed legislation is "simply a public relations facade intended to forestall real criticism and change." He argues, in part, that the proposal does not establish time limits on welfare, that the proposal requires few welfare recipients to work, that the proposal's minimal work requirements are not properly targeted, and that the proposal really does not attempt to control increasing welfare costs. Rector concludes that the reason the Clinton welfare proposal fails to accomplish meaningful reform is that liberals are not really interested in true reform but in increasing the social welfare bureaucracy.

Addressing the problems of those in need is well documented in the literature. Certainly, one place to begin is with those who contributed to two turning points in welfare policy—one to the Left and one to the Right: see Michael Harrington, *The Other American* (Macmillan, 1962) and Charles Murray, *Losing Ground: American Social Policy 1950–1980* (Basic Books, 1984). Lawrence Mead has written two books consistent with the arguments advanced by Murray called *Beyond Entitlements: The Social Obligations of Citizenship* (The Free Press, 1985) and *The New Politics of Poverty: The Nonworking Poor in America* (Basic Books, 1992). More current readings include "The Route to Welfare Reform," by Judith M. Gueron, *The Brookings Review* (Summer 1994); "Old Traps, New Twists," by Kent Weaver, *The Brookings Review* (Summer 1994); "Rethinking Welfare Reform," by Jared Bernstein, *Dissent* (Summer 1993); "The War on Welfare: Clinton's Carrots and Sticks," by Teresa Amott, *Dollars and Sense* (November/December 1993); and "The End of Welfare—Sort Of," by David Whitman and Matthew Cooper, *U.S. News & World Report* (June 20, 1994).

PART 3

The World Around Us

For many years America held a position of dominance in international trade. That position has been changed by time, events, and the emergence of other economic powers in the world. Decisions that are made in the international arena will, with increasing frequency, influence our lives. Protectionist measures are being discussed in Congress, and the jobs of many Americans may depend on the outcome of those discussions. Relations between the United States and Japan seem to make media headlines every week. The environment is also a major concern for economists and other analysts today.

- Should the United States Protect Domestic Industries from Foreign Competition?

- Is Japan a Threat to America's Economic and National Security?

- Does Global Warming Require Immediate Government Action?

- Should Pollution Be Put to the Market Test?

- Has Capitalism Defeated Socialism?

ISSUE 16

Should the United States Protect Domestic Industries from Foreign Competition?

YES: Robert Kuttner, from "The Free Trade Fallacy," *The New Republic* (March 28, 1983)

NO: Michael Kinsley, from "Keep Free Trade Free," *The New Republic* (April 11, 1983)

ISSUE SUMMARY

YES: Columnist Robert Kuttner alleges that David Ricardo's eighteenth-century view of the world does not "describe the global economy as it actually works" in the twentieth century. He says that, today, "comparative advantage" is determined by exploitative wage rates and government action; it is not determined by free markets.

NO: Social critic Michael Kinsley replies that we do not decrease American living standards when we import the products made by cheap foreign labor. He claims protectionism today, just as it did in the eighteenth century, weakens our economy and only "helps to put off the day of reckoning."

The basic logic of international trade has not changed over time. The villains change, the winners and losers change, but the theory remains the same. Thus, do not be alarmed that the readings that follow refer to 10-year-old editorials that appeared in the *Wall Street Journal*, the *New York Times*, or the *Village Voice*. The pleadings made in these articles are almost identical to those that are now being made in the newspapers of the 1990s. As the saying goes, "The more things change, the more they stay the same." It is because of the timelessness of the free trade versus protectionism debate that we have included the Kuttner/Kinsley selections, even though these essays first appeared in print a decade ago. Not only does the basic logic of international trade not change over time, it is indistinguishable from domestic trade: Both domestic and international trade must answer the fundamental economic questions: *"What* to produce?" *"How* to produce it?" and *"For whom* to produce?" The distinction is that the international trade questions are posed in an international arena. This is an arena filled with producers and consumers who speak different languages, use different currencies, and are often suspicious of the actions and reactions of foreigners.

If markets work the way they are expected to work, free trade simply increases the extent of a purely domestic market and, therefore, increases the advantages of specialization. Market participants should be able to buy and consume a greater variety of inexpensive goods and services after the establishment of free trade than they could before free trade. You might ask, Then why do some wish to close the borders and deny Americans the benefits of free trade? The answer to this question is straightforward. These benefits do not come without a cost.

There are two sets of winners and two sets of losers in this game of free trade. The most obvious winners are the consumers of the less expensive imported goods. These consumers are able to buy the low-priced color television sets, automobiles, or steel that is made abroad. Another set of winners are the producers of the exported goods. All the factors in the export industry, as well as those in industries that supply to the export industry, experience an increase in their market demand. Therefore, their income increases. In the United States, agriculture is one such export industry. As new foreign markets are opened, farmers' incomes increase, as do the incomes of those who supply the farmers with fertilizer, farm equipment, gasoline, and other basic inputs.

On the other side of this coin are the losers. The obvious losers are those who own the factors of production that are employed in the import-competing industries. These factors include the land, labor, and capital that are devoted to the production of such items as U.S.–made color television sets, U.S.–made automobiles, and U.S.–made steel. The less expensive foreign imports displace the demand for these products. The consumers of exported goods are also losers. For example, as U.S. farmers sell more of their products abroad, less of this output is available domestically. As a result, the domestic prices of these farm products and other export goods and services rise.

The bottom line is that there is nothing "free" in a market system. Competition—whether it is domestic or foreign—creates winners and losers. Historically, we have sympathized with the losers when they suffer at the hands of foreign competitors. However, we have not let our sympathies seriously curtail free trade. Robert Kuttner argues that we can no longer afford this policy. He maintains that U.S. workers face "unfair foreign competition" and that the international rules of the game have changed. Michael Kinsley replies that this is pure, unadorned protectionism. He concludes that "each job 'saved' will cost other American workers far more than it will bring the lucky beneficiary."

YES

Robert Kuttner

THE FREE TRADE FALLACY

In the firmament of American ideological convictions, no star burns brighter than the bipartisan devotion to free trade. The President's 1983 Economic Report, to no one's surprise, sternly admonished would-be protectionists. An editorial in *The New York Times*, midway through an otherwise sensibly Keynesian argument, paused to add ritually, "Protectionism might mean a few jobs for American auto workers, but it would depress the living standards of hundreds of millions of consumers and workers, here and abroad."

The Rising Tide of Protectionism has become an irresistible topic for a light news day. Before me is a thick sheaf of nearly interchangeable clips warning of impending trade war. With rare unanimity, the press has excoriated the United Auto Workers for its local content legislation. *The Wall Street Journal*'s editorial ("Loco Content") and the *Times*'s ("The Made-in-America Trap") were, if anything, a shade more charitable than Cockburn and Ridgeway in *The Village Voice* ("Jobs and Racism"). And when former Vice President Mondale began telling labor audiences that America should hold Japan to a single standard in trade, it signaled a chorus of shame-on-Fritz stories.

The standard trade war story goes like this: recession has prompted a spate of jingoistic and self-defeating demands to fence out superior foreign goods. These demands typically emanate from overpaid workers, loser industries, and their political toadies. Protectionism will breed stagnation, retaliation, and worldwide depression. Remember Smoot-Hawley!

Perhaps it is just the unnerving experience of seeing *The Wall Street Journal* and *The Village Voice* on the same side, but one is moved to further inquiry. Recall for a moment the classic theory of comparative advantage. As the English economist David Ricardo explained it in 1817, if you are more efficient at making wine and I am better at weaving cloth, then it would be silly for each of us to produce both goods. Far better to do what each does best, and to trade the excess. Obviously then, barriers to trade defeat potential efficiency gains. Add some algebra, and that is how trade theory continues to be taught today.

To bring Ricardo's homely illustration up to date, the economically sound way to deal with the Japanese menace is simply to buy their entire

From Robert Kuttner, "The Free Trade Fallacy," *The New Republic*, vol. 188, no. 12 (March 28, 1983). Copyright © 1983 by The New Republic, Inc. Reprinted by permission of *The New Republic*.

cornucopia—the cheaper the better. If they are superior at making autos, TVs, tape recorders, cameras, steel, machine tools, baseballs, semiconductors, computers, and other peculiarly Oriental products, it is irrational to shelter our own benighted industries. Far more sensible to buy their goods, let the bracing tonic of competition shake America from its torpor, and wait for the market to reveal our niche in the international division of labor.

But this formulation fails to describe the global economy as it actually works. The classical theory of free trade was based on what economists call "factor endowments"—a nation's natural advantages in climate, minerals, arable land, or plentiful labor. The theory doesn't fit a world of learning curves, economies of scale, and floating exchange rates. And it certainly doesn't deal with the fact that much "comparative advantage" today is created not by markets but by government action. If Boeing got a head start on the 707 from multibillion-dollar military contracts, is that a sin against free trade? Well, sort of. If the European Airbus responds with subsidized loans, is that worse? If only Western Electric (a U.S. supplier) can produce for Bell, is that protection? If Japan uses public capital, research subsidies, and market-sharing cartels to launch a highly competitive semiconductor industry, is *that* protection? Maybe so, maybe not.

Just fifty years ago, Keynes, having dissented from the nineteenth-century theory of free markets, began wondering about free trade as well. In a 1933 essay in the *Yale Review* called "National Self-Sufficiency," he noted that "most modern processes of mass production can be performed in most countries and climates with almost equal efficiency." He won-

dered whether the putative efficiencies of trade necessarily justified the loss of national autonomy. Today nearly half of world trade is conducted between units of multinational corporations. As Keynes predicted, most basic products (such as steel, plastics, microprocessors, textiles, and machine tools) can be manufactured almost anywhere, but by labor forces with vastly differing prevailing wages.

With dozens of countries trying to emulate Japan, the trend is toward worldwide excess capacity, shortened useful life of capital equipment, and downward pressure on wages. For in a world where technology is highly mobile and interchangeable, there is a real risk that comparative advantage comes to be defined as whose work force will work for the lowest wage.

In such a world, it is possible for industries to grow nominally more productive while the national economy grows poorer. How can that be? The factor left out of the simple Ricardo equation is idle capacity. If America's autos (or steel tubes, or machine tools) are manufactured more productively than a decade ago but less productively than in Japan (or Korea, or Brazil), and if we practice what we preach about open trade, then an immense share of U.S. purchasing power will go to provide jobs overseas. A growing segment of our productive resources will lie idle. American manufacturers, detecting soft markets and falling profits, will decline to invest. Steelmakers will buy oil companies. Consumer access to superior foreign products will not necessarily compensate for the decline in real income and the idle resources. Nor is there any guarantee that the new industrial countries will use their burgeoning income from American sales to buy American capital equipment (or computers, or even coal), for they are all striving to develop their own advanced, diversified economies.

Against this background of tidal change in the global economy, the conventional reverence for "free trade" is just not helpful. As an economic paradigm, it denies us a realistic appraisal of second bests. As a political principle, it leads liberals into a disastrous logic in which the main obstacle to a strong American economy is decent living standards for the American work force. Worst of all, a simple-minded devotion to textbook free trade in a world of mercantilism assures that the form of protection we inevitably get will be purely defensive, and will not lead to constructive change in the protected industry.

The seductive fallacy that pervades the hand-wringing about protectionism is the premise that free trade is the norm and that successful foreign exporters must be playing by the rules. Even so canny a critic of political economy as Michael Kinsley wrote in these pages that "Very few American workers have lost their jobs because of unfair foreign trade practices, and it is demagogic for Mondale and company to suggest otherwise." But what is an unfair trade practice? The Common Market just filed a complaint alleging that the entire Japanese industrial system is one great unfair trade practice!

To the extent that the rules of liberal trade are codified, they repose in the General Agreement on Tariffs and Trade (stay awake, this will be brief). The GATT is one of those multilateral institutions created in the American image just after World War II, a splendid historical moment when we could commend free trade to our allies the way the biggest kid on the block calls for a fair fight.

The basic GATT treaty, ratified in 1947, requires that all member nations get the same tariff treatment (the "most favored nation" doctrine), and that tariffs, in theory at least, are the only permissible form of barrier. Governments are supposed to treat foreign goods exactly the same as domestic ones: no subsidies, tax preferences, cheap loans to home industries, no quotas, preferential procurement, or inspection gimmicks to exclude foreign ones. Nor can producers sell below cost (dumping) in foreign markets....

In classical free trade theory, the only permissible candidate for temporary protection is the "infant industry." But Japan and its imitators, not unreasonably, treat every emerging technology as an infant industry. Japan uses a highly sheltered domestic market as a laboratory, and as a shield behind which to launch one export winner after another. Seemingly, Japan should be paying a heavy price for its protectionism as its industry stagnates. Poor Japan! This is not the place for a detailed recapitulation of Japan, Inc., but keep in mind some essentials.

The Japanese government, in close collaboration with industry, targets sectors for development. It doesn't try to pick winners blindfolded; it creates them. It offers special equity loans, which need be repaid only if the venture turns a profit. It lends public capital through the Japan Development Bank, which signals private bankers to let funds flow. Where our government offers tax deductions to all businesses as an entitlement, Japan taxes ordinary business profits at stiff rates and saves its tax subsidies for targeted ventures. The government sometimes buys back outdated capital equipment to create markets for newer capital.

The famed Ministry of International Trade and Industry has pursued this essential strategy for better than twenty years, keeping foreign borrowers out of cheap Japanese capital markets, letting in foreign investors only on very restricted terms, moving Japan up the product ladder from cheap labor intensive goods in the 1950s to autos and steel in the 1960s, consumer electronics in the early 1970s, and computers, semiconductors, optical fibers, and just about everything else by 1980. The Japanese government also waives antimonopoly laws for development cartels, and organizes recession cartels when overcapacity is a problem. And far from defying the discipline of the market, MITI encourages fierce domestic competition before winnowing the field down to a few export champions....

The Japanese not only sin against the rules of market economics. They convert sin into productive virtue. By our own highest standards, they must be doing something right. The evident success of the Japanese model and the worldwide rush to emulate it create both a diplomatic crisis for American trade negotiators and a deeper ideological crisis for the free trade regime. As Berkeley professors John Zysman and Steven Cohen observed in a careful study for the Congressional Joint Economic Committee last December, America, as the main defender of the GATT philosophy, now faces an acute policy dilemma: "how to sustain the open trade system and promote the competitive position of American industry" at the same time.

Unfortunately, the dilemma is compounded by our ideological blinders. Americans believe so fervently in free markets, especially in trade, that we shun interventionist measures until an industry is in deep trouble. Then we build it half a bridge.

There is no better example of the lethal combination of protectionism plus market-capitalism-as-usual than the steel industry. Steel has enjoyed some import limitation since the late 1950s, initially through informal quotas. The industry is oligopolistic; it was very slow to modernize. By the mid-1970s, world demand for steel was leveling off just as aggressive new producers such as Japan, Korea, and Brazil were flooding world markets with cheap, state-of-the-art steel.

As the Carter Administration took office, the American steel industry was pursuing antidumping suits against foreign producers—an avenue that creates problems for American diplomacy. The new Administration had a better idea, more consistent with open markets and neighborly economic relations. It devised a "trigger price mechanism," a kind of floor price for foreign steel entering American markets. This was supposed to limit import penetration. The steelmakers withdrew their suits. Imports continued to increase.

So the Carter Administration moved with characteristic caution toward a minimalist industrial policy. Officials invented a kind of near-beer called the Steel Tripartite. Together, industry, labor, and government would devise a strategy for a competitive American steel industry. The eventual steel policy accepted the industry's own agenda: more protection, a softening of pollution control requirements, wage restraint, new tax incentives, and a gentlemen's agreement to phase out excess capacity. What the policy did not include was either an enforceable commitment or adequate capital to modernize the industry. By market standards, massive retooling was not a rational course, because the return on steel investment was well below prevailing yields on other investments. Moreover, government officials had neither the ideological mandate nor adequate information to tell the steel industry how to invest. "We would sit around and talk about rods versus plate versus specialty steel, and none of us in government had any knowledge of how the steel industry actually operates," confesses C. Fred Bergsten, who served as Treasury's top trade official under Carter. "There has never been a government study of what size and shape steel industry the country needs. If we're going to go down this road, we should do it right, rather than simply preserving the status quo." ...

The argument that we should let "the market" ease us out of old-fashioned heavy industry in which newly industrialized countries have a comparative advantage quickly melts away once you realize that precisely the same nonmarket pressures are squeezing us out of the highest-tech industries as well. And the argument that blames the problem on overpaid American labor collapses when one understands that semiskilled labor overseas in several Asian nations is producing advanced products for the U.S. market at less than a dollar an hour. Who really thinks that we should lower American wages to that level in order to compete?

In theory, other nations' willingness to exploit their work forces in order to provide Americans with good, cheap products offers a deal we shouldn't refuse. But the fallacy in that logic is to measure the costs and benefits of a trade transaction only in terms of that transaction itself. Classical free-trade theory assumes full employment. When foreign, state-led competition drives us out of industry after industry, the costs to the economy as a whole can easily outweigh the benefits. As Wolfgang Hager, a consultant to the Common Market, has written, "The cheap [imported] shirt is paid for several times: once at the counter, then again in unemployment benefits. Secondary losses involve input industries ... machinery, fibers, chemicals for dyeing and finishing products."

As it happens, Hager's metaphor, the textile industry, is a fairly successful example of managed trade, which combines a dose of protection with a dose of modernization. Essentially, textiles have been removed from the free-trade regime by an international market-sharing agreement. In the late 1950s, the American textile industry began suffering insurmountable competition from cheap imports. The United States first imposed quotas on imports of cotton fibers, then on synthetics, and eventually on most textiles and apparel as well. A so-called Multi-Fiber Arrangement eventually was negotiated with other nations, which shelters the textile industries of Europe and the United States from wholesale import penetration. Under M.F.A., import growth in textiles was limited to an average of 6 percent per year.

The consequences of this, in theory, should have been stagnation. But the result has been exactly the opposite. The degree of protection, and a climate of cooperation with the two major labor unions, encouraged the American textile industry to invest heavily in modernization. During the 1960s and 1970s, the average annual productivity growth in textiles has been about twice the U.S. industrial average, second only to electronics. According to a study done for the Common Market, productivity in the most efficient American weaving operations is 130,000 stitches per worker per hour—twice as high as France and three times as high as Britain. Textiles, surprisingly enough, have remained an export winner for the United States, with net exports regularly exceeding imports. (In 1982, a depressed year that saw renewed competition from China, Hong Kong, Korea, and Taiwan, exports just about equaled imports.)

But surely the American consumer pays the bill when the domestic market is sheltered from open foreign competition. Wrong again. Textile prices have risen at only about half the average rate of the producer price index, both before and after the introduction of the Multi-Fiber Arrangement.

Now, it is possible to perform some algebraic manipulations and show how much lower textile prices would have been without any protection. One such computation places the cost of each protected textile job at several hundred thousand dollars. But these static calculations are essentially useless as practical policy guides, for they leave out the value over time of maintaining a textile industry in the United States. The benefits include not only jobs, but contributions to G.N.P., to the balance of payments, and the fact that investing in this generation's technology is the ticket of admission to the next.

Why didn't the textile industry stagnate? Why didn't protectionism lead to higher prices? Largely because the textile industry is quite competitive domestically. The top five manufacturers have less than 20 percent of the market. The industry still operates under a 1968 Federal Trade Commission consent order prohibiting any company with sales of more than $100 million from acquiring one with sales exceeding $10 million. If an industry competes vigorously domestically, it can innovate and keep prices low, despite being sheltered from ultra- low-wage foreign competition—or rather, thanks to the shelter. In fact, students of the nature of modern managed capitalism should hardly be surprised that market stability and new investment go hand in hand.

The textile case also suggests that the sunrise industry/sunset industry distinction is so much nonsense. Most of America's major industries can be winners *or* losers, depending on whether they get sufficient capital investment. And it turns out that many U.S. industries such as textiles and shoes, which conventionally seem destined for lower-wage countries, can survive and modernize given a reasonable degree of, well, protection.

What, then, is to be done? First, we should acknowledge the realities of international trade. Our competitors, increasingly, are not free marketeers in our own mold. It is absurd to let foreign mercantilist enterprise overrun U.S. industry in the name of free trade. The alternative is not jingoist protectionism. It is managed trade, on the model of the Multi-Fiber Arrangement. If domestic industries are assured some limits to import growth, then it becomes rational for them to keep retooling and modernizing.

It is not necessary to protect every industry, nor do we want an American MITI. But surely it is reasonable to fashion plans for particular key sectors like steel, autos, machine tools, and semiconductors. The idea is not to close U.S. markets, but to limit the rate of import growth in key industries. In exchange, the domestic industry must invest heavily in modernization. And as part of the bargain, workers deserve a degree of job security and job retraining opportunities.

Far from being just another euphemism for beggar-thy-neighbor, a more stable trade system generally can be in the interest of producing countries. Universal excess capacity does no country much of a favor. When rapid penetration of the U.S. color TV market by Korean suppliers became intolerable, we slammed shut an open door. Overnight, Korean color TV production shrank to 20 percent of capacity. Predictable, if more gradual, growth in sales would have been preferable for us and for the Koreans.

Second, we should understand the interrelationship of managed trade, industrial policies, and economic recovery. Without a degree of industrial planning, limiting imports leads indeed to stagnation. Without restored world economic growth, managed trade becomes a nasty battle over shares of a shrinking pie, instead of allocation of a growing one. And without some limitation on imports, the Keynesian pump leaks. One reason big deficits fail to ignite recoveries is that so much of the growth in demand goes to purchase imported goods.

Third, we should train more economists to study industries in the particular. Most economists dwell in the best of all possible worlds, where markets equilibrate, firms optimize, the idle resources re-employ themselves. "Microeconomics" is seldom the study of actual industries; it is most often a branch of arcane mathematics. The issue of *whether* governments can sometimes improve on markets is not a fit subject for empirical inquiry, for the paradigm begins with the assumption that they cannot. The highly practical question of *when* a little protection is justified is ruled out *ex ante*, since neoclassical economics assumes that less protection is always better than more.

Because applied industrial economics is not a mainstream concern of the economics profession, the people who study it tend to come from the fields of management, industrial and labor relations, planning, and law. They are not invited to professional gatherings of economists, who thus continue to avoid the most pressing practical questions. One economist whom I otherwise admire told me he found it "seedy" that high-wage autoworkers would ask consumers to subsidize their pay. Surely it is seedier for an $800-a-week tenured economist to lecture a $400-a-week autoworker on job security; if the Japanese have a genuine comparative advantage in anything, it is in applied economics.

Fourth, we should stop viewing high wages as a liability. After World War II, Western Europe and North America evolved a social contract unique in the history of industrial capitalism. Unionism was encouraged, workers got a fair share in the fruits of production, and a measure of job security. The transformation of a crude industrial production machine into something approximating social citizenship is an immense achievement, not to be sacrificed lightly on the altar of "free trade." It took one depression to show that wage cuts are no route to recovery. Will it take another to show they are a poor formula for competitiveness? Well-paid workers, after all, are consumers.

NO
Michael Kinsley

KEEP FREE TRADE FREE

Free trade is not a religion—it has no spiritual value—and Bob Kuttner is right to insist, as he did in TNR two weeks ago, that if it is no longer good for America in practical terms, it is not a sensible policy for liberals anymore. He and I would also agree that a liberal trade policy ought to be good for working people in particular (including people who would like to be working but aren't). The question is whether free trade is just a relic from two happier eras—the period of liberal clarity two centuries ago when Adam Smith and David Ricardo devised the theories of free enterprise and free trade, and the period of American hegemony after World War II when we could dominate world markets—or whether it is still a key to prosperity.

Kuttner argues that Ricardo's theory of "comparative advantage"—that all nations are better off if each produces and exports what it can make most efficiently—no longer applies. Local factors such as climate and natural resources don't matter much anymore. As a result, "most basic products... can be manufactured almost anywhere" with equal efficiency. This means, Kuttner says, that the only ways one nation (e.g., Japan) gains comparative advantage over another (e.g., us) these days are through low wages or "government action." Either of these, he says, makes nonsense of Ricardo's theory. In addition, Kuttner says, Ricardo didn't account for the problem of "idle capacity"—expensive factories sitting unused.

"Idle capacity" is an argument against any competition at all, not just from abroad, and has a long history of being carted out whenever established companies (the airlines, for example) want the government to prevent newcomers from horning in on their turf. If you believe in capitalism at all, you have to believe that the temporary waste of capital that can result from the turmoil of competition is more than outweighed by the efficiency of competition in keeping all the competitors on their toes. A capitalist who builds a plant knowing (or even not knowing) that it is less efficient than a rival abroad deserves whatever he gets. As for older plants that are already built—that capital is sunk. If the cost of running those plants is higher than the cost of buying the same output from abroad, keeping them running is more wasteful than letting them sit idle.

This brings us to the real problem; not sunk capital but sunk lives. The middle-class living standard achieved by much of the United States working class is one of the glories of American civilization. Yet Kuttner says, "semi-skilled labor overseas is producing advanced products for the U.S. market at less than a dollar an hour. Who really thinks that we should lower American wages to that level in order to compete?"

We shouldn't, of course. But importing the products of cheap foreign labor cannot lower American living standards as a whole, and trade barriers cannot raise living standards. This is not a matter of morality: it is a matter of mathematics. If widgets can be imported from Asia for a price reflecting labor costs of $1 an hour, then an hour spent making widgets adds a dollar of value to the economy. This is true no matter what American widget makers are being paid. If foreign widgets are excluded in order to protect the jobs of American widget makers getting $10 an hour, $1 of that $10 reflects their contribution to the economy and $9 is coming out of the pockets of other workers who have to pay more for widgets. Nice for widget makers, but perfectly futile from the perspective of net social welfare.

After all, if this economic alchemy really worked, we could shut our borders to all imports, pay one another $1,000 an hour, and we'd all be rich. It doesn't work that way. In fact, as a society, we're clearly better off taking advantage of the $1 widgets. The "comparative advantage" of cheap Asian labor is an advantage to *us* too. That's why trade is good.

But what about the poor widget makers? And what about the social cost of unemployment? If former widget makers aren't working at all, they aren't even adding a dollar's worth to the economy. Protectionism is, in effect, a "make work" jobs program—but a ridiculously expensive one, both directly and indirectly. The direct cost, in this example, is $9 an hour. The indirect cost is in reducing the efficiency of the economy by preventing international specialization.

If the disparity between American and foreign wages is really that great, Americans just shouldn't be making widgets. We could pay widget workers at $8 an hour to do nothing, and still be better off. We could put them to work at their current wage doing anything worth more than a dollar an hour. We could spend the equivalent of $9 an hour on retraining. And we owe it to widget workers to try all these things if necessary, because they are the victims of a change that has benefited all the rest of us by bringing us cheaper widgets (and because, as Lester Thurow points out, doing these things will discourage them from blocking the needed change). To protect them while they keep on making widgets, though, is insane.

These suggestions are, of course, overt tax-and-spend government programs, compared to the covert tax-and-spend program of protectionism. In a period of political reaction, the covert approach is tempting. But hypocrisy is not a sensible long-term strategy for liberals, nor is willfully ignoring the importance of economic productivity.

In many basic industries, American wages are not all that far out of line, as Bob Kuttner seems to acknowledge in the case of autos. Modest wage adjustments can save these jobs and these industries for America. It is uncomfortable for a well-paid journalist to be urging pay cuts for blue-collar workers. On the other hand, steelworkers (when they are working) make more than the median American income. Protectionism to preserve wage levels is just a redistribution of national wealth; it creates no new wealth. Nothing is wrong with redistribution, but in any radical socialist redistribution of wealth, the pay of steelworkers would go down, not up. So it's hard to see why the government should intervene to protect steelworkers' wages at the expense of general national prosperity. This is especially true when millions are unemployed who would happily work for much less, and there is no jobs program for them.

But Bob Kuttner believes that protection can be good for general national prosperity even apart from the wage question, in an age when other nations' "comparative advantage" comes from government policies that include protectionism. It is important to separate different strands in the common protectionist argument that we have to do it because Japan does it. Many politicians of various stripes, and William Safire in a recent column, argue (on an implicit analogy between trade war and real war) that only by threatening or building trade barriers of our own can we persuade the Japanese to dismantle theirs and restore free trade. Kuttner, by contrast, thinks that the idea of free trade is outmoded; that the Japanese are *smart* to restrict imports and we would be smart to do the same as part of an "industrial policy."

Both Safire and Kuttner assume incorrectly that free trade needs to be mutual. In fact, the theory of free trade is that nations benefit from their own open borders as well as the other guy's. This may be right or wrong, but the mere fact that Japan is protectionist does not settle the question of what our policy should be.

Certainly, it's worth looking at Japan for clues about how to succeed in the world economy, and certainly one key to Japan's success seems to be a government-coordinated industrial policy. (The current vogue for "industrial policy" is assessed by my colleague Robert Kaus in the February *Harper's*—forgive the plug.) But why must such a policy include trade barriers? One reason Japan thwarts imports is a conscious decision to reduce workers' living standards in order to concentrate national resources on industrial investment. I presume this isn't what Kuttner and other liberal trade revisionists have in mind. Kuttner and others include protectionism in their "industrial policy" for two other reasons. First, as a sort of bribe to get unions to go along with sterner measures—possibly necessary, but not a case for protection on its own merits. Second, to give promising industries a captive market in which to incubate and gather strength before taking on the world.

The trouble with this "nurture" argument is that there's no end to it. Kuttner himself says that it's "not unreasonable" to "treat every emerging technology" this way, and also says that "most of America's major industries can be winners" with the right treatment. After you add the few hopeless loser industries where we must allegedly create barriers to save American wages, you've got the whole economy locked up, and whether this will actually encourage efficiency or the opposite is, at the very least, an open question. And if every major country protects every major industry, there will be no world market for any of them to conquer.

Kuttner's model for "managed trade" is the Multi-Fiber Arrangement, an international agreement that restricts imports of textiles. This, according to Kuttner, permitted the American textile industry to modernize and become productive, to the point where exports exceeded imports—a less impressive accomplishment if you recall that the M.F.A. *restricts* imports.

Kuttner concedes that, despite the productivity gains, textile prices are higher than they would be without protection from cheap foreign labor. (Indeed, the current situation in the textile industry, as Bob Kuttner describes it, seems to vindicate Luddites, who got their start in textiles; human beings could do the work more efficiently, but machines are doing it anyway.) So what's the point? According to Kuttner, "The benefits include not only jobs, but contributions to G.N.P., to the balance of payments, and the fact that investing in this generation's technology is the ticket of admission to the next." Yet Kuttner does not challenge the "algebraic manipulations" he cites that show how each job saved costs the nation "several hundred thousand dollars" in higher textile prices. The only "contribution to G.N.P." from willful inefficiency like this can be the false contribution of inflation. The balance of payments is a measure of economic health, not a cause of it; restricting imports to reduce that deficit is like sticking the thermometer in ice water

to bring down a feverish temperature. As for the suggestion that the *next* generation of technology will bring the *real* payoff—well, they were probably promising the same thing two decades ago when the Multi-Fiber Arrangement began.

Kuttner also worries that "without some limitation on imports," Keynesian fiscal policies don't work. This is like the monetarists who worry that financial advances such as money market funds will weaken the connection between inflation and the money supply. Unable to make their theory accord with life, they want the government to make life accord with their theory. There *is* a world economy—which Bob Kuttner seems to recognize as a good thing— and this means Keynesian techniques will increasingly have to be applied internationally....

There can be no pretense that domestic content legislation has anything to do with "industrial policy"—improving the competitive ability of American industry. It is protectionism, pure and unadorned, and each job "saved" will cost other American workers far more than it will bring the lucky beneficiary. Like most protectionist measures, far from aiding America's adjustment to world competition, it just helps put off the day of reckoning.

POSTSCRIPT

Should the United States Protect Domestic Industries from Foreign Competition?

The desirability of free trade is one of few issues on which a large majority of professional economists agree. Survey after survey confirms this: Economists are ardent supporters of free trade. In spite of this general consensus, protectionism is hotly debated. This certainly is the case in these two essays.

Kuttner argues two basic points in his essay. First, he contends that the world that English economist David Ricardo modeled in 1817 is starkly different than the world we know today. He describes our world as "a world of learning curves, economies of scale, and floating exchange rates." It is a world where comparative advantage "is created not by markets but by government action." Second, he maintains that although free markets will lead to factor price equalization—that is, wage rates in developing countries will rise and U.S. wage rates will fall as long as there is a differential—we should not, and cannot, allow this to happen. He asks: Do we want wage levels in the United States to fall to a dollar an hour?

Kinsley does not believe that free trade is a relic from the past. After looking at the simple mathematics of Kuttner's proposal, Kinsley contends: "Protectionism is, in effect, a 'make work' jobs program—but a ridiculously expensive one, both directly and indirectly." He believes we can achieve the same end without sacrificing the benefits of "international specialization." Kinsley goes on to argue that when "every major country protects every major industry"—the natural consequence of Kuttner's national industrial policy—"there will be no world market for any of them to conquer." He contends that we will return to the isolationists' world, a world that is poorer than it need be.

Since the majority of economists support the notion of free trade, readings supporting this position are very easy to identify. However, if you would like to read an extreme position paper, you might try Paula Stern's "Ronald Reagan: The International Bad Boy on Trade," *The International Economy* (July/August 1991). In this essay she argues that "the essence of Reagan's trade policy became clear: Espouse free trade, but find an excuse on every occasion to embrace the opposite." For a more scholarly discourse, you might read Douglas Irwin's "Retrospectives: Challenges to Free Trade," *Journal of Economic Perspectives* (Spring 1991). Irwin concludes that when all is said and done, the charges leveled at free trade "will not fundamentally challenge the belief of economists in free trade."

ISSUE 17

Is Japan a Threat to America's Economic and National Security?

YES: Stephen D. Cohen, from "United States–Japanese Trade Relations," *Proceedings of the Academy of Political Science* (vol. 37, no. 4, 1990)

NO: Philip H. Trezise, from "Japan, the Enemy?" *The Brookings Review* (Winter 1989/1990)

ISSUE SUMMARY

YES: Professor of international economic relations Stephen D. Cohen concludes that a continuation of our "inferior industrial performance relative to Japan" is a threat to both the "economic [and] national security interests of the United States."

NO: Philip H. Trezise, a senior fellow of the Brookings Institution, replies that "on any rational calculation, economic competition from Japan does not threaten America's national security" or its long-run economic vitality.

In the post–World War II period, Japan flooded the free world market with cheap imitations of American-made goods. There were toy cars and airplanes made out of tin, flimsy dolls dressed in gaudy, rough cotton, watches and clocks that rarely lasted through a year of service, and many, many other consumer items all boldly stamped "made in Japan." In the eyes of most consumers, "made in Japan" was synonymous with "second rate." This was poor-quality merchandise that rarely, if ever, commanded respect.

Gradually, however, this reputation faded. The Japanese genius for copying, modifying, and producing at low cost simple consumer goods was directed toward more sophisticated items. No longer were Japanese industrialists content with competing for the "low end" of the consumer market; they set their sights on the "high end." The transistor, which was first developed in the United States in the early 1960s and licensed to Japanese firms, became the vehicle. This technology was first applied to the radio. Portable radios that were once the size of large suitcases suddenly were squeezed into remarkably small boxes that became extremely popular among beach-goers. The rest of the electronic industry was soon to follow. Relatively inexpensive state-of-the-art television sets, cameras, tape recorders, and calculators produced in Japan literally drove their American counterparts out of the market. For all practical purposes, by the mid-1970s, the U.S. electronics industry was dead.

Other Japanese industrialists turned their attention to the automobile market—an industry dominated by the Big Three American auto makers (General Motors, Ford, and Chrysler). The energy crisis that was initiated by the Organization of Petroleum Exporting Countries (OPEC) in 1973 and 1979 opened the trade door for Japan. From a negligible market share, Japanese exports to the United States rose to 1.2 million cars in 1973, as consumers turned their backs on the American-built gas-guzzlers. By the time the second wave of the energy crisis hit the American coastline, Japanese sales in the United States had risen to 1.7 million cars. This market penetration whetted the American appetite for the fuel-efficient, low-maintenance, inexpensive alternative to the automobiles produced by the Big Three. By 1986, Japanese auto sales rose to a remarkable 3.6 million cars, signaling to all that the U.S. automobile industry was under a direct attack.

Japanese success in the world marketplace is reflected in its trade balances. In 1963, the value of Japanese merchandise exports to North America was essentially equal to the value of Japan's imports from North America. By 1973 this ratio rose to 1.1, or slightly more exports to North America than imports to Japan. Over the next 13 years this ratio grew markedly, so that by 1986 Japan was exporting to North America 3.3 times more than it was importing. This imbalance excited much concern over "American competitiveness" and "Japanese unfair trade practices."

These concerns eventually led to a series of trade concessions on the part of Japan. Most importantly, they agreed to voluntary export quotas on certain commodities, such as automobiles, and explicit policies to open their domestic markets to American firms. Gradually the ratio of Japanese merchandise exports to imports began to fall. By 1989 it was back down to 1.9; but this still represented nearly twice the value of exports to North America compared to the value of her imports from North America.

In the selections that follow, the wisdom of seeking trade concessions is debated. Stephen D. Cohen argues that the presence of Japan's trade surplus is a threat to America's international strength—both military and economic strength. Philip H. Trezise, on the other side, maintains that Japanese success in the world marketplace is beneficial not only to the Japanese but also to Americans.

YES

Stephen D. Cohen

UNITED STATES–JAPANESE TRADE RELATIONS

With the waning of the cold war and the reduced threat of confrontation between the global military superpowers, the United States and Japan arguably
constitute the world's most important bilateral relationship. This relationship
now consists of a struggle—peaceful to be sure, but for enormous stakes—
between economic superpowers. Relations between the United States and
Japan feature a close political and military friendship that is being strained
by a long-running series of economic frictions. To the dismay of political scientists, most American businesspeople and many American economists are
urging their government to take an increasingly harder line with Japan in
an effort to receive equitable treatment in what has long been viewed as an
unbalanced, inequitable trading relationship.

The economic arguments between the United States and Japan have extraordinary significance. These two countries formed the world's newest and
most important bilateral relationship not because of political or military considerations but because global power and influence among nations in the
twenty-first century will be determined more by economic and technological
strength than by the size and sophistication of weapons stockpiles. Japan
and the United States, as the world's largest and strongest economies, will
inevitably be the two forces to be most reckoned with in what may be the
continuing evolution into a postmilitary international system. This is why
the majority of respondents in some recent United States public opinion polls
indicated that Japan, not the Soviet Union, represents the greatest long-term
threat to American national security. There is an intuitive recognition (not yet
fully shared by the United States government) that national security must be
defined broadly to include industrial and financial strength.

Japan is the most significant foreign competitor of the United States and vice
versa. No other country has mounted such a comprehensive and successful
assault on the competitiveness of American industry, once the undisputed
colossus of the world. No other country has in so many instances caught up
to and surpassed the once unassailable American leading-edge superiority in
the high-tech sector. No other country comes close to Japan in representing

From Stephen D. Cohen, "United States–Japanese Trade Relations," *Proceedings of the Academy
of Political Science*, vol. 37, no. 4 (1990). Copyright © 1990 by The Academy of Political Science.
Reprinted by permission.

a future challenge to United States competitiveness in the critically important new technologies: supercomputers, semiconductors, superconductivity, composite materials, telecommunications equipment and so on.

For most Japanese, friendship with the United States represents political security to a country with a still undefined sense of international mission or function. The United States is also Japan's most important foreign market and a key determinant of its continued prosperity. At the same time, American industry has been a symbolic target for a country that wished to bypass it on the way to becoming an internationally dominant industrial power.

The importance and mutual rewards of the world's largest bilateral trade relationship are not in question. What is in question is whether the likely further escalation of bilateral trade conflict will erupt into damaging unilateral economic actions that in turn will lead to political estrangement. There can be no assurance that the previously successful record of trade-conflict management can continue indefinitely, especially in view of a possible expansion of Japan's industrial superiority in the future. Also not in question is whether, by conventional measurements, the Japanese trade performance has been superior to that of the United States.

What is in question is how the two countries should best respond to a state of affairs that tries everyone's patience. Japan's trade policy has centered on a flurry of activity designed to demonstrate responsiveness to United States demands but not necessarily to induce adjustment in the bilateral disequilibrium. From the American viewpoint, the specter of Japan's unbroken winning streak in trade competition was at the focus of virtually every new concept and proposed initiative introduced in United States trade policy in the 1980's. Possible responses to reverse its deteriorating trade position include reciprocity, industrial policy, results-oriented trade talks, and reinvigorated American industrial competitiveness.

There is a serious, systemic trade problem between the two countries that is seriously misunderstood, underestimated and inadequately addressed. It arises from political, cultural and economic forces. The trade disequilibrium is best viewed as the tip of the iceberg, with domestic factors as the main underlying causal factors. With both countries continuing to treat symptoms rather than causes, it is no surprise that trade conflict has occurred on a nonstop basis since 1969. To the extent that the diagnosis offered here is correct, neither an end nor a plateau in trade frictions is in sight.

Economic conflict begins with accusations by the United States and other countries that Japan is an unfair, adversarial trader that does not play by conventional international rules in order to pursue a mercantile policy of self-aggrandizement. Critics allege that Japanese markets remain largely closed, albeit informally, to imports of manufactured goods. Its exporting companies are said to be avaricious predators intent on building market share and destroying their foreign competition. The more rabid critics of Japan accuse it of continuing to fight World War II through economic means.

Japan, in turn, is tired of what has become an unbroken record of United States whining. It accuses the United States of excessive consumption, an inadequate effort to improve its own industrial productivity, and not trying hard enough to sell in the Japanese market. The boom in Japan's exports to the United States, according to Japanese critics, reflects the preferences of American consumers for low-cost, high-quality goods, some of which are not even manufactured in the United States. The more extreme critics consider the United States to be in permanent decline, a country that is burdened by poor economic policy management, an excessively heterogeneous population, an excessive need for instant gratification, and shockingly bad business practices.

The proximate cause of the trade frictions is the large, seemingly permanent United States bilateral deficits with Japan (see Table 1). It is legitimate to state unequivocally that these deficits have produced a genuine disequilibrium in political terms, that is, an American belief that something is grievously wrong and urgently needs rectification, mainly through adjustments by Japan. It is *not* legitimate to state unequivocally that these deficits represent an absolutely unacceptable economic disequilibrium. Bilateral deficits per se, as the Japanese are quick to point out, are relatively insignificant. It is multilateral trade balances that matter.

It is the sources of the bilateral trade imbalance that must be of central concern. Here again, there are many opinions but no genuine consensus. Conflicting perceptions are an inherent part of bilateral trade disputes. Some argue that the culprit is Japanese industrial policy, in which close government-business relations have built a mighty anti-import fortress known colloquially as Japan, Incorporated. Others contend that the culprit is the simple manufacturing ineptitude of the United States, a country alleged, but not proved, to be in the advanced stages of moving into a postindustrial services-oriented economy.

The systemic source of the imbalance is best viewed as a divergence in ends (priorities and values) and therefore a divergence in means (domestic, economic and trade policies). The American system is weighted in favor of the individual and consumption. The Japanese system is weighted in favor of the corporation and production. American ideology favors the free market and cheap imports. Japanese ideology favors government enhancement of market forces, industrial self-sufficiency, and world-class strength in the manufacturing sector. The United States prints money to finance the world's largest trade deficit and in turn consumes more as a country than it produces. Japan saves like mad, accepts relatively poor housing and an inadequate infrastructure, and continues sending massive amounts of capital earned from its trade surpluses back to the United States, the effect of which is to compensate for this country's inadequate savings rate. American foreign relations for half a century have centered on political and military goals. Since 1945, Japan's foreign relations have sought to maximize exports [see Table 2 for a summary of Japan's trade structure as compared to that of the West]. . . .

ORIGINS OF THE TRADE DISPUTE

As a Japanese surplus became a fixture in the bilateral trade relationship, the United States successfully induced Japan to take sustained actions on two fronts. The first involved additional "voluntary" export restraints in a number of sectors, including textiles, automobiles, steel, color televisions, and machine tools. The second involved Japan's initiation of

Table 1

Bilateral United States–Japan Trade Balances, 1981–1990

	U.S. Bilateral Deficit ($ billion)	U.S. Imports From Japan ($ billion)	U.S. Exports to Japan ($ billion)
1981	$15.8	$37.6	$21.8
1982	16.7	37.7	21.0
1983	19.3	41.2	21.9
1984	33.6	57.1	23.6
1985	46.2	68.8	22.6
1986	55.0	81.8	26.9
1987	56.3	84.6	28.2
1988	52.1	89.8	37.7
1989	49.0	93.5	44.5
1990	41.1	89.6	48.6

Source: United States Department of Commerce

an unprecedented series of unilateral measures that eliminated or reduced hundreds of overt tariff and nontariff trade barriers. The result was an eventual Japanese contention that it had become the world's most open market (a valid claim, at least in regard to formal import restrictions). This assertion was not widely accepted in the United States, where complaints about the difficulty of succeeding in the Japanese market are still voiced by many American companies.

Bilateral consultations and negotiations continued throughout the 1980's amid continuous proposals by various members of Congress to pass harsh, retaliatory legislation as leverage to force genuine reciprocity in market access. As the "Japan problem" worsened, new forms of agreements were pursued. They included altering macroeconomic policies in an effort to increase the value of the yen's exchange rate relative to the dollar. Instead of a piecemeal approach to addressing United States corporate complaints, market-oriented,

sector-selective (MOSS) talks were convened in 1985 to focus on all the alleged market-access problems for four specially designated goods in which the United States retained a comparative advantage (electronics, pharmaceuticals/medical equipment, telecommunications, forestry products, and, later, automobile parts). One year later, the two governments concluded a groundbreaking agreement involving trade in semiconductors; it sought to shelter the American industry from Japanese "dumping" (selling below production cost) of chips both in the United States and in third countries, and it sought to provide the American industry with a specific percentage (20 percent) of the Japanese market in lieu of any further Japanese promises of market-opening measures.

STRUCTURAL IMPEDIMENTS INITIATIVE

More new forms of negotiating modalities were introduced in 1989. The first was

Table 2

Comparing Japan's Trade Structure With the West

Category	Japan				West Germany		United States		North America		European Community	
	1980	1987	1988	1989	1980	1987	1980	1987	1980	1987	1980	1987
Manufactured goods *(as percentage of GDP)*												
Exports	11.9	9.5	9.1	9.6	20.9	24.2	5.5	4.3	4.4	3.0	8.5	8.1
Imports	2.9	2.8	3.2	3.5	13.3	14.8	5.1	7.5	4.3	6.3	5.3	5.3
Balance	9.0	6.7	5.9	6.1	7.6	9.4	0.4	− 3.2	0.1	− 3.2	2.9	2.3
Non-Manufactured goods *(as percentage of GDP)*												
Exports	0.2	0.1	0.1	0.1	1.6	1.0	1.3	0.7	1.4	0.8	1.0	0.7
Imports	9.0	3.5	3.3	3.6	7.3	3.5	3.6	1.4	3.0	1.1	6.0	2.6
Balance	− 8.8	− 3.4	− 3.2	− 3.5	− 5.7	− 2.5	− 2.3	− 0.7	− 1.6	− 0.3	− 5.0	− 1.9

Source: Organization for European Cooperation and Development, *Summary Report on Trade of Japan* (Paris: OECD, 1990), *Far Eastern Economic Review* (Hong Kong), June 21, 1990, p. 47.

a direct outgrowth of Japan's being identified as a "priority" source of foreign-trade barriers against American goods under the Super 301 amendment to the Omnibus Trade and Competitiveness Act of 1988. Acting under the law, the administration of President George Bush named three areas—supercomputers, communications satellites, and wood products—that required either productive bilateral negotiations (read foreign concessions would be forthcoming) or eventual United States retaliation in kind against Japanese goods. The second, the so-called Structural Impediments Initiative (SII), was an indirect outgrowth of the Super 301 and marked a major conceptual breakthrough. The original American idea was to discuss the big picture for the first time by addressing such structural barriers to imports as the Japanese distribution system, the industrial structure (whereby companies in an extended consortium, such as Mitsui or Mitsubishi, tend to buy from one another), and the rigid pricing system for imports. But Japan insisted that the agenda be

expanded to include its charges about the structural weaknesses in the United States that are allegedly the principal sources of the trade disequilibrium.

The contradictory positions that were subsequently introduced in the SII are a perfect microcosmic symbol of the near 180-degree difference in the way each country (and Japan's supporters in the United States) apportion blame for generating bilateral economic antagonisms. In this regard, the debate over causality becomes a kind of Rorschach test. Both of the main contending views on causality are rational. But, given the absence of incontrovertible scientific methodology to determine precise cause and effect, individuals unconsciously fall back on previous experiences, prejudices, and preconceived notions in identifying with one side over the other.

While both sides continue hurling charges at each other, the festering trade dispute has begun to spill over into other economic issues. The agenda now includes the concerns of some Americans about Japan's allegedly excessive investment in the United States, its rising political influence in the United States, and the wisdom of Japan's independent development of advanced military weapons like the FSX fighter.

FLAWS IN JAPAN'S ECONOMIC CASE

An economic maxim applies to Japan: for society as a whole, there is no such thing as a free lunch. There can be no denying that Japan has achieved an economic miracle in its industrial sector since the 1950's. The miracle received crucial assistance from a seemingly universal consensus in the country that individual sacrifices had to be made in order to accomplish the priority goal of industrial recovery, a concept that could easily be embraced in a society that emphasized a group orientation. Japan's unprecedented industrial success, the springboard for its unprecedented trade success, also flowed from unexpectedly successful official policies and from unexpectedly brilliant accomplishments by private industry.

The major flaw in Japanese international economic relations continues to be the inhospitable atmosphere accorded to imports of sophisticated manufactured goods. Japan can honestly boast of having the lowest level of overt barriers and point to recent sharp upturns in its level of manufactured imports. Nevertheless, it has a surplus in manufactured goods so large (a world-record-shattering $172 billion in 1988) that it renders absurd the often heard Japanese claim that it must export a lot of manufactured goods in order to pay for its imports of raw materials. Japan's trade pattern continues to be in a class by itself in terms of the low figure for imports of manufactures as a percent of gross national product and its relatively low volume of intraindustry trade, that is, importing the same kinds of products that are exported, such as cars.

Japan poses an extraordinary problem for the United States in that a nearly complete array of the traditional techniques utilized in economics to redress a trade disequilibrium has been tried and has failed: relaxation of import barriers, exchange rate appreciation, accelerated domestic demand, politicians' exhortations to import more, and so on. Japan's argument about the true openness of its markets would be a lot more convincing if most of its trading partners were not voicing the same market-access complaints as the admittedly export-indifferent United States.

Although there is a dearth of smoking guns, circumstantial evidence, anecdotal evidence, and plain common sense collectively suggest that in the case of sophisticated manufactured goods, especially those in the targeted industries of the future, Japanese companies do prefer to keep the market share of imports to a "moderate" level. The market is not closed. It is, however, an extraordinary uphill battle by foreign exporters for more than a nominal market share in Japan. Even foreign companies that have a long-term, strong commitment to doing everything right in selling in Japan encounter levels of difficulty and frustration not experienced in countries with less of a history of keeping the rest of the world at a distance.[1]

Japan's efforts at "internationalization" have fallen far short of the mark. The country's retention of its insular, tradition-bound mentality has collided with the sheer magnitude of its export success, as well as with what is arguably the most pervasive international trend of the late twentieth century: accelerated economic interdependence. With its new role as the world's largest creditor nation come new responsibilities and the need for greater empathy for the economic needs and interests of its major trading partners and the poorer countries of the Southern Hemisphere.

Forecasts of the imminent peaking of Japan's economic success are, as they have been for almost 20 years, more wishful thinking and economic fallacy than truth. Japanese society may be aging, and a new generation born into relative affluence may not retain the same commitment to the work ethic as previous generations. But that will not prevent people from working harder. The idea that Japan has come to a plateau because it is not good at innovation flies in the face of the economic data showing massive outpourings of capital for investment in new plants and for research and development by Japanese corporations, as well as an upsurge in new patent applications.

UNITED STATES ECONOMIC FLAWS

The continuing difficulty in exporting sophisticated capital goods to the Japanese market is the first of two distinct, though interrelated, problems that constitute the essence of contemporary United States–Japan trade relations. The second problem is the inadequacies of both the domestic and external American economic performance. These collective inadequacies would perpetuate a large bilateral trade disequilibrium even if Japan were to undertake a radical restructuring of its attitudes toward dependency on foreigners for key technologies, its distribution system, its industrial structure, its willingness to abandon old business relations just to obtain cheaper products, and so forth.

The counterparts of Japan's record-setting trade surpluses are the unprecedented United States deficits that turned the American trade account in the 1980's into a sea of red ink. An important source of the deficits in the first half of the decade was not of Japanese origin: the overvaluation of the dollar's exchange rate made imports a bargain and reduced the competitiveness of American exports on a global basis. Large federal budget deficits following the tax cut induced by Reaganomics combined with falling savings rates to produce an internal United States disequilibrium that inevitably caused a net inflow of capital from abroad and a deficit in the current account (goods and services) of the balance of payments. Until savings increase or the budget deficit is reduced, a United States trade deficit will remain, not of Japanese doing but one that is largely self-inflicted.

When competing head-on with the industrial giants of Japan, the weaknesses of American management practices and production techniques are painfully magnified. The American reward system, which instills myopia among business executives about the value of immediate profits, does not hold up well against the long-term time horizon of Japanese managers willing to invest years of effort and lose hundreds of millions of dollars to maximize global market share. Ironically, several of the "innovations" of Japanese management, such as statistical procedures to enhance quality control, were devised by Americans whose countrymen originally had no interest in their ideas. It was not until recent years that most American business executives switched from the argument that the Japanese were competing mainly through unfair practices to the position that even the mightiest, proudest American industrial company would do well to replicate the perfectly fair and quite clever strategies being practiced by their Japanese competition. Hence, many American companies learned that assembling goods right the first time is cheaper than repairing defects later on, that is, vigorous quality control is effectively free.

Many American factories have switched to the Japanese system of "just in time delivery," by which inventory costs and the need for storage space are reduced by having suppliers deliver components only hours before they are actually needed on the production line. A number of American manufacturing companies have adopted the Japanese model of minimizing layers of middle management and maximizing attention paid to the ideas of production-line workers.

American companies are slowly absorbing the brilliant approach of their Japanese competitors to "process technology," the art of designing the production line for maximum efficiency. As exemplified by the unsuccessful multibillion-dollar retooling by General Motors in the 1980's, maximum efficiency on the production line means more than simple installation of labor-saving devices. It requires a proper configuration of flexible machinery on the production line and cooperation in the design phase among engineers, assembly-line workers, and even suppliers. Maximum efficiency also requires the ability to adjust machinery quickly and simply to turn out different models of the same products, be they automobiles or household appliances.

However, this is not to suggest the beginning of a turnaround in the bilat-

eral trade disequilibrium. Even a more vigorous turnaround by American industry would be insufficient to overcome the disadvantages imposed by the fact that American economic policymaking does not put nearly enough emphasis on enhancing industrial competitiveness as Japan does. For example, the Japanese government has always put a major emphasis on ensuring that high-growth industries have ample amounts of low-cost capital. In the United States, government and business remain adversaries instead of trying jointly to forecast what goals and important new technologies the country's private sector should be pursuing. The American political establishment remains stubbornly opposed to any form of industrial policy in the increasingly important sector of commercial high technology, while mysteriously embracing it in sectors like agriculture and military aerospace. United States tax laws still encourage companies to go into debt to make acquisitions or engage in leveraged buy-outs.

While those presumed to be America's best and brightest are speculatively buying and selling corporate assets and issuing junk bonds of questionable value, the Japanese methodically go about the business of expanding sales through efficient, high-volume, low-defect production methods. While the United States focuses on how to carve up the existing national economic pie, the Japanese seek to enlarge it. While American executives try to please shareholders and maximize their incomes—admittedly a very efficient system—their Japanese competition is trying to please customers and maximize market share—sometimes an even better system.

The Japanese government has the simpler task in designing an optimal negotiating strategy with its United States counterpart. First, it relies on its vast commercial intelligence network in Washington to determine when United States threats are genuine. Second, the Japanese government relies on an even vaster public relations and lobbying network in the United States to get articulate, highly visible versions of Japanese viewpoints and rebuttals before United States officials as well as the general public. Third, it continues to find scattered import barriers to reduce. Japan's nearly quarter century of import liberalization is unique for more than just its extent; it has had the singular motive of seeking not to give lower prices to Japanese consumers but to please American demands. The potential for cheaper imports has been deemed a sacrifice, not an economic bonanza as it would in the United States. Fourth, when United States pressures intensify, the Japanese government pressures the appropriate Japanese companies to ease off on further export growth.

Japan's official trade agenda is basically reactive; the private sector takes the initiative and sets the tone. Most Japanese are satisfied with their country's trade performance and trade surplus. They prefer to stick with a winning formula, wanting nothing basic to change other than for the United States and other trading partners to be more understanding, to stop making threats, and not to pester them for ever more concessions. Japan's mounting global industrial and technological strength is accomplishing one of the transcendent goals of 2,000 years of Japanese history: retaining its political and cultural independence by carefully controlling and limiting foreign intrusion and leverage.

The United States government has found it much more difficult to set an effective bilateral trade agenda because its industry remains on the defensive. In lieu of adopting a grand strategy of homing in on the systemic problem, however, it has pursued piecemeal tactics aimed at changing trading conditions on a product-by-product basis. It has never known exactly how far to push Japan, fearing the triggering of protectionist trade actions or, even worse, political strains. Internal economic shortcomings have always been recognized as contributing to the trade disequilibrium, but for the past decade most of them have been attributed to government interference, not the lack of effective government initiatives or existing mistakes.

The net result is that United States trade policy toward Japan is the worst of both worlds. On the one hand, strident demands make the United States look like a bully with an unending request list. On the other hand, the lack of determination and consistency in United States policy has yielded wholly inadequate results. American negotiating strategy has been largely reduced to a repeated and somewhat predictable version of the good-cop/bad-cop routine of old Hollywood movies. After a ritualistic warning by the liberal trade-loving executive branch that the protectionist ogres in Congress are on the brink of passing restrictive trade legislation, Japan produces a ritualistic market-opening measure or export-restraint agreement, depending on the situation.

When the administration relies on the "congressional card," it implicitly links itself with purportedly fellow free traders in Japan in order to fight villains in another part of the United States government. In the words of a former United

States negotiator: "The negotiation thus changed direction: originally a matter of U.S. government requests, it became one of mutually calibrating just how much action would be necessary to keep Congress leashed. Instead of a negotiator, the U.S. trade team became an adviser to the government of Japan on how to handle the U.S. Congress."[2]

The United States government would be well advised to develop a consensus on its needs and goals in the bilateral trade relationship, as well as how hard it is willing to press to achieve them. A unified strategy must come from the Office of the President, and it is unlikely to be produced by conventional policymaking forums....

The first stage of a more effective United States Japanese trade dialogue would consist of both countries formally acknowledging the applicability of the Japanese proverb that when two men fight, both are at fault. Japan needs to accept the fact that selling advanced manufactured goods to its market still poses extraordinary difficulties to most foreigners. Pointing to its increased imports of consumer goods or to healthy sales and profits by United States corporate subsidiaries producing in Japan is not the same thing as demonstrating that the Japanese market for high-tech goods is "reasonably" open in regard to cost, energy, and effort. Japan's industrial policy tends to target the same high-tech industries—such as computers, semiconductors, telecommunications equipment, and biotechnology—in which the United States has (or had) international competitive strength. The United States should not be content with even a bilateral trade surplus with Japan if it was caused by a boom in exports of agricultural and other primary products. Japan ought to realize

that the more it discusses its "internationalization," the less likely it truly exists.

The United States needs to accept the fact that, quite apart from its legitimate complaints about the relative difficulty and cost of exporting to Japan, its lack of competitiveness vis-à-vis Japanese products, especially in its home market, is primarily the result of shortcomings in United States domestic economic policies, management practices, and production skills. The United States needs to accept the costly nature of protectionist trade policies, inasmuch as they tend to dissipate pressures on American producers to continue cutting costs and raising quality. Furthermore, restrictions on Japanese goods have already been shown to be harmful to the increasing number of American companies using Japanese-made capital goods and components. At the same time, the United States government must realize that more of the same is not an optimal strategy.

As long as it avoids the somewhat arbitrary idea of putting specific numbers on what Japan should be buying, the United States would be well advised to follow the basic recommendation of the 1989 report to the United States Trade Representative by the Advisory Committee for Trade Policy and Negotiations: the United States should

structure a program of action that pursues change on multiple fronts, commits adequate resources over a 4–5-year period, is strategically focused, and is results-oriented. This program we see as a natural evolution of U.S. trade policy from a more or less reactive response to the damage wrought by the strong dollar in the early 1980's, to active efforts to create the conditions necessary for the growth of industries and sectors critical to the nation's long-term economic vitality.[3]

Japan should embrace as an integral part of its trade policy the belief that, in the long run, its national security is more likely to be enhanced by the friendship of trading partners than by the size of its trade surplus. The Japanese government needs to promote a whole new mind-set in Japan that encourages more attention to the Japanese consumer. This effort would need to be supported by such reforms as a more vigorous legal challenge to cartels and the easing of restrictions on large chain stores (they are more attracted to imports than the small stores effectively controlled by Japanese manufacturers). Furthermore, the government needs to go beyond slogans to generate a genuine consensus among Japanese industries that it is no longer in the national interest to discriminate against imports.

No matter how open the Japanese market becomes (or how much additional leisure time Japanese workers opt for), there is no reason to expect a diminution of Japan's increasing excellence in advanced technologies. If American exports to Japan are to rise and if American imports from Japan are not to swamp important high-tech industries, the United States clearly needs to improve its business environment. The appropriate starting point is an immediate, genuine (as opposed to accounting smoke and mirrors) reduction in the United States budget deficit. By reducing the government's absorption of the available capital pool, productive investment in the industrial sector would be encouraged by the assumed reduction in interest rates that would occur with a reduced federal budget deficit.

Furthermore, the government needs to realize that the nature of modern economics and the fading dividing line between military and civilian technology justify increased official funding of expensive or risky, but promising, new commercial technologies. While the United States does not need a comprehensive "industrial policy" to replace its basic dependence on corporate investment and venture capital, it does need additional government seed money to help entrepreneurial companies compete with the deep pockets of their larger, better financed, vertically integrated Japanese competitors.

No matter what Washington does to improve the domestic business environment, it will not be enough unless American business executives alter their behavior. They must place less emphasis on short-term profits, year-end bonuses, and wheeling and dealing in mergers, acquisitions and leveraged buy-outs. A significant part of the trade battle with Japan continues to be lost on the factory floor.

Official encouragement of dollar depreciation to an exchange rate of between 100 yen and 200 yen would aid American competitiveness, but it is not a panacea. Yen appreciation has not and will not keep Americans from buying high-quality Japanese goods, nor will it open the floodgates in Japan to imports of American-made manufactured goods.

There are two problems with this list of proposed policy and program reforms. First, it is far from definitive. At the same time, however, neither country is likely to act quickly on its contents. A resolution in the underlying causes of the trade disequilibrium can only be foreseen by optimists. More likely than not, the systemic causes of frictions will remain unaddressed. United States industry may well do better in the competitiveness race but not as well as Japan in the pursuit of excellence in the important new technologies. There is no reason to expect the industrial competitiveness gap to narrow significantly. It therefore appears that during the 1990's Japan is fated to remain America's number-one foreign competitor, number-one illuminator of shortcomings in United States economic policies and business practices, and the principal source of frustration to American trade policymakers.

Continuation of an inferior industrial performance relative to Japan is not conducive either to the long-term economic prosperity or national security interests of the United States. Regrettably, in its successful but short-sighted pursuit of profit and consumption maximization, America cannot be bothered to respond more effectively to the long-term challenges of the alternative model of capitalist power being pursued in Japan. Also regrettably, Japan is not likely to find increased economic success a reason to become truly less insular. By the turn of the century, the inadequacies of United States

trade and economic policies may cause this country to fail two key tests cited by Paul Kennedy in *The Rise and Fall of the Great Powers:*

> whether, in the military/strategical realm, it can preserve a reasonable balance between the nation's perceived defense requirements and the means it possesses to maintain those commitments; and whether, as an intimately related point, it can preserve the technological and economic bases of its power from relative erosion in the face of the ever-shifting patterns of global production.[4]

NOTES

1. See for example the report of the sales failure in high-tech goods by a native-born Japanese émigré sent back to live in Japan by Allied-Signal, Inc., in "Hidden Wall: A Native Son Battles Japan's Trade Barriers," *Washington Post*, June 23, 1989.

2. Clyde Prestowitz, Jr., *Trading Places* (New York: Basic Books, 1988), p. 281.

3. "Analysis of the U.S.–Japan Trade Problem" (Report of the Advisory Committee for Trade Policy and Negotiations, Washington, D.C., February, 1989), p. ix.

4. Paul Kennedy, *The Rise and Fall of the Great Powers* (New York: Random House, 1987), pp. 514–515.

NO
Philip H. Trezise

JAPAN, THE ENEMY?

Does Japanese economic competition present a greater threat to American security than Soviet military power? Is Japan a "systematically predatory actor" on the international economic scene? Is it an authoritarian state under irresponsible and corrupt rule? Must we devise a new policy to "contain" a rogue Japan? Is it time for the Pentagon to draw up plans for an eventual war with Japan?

According to opinion polls, a majority of Americans say yes to the first of these questions. Many supposedly well-informed people also respond affirmatively to the next three. The idea of planning for a war with Japan is no doubt remote from most Americans' minds, but it is said to be whispered among those whose profession is to reflect on the contingencies of the future.

To be sure, the actual state of U.S.–Japan relations is less bleak than the news media or the magazine and book authors would have it. The situation is not analogous to the second half of the 1930s. Japan is not rampaging in China or anywhere else. Official relations between Japan and the United States remain close and in the main cordial. Although squabbles over trade policy are chronic, each side treats the other with reasonable regard for the civilities. The American public may view Japan's economic accomplishments and capacities with alarm, but it does not boycott Japanese goods, rather the contrary.

Still something is very wrong with the domestic dialogue. In Congress Japan-bashing is obviously considered to be an appropriate and electorally risk-free activity. Little consideration seems to be given to the thought that any serious rift between the world's two largest economies would hurt mutual and global welfare. That the U.S.–Japanese military alliance has been a force for stability in East Asia for nearly four decades goes largely unspoken, while Japan's low defense budget is a standard target for attacks. And the current polemics carry an undercurrent of racism, not overwhelming, perhaps, but not pleasant either.

Yet on any rational calculation, economic competition from Japan does not threaten America's national security. If Japanese government and industry engage in conduct contrary to international rules or norms, ample legal,

From Philip H. Trezise, "Japan, the Enemy?" *The Brookings Review* (Winter 1989/1990). Copyright © 1989 by The Brookings Institution. Reprinted by permission.

administrative, and economic remedies are available. Japan's democracy has its warts, as whose does not, but it functions effectively in a society that is in all fundamentals free. "Containing" Japan is the offering of a journalist who sees American vulnerabilities that do not exist. Another Pacific war? More remote eventualities can be imagined, but not readily.

These are assertions. Let us see if they can be fortified with arguments and facts.

DEFICITS AND DEBT

Current problems between the two countries obviously derive principally from their economic relationship. That has been the case virtually since the signing of the peace treaty in 1951. The difference today is that the relations are more complex and the interdependence of the two economies is much greater. Whether this greater involvement threatens our well-being is quite another matter.

Some see a threat in our trade imbalance with Japan. The U.S. external deficit has been running at unprecedented heights. Foreign trade in goods accounts for the largest part, and of that, trade with Japan stands out. The total trade deficit peaked in 1987 at $159.5 billion; 36 percent represented the deficit with Japan. The U.S. trade deficit with the world promises to be more nearly $100 billion in 1989, while Japan's share is likely to be close to 50 percent. Inevitably, the size and the seemingly intractable character of Japan's trade surplus with us has been politicized. Thus Representative Richard A. Gephardt in 1988 almost succeeded in writing into law a provision penalizing nations with "excessive" trade surpluses, to wit, Japan.

A deficit must be covered by borrowing, and the United States has quickly acquired the world's largest-ever external debt, currently estimated at half a trillion dollars, much of it owed to Japan. A relatively small part of the Japanese-owned assets in the United States is in the form of real estate and industrial plant. It turns out, however, that Americans are no less prone than Europeans, Canadians, Mexicans—and Japanese—to anxieties at observing that land, office buildings, and factories are being bought or built by foreigners. Other, less visceral, concerns arise about the much greater sum of foreign capital invested in Treasury securities and the bond and stock markets. Take together these debts provide another element in what has become, at a minimum, a worrisome matter of international public relations.

Underlying all else is the perception that Japan's trade and economic policies are unfair. It is a perception that finds support in a mass of anecdotal material and in a few more rigorous studies of the trade data. In the popular version, Japan's market is said to be closed to American exports while Japanese exports have flourished in the American market. The government of Japan is supposed to subsidize and otherwise coddle the export industries, with special attention to the now and future high-technology sectors. Credit for business and industry is cheap because the Ministry of Finance and the Bank of Japan will it so, mainly in the interest of exports. Although Japanese firms can readily establish themselves in the United States, American businesses encounter high barriers to entry into Japan. The catalogue of the imputed offenses against fairness is extensive. It unquestionably has achieved a wide measure of acceptance.

Well, the U.S. external deficit is real, the growing debt to foreigners is breathtakingly large, and critical views of Japanese economic policies and practices are not always, as some Japanese insist, self-serving or based on misunderstandings. The United States does have problems in its economic relations with Japan, not all of them trivial.

But do those problems make Japan a consequential, not to say a mortal, danger to American interests or security? Has the Japanese economic miracle, once looked upon as witness to the wisdom of U.S. postwar policy, brought into being a monster?

If the foreign deficit is part of the case against Japan, then one must ask how it came about and what damage it has wrought.

In a sense the deficit, which began its surge in 1982, was intended by nobody and caused by everybody. Before 1982 U.S. deficits on merchandise trade (themselves a phenomenon that did not appear in this century until the 1970s) normally were balanced or overbalanced by earnings from American investments abroad. After the 1981 tax cuts and the subsequent unplanned federal budget deficits, the overall external deficit—goods and services—soared (from less than $9 billion in 1982 to $153 billion in 1987), driven by a rapidly rising trade imbalance and a declining net position on returns from foreign investments.

Conventional wisdom, which in this case is also true wisdom, says that these developments reflected higher rates of savings and fewer desirable investment opportunities abroad than in the United States. Private savings rates in the United States have been among the lowest in the industrial world. The post-1981 federal budget deficits preempted for govern-

ment use a historically large part of these savings, three-fifths between 1984 and 1988. Shrinking domestic savings and the growing demand for investment pushed up real interest rates and drew foreign savings to U.S. financial markets. In the predictable course of events, this expanding demand for dollars caused the exchange value of the dollar to rise sharply. Just as predictable, the strong dollar attracted imports and put the export industries at severe disadvantage. Hence the massive trade deficits of the 1980s.

It can be and was argued that this sequence could have been slowed or interrupted if the high-savings countries —particularly Japan and Germany—had chosen to emulate the United States by using more of their peoples' savings for public purposes. Germany with very high unemployment and Japan with manifestly large unfilled needs for public facilities might have attacked these domestic issues by lifting the lid on government spending, at the price of bigger budget deficits. They did not do so, for what they saw as compelling economic and political reasons. Had they indeed opted to absorb more of their nations' savings for domestic use, the U.S. consumption and investment boom could not have run unchecked. The practical choices would have been to do something real about cutting the budget deficit or living with interest rates that would have curbed the expansion.

These reflections are germane to the question of the trade deficit's effect on the national welfare. No one can doubt that the strong dollar of the early 1980s hurt U.S. export and import-competing industries. To workers who lost high-paying jobs in these industries, it is little comfort that the national unemployment rate fell steadily to virtually full employment levels while total civilian employment grew at a very satisfactory pace. Nor, presumably, do managements pressured by foreign competition to restructure their companies look back with undiluted pleasure at the experience.

Nevertheless, it is the fact that the trade and overall deficits were accompanied by strongly rising employment and that the growth of productivity per man-hour in the American manufacturing industry from 1981 through 1987 was roughly one and one-half times the 1948–81 average. The reality is that the capital inflow from Japan and elsewhere served to sustain American levels of investment that could not have been reached otherwise. These were voluntary flows, made in response to explicable economic incentives. In short, the United States is richer and more productive because Japanese and other foreigners found it in their interest to send their excess savings here.

Some observers who are not given to demoniac views of foreign investment nonetheless worry that capital inflows might substantially diminish well before American net savings have recovered. In that event, they speculate, interest rates would have to rise, precipitating a U.S. recession. That has not happened, and fears that it will have subsided. It could occur, though, which is one reason why public policy should be focused more than it is on our low savings.

A nonhypothetical reason for concern about U.S. reliance on foreign capital is the external debt that is the counterpart of the borrowing. Payments of interest and dividends on the debt must come out of current American income. In 1988 these payments exceeded $100 billion, almost equaling receipts from accumulated U.S. investments abroad. This year the payments will exceed receipts. Clearly enough, the nation would be better off if these payments were made to other Americans rather than to foreigners. If Americans can cease accumulating debt —which means, remember, restoring the savings rate to more normal levels—disposable incomes will be the higher for it.

But it is well to recognize that the nation's capital stock is larger than it would have been without the foreign inflows that now constitute the external debt. The income generated by that larger stock provides the wherewithal to meet the costs of servicing the borrowings. While it is anomalous and perhaps immoral for the world's richest country to be absorbing so much of the world's savings, the United States is not in danger of being impoverished by the costs of carrying its debt.

FOREIGN DIRECT INVESTMENT

The presence of visible foreign investment seems to make for domestic uneasiness almost everywhere. What is troubling about that uneasiness in the United States is its focus on Japanese direct investment, which still lags behind the British. Some adverse reaction had to be expected as Japanese investors bought real estate in New York and Los Angeles, built auto plants in Ohio, Tennessee, Illinois, and Michigan, and took over textile mills in the Carolinas. The facts hardly warrant hysteria or even mild worry, however. We are not being "colonized" by Japan or anyone else.

The national wealth of the United States is estimated to be $15 trillion. Assets—securities and direct investments in land, structures, and equipment—owned by foreigners at the end of 1988 were valued at $1.3 trillion, or 8.7 percent. (U.S.–

owned assets abroad were valued, actually undervalued, at $700 billion.) Foreign direct investment in the United States was $329 billion (slightly greater than the book value of U.S. direct investment abroad) or 2.2 percent of the nation's stock of resources exclusive of people. Japanese direct investments totalled $53 billion, or slightly more than three-tenths of a percent of our national wealth. These are not numbers that would imply the imminent domination of American economic or political life by Japan or by foreigners generally.

It is not always recognized, either, that foreign firms establishing themselves in the United States become American firms, liable for American taxes, required to observe American laws and regulations, and subject to the peculiarities and pressures of American community life. Their interest is to be seen as good corporate citizens here, as is true of American multinationals abroad. Their interest, and ours, is also that they be profitable, for that is the indicator that their and our resources are being used efficiently.

In 1985 a Japanese investor needed, on average, 238 yen to buy a dollar's worth of U.S. assets. In 1988 he needed only 128 yen. This depreciation of the dollar has led to complaints that Japan is buying into America on the cheap. But as depreciation has lowered the yen cost of acquiring land, facilities, and securities in the United States, it has equally lowered the yen income to be earned here. Japanese investors cannot have failed to observe this relationship. The reasons for the present flow of foreign investment into the United States are its good economic performance, its political stability, and, possibly, worries that its xenophobes may eventually succeed in writing laws that would block future inflows of capital.

JAPAN'S ECONOMIC INHOSPITALITY

That Japan itself has been less than hospitable to foreign investment is a further source of grievance—part and parcel of the more general indictment of the Japanese government and its businesses for allegedly ignoring claims to reciprocity and equal treatment or, in the more extreme form, for calculated economic aggression against the United States.

A full treatment of that indictment is beyond the scope or purpose of this essay. Some of its points should be mentioned, however. American direct investment in Japan was valued at $17 billion in 1988. In the United Kingdom it was $49 billion. Of course language and acquaintance favor investment in the U.K. But Japan's postwar economic growth was explosive, while the British economy stagnated. Had entry into Japan been as easy as into the U.K., more American firms would surely have overcome language and like barriers—as, of course, many did.

Japan's tariffs were drastically lowered in the 1970s and 1980s, and quota restrictions, except for agricultural imports, largely removed. Nevertheless, Europeans and Americans say the Japanese market is less open than those of the other major industrial powers. A persuasive piece of evidence is Japan's exceptionally low volume of imports of manufactured goods, relative to gross national product or as a share of total imports. Even after allowing for Japan's dependence on imports of foodstuffs, raw materials, and fuel, and for its distance from suppliers, the comparisons are striking. As recently as 1985, only a quarter of Japanese imports were in manufactures; in contrast, fully 70 percent of U.S. imports were manufactured goods. Japan's ratio of manufactures imports to GNP was 2.6 percent; in West Germany, which is also heavily dependent on imports of primary products, the ratio was 14.9 percent.

Since 1985 the strengthening yen has made foreign manufactures cheaper, and imports have risen; between 1985 and 1988 American exports of manufactures to Japan rose by 79 percent, compared with 49 percent to the rest of the world. Manufactures accounted for almost 50 percent of all of Japan's imports in 1988. Yet the ratio to national expenditure was less than half that of the United States, which itself is a modest importer in relation to GNP.

Why Japan's manufactured imports are comparatively low has been the subject of debate among economists, Japanese and American, with no fully conclusive answers. But anomalies in Japan's trade structure give credibility to the existence of an anti-import bias, whether enforced by custom or by rules and regulations.

An example: Japan is a very large importer of raw logs and a small importer of manufactures of wood, although its wood products manufacturing sector is not an obviously efficient processor of the raw materials; it ranks ahead only of apparel and leather in value added per worker. Similarly, Japan imports metal ores and concentrates in quantity, and metal manufactures and semi-manufactures in comparatively inconsiderable lots; no other industrial country exhibits this pattern of trade.

A reasonable assumption is that these seeming oddities (in economic terms) reflect a reluctance to accept the political costs that a contraction of these processing industries would entail. American admirers of Japan's industrial policies like to cite the readiness of the Ministry of Trade and Industry (MITI) to "phase out" aging, inefficient industries. This readiness is pure myth. Japan is no different from other countries in wishing to preserve established industries, and it may well be more diligent at pursuing that objective.

Japan is the largest foreign market for America's farmers. It is also a closed market for rice and a restricted market for a number of other agricultural commodities. These restrictions are required because most of Japanese agriculture is high cost and must be supported by public subsidies. Unrestricted imports would be budgetarily impossible.

Agricultural policy in Japan is unique only in the sense that the costs to taxpayers and consumers are relatively much higher than in other major countries. In some details it seems unusually excessive, however. Wheat is a crop poorly suited to Japan's small-scale farms. Wheat imports are sizable but in quantities carefully controlled to shield rice from undue competition.

In the 1970s, when surpluses caused a decision to retire land from rice production, the Ministry of Agriculture chose to offer truly extraordinary subsidies to farmers who would convert this land to wheat, soybeans, barley, or sugar beets, all import-displacing crops. In the case of wheat, a farmer eligible for all the available benefits could receive payments equal to 13 or 14 times the cost of foreign wheat delivered in Japan. This policy, which in its essentials continues today, actually brought only rather modest acreage into production of the heavily subsidized crops. What it seems to have represented was an unusually committed mindset against imports.

One of the counts in the foreign indictment of Japanese economic policies is the use of subsidies to foster selected industries, particularly the high-tech sectors. This is a much overdrawn matter. An overwhelming share of public subsidies goes to agriculture, followed, now that the money-draining national railways have been privatized, by energy and small business. The amounts going to industry may have served as useful catalysts for ventures targeted by MITI, semiconductors, for example, but they have been tiny in comparison with, say, the funds lavished on the Airbus or the Concorde in Europe. And a number of MITI's long-term targets have been missed altogether. Still, subsidies, together with other features of industrial policy, doubtless have helped to give some Japanese industries a competitive edge not otherwise attainable.

Other unfair or questionable practices are alleged. The industrial/banking groupings (*keiretsu*)—Mitsubishi, Mitsui, Sumitomo, et al.—are said to give preference to group members, perhaps particularly when the competing product or firm is foreign. Some people believe that the banking system, at government direction, subsidizes industry, or some sectors of industry, in the form of credit on below-market terms. These accusations are not easily substantiated. The second of them indeed seems to run counter to the increasing practice among major Japanese corporations of borrowing against their own commercial paper or in the Euro-markets rather than from the domestic banks.

THE PRICE OF UNFAIR PRACTICES

Supposing, in any case, that at least a significant part of the total indictment has merit, what conclusions are to be drawn?

One is that the losers include those competitive foreign suppliers who encounter a protected and circumscribed market and would-be investors who are denied potentially profitable opportunities. Americans are very important among these losers, but they also number Europeans, Australians, Koreans, and so on. The economic penalties imposed on all of them detract from global welfare, as does protectionism anywhere.

More substantial losers still are the citizens of Japan. As consumers they pay higher-than-necessary prices and have a more limited range of choice. As taxpayers they are required to help finance activities that use the nation's resources wastefully. If they are among the country's efficient producers, they must absorb costs that reduce their returns and worsen their competitive positions.

An economists' aphorism says that a tax on imports is a tax on exports. The argument in essence says that protection raises general money wages. Sectors producing import substitutes or wholly domestic goods can pass on the higher wage costs to consumers. The export industries, facing a world market, cannot, so profits and employment in the export sector decline. In brief, protection diverts resources from export sectors, actual or potential, to sectors where they are or will be used less efficiently. The long-run effect on economic growth is, of course, negative. As remaining protection comes down, Japan's export industries will be the stronger for it. Any improvement in the U.S. trade balance to be gained from greater access to Japan's market is thus likely to be for the short term. A lasting change in the Japanese trade surplus will depend on changes in relative savings/investment ratios.

Nevertheless, a Japan that imports more and exports more is to be desired. The United States has been right to seek greater market access and not only because U.S. exporters stand to benefit. To the extent that Japan is more protectionist than other countries, its contribution to world economic growth and welfare, considerable as it surely has been, is below potential.

A FITTING TRADE PARTNER?

Some of Japan's critics see in its formidable export performance and its outsized trade surplus a danger to the relatively open trading system that has helped to foster and sustain the remarkable gains made in world economic growth since World War II. They point to the import restrictions already imposed on Japanese goods in North America and Western Europe as indicative of a trend that is bound to take on momentum. The end result, presumably, would be to undo completely the international consensus on liberal trade that is represented by the General Agreement on Tariffs and Trade (GATT). In its extreme form, the argument goes that Japan simply does not fit and that the survival of the trading system would be best ensured by its exclusion.

These views have made little evident impression on the political leaders of Japan's trading partners. Far from seeking to isolate Japan, they have the MITI minister as a charter member of the "Quad," the inner group of the GATT composed of American, European Com-

munity, Canadian, and Japanese trade officials. In 1986, when Japan's export surplus was nearing its highest point, the GATT membership agreed at Punta del Este to launch the Uruguay Round, with perhaps the most ambitious agenda of any of the multilateral tariff and trade policy negotiations. The objectives include tightening the GATT rules that have been ignored or evaded by the protective measures taken against Japanese exports. The final returns will not be in until 1990 or later, but the Uruguay Round bargainers thus far have registered anything but despair for the GATT and its future.

One reason may be that the macroeconomic effects of Japan's outsized trade surpluses have been less disruptive than might have been feared. The surplus reached a peak in 1987 at $96 billion. Three quarters of it was with the United States and the European Community. These enormous economies, with a combined GNP of well over $9 trillion, seem to have adjusted quite smoothly to the unprecedentedly large trade deficits. In the United States, where the cumulative trade deficit from 1981 through 1988 was $750 billion (40 percent of it in trade with Japan), the march to virtual full employment went largely unchecked. Europe's troubling employment problems began in the early 1970s, long before the surge in Japan's surpluses, and clearly are caused far more by rigidities in the individual national economies than by imports from Japan. West Germany, which has had trade surpluses that in some years were relatively larger than Japan's, has had unemployment levels comparable to those of its fellow EC members.

Of course Japan's export successes have imposed painful adjustment costs on American firms and their workers in certain industries, among them semiconductors, steel, autos, machine tools, and consumer electronics. Against these costs are arrayed gains to consumers, not only from lower prices but also from advances in quality or performance of the product involved, domestic and Japanese. The case for engaging in trade is that its benefits are widely shared and continuing, whereas the costs are local and temporary.

There remain the arguments that Japan is a predatory trader and that national security is about to be imperiled by U.S. dependence on Japanese high-tech goods.

OVERBLOWN FEARS OF PREDATION...

Predation can be defined as a policy aimed systematically at eliminating competitors in order to create the conditions for monopoly pricing. That is the classic case for resisting export dumping. As a defense against this putative threat, the GATT allows, and most trading nations including the United States have, antidumping statutes. Japanese goods offered in the United States at below the home market price or below average cost are liable to penalty duties. The economics of that law are open to debate, but its availability is not in question. Nor is its use. At the end of 1987, 158 antidumping findings and orders were outstanding, covering products from 23 countries, Japan most prominent among them, followed by Canada.

Dumping is typically a marketing decision by a private firm or firms. "Unfair" pricing, with its implications of predatory intent, can be facilitated by official subsidies to producers. Here again the United States has a legal defense. Its countervailing duty law, which is sanctioned by the GATT, provides for penalty duties when foreign government subsidies are found to cause or threaten "material injury" to a domestic industry or to materially retard its establishment. Seventy-four countervailing duty orders were in effect at the end of 1987 on goods from 31 countries, none including Japan.

... AND HIGH-TECH DEPENDENCE

The existence of antidumping and countervailing duty laws makes a successful predation policy unlikely, if indeed such a policy ever has been considered to be practicable in the American market. Japan, however, has achieved a dominant position in the U.S. market for three major products: video cassette recorders, facsimile machines, and memory chips. Experience with VCRs and Fax hardly bears out fears about exploitation of American consumers. The Japanese makers have been competing vigorously with one another here, the conclusive manifestation being the steady downward course of prices. Moreover, they have moved some of their production to the United States and have established marketing facilities here, where they unquestionably come under the jurisdiction of the antitrust unit of the Department of Justice.

Memory chips are a different story. U.S. market conditions in 1987 and 1988 give convincing evidence of cartel pricing by the Japanese chip industry, to the considerable unhappiness of U.S. users. No sleuthing was necessary to determine the cause. The 1986 Semiconductor Trade Arrangement (STA) negotiated between the two governments provided that the Japanese authorities would ensure that chip prices would be raised to levels determined by the United States to reflect full, nondumping costs. A leading writer on the economic threat from Japan has described the result: "This [the STA] amounted to getting the Japanese government to force its companies to make a profit and even to impose controls to avoid excess production—in short a government-led cartel."

Memory chips are vital to computers, which in turn have manifold military applications. Japanese advances in this category of semiconductors and in the electronics industry generally have been the grounds for the perceived menace to American national security. The Defense Department's Defense Science Board in 1987 found it "an unacceptable situation" that "U.S. defense will soon depend on foreign sources for state-of-the-art technology in semiconductors." Why such dependence should be unacceptable is arguable. The United States depends on foreign sources for other things important to defense, oil for example. The probability that Japan would withhold its semiconductors from its American ally is extremely small.

Nevertheless, the case has been essentially decided. Government subsidies and freedom from antitrust strictures are now to assist American industry to challenge and outdo its Japanese rivals. If the premise is granted that there is a high-tech problem immediately or predictably related to the nation's security, then a response is warranted. One hopes that the response that has been chosen will succeed. In any event, the most productive country in the world is hardly a helpless giant.

PERSPECTIVE ON SUCCESS

Nor should Americans be mesmerized by Japan's economic successes. In the 1960s when Japan's GNP was growing at 10–11 percent annually, many expected that growth to continue more or less indefinitely. In the 1970s the growth rate fell to an average annual 4.5 percent, and it has slowed further to a little more than 4 percent in the 1980s. Nothing about the slowdown is the least bit mysterious. Japan in the 1950s and 1960s was able to employ a growing labor force, including its otherwise jobless and underemployed workers. Its enterprising business class was investing the nation's high savings in the facilities needed to raise the productivity of these workers. As the pool of unemployed declined and population growth tailed off and as the managerial and technical catch-up with Western Europe and the United States came nearer, growth had to slow.

Catch-up is some distance from being complete, moreover. Japanese workers today produce on average about 70 percent as many real goods and services as do American workers. Canadians are at 95 percent of the U.S. level, while the West Europeans fall between the Japanese and the Canadians. Japan and West Germany—and many others—will probably move closer to the United States and Canada over time. But as they achieve parity or superiority by this measure, Americans will not thereby be poorer—any more than they are less well off because Canadians are almost as productive as they are.

If comfort is needed, Japan has an ongoing, basic, and serious economic (and social) problem: Its population is aging much faster than the population of other major industrialized countries.

Demographic projections for the year 2000 put Japan's over-65 population at 16.2 percent (West Germany's is projected at 15.0 percent; the United States' at 12.0 percent). In 1950 the over-65 cohort was 4.9 percent of Japan's population; it is expected to be almost a quarter in 2020. The implications of this for the economic fundamentals—the labor force and the savings rate—have to be negative. Japan's has proven to be a remarkably resilient society, and it can be expected to rise to this new challenge. But a nation with a sharply rising ratio of nonworkers to workers is not likely to have the economic dynamism it had in earlier times.

In the end, however, developments in Japan cannot provide solutions for America's own problems. The United States has had an extended economic expansion, supported in important measure by Japanese and other lenders and investors. The U.S. trade deficit and foreign debt are the counterparts of these investments. Even as rich and reliable a borrower as the United States cannot continue acquiring debt at recent rates indefinitely. Market forces along with federal budget decisions have begun to be registered in a declining trade deficit. This decline needs to be continued for our peace of mind and because we probably have been preempting too much of the world's savings. Japan's cooperation will aid the adjustment process. But the critical choices to be made will be ours.

Meanwhile, separately, we can pursue the microeconomic issues we have with Japan. From the U.S. perspective, these primarily involve Japanese protectionism, in which we have a legitimate interest because we can expect to have a more efficient economy if remaining restrictions on access to Japan's market can be reduced or removed. Since Japan's economy will also be made more efficient, there can be no assurance about the effect on our trade imbalance. But the shared gains will be real—as real and desirable as would be those realizable from a successful attack on the protectionism we have at home.

POSTSCRIPT

Is Japan a Threat to America's Economic and National Security?

In the February 1992 issue of *International Economic Conditions*, published by the Federal Reserve Bank of St. Louis, Alison Butler makes a series of insightful comments. She notes that except for a superficial increase in 1991, Japan's bilateral surplus with the United States decreased throughout the late 1980s and early 1990s. In very large measure this is due to the fact that U.S. exports to Japan have grown about seven times faster than the growth rate of Japan's exports to the United States. If this pattern continues for the next five years, the value of Japan's merchandise exports to the United States will about equal the value of her imports from the United States!

In light of this prediction, we must ask a series of questions: (1) Is a trade deficit between two countries such as the United States and Japan a problem? (2) Does the decline in the U.S. auto industry or electronics industry reflect shifting "comparative advantages," or are these losses reflective of "unfair trade practices"? (3) How can the United States improve its economic performance in light of its experiences with modern-day Japan? (4) Should the United States modify its trade policy toward Japan?

If you have lingering questions, you might care to read other works by the two authors. Trezise has written widely in the area of international economics. One of the several books he has coedited or coauthored is *The Future Course of U.S.–Japan Economic Relations* (Brookings Institution, 1983). Likewise, Cohen has written extensively on various international trade and monetary policy issues. Several of his more important contributions are *The Making of United States International Economic Policy: Principles, Problems, and Proposals for Reform*, 3rd ed. (Praeger, 1988) and *Cowboys and Samurai: Why the United States Is Losing the Industrial Battle and Why It Matters* (1991). But do not limit yourself to only Trezise and Cohen. Tens of thousands of pages have been written about U.S.–Japan economic relations. For example, the April 1991 issue of *Current History* is devoted to a discussion of Japan as a world power and its relations with the United States, the Koreas, the former Soviet Union, and other countries. Alison Butler provides a banker's view in an article entitled "Trade Imbalances and Economic Theory: The Case for a U.S.–Japan Trade Deficit," *Federal Reserve Bank of St. Louis Review* (March/April 1991). Finally we suggest a third-party view of this issue—an Australian's opinion: Aurelia George, "Japan's American Problem: The Japanese Response to U.S. Pressure," *The Washington Quarterly* (Summer 1991).

ISSUE 18

Does Global Warming Require Immediate Government Action?

YES: Cynthia Pollock Shea, from "Protecting Life on Earth: Steps to Save the Ozone Layer," *Worldwatch Paper 87* (1988)

NO: Lester B. Lave, from "The Greenhouse Effect: What Government Actions Are Needed?" *Journal of Policy Analysis and Management* (vol. 7, no. 3, 1988)

ISSUE SUMMARY

YES: Cynthia Pollock Shea, a senior researcher with the Worldwatch Institute, pleads with governments and industries to initiate a "crash program" designed to halt emissions of chemicals that deplete the ozone, such as chlorofluorocarbons, before irreparable damage is done to world agriculture, marine life, and human health.

NO: Professor of economics Lester B. Lave warns against drastic solutions that could themselves be harmful or, at a minimum, "costly if the greenhouse consequences are more benign than predicted."

Few of us can forget the heat wave of the summer of 1988. Electric bills skyrocketed as air conditioners ran day and night. Bright green lawns turned yellow-brown. Lakes, streams, and reservoirs fell to critically low levels; car washing was discouraged, lawn sprinkling was banned, and toilets were bricked. Citizens and policymakers alike were concerned that the world was entering the long-predicted and much-feared period of global warming associated with the greenhouse effect.

As summer turned to fall, then–presidential candidate Bush promised voters that if he were elected, he would become the "environmental president." He would protect the environment from the advancing global warming— at least he would attempt to slow its progress. Once elected he joined other heads of state in a Paris environmental summit. This, in turn, led to the policy prescriptions that he introduced in a speech delivered at Georgetown University in early February 1990. Four broad policies were detailed in this speech:

1. *Increase the information base.* He proposed a sharp increase in U.S. expenditures on studies focused on "global climate change."
2. *Redirect and increase expenditures on basic energy research and development from $16.4 billion to $17.5 billion.* This represented a modest 6.4 percent

increase in the Department of Energy's budget and some redistribution of funds from civilian applied research and development programs to grants for basic research.

3. *A phaseout of most chlorofluorocarbons.* In line with a 1987 international agreement, the Montreal Protocol, President Bush proposed a 50 percent cut in the production of these powerful greenhouse gases that attack the ozone layer.

4. *A "plant-a-tree" program.* The Bush administration proposed planting a billion trees each year at a cost of $170 million annually.

The question we must ask is whether or not these presidential initiatives are appropriate in light of the costs and benefits of public action to slow or reverse the progress of global warming. Once again we must turn to our marginal analysis to determine how aggressive public policy should be in slowing the progress of global warming. We can anticipate that alternative policies will have increasing marginal costs and decreasing marginal benefits as more ambitious programs are employed. Two views of these costs and benefits are provided in the following essays. Cynthia Pollock Shea warns that if decisive action is not taken immediately to protect the ozone layer, we will face serious health hazards, reduced crop yields, decreased fish populations, and industrial damage. Lester B. Lave, on the other hand, argues that there is too much uncertainty to rush forward with sweeping policy action. He preaches moderation.

Since the consequences of these policy decisions may be irreversible and not fully felt for many decades in the future, extreme care must be taken. Older generations may be totally immune from the consequences. It is the younger generations that will pay for the mistakes made in the early 1990s.

YES

Cynthia Pollock Shea

PROTECTING LIFE ON EARTH: STEPS TO SAVE THE OZONE LAYER

When British scientists reported in 1985 that a hole in the ozone layer had been occurring over Antarctica each spring since 1979, the news came as a complete surprise. Although the theory that a group of widely used chemicals called chlorofluorocarbons (CFCs) would someday erode upper atmospheric ozone had been advanced in the mid-1970s, none of the models had predicted that the thinning would first be evident over the South Pole—or that it would be so severe.

Ozone, the three-atom form of oxygen, is the only gas in the atmosphere that limits the amount of harmful solar ultraviolet radiation reaching the earth. Most of it is found at altitudes of between 12 and 25 kilometers. Chemical reactions triggered by sunlight constantly replenish ozone above the tropics, and global air circulation transports some of it to the poles.

By the Antarctic spring of 1987, the average ozone concentration over the South Pole was down 50 percent. Although the depletion was alarming, many thought that the thinning was seasonal and unique to Antarctica. But an international group of more than 100 experts reported in March 1988 that the ozone layer around the globe was eroding much faster than models had predicted. Between 1969 and 1986, the average concentration of ozone in the stratosphere had fallen by approximately 2 percent.

As ozone diminishes, the earth receives more ultraviolet radiation, which promotes skin cancers and cataracts and depresses the human immune system. As more ultraviolet radiation penetrates the atmosphere, it will worsen these health effects, reduce crop yields and fish populations, damage some materials such as plastics, and increase smog. Compounds containing chlorine and bromine, which are released from industrial processes and products, are now widely accepted as the primary culprits in ozone depletion. Most of the chlorine comes from CFCs; the bromine originates from halons used in fire extinguishers.

Spurred to action by the ozone hole, 35 countries have signed an international agreement—the Montreal Protocol—aimed at halving most CFC emissions by 1998 and freezing halon emissions by 1992. But the agreement is so riddled with loopholes that its objectives will not be met. Furthermore, scientific findings subsequent to the negotiations reveal that even if the treaty's goals were met, significant further deterioration of the ozone layer would still occur.

New evidence that a global warming may be under way strengthens the need to further control and phase out CFC and halon emissions. With their strong heat-absorbing properties, CFCs and halons are an important contributor to the greenhouse effect. Currently available control technologies and stricter standards governing equipment operation and maintenance could reduce CFC and halon emissions by some 90 percent. But effective government policies and industry practices to limit and ultimately phase out chlorine and bromine emissions have yet to be formulated. Just as the effects of ozone depletion and climate change will be felt worldwide, a lasting remedy to these problems must also be global.

THE OZONE DEPLETION PUZZLE

As a result of the efforts of many scientists, the pieces of the ozone depletion puzzle have gradually been falling into place. During the long, sunless Antarctic winter—from about March to August—air over the continent becomes isolated in a swirling polar vortex that causes temperatures to drop below -90 degrees Celsius. This is cold enough for the scarce water vapor in the dry upper atmosphere to freeze and form polar stratospheric clouds. Chemical reactions on the surface of the ice crystals convert chlorine from nonreactive forms such as hydrogen chloride and chlorine nitrate into molecules that are very sensitive to sunlight. Gaseous nitrogen oxides, ordinarily able to inactivate chlorine, are trans-formed into frozen, and therefore nonreactive, nitric acid.

Spring sunlight releases the chlorine, starting a virulent ozone-destroying chain reaction that proceeds unimpeded for five or six weeks. Molecules of ozone are transformed into molecules of ordinary, two-atom oxygen. The chlorine emerges unscathed, ready to attack more ozone. Diminished ozone in the vortex means the atmosphere there absorbs less incoming solar radiation, thereby perpetuating lower temperatures and the vortex itself.

Paradoxically, the phenomenon of global warming encourages the process. Higher concentrations of greenhouse gases are thought to be responsible for an increase in the earth's surface temperature and a decrease in the temperature of the stratosphere. In addition, methane, one of the primary greenhouse gases, is a significant source of stratospheric water vapor. Colder temperatures and increased moisture both facilitate the formation of stratospheric clouds.

While many of the meteorological and chemical conditions conducive to ozone depletion are unique to Antarctica, ground-based research in Greenland in the winter of 1988 found elevated chlorine concentrations and depressed ozone levels over the Arctic as well. Although a strong vortex does not develop there and temperatures are not as low, polar stratospheric clouds do form.

The theories on how chlorine interacts on the surface of particles in polar stratospheric clouds are leading to worries that similar ozone-depleting reactions may occur around the globe. If chemicals such as sulfate aerosols from volcanoes and human-made sulfurs are capable of hosting the same catalytic reactions, global ozone depletion may accelerate even more rapidly than anticipated.

Consensus about the extent of ozone depletion and its causes strengthened with the release of the NASA Ozone Trends Panel report on March 15, 1988. Ozone losses were documented around the globe, not just at the poles. The blame was firmly placed on chlorofluorocarbons. The panel reported that between 30 and 64 degrees north latitude, where most of the world's people live, the total amount of ozone above any particular point had decreased by between 1.7 and 3 percent in the period from 1969 to 1986 (Table 1). The report further stated that while the problem was worst over Antarctica during the spring, "ozone appears to have decreased since 1979 by 5 percent or more at all latitudes south of 60 degrees south throughout the year." The hole alone covers approximately 10 percent of the Southern Hemisphere.

Within a matter of weeks the report's conclusions were widely accepted, and public debate on the issue began to build. Ozone depletion is occurring far more rapidly and in a different pattern than had been forecast. Projections of the amount and location of future ozone depletion are still highly uncertain. Although the fundamental mechanisms of ozone depletion are generally understood, the effect of cloud surface chemistry, the rate of various chemical reactions, and the specific chemical pathways are still in doubt. According to Sherwood Rowland, one of the first to sound a warning, policy decisions now and for at least another decade must be made without good quantitative guidelines of what the future holds.

Table 1

Global Decline in Atmospheric Ozone, 1969–1986*

Latitude	Year-round decrease (percent)	Winter decrease (percent)
53–64° N	−2.3	−6.2
40–53° N	−3.0	−4.7
30–40° N	−1.7	−2.3
19–30° N	−3.1	n.a.
0–19° N	−1.6	n.a.
0–19° S	−2.1	n.a.
19–29° S	−2.6	n.a.
29–39° S	−2.7	n.a.
39–53° S	−4.9	n.a.
53–60° S	−10.6	n.a.
60–90° S	−5.0 or more	n.a.

*Data for the area 30 to 64 degrees north of the equator are based on information gathered from satellites and ground stations from 1969 to 1986. Data for the area from 60 degrees south to the South Pole are based on information gathered from satellites and ground stations since 1979. All other information was compiled after November 1978 from satellite data alone.

Sources: U.S. National Aeronautics and Space Administration, Ozone Trends Panel; Cass Peterson, "Evidence of Ozone Depletion Found Over Big Urban Areas," The Washington Post, March 16, 1988.

EFFECTS OF ULTRAVIOLET RADIATION

At present, ozone absorbs much of the ultraviolet light that the sun emits in wavelengths harmful to humans, animals, and plants. The most biologically damaging wavelengths are within the 290- to 320-nanometer band, referred to as UV-B. But according to uncertain projections from computer models, erosion of the ozone shield could result in 5 to 20 percent more ultraviolet radiation reaching populated areas within the next 40 years—most of it in the UV-B band.

In light of the findings of the NASA Ozone Trends Panel, the U.S. Environmental Protection Agency (EPA) damage projections cited in this section are conservative. Although the EPA ranges are based on current control strategies, they assume ozone depletion levels of 1.2 to 6.2 percent. Yet all areas of the globe have already suffered depletion beyond this lower bound.

Globally, skin cancer incidence among Caucasians is already on the rise, and it is expected to increase alarmingly in the presence of more UV-B. Some 600,000 new cases of squamous and basal cell carcinoma—the two most common but rarely fatal skin cancer types—are reported each year in the United States alone. Worldwide, the number of cases is at least three times as high. Each 1 percent drop in ozone is projected to result in 4 to 6 percent more cases of these types of skin cancer. The EPA estimates that ozone depletion will lead to an additional 31,000 to 126,000 cases of melanoma—a more deadly form of skin cancer—among U.S. whites born before 2075, resulting in an additional 7,000 to 30,000 fatalities.

Under the same EPA scenarios, from 555,000 to 2.8 million Americans born before 2075 will suffer from cataracts of the eyes who would not have otherwise. Victims will also be stricken earlier in life, making treatment more difficult.

Medical researchers also fear that UV-B depresses the human immune system, lowering the body's resistance to attacking micro-organisms, making it less able to fight the development of tumors, and rendering it more prone to infectious diseases. In developing countries, particularly those near the equator that are exposed to higher UV-B levels, parasitic infections could become more common. The response may even decrease the effectiveness of some inoculation programs, such as those for diphtheria and tuberculosis.

Terrestrial and aquatic ecosystems are also affected. Screenings of more than 200 plant species, most of them crops, found that 70 percent were sensitive to UV-B. Increased exposure to radiation may decrease photosynthesis, water-use efficiency, yield, and leaf area. Soybeans, a versatile and protein-rich crop, are particularly susceptible. One researcher at the University of Maryland discovered that a simulated ozone loss of 25 percent reduced the yield of one important soybean species by as much as 25 percent. He also found that plant sensitivity to UV-B increased as the phosphorus level in the soil increased, indicating that heavily fertilized agricultural areas may be the most vulnerable.

Aquatic ecosystems may be the most threatened of all. Phytoplankton, the one-celled microscopic organisms that engage in photosynthesis while drifting on the ocean's surface, are the backbone of the marine food web. Because they require sunlight, they cannot escape incoming ultraviolet radiation and continue to thrive. Yet if they remain at the water's surface, studies show that a 25 percent reduction in ozone would decrease their productivity by about 35 percent. A significant destruction of phytoplankton and its subsequent decomposition could even raise carbon dioxide levels, speeding the warming of the atmosphere.

Zooplankton and the larvae of several important fish species will be doubly strained: Their sole food supply, phytoplankton, will be scarcer. For some shellfish species, a 10 percent decrease in ozone could result in up to an 18 percent increase in the number of abnormal larvae. Commercial fish populations already threatened by overharvesting may have more difficulty rebuilding due to effects of increased UV-B. Some species will undoubtedly be more vulnerable to increased ultraviolet radiation than others, and the changes are likely to be dramatic. Ultimately, entire ecosystems may become more unstable and less flexible.

Increased UV-B levels also affect synthetic materials, especially plastics, which become brittle. Studies conducted for the EPA estimated that without added chemical stabilizers, the cumulative damage to just one polymer, polyvinyl chloride, could reach $4,700 million by 2075 in the United States alone.

Ironically, as more ultraviolet radiation reaches the ground, the photochemical process that creates smog will accelerate, increasing ground-level ozone. Studies show that ground-level ozone retards crop and tree growth, limits visibility, and impairs lung functions. Urban air quality, already poor in most areas of the world, will worsen. In addition, stratospheric ozone decline is predicted to increase tropospheric amounts of hydrogen peroxide, an acid rain precursor.

Despite the many uncertainties regarding the amount of future ozone depletion, rising UV-B levels, and their biological effects, it is clear that the risks to aquatic and terrestrial ecosystems and to human health are enormous. The central conclusion of the EPA studies is that "the benefits of limiting future CFC/halon use far outweigh the increased costs these regulations would impose on the economy."

CHEMICAL WONDERS, ATMOSPHERIC VILLAINS

Chlorofluorocarbons are remarkable chemicals. They are neither toxic nor flammable at ground levels, as demonstrated by their discoverer, Thomas Midgley, Jr., in 1930, when he inhaled vapors from a beaker of clear liquid and then exhaled to extinguish a candle. A safe coolant that was inexpensive to produce was exactly what the refrigeration industry needed. E.I. du Pont de Nemours & Company marketed the compound under the trademark Freon. (In chemical shorthand, it is referred to as CFC-12). International production soared, rising from 545 tons in 1931 to 20,000 tons in 1945. Another use for the chemical, as a blowing agent in rigid insulation foams, was discovered in the late 1940s.

Over time, the versatility of the various CFCs seemed almost endless. CFC-11 and CFC-12 were first used as aerosol propellants during World War II in the fight against malaria. In the postwar economy, they were employed in aerosol products ranging from hairspray and deodorant to furniture polish. By the late 1950s, a combination of blowing agents CFC-11 and carbon dioxide was used to make softer furniture cushions, carpet padding, and automobile seats.

Many social and technological developments in recent decades were assisted by the availability of CFCs. Air conditioners made it possible to build and cool shopping malls, sports arenas, high-rise office buildings, and even automobiles. Artificial cooling brought comfort, business, and new residents to regions with warm climates. And healthier, more interesting diets are now available because food can be refrigerated in the production and distribution chain.

Even the computer revolution was aided by CFCs. As microchips and other components of electronic equipment became smaller and more sophisticated, the need to remove the smallest contami-

Table 2

Global CFC Use, by Category, 1985

Use	Share of total (percent)
Aerosols	25
Rigid-foam insulation	19
Solvents	19
Air conditioning	12
Refrigerants	8
Flexible foam	7
Other	10

Source: Daniel F. Kohler and others, *Projections of Consumption of Products Using Chlorofluorocarbons in Developing Countries*, Rand N-2458-EPA, 1987.

Table 3

Per Capita Use of CFC-11, CFC-12, and CFC-113, 1986 (Kilograms Per Capita)

	CFC-11	CFC-12	CFC-113	Total*
United States	.34	.58	.31	1.22
Europe	.47	.34	.12	.93
Japan	.23	.29	.43	.91

*Rows not completely additive due to trade.

Source: U.S. Environmental Protection Agency, *Regulatory Impact Analysis: Protection of Stratospheric Ozone*, 1987.

nants became critical. CFC-113 is used as a solvent to remove glue, grease, and soldering residues, leaving a clean, dry surface. CFC-113 is now the fastest growing member of the CFC family; worldwide production exceeds 160,000 tons per year.

An industry-sponsored group, the Alliance for Responsible CFC Policy, pegs the market value of CFCs produced in the United States at $750 million annually, the value of goods and services directly dependent on the chemicals at $28,000 million, and the end-use value of installed equipment and products at $135,000 million. Around the world, aerosols are still the largest user of CFCs, accounting for 25 percent of the total (Table 2). Rigid-foam and solvent applications, the fastest growing uses for CFCs, are tied for second place.

In 1987, global CFC production (excluding the People's Republic of China, the Soviet Union, and Eastern Europe) came close to 1 million tons. Combined production of CFC-11 and CFC-12 accounts for at least three-fourths of this total. Total per capita use of the three most common CFCs is highest in the United States—at 1.22 kilograms—but Europe and Japan are not far behind (Table 3).

From 1931 through 1986, virtually all the CFC-11 and CFC-12 produced was sold to customers in the Northern Hemisphere. Since raw chemicals and products made with and containing CFCs were then exported, in part to developing countries, final usage was not quite as lopsided. Indeed, the Third World accounted for 16 percent of global CFC consumption in 1986 (Table 4). As populations, incomes, and the manufacturing base grow in developing countries, CFC use there is projected to rise.

Halons, which are used in fighting fires in both hand extinguishers and total-flooding systems for large enclosed areas, contain bromine, a more effective ozone destroyer than chlorine. Demand for halons, which were developed in the 1940s, quadrupled between 1973 and 1984 and is still growing at a rate of 15 percent annually.

Alarming though the latest ozone measurements are, they reflect only the responses to gases released through the early 1980s. Gases now rising through the lower atmosphere will take up to

Table 4

CFC Consumption by Region, 1986

Region	Share of total (percent)
United States	29
Other industrial countries*	41
Soviet Union, Eastern Europe	14
Other developing countries	14
People's Republic of China, India	2

*The European Community accounts for more than half, followed by Japan, Canada, Australia, and others.

Source: "The Ozone Treaty: A Triumph for All," *Update from State*, May/June 1988.

eight years to reach the stratosphere. And an additional 2 million tons of substances containing chlorine and bromine are still on the ground, trapped in insulation foams, appliances, and fire-fighting equipment.

Chlorine concentrations in the upper atmosphere have grown from 0.6 to 2.7 parts per thousand million in the past 25 years. Under even the most optimistic regulatory scenarios, they are expected to triple by 2075. Bromine concentrations are projected to grow considerably faster. Without a complete and rapid phaseout of CFC and halon production, the real losers will be future generations who inherit an impoverished environment.

REDUCING EMISSIONS

On September 16, 1987, after years of arduous and heated negotiation, the Montreal Protocol on Substances That Deplete the Ozone Layer was signed by 24 countries. Provisions of the agreement include a freeze on CFC production (at 1986 levels) by 1989, a 20 percent decrease in production by 1993, and another 30 percent cut by 1998. Halon production is subject to a freeze based on 1986 levels starting in 1992....

The means to achieve these reductions are left to the discretion of individual nations. Most signatory countries are responding with production limits on chemical manufacturers. Although this approach complies with treaty guidelines, it effectively ensures that only those willing to pay high prices will be able to continue using CFCs. It also places the onus of curbing emissions on the myriad industrial users of the chemicals and on the consumers of products that incorporate them. Moving quickly to protect the ozone layer calls for a different approach —one that targets the largest sources of the most ozone-depleting chemicals.

When concern about the ozone layer first emerged in the 1970s, some industrial country governments responded. Since 56 percent of combined CFC-11 and CFC-12 production in 1974 was used in aerosols, spray cans were an obvious target. Under strong public pressure, Canada, Norway, Sweden, and the United States banned CFC propellants in at least 90 percent of their aerosol products. The change brought economic as well as environmental benefits. Hydrocarbons, the replacement propellant, are less expensive than CFCs and saved the U.S. economy $165 million in 1983 alone. The European Community adopted a different approach. In 1980, the member countries agreed not to increase their capacity to produce these two CFCs and called for a 30 percent reduction in their use in aerosol propellants by 1982 (based on 1976 consumption figures).

Despite rapid growth, CFC-113 emissions may be some of the easiest and most economical to control. The chemical is only used to clean the final product and is not incorporated in it. Thus emissions are virtually immediate; three-fourths result from vapor losses, the remainder from waste disposal. A U.S. ban on land disposal of chlorinated solvents that took effect in November 1986, consideration of similar regulations elsewhere, the high cost of incinerating CFC-113 (because it contains toxic fluorine), and accelerating concern about ozone depletion have all created strong incentives for solvent recovery and recycling.

Since CFC-113 costs about twice as much as other CFCs, investments in recovery and recycling pay off more quickly. Recycling of CFC-113 is now practiced on-site at many large computer companies. Smaller electronics firms, for which in-house recycling is not economical, can sell their used solvents to commercial recyclers or the distributors of some chemical manufacturers.

Capturing CFC emissions from flexible-foam manufacturing can also be accomplished fairly quickly but requires investment in new ventilation systems. New suction systems coupled with carbon adsorption technologies are able to recover from 40 to 90 percent of the CFCs released.

Another area that offers significant savings, at a low cost, is improved design, operating, and maintenance standards for refrigeration and air conditioning equipment. Codes of practice to govern equipment handling are being drawn up by many major trade associations. Key among the recommendations are to require worker training, to limit maintenance and repair work to authorized personnel, to install leak detection systems, and to use smaller refrigerant charges. Another recommendation, to prohibit venting of the refrigerant directly to the atmosphere, requires the use of recovery and recycling technologies.

Careful study of the automobile air conditioning market in the United States, the largest user of CFC-12 in the country, has found that 34 percent of emissions can be traced to leakage, 48 percent occur during recharge and repair servicing, and the remainder happen through accidents, disposal, and manufacturing, in that order. Equipment with better seals and hoses would reduce emissions and result in less need for system maintenance.

Over the longer term, phasing out the use and emissions of CFCs will require the development of chemical substitutes that do not harm the ozone layer. The challenge is to find alternatives that perform the same function for a reasonable cost, that do not require major equipment modifications, that are nontoxic to workers and consumers, and that are environmentally benign....

The time has come to ask if the functions performed by CFCs are really necessary and, if they are, whether they can be performed in new ways. If all known technical control measures were used, total CFC and halon emissions could be reduced by approximately 90 percent. Many of these control strategies are already cost-effective, and more will become so as regulations push up the price of ozone-depleting chemicals. The speed with which controls are introduced will determine the extent of ozone depletion in the years ahead and when healing of the ozone layer will begin.

BEYOND MONTREAL

An international treaty to halve the production of a chemical feared responsible for destroying an invisible shield is unprecedented. But unfortunately, for several reasons, the Montreal Protocol will not save the ozone layer.

First, many inducements were offered to enhance the treaty's appeal to prospective signatories—extended deadlines for developing and centrally planned economies, allowances to accommodate industry restructuring, and loose definitions of the products that can legitimately be traded internationally. The cumulative effect of these loopholes means that, even with widespread participation, the protocol's goal of halving worldwide CFC use by 1998 will not be met.

Second, recent scientific findings show that more ozone depletion has already occurred than treaty negotiators assumed would happen in 100 years. A recent EPA report concluded that by 2075, even with 100 percent global participation in the protocol, chlorine concentrations in the atmosphere would triple. The agreement will not arrest depletion, merely slow its acceleration.

Third, several chemicals not regulated under the treaty are major threats to the ozone layer. Methyl chloroform and carbon tetrachloride together contributed 13 percent of total ozone-depleting chemical emissions in 1985. As the use of controlled chemicals diminishes, the contribution of these two uncontrolled compounds will grow.

The recognition that global warming may have already begun strengthens the case for further and more rapid reductions in CFC emissions. CFCs currently account for 15 to 20 percent of the greenhouse effect and absorb wavelengths of infrared radiation that other greenhouse gases allow to escape. Indeed, one molecule of the most widely used CFCs is as effective in trapping heat as 15,000 molecules of carbon dioxide, the most abundant greenhouse gas. In light of these findings, logic suggests a virtual phaseout of CFC and halon emissions by all countries as soon as possible. Releases of other chlorine and bromine-containing compounds not currently covered under the treaty also need to be controlled and in some cases halted.

The timing of the phaseout is crucial. Analysts at EPA examined the effects of a 100 percent CFC phaseout by 1990 and a 95 percent phaseout by 1998. Peak chlorine concentrations would differ by 0.8 parts per thousand million, some one-third of current levels. And under the slower phasedown, atmospheric cleansing would be prolonged considerably: Chlorine levels would remain higher than the peak associated with the accelerated schedule for at least 50 years.

As noted, it is technically feasible to reduce CFC and halon emissions by at least 90 percent. Sweden is the first country to move beyond endorsing a theoretical phaseout. In June 1988 the parliament, after extensive discussions with industry, passed legislation that includes specific deadlines for banning the use of CFCs in new products. Consumption is to be halved by 1991 and virtually eliminated by 1995. Environmental agencies in Britain, the United States, and the Federal Republic of Germany have endorsed emissions reductions of at least 85 percent. Chemical producers in these three countries account for over half the global output of controlled substances.

Levying a tax on newly manufactured CFCs and other ozone-depleting substances is one way governments can cut emissions and accelerate the adoption of alternative chemicals and technologies. If the tax increased in step with mandatory production cutbacks, it would eliminate windfall profits for producers, encourage recovery and recycling processes, stimulate use of new chemicals, and provide a source of funding for new technologies and for needed research. Encouraging investments in recycling networks, incinerators for rigid foams, and collection systems for chemicals that would otherwise be discarded could substantially trim emissions from existing products, from servicing operations, and from new production runs. Research on new refrigeration, air conditioning, and insulation processes is worthy of government support. Unfortunately, international funding for developing such technologies totals less than $5 million.

As mentioned in the text of the Montreal Protocol, results of this research, as well as new technologies and processes, need to be shared with developing countries. Ozone depletion and climate warming are undeniably global in scope. Not sharing information on the most recent developments ensures that environmentally damaging and outdated equipment will continue to be used for years to come, further eroding the Third World technology base....

The scientific fundamentals of ozone depletion and climate change are known, and there is widespread agreement that both have already begun. Although current models of future change vary in their predictions, the evidence is clear enough to warrant an immediate response. Because valuable time was lost when governments and industries relaxed their regulatory and research efforts during the early 1980s, a crash program is now essential. Human health, food supplies, and the global climate all hinge on the support that can be garnered for putting an end to chlorine and bromine emissions.

NO
Lester B. Lave

THE GREENHOUSE EFFECT: WHAT GOVERNMENT ACTIONS ARE NEEDED?

Human beings are causing global-scale changes for the first time.... [A]rticles by Gordon MacDonald and Irving Mintzer document the "greenhouse" effect and give some indications of the environmental changes that will result. The possibility of such global changes rouses deep emotions in people: awe that humans have become so powerful, rage that we are tampering with the natural environment on a large scale, and fear that we might create an environment hostile to our progeny. Technologists tend to focus on the first emotion with the optimism that we can also find ways to head off or solve the problems. Environmentalists fix on the second, fearing that humans can only ruin nature. This article focuses on the third, asking what governmental or other social actions are possible and warranted. What should be done now and in the foreseeable future as a result of what is currently known about the atmospheric concentration of greenhouse gases, the resulting climate change, and the consequences for people?

WHY DOES THE GREENHOUSE EFFECT RECEIVE SO MUCH ATTENTION?

Scientists have been giving great attention to the greenhouse effect for more than a decade, despite the vast qualitative and quantitative uncertainties. The public joins scientists in the concern that current activities could create a much less hospitable planet in the future. Congress has also directed its concern to these issues. Congress generally regards programs whose impact is more than three to ten years in the future as hopelessly long term; it seems bizarre that greenhouse effects, which are a century or so into the future, have received major Congressional attention....

Greenhouse effects have the attributes of being (1) global (in the sense that all regions are affected), (2) long term (in the sense that near-term effects are undetectable and important effects on people and their well being are perhaps a century in the future), (3) ethical (in the sense that they involve the preferences and well being of people who have not been born yet, as

From Lester B. Lave, "The Greenhouse Effect: What Government Actions Are Needed?" *Journal of Policy Analysis and Management*, vol. 7, no. 3 (1988). Copyright © 1988 by John Wiley & Sons, Inc. Reprinted by permission. Notes omitted.

well as plants, animals, and the environment more generally), (4) potentially catastrophic (in the sense that large changes in the environment might result, as well as massive loss of human life and property), and (5) contentious (in the sense that coming to decisions, translating these into agreements, and enforcing agreements would be difficult due to important "spillover" or external effects, uncertainty, the incentives for individual nations to cheat, the difficulty of detecting cheating, and the difficulty of enforcing agreements even after cheating is detected). In addition, many of the likely public investments such as attempts to substitute for carbon dioxide producing activities would be expensive and disruptive. In other words, this set of issues exercises almost all of the tools of policy analysis and poses deep problems to decision analysts. Below, I point out some particularly attractive research areas, such as behavioral reactions, crucial to formulating policy regarding greenhouse gases.

Uncertainty. A dominant question in formulating greenhouse policy is: What is the uncertainty concerning current statements about emissions, atmospheric accumulation, resulting climate changes, and resulting effects on the managed and unmanaged biospheres? . . .

The Department of Energy has put major resources over the past decade into understanding the carbon cycle, the current sources and sinks of carbon in the environment and the mechanisms that handle increasing carbon emissions into the environment. It is safe to say that the carbon cycle is not understood well, with uncertainty regarding perhaps 20% of total sources and sinks of carbon entering the environment. Controversies surround the importance of deforestation, the amount of carbon retained in the at-

mosphere, the amount being absorbed by the oceans, and the amount being taken up in plants.

The dynamics can be even more difficult to understand, because the oceans hold less carbon as they warm. Thus, there could be a destabilizing feedback of a warmer atmosphere leading to ocean warming, which induces release of carbon to the atmosphere. With the oceans becoming a net source rather than a sink, atmospheric concentrations would increase more rapidly, leading to rapidly increasing atmospheric temperatures, which induce ocean warming and carbon release. Is this scenario one that leads to disaster—or one where the ocean warming takes so long that fossil fuels are fully used and the increased carbon taken up by plants before the oceans warm enough to release appreciable carbon dioxide to the atmosphere? To what extent, and how quickly, would increased plant growth, due to a warmer climate, more rain, and higher atmospheric concentrations of carbon dioxide, absorb much more of the atmospheric carbon and slow or stop atmospheric warming?

The speed with which natural ecosystems can adapt to climate change is also a matter of concern. A large-scale climate change, comparable to a carbon dioxide doubling, has occurred over the last 18,000 years since the end of the last great ice age. While the temperature changes are comparable, the previous change occurred over 18,000 years while the change due to the greenhouse effect would occur over a century or so, perhaps one-hundred times faster. This rate of change could exceed the abilities of natural ecosystems to adapt. The amount of change is small, however, compared to what is currently experienced for the changes from day to night or season to season.

The issues related to carbon dioxide are much different from the issues related to other greenhouse gases. Neither of the two feedback mechanisms sketched above apply to CFC (chlorofluorucarbons) or methane. The Environmental Protection Agency estimates that about half of the atmospheric warming, after a century, would be attributed to gases other than carbon dioxide—an estimate that is markedly different from those of ten years ago. Much needs to be done to understand feedback mechanisms for the other greenhouse gases and to investigate possible interactions among the gases. For example, atmospheric warming is likely to increase the demand for air conditioning, which would lead to greater electricity use (resulting in increased carbon dioxide emissions) and to greater emissions of CFC from compressor leaks. The warming would also increase the demand for insulation, some of which would be foam insulation made with CFC, releasing much more of this gas to the atmosphere.

The current global circulation models are magnificent examples of technical virtuosity. The physical movements and energy fluxes of the atmosphere are described by partial differential equations that are too complicated to be solved explicitly. Thus the models depend upon expert judgment to decide what aspects of the problem should be treated explicitly within the model and how much attention each aspect should get. The current predictions of the consequences of doubling atmospheric carbon dioxide come mainly from models that treat the oceans as if little mixing occurred and there were no currents. The models also ignore many chemical reactions in the atmosphere.

Clearly, these models are "wrong" in the sense of being bad examples of reality. But the central question is whether failing to include these elements results in an error of 10% or whether the models could be wrong to the extent of predicting warming when these gases actually result in atmospheric cooling....

As shown below, exploring the consequences of this warming requires detailed predictions or assumptions for each area about climate, storm patterns, and the length of the growing season. These predictions are little more than educated guesses. For the modelers, this uncertainty is a stimulus to do better. For the policy analyst, the uncertainty must be treated explicitly in deciding what actions are warranted now and in the future.

Even vast uncertainty need not preclude taking preventive action. Uncertainty should induce caution and prevent decision makers from rushing into actions and commitments, however. For example, precipitous action would have led to forbidding military and 747 flights in the stratosphere in the early 1970s. Then, in the late 1970s, precipitous action might have led to building aircraft to fly in the stratosphere as much as possible. Finally, today aircraft flights in the stratosphere are regarded as irrelevant to stratospheric ozone levels.

It is prudent to be concerned about potentially disastrous effects and to be willing to take some actions now, even given the uncertainty. For example, American regulators insisted on building strong containment vessels around civilian nuclear reactors, even though they regarded the chance of a mishap that would require the containment vessel as remote. The USSR regulators did not insist on such safeguards, with quite different results between the problems at Three Mile Island and the tragedy at Chernobyl.

While there is major uncertainty, the policy conclusions about CFC emissions are different today from those about carbon dioxide emissions, as I discuss below.

Accounting for the Uncertainty. The long-term effects of an increase in greenhouse gases are unknown and almost certainly unknowable. The physical changes, such as the gross increase in temperature for each latitude might be predicted, but it is unlikely that the dates of last frost and first freeze and detailed patterns of precipitation will be known for each growing area. Still more difficult to forecast is the adaptive behavior of individuals and governments. The accumulation of greenhouse gases could be enormously beneficial or catastrophic for humans. Or more likely, it would be beneficial at some times and places and catastrophic at others.

Preventive actions are akin to purchasing an insurance policy against potentially catastrophic greenhouse effects. Most people voluntarily purchase life insurance, even though the likelihood of dying in a particular year is very small. I suspect that people would be willing to pay a premium for a policy that would protect against an inhospitable Earth a century or so hence. But, the question is what type of insurance policy is most attractive and how much of a premium are people willing to pay.

Preventing all greenhouse effects is virtually impossible. If the climate changes and resultant human consequences are to be headed off, then heroic actions would be required immediately to reduce emissions of all the greenhouse gases throughout the world. For example, nuclear plants could be built to phase out all coal-burning plants within several decades. The decision to do that would be enormously expensive and disruptive. Such a decision would have to be agreed to in every country and enormous resources would be required to implement it. I would not support such a decision for many reasons.

Short of such heroic measures, are there any actions that might be taken now, even though uncertainty dominates the predictions of effects? Prudence would dictate that we should take actions that might prove highly beneficial, even if they are unlikely to be needed, if their cost is small. Proscribing coal use is not an attractive insurance policy, but we should give serious consideration to limiting the growth rate of coal use. The world discovered after 1974 that there was not a one-to-one coupling of energy use and economic activity. Since then, the developed countries have experienced a considerable increase in economic activity while most countries use little or no more energy than in 1974. Reducing the emissions of other greenhouse gases would be less difficult and disruptive than large reductions in coal use. In particular, it is not difficult or expensive to switch to CFC substitutes that are less damaging and to stop using these chemicals as foaming agents for plastics and in consumer products.

Thus, one of the best ways to deal with uncertainty is to look for robust actions, actions that would be beneficial in the worst case, not harmful in other cases, and not very costly to take. Emphasizing energy conservation is perhaps the best example of a prudent policy. Conservation makes sense without any appeal to greenhouse effects, given the deaths and disease associated with mining, transport, and air pollution from coal. The greenhouse effects simply underline what is already an obvious conclusion, but not one that is being pursued vigorously. So much energy could be saved by adjusting fully to current market prices that sufficient conservation might be attained merely by encouraging this adjustment. In particular, large subsidies to energy use distort resource-allocation decisions significantly.

A second example of an inexpensive insurance policy is switching to less damaging CFCs and using less of them.

Another approach is to develop a strategy of reevaluation at fixed intervals or as new information becomes available. Instead of viewing the current decision as the only opportunity to worry about greenhouse issues, one can attempt to clarify which particular outcomes would cause greatest concern. Then one could revisit the issues periodically to see if uncertainty has been resolved or at least substantially diminished.

SOCIAL AND ECONOMIC CONSEQUENCES OF CLIMATE CHANGE

Announcement of an invention, such as a new drug, is generally greeted with public approval. Certainly there is recognition that innovations may bring undesired consequences, such as occurred with Thalidomide, and so premarket testing and technology assessment have been established and emphasized in many regulatory areas. An innovation seems to be defined in terms of the intent of the inventor to produce something that will make society better or at least to make him richer. On net, it is fair to say that such innovations are viewed positively, with the untoward consequences to be dealt with if they arise.

In contrast, an environmental change such as the greenhouse effect is viewed with horror. Such changes are generally not desired by anyone, but rather emerge as the unintended consequences of society's actions. Those who are horrified might admit that there are some changes that are likely to be beneficial, but they would still regard the overall effect as catastrophic. People tend to be more alarmed by large-scale, rapid environmental changes because the consequences would be important and uncontrollable.

Why are Americans such determined optimists about new technology and such determined pessimists about environmental changes? I suspect that much of the difference is explained by the good intent of the inventor versus the unintended nature of the environmental change. If so, this suggests that people have unwarranted faith in the good intentions of inventors, compared to the unintended changes from taking resources or using the environment as a garbage pail.

Deriving the social and economic consequences of climate change is more difficult than might appear. To be sure, if an area becomes so hot or dry that habitation is impossible, or if an area is under water, the consequences are evident. Thus, if sea level rose, the low-lying parts of Louisiana, Florida, Bangladesh, and the Netherlands would be drastically affected. The vast number of short-term effects are difficult to predict and evaluate. Furthermore, the long-term changes are likely to be less drastic (adjustment occurs to mitigate the difficulties, although this might take a long term for an ecosystem), and so the consequences will be even more difficult to infer.

In particular, a change in climate presents a challenge to farmers. If summers are hotter and drier in the corn belt, then a farmer growing corn in Illinois is going to experience crop failure more frequently, due both to droughts and to heat damage. As the climate changes, rare crop damage will give rise to occasional and then frequent damage. Will the Illinois farmer keep planting corn, surviving with the aid of ever-larger government subsidies? Or will he plant new crops that flourish under the hotter, drier climate?

Climate change also presents an opportunity. Sylvan Wittwer, a noted agronomist, observed that "... the present level of atmospheric carbon dioxide is suboptimal, and the oxygen level is supraoptimal, for photosynthesis and primary productivity in the great majority of plants." The increased atmospheric carbon dioxide concentrations would enhance growth and water-use efficiency, leading to more and faster growth. Charles Cooper remarks that a doubled atmospheric concentration of carbon dioxide "... is about as likely to increase global food, at least in the long run, as to decrease it. It is certain though, that some nations, regions, and people will gain and others will lose." A new climate regime with more precipitation and a longer growing season bodes well for agriculture—if we figure out what crops to plant and figure out generally how to tailor agriculture to the new climate regime, and how to deal with new pests.

The midcontinental drying, if it occurs, could mean the end of current agricultural practices in the midwest. This climate change might induce more irrigation, dry farming practices such as have been demonstrated in Israel, new cultivars, different crops, or even ceasing to cultivate this land. The increased rains might mean there was sufficient winter precipitation to provide water for summer irrigation; it would certainly mean that there was sufficient water elsewhere in the country to be transported to the midwest for irrigation. Large dams and canals might be required, but the technology for this is available. Certainly this water would be more expensive than that currently available, but there is no reason to be concerned about starvation or even large increases in food prices for the U.S. On net, food and fibers might be slightly more expensive or less expensive in the U.S. under the new climate, but the change is almost certain to be small compared to other economic changes.

For the U.S., there is no difficulty with finding the appropriate technology for breeding new crops that fit the climate, developing a less water-intensive agriculture, or for moving water for irrigation. The difficulty would be whether agronomists are given the right tasks, whether farmers give up their old crops and farming methods, and whether society can solve the myriad social problems associated with damming newly enlarged rivers and moving the water to where it is needed.

The "less managed" areas, including forests, grasslands, and marsh, might experience large changes and a system far from long-term equilibrium. These effects would be scarcely discernable in measured gross national product, but would be viewed as extremely important by many environmentalists.

Water projects and resources more generally might pose a greater problem. Large-scale water projects, such as dams and canals, are built to last for long periods. Once built, they are not easily changed. Thus, major climate change could lead to massive dams fed by tiny streams or dams completely inadequate for the rivers they are designed to control. Similarly, treaty obligations for the Colorado are inflexible and could pose major problems if there is less water flowing down the river. Similarly, the climate change would induce migration, both across areas in the U.S. and from other countries. The legal and illegal migration could pose major problems. Finally, Americans treasure certain natural resources, such as waterfalls. Climate change that stopped the flow at popular falls would be regarded seriously.

Commenting on energy modeling, Hans Landsberg wrote: "... all of us who have engaged in projecting into the more distant future take ourselves too seriously.... What is least considered is how many profound turns in the road one would have missed making 1980 projections in 1930! I am not contending that the emperor is naked, but we surely overdress him."

REPRISE: WHY SO MUCH CONCERN FOR THE GREENHOUSE EFFECT?

It is the symbolic nature of the issues that has drawn attention to the greenhouse effect. Anyone who thinks he can see 100 years into the future is mad. If humans have now acquired the power to influence the global environment, then it is likely that we will cause changes even larger than those discussed here within the next century or so. Both the greenhouse effect and other global changes could be predominantly beneficial or harmful to humans and various aspects of the environment, although they are likely to be beneficial in some times and places and detrimental in others. But a large element of the public debate is almost scandalized at the notion

that the changes might be beneficial or made beneficial by individual actions and government policies.

The difficulty is public concern that global scale effects are now possible; we have had a "loss of innocence." In the past, if an individual ruined a plot of land, he could move on. If human actions caused major problems such as the erosion of the Dalmatian coast of Yugoslavia, there was always other inviting land. But, if the Earth is made inhospitable, there is no other inviting planet readily at hand.

I share this concern, but find it naive. Having acquired the power to influence the global environment, there is no way to relinquish it. No one intends to change the global environment by emitting greenhouse gases. Rather, the change is an inadvertent consequence of business as usual. The culprit is not a malevolent individual or rapacious company. Instead, it is the scope of human activities stemming from a large population, modern technology, and an unbelievable volume of economic activity. These culprits are not going to disappear, however much we might all wish that people did not have the ability to affect our basic environment. In this sense, the human race has lost its environmental innocence.

The symbolism is important because of the need to educate the public and government and gauge their reactions to this first global environmental issue. If people and governments show themselves to be concerned and willing to make sacrifices, the prospect for the future looks brighter. If instead, each individual and nation regards the effects as primarily due to others, and as someone else's problem, the increases in economic activity and advances in technology promise a future with major unintended changes in the Earth's environment.

Such changes could be dealt with by concerned global action to stop the stimulus and thus the response. Or they could be dealt with by individual and national actions to adapt to the consequences. However much I might wish for concerted action among countries, I do not believe this is likely to occur. There are too many disparate interests, too much to be gained by cheating, too much suspicion of the motives of others, and too little control over all the relevant actors. Thus, reluctantly, I conclude that mitigation through adaptation must be our focus.

For example, within the United States, federal environmental laws have been only a modest success in preventing environmental pollution. Ozone problems have worsened, ground water has become more polluted, and we seem no closer to dealing with radioactive and toxic wastes. When the scope of the problem becomes international, as with acid rain, there is little or no progress. Curtailing sulfur oxides emissions into the air necessarily involves promoting some interests while hurting others. Those who would be hurt are, not surprisingly, more skeptical about whether low levels of acid sulfate aerosols cause disease than those who believe that they would benefit. Getting agreement on action has proven essentially impossible for abating sulfur ox-

ides. It is hard to imagine that a debate among 140 nations on the greenhouse effect would lead to an agreement to adopt binding programs to abate emissions.

A multinational agreement on controlling CFC has been negotiated in 1987. This is an extremely encouraging, and surprising development. There are many obstacles to effective implementation, however, from ratification by each country to best faith efforts to abide by the sense of the agreement.

CONCLUSION

The greenhouse effect is the first of what are likely to be many long-term, global problems. Analysis is difficult because of the vast uncertainty about causes and effects, as well as of the consequences of the resulting climate change. The current uncertainties together with the costs of precipitous action imply that heroic actions to curtail the emissions of all greenhouse gases are not justified. Nonetheless, the current facts support a program of energy conservation, abatement, research, and periodic reconsideration that is far more activist than the current policy of the U.S. government.

I would like to thank Stephen Schneider and Jesse Ausubel for comments. This work was supported in part by the National Science Foundation (Grant No. SES-8715564).

POSTSCRIPT

Does Global Warming Require Immediate Government Action?

The harsh reality is that the environment is deteriorating. Very few, if any, physical scientists dispute this fact. What is disputed is the rate of decline in the global environment and whether or not citizens acting at the end of the twentieth century should try to alter this process. Do we have enough knowledge of the future to take dramatic steps today that will reshape the world of tomorrow? These are hard questions. If we answer incorrectly, our children and our children's children may curse us for our lack of resolve to solve environmental problems that were clear for all to see.

Shea and Lave both agree that there is a clear and present danger associated with ozone-depleting chemicals, such as chlorofluorocarbons, which are also the gases that contribute to the greenhouse effect. What they disagree upon is whether or not we know enough today to take immediate, decisive action. Do *you* know enough? If you do not, we suggest that you read further in this area. *It is your future that is being discussed here.*

A brief history of scientific concerns about the greenhouse effect, which stretches back to the late nineteenth century, is found in Jesse H. Ausubel, "Historical Note," in the National Research Council's *Changing Climate: Report of the Carbon Dioxide Assessment Committee* (National Academy Press, 1983). We should note that there are a number of other essays in *Changing Climate* that may be of interest to you. The Environmental Protection Agency (EPA) has published many studies you might want to examine. See, for example, the EPA's study entitled *The Potential Effects of Global Climate Change on the United States* (December 1989) or *Policy Options for Stabilizing Global Climate* (February 1989). An extensive analysis of the scientific, economic, and policy implications are also found in the *1990 Economic Report of the President.*

ISSUE 19

Should Pollution Be Put to the Market Test?

YES: Alan S. Blinder, from *Hard Heads, Soft Hearts* (Addison-Wesley, 1987)

NO: David Moberg, from "Environment and Markets: A Critique of 'Free Market' Claims," *Dissent* (Fall 1991)

ISSUE SUMMARY

YES: Alan S. Blinder, a member of the Board of Governors of the Federal Reserve System, urges policymakers to use the energy of the market to solve America's environmental problems.

NO: Social critic David Moberg warns against giving businesses more flexibility and economic incentives, and he argues that clear public policy and direct government intervention will have the most positive effects on the environment.

Markets sometimes fail. That is, markets sometimes do not automatically yield optimum, economically efficient answers. This is because prices sometimes do not reflect the true social costs and benefits of consumption and production. The culprit here is the presence of externalities. Externalities are spillover effects that impact third parties who had no voice in the determination of an economic decision.

If, for example, my friend and coeditor Frank J. Bonello decided to "cut a few corners" to hold down the costs of his commercially produced banana cream pies, he might well create a *negative externality* for his neighbors. That is, if in the dark of night, Bonello slipped to the back of his property and dumped his banana skins, egg shells, and other waste products into the St. Joe River that borders his property, part of the cost of producing banana cream pies would be borne by those who live downstream from the Bonello residence. Since the full costs of production are not borne by Bonello, he can set a competitively attractive price and sell many more pies than his competitors, whom we assume must pay to have their waste products carted away.

If Bonello is not forced to internalize the negative externality associated with his production process, the price attached to his pies gives an improper market signal in regard to the true scarcity of resources. In brief, because Bonello's pies are cheaper than his competitors, demanders will flock to his doorstep to demand more and more of his pies, unknowingly causing him to dump more and more negative externalities on his neighbors downstream.

In this case, as in other cases of firms casting off negative externalities, the public sector may have to intervene and mandate that these externalities be internalized. This is not always an easy task, however. Two difficult questions must be answered: (1) Who caused the external effect? Was it only Bonello's banana cream pie production? and (2) Who bore the costs of the negative external, and what are their losses? These questions require detective work. We must not only identify the source of the pollution, but we must also identify the people who have been negatively affected by its presence and determine their "rights" in this situation. Once this has been achieved, the difficult task of evaluating and measuring the negative effects must be undertaken.

Even if this can be successfully negotiated, one last set of questions remains: What are the alternative methods that can be used to force firms to internalize their externalities, and which of these methods are socially acceptable and economically efficient? This is the subject of the debate that follows.

Alan S. Blinder warns against the limitations inherent in a market solution to this problem; however, he still supports harnessing the power of the market in order to rid the world of the harmful effects of pollution. David Moberg, on the other hand, takes care to note that private market solutions can be effective. But he maintains that many times, old-fashioned regulation can be even more effective.

YES

Alan S. Blinder

CLEANING UP THE ENVIRONMENT: SOMETIMES CHEAPER IS BETTER

We cannot give anyone the option of polluting for a fee.

—Senator Edmund Muskie
(in Congress, 1971)

In the 1960s, satirist Tom Lehrer wrote a hilarious song warning visitors to American cities not to drink the water or breathe the air. Now, after the passage of more than two decades and the expenditure of hundreds of billions of dollars, such warnings are less appropriate—at least on most days! Although the data base on which their estimates rest is shaky, the Environmental Protection Agency (EPA) estimates that the volume of particulate matter suspended in the air (things like smoke and dust particles) fell by half between 1973 and 1983. During the same decade, the volume of sulfur dioxide emissions declined 27 percent and lead emissions declined a stunning 77 percent. Estimated concentrations of other air pollutants also declined. Though we still have some way to go, there is good reason to believe that our air is cleaner and more healthful than it was in the early 1970s. While the evidence for improved average water quality is less clear (pardon the pun), there have at least been spectacular successes in certain rivers and lakes.

All this progress would seem to be cause for celebration. But economists are frowning—and not because they do not prize cleaner air and water, but rather because our current policies make environmental protection far too costly. America can achieve its present levels of air and water quality at far lower cost, economists insist. The nation is, in effect, shopping for cleaner air and water in a high-priced store when a discount house is just around the corner. Being natural cheapskates, economists find this extravagance disconcerting. Besides, if we shopped in the discount store, we would probably buy a higher-quality environment than we do now....

IS POLLUTION AN ECONOMIC PROBLEM?

... Nothing in this discussion ... implies that the appropriate level of environmental quality is a matter for the free market to determine. On the contrary, the market mechanism is ill suited to the task; if left to its own devices, it will certainly produce excessive environmental degradation. Why? Because users of clean air and water, unlike users of oil and steel, are not normally made to pay for the product.

Consider a power plant that uses coal, labor, and other inputs to produce electricity. It buys all these items on markets, paying market prices. But the plant also spews soot, sulfur dioxide, and a variety of other undesirables into the air. In a real sense, it "uses up" clean air—one of those economic goods which people enjoy—without paying a penny. Naturally, such a plant will be sparing in its use of coal and labor, for which it pays, but extravagant in its use of clean air, which is offered for free.

That, in a nutshell, is why the market fails to safeguard the environment. When items of great value, like clean air and water, are offered free of charge it is unsurprising that they are overused, leaving society with a dirtier and less healthful environment than it should have.

The analysis of why the market fails suggests the remedy that economists have advocated for decades: charge polluters for the value of the clean air or water they now take for free. That will succeed where the market fails because an appropriate fee or tax per unit of emissions will, in effect, put the right price tag on clean air and water—just as the market now puts the right price tag on oil and steel. Once our precious air and water resources are priced correctly, polluters will husband them as carefully as they now husband coal, labor, cement, and steel. Pollution will decline. The environment will become cleaner and more healthful....

The Efficiency Argument

It is now time to explain why economists insist that emissions fees can clean up the environment at lower cost than mandatory quantitative controls. The secret is the market's unique ability to accommodate individual differences—in this case, differences among polluters.

Suppose society decides that emissions of sulfur dioxide must decline by 20 percent. One obvious approach is to mandate that every source of sulfur dioxide reduce its emissions by 20 percent. Another option is to levy a fee on discharges that is large enough to reduce emissions by 20 percent. The former is the way our current environmental regulations are often written. The latter is the economist's preferred approach. Both reduce pollution to the same level, but the fee system gets there more cheaply. Why? Because a system of fees assigns most of the job to firms that can reduce emissions easily and cheaply and little to firms that find it onerous and expensive to reduce their emissions.

Let me illustrate how this approach works with a real example. A study in St. Louis found that it cost only $4 for one paper-products factory to cut particulate emissions from its boiler by a ton, but it cost $600 to do the same job at a brewery. If the city fathers instructed both the paper plant and the brewery to cut emissions by the same amount, pollution abatement costs would be low at the paper factory but astronomical at the brewery. Imposing a uniform emissions tax is a more cost-conscious strategy. Suppose a $100/ton tax is announced. The paper company will see an opportunity to save $100 in taxes by spending $4 on cleanup, for a $96 net profit. Similarly, any other firm whose pollution-abatement costs are less than $100 per ton will find it profitable to cut emissions. But firms like the brewery, where pollution-abatement costs exceed $100 per ton, will prefer to continue polluting and paying the tax. Thus the profit motive will automatically assign the task of pollution abatement to the low-cost firms—something no regulators can do.

Mandatory proportional reductions have the seductive appearance of "fairness" and so are frequently adopted. But they provide no incentive to minimize the social costs of environmental clean-up. In fact, when the heavy political hand requires equal percentage reductions by every firm (or perhaps from every smokestack), it pretty much guarantees that the social clean-up will be far more costly than it need be. In the previous example, a one-ton reduction in annual emissions by both the paper factory and the brewery would cost $604 per year. But the same two-ton annual pollution abatement would cost only $8 if the paper factory did the whole job. Only by lucky accident will equiproportionate reductions in discharges be efficient.

Studies that I will cite later... suggest that market-oriented approaches to pollution control can reduce abatement costs by 90 percent in some cases. Why, economists ask, is it more virtuous to make pollution reduction hurt more? They have yet to hear a satisfactory answer and suspect there is none. On the contrary, virtue and efficiency are probably in harmony here. If cleaning up our air and water is made cheaper, it is reasonable to suppose that society will buy more clean-up. We can have a purer environment and pay less, too. The hard-headed economist's crass means may be the surest route to the soft-hearted environmentalist's lofty ends.

The Enforcement Argument

Some critics of emissions fees argue that a system of fees would be hard to enforce. In some cases, they are correct. We obviously cannot use effluent charges to reduce concentrations of the unsightly pollutant glop if engineers have yet to devise an effective and dependable devise for measuring how much glop firms are spewing out. If we think glop is harmful, but are unable to monitor it, our only alternative may be to require firms to switch to "cleaner" technologies. Similarly, emissions charges cannot be levied on pollutants that seep unseen —and unmeasured—into groundwater rather than spill out of a pipe.

In many cases, however, those who argue that emissions fees are harder to enforce than direct controls are deceiving themselves. If you cannot measure emissions, you cannot charge a fee, to be sure. But neither can you enforce mandatory standards; you can only delude yourself into thinking you are enforcing them. To a significant extent, that is precisely what the EPA does now. Federal antipollution regulations are poorly policed; the EPA often declares firms in compliance based on nothing more than the firms' self-reporting of their own behavior. When checks are made, noncompliance is frequently uncovered. If emissions can be measured accurately enough to enforce a system of quantitative controls, we need only take more frequent measurements to run a system of pollution fees.

Besides, either permits or taxes are much easier to administer than detailed regulations. Under a system of marketable permits, the government need only conduct periodic auctions. Under a system of emissions taxes, the enforcement mechanism is the relentless and anonymous tax collector who basically reads your meter like a gas or electric company. No fuss, no muss, no bother—and no need for a big bureaucracy. Just a bill. The only way to escape the pollution tax is to exploit the glaring loophole that the government deliberately provides: reduce your emissions.

Contrast this situation with the difficulties of enforcing the cumbersome command-and-control system we now operate. First, complicated statutes must be passed; and polluting industries will use their considerable political muscle in state legislatures and in Congress to fight for weaker laws. Next, the regulatory agencies must write detailed regulations defining precise standards and often prescribing the "best available technology" to use in reducing emissions. Here again industry will do battle, arguing for looser interpretations of the statutes and often turning the regulations to their own advantage. They are helped in this effort by the sheer magnitude of the information-processing task that the law foists upon the EPA and state agencies, a task that quickly outstrips the capacities of their small staffs.

Once detailed regulations are promulgated, the real problems begin. State and federal agencies with limited budgets must enforce these regulations on thousands, if not millions, of sources of pollution. The task is overwhelming. As one critic of the system put it, each polluter argues:

(1) he is in compliance with the regulation; (2) if not, it is because the regulation is unreasonable as a general rule; (3) if not, then the regulation is unreasonable in this specific case; (4) if not, then it is up to the regulatory agency to tell him how to comply; (5) if forced to take the steps recommended by the agency, he cannot

be held responsible for the results; and (6) he needs more time....

Other Reasons to Favor Emissions Fees

Yet other factors argue for market-based approaches to pollution reduction.

One obvious point is that a system of mandatory standards, or one in which a particular technology is prescribed by law, gives a firm that is in compliance with the law no incentive to curtail its emissions any further. If the law says that the firm can emit up to 500 tons of glop per year, it has no reason to spend a penny to reduce its discharges to 499 tons. By contrast, a firm that must pay $100 per ton per year to emit glop can save money by reducing its annual discharges as long as its pollution-abatement costs are less than $100 per ton. The financial incentive to reduce pollution remains.

A second, and possibly very important, virtue of pollution fees is that they create incentives for firms to devise or purchase innovative ways to reduce emissions. Under a system of effluent fees, businesses gain if they can find cheaper ways to control emissions because their savings depend on their pollution abatement, not on how they achieve it. Current regulations, by contrast, often dictate the technology. Firms are expected to obey the regulators, not to search for creative ways to reduce pollution at lower cost.

For this and other reasons, our current system of regulations is unnecessarily adversarial. Businesses feel the government is out to harass them—and they act accordingly. Environmental protection agencies lock horns with industry in the courts. The whole enterprise takes on the atmosphere of a bullfight rather than that of a joint venture. A market-based approach, which made clear that the government wanted to minimize the costs it imposed on business, would naturally create a more cooperative spirit. That cannot be bad.

Finally, the appearance of fairness when regulations take the form of uniform percentage reductions in emissions, as they frequently do, is illusory. Suppose Clean Jeans, Inc. has already spent a considerable sum to reduce the amount of muck it spews into the Stench River. Dirty Jeans, Inc., just downriver, has not spent a cent and emits twice as much. Now a law is passed requiring every firm along the Stench to reduce its emissions by 50 percent. That has the appearance of equity but not the substance. For Dirty Jeans, the regulation may be a minor nuisance. To comply, it need only do what Clean Jeans is already doing voluntarily. But the edict may prove onerous to Clean Jeans, which has already exploited all the cheap ways to cut emissions. In this instance, not only is virtue not its own reward—it actually brings a penalty! Such anomalies cannot arise under a system of marketable pollution permits. Clean Jeans would always have to buy fewer permits than Dirty Jeans....

OBJECTIONS TO "LICENSES TO POLLUTE"

Despite the many powerful arguments in favor of effluent taxes or marketable emissions permits, many people have an instinctively negative reaction to the whole idea. Some environmentalists, in particular, rebel at economists' advocacy of market-based approaches to pollution control—which they label "licenses to pollute," a term not meant to sound complimentary. Former Senator Muskie's dictum, quoted at the beginning of this chapter, is an example. The question is: Are the objections to "licenses to pollute" based on coherent arguments that should sway policy, or are they knee-jerk reactions best suited to T-shirts?* My own view is that there is little of the former and much of the latter. Let me explain.

Some of the invective heaped upon the idea of selling the privilege to pollute stems from an ideologically based distrust of markets. Someone who does not think the market a particularly desirable way to organize the production of automobiles, shirts, and soybeans is unlikely to trust the market to protect the environment. As one congressional staff aide put it: "The philosophical assumption that proponents of [emissions] charges make is that there is a free-market system that responds to ... relative costs.... I reject that assumption." This remarkably fatuous statement ignores mountains of evidence accumulated over centuries. Fortunately, it is a minority view in America. Were it the majority view, our economic problems would be too severe to leave much time for worry about pollution.

Some of the criticisms of pollution fees are based on ignorance of the arguments or elementary errors in logic. As mentioned earlier, few opponents of market-based approaches can even explain why economists insist that emissions fees will get the job done more cheaply.

One commonly heard objection is that a rich corporation confronted with a pollution tax will pay the tax rather than reduce its pollution. That belief shows an astonishing lack of respect for avarice. Sure, an obstinate but profitable company *could* pay the fees rather

*[Earlier in his book, Blinder warns his readers about simplistic answers to complex questions. He concludes that "if it fits on a T-shirt, it is almost certainly wrong."—Eds.]

than reduce emissions. But it would do that only if the marginal costs of pollution abatement exceed the fee. Otherwise, its obduracy reduces its profits. Most corporate executives faced with a pollution tax will improve their bottom lines by cutting their emissions, not by flouting the government's intent. To be sure, it is self-interest, not the public interest, that motivates the companies to clean up their acts. But that's exactly the idea behind pollution fees....

One final point should lay the moral issue to rest. Mandatory quantitative standards for emissions are also licenses to pollute—just licenses of a strange sort. They give away, with neither financial charge nor moral condemnation, the right to spew a specified amount of pollution into the air or water. Then they absolutely prohibit any further emissions. Why is such a license morally superior to a uniform tax penalty on all pollution? Why is a business virtuous if it emits 500 tons of glop per year but sinful if it emits 501? Economists make no claim to be arbiters of public morality. But I doubt that these questions have satisfactory answers.

The choice between direct controls and effluent fees, then, is not a moral issue. It is an efficiency issue. About that, economists know a thing or two.

Having made my pitch, I must confess that there are circumstances under which market-based solutions are inappropriate and quantitative standards are better. One obvious instance is the case of a deadly poison. If the socially desirable level of a toxin is zero, there is no point in imposing an emission fee. An outright ban makes more sense.

Another case is a sudden health emergency. When, for example, a summertime air inversion raises air pollution in Los Angeles or New York to hazardous levels, it makes perfect sense for the mayors of those cities to place legal limits on driving, on industrial discharges, or on both. There is simply no time to install a system of pollution permits.

A final obvious case is when no adequate monitoring device exists, as in the case of runoff from soil pollution. Then a system of emissions fees is out of the question. But so also is a system of direct quantitative controls on emissions. The only viable way to control such pollution may be to mandate that cleaner technologies be used.

But each of these is a minor, and well recognized, exception to an overwhelming presumption in the opposite direction. No sane person has ever proposed selling permits to spill arsenic into water supplies. None has suggested that the mayor of New York set the effluent tax on carbon monoxide anew after hearing the weather forecast each morning. And no one has insisted that we must meter what cannot be measured. Each of these objections is a debater's point, not a serious challenge to the basic case for market-oriented approaches to environmental protection....

RAYS OF HOPE: EMISSIONS TRADING AND BUBBLES

There are signs, however, that environmental policy may be changing for the better. The EPA seems to be drifting slowly, and not always surely, away from technology-driven direct controls toward more market-oriented approaches. But not because the agency has been convinced by the logic of economists' arguments. Rather, it was driven into a corner by the inexorable illogic of its own procedures. Necessity proved to be the midwife of common sense.

The story begins in the 1970s, when it became apparent that many regions of the country could not meet the air quality standards prescribed by the Clean Air Act. Under the law, the prospective penalty for violating of the standards was Draconian: no new sources of pollution would be permitted in these regions and existing sources would not be allowed to increase their emissions, implying a virtual halt to local economic growth. The EPA avoided the impending clash between the economy and the environment by creating its "emissions-offsets" program in 1976. Under the new rules, companies were allowed to create new sources of pollution in areas with substandard air quality as long as they reduced their pollution elsewhere by greater amounts. Thus was emissions trading born.

The next important step was invention of the "bubble" concept in 1979. Under this concept, all sources of pollution from a single plant or firm are imagined to be encased in a mythical bubble. The EPA then tells the company that it cares only about total emissions into the bubble. How these emissions are parceled out among the many sources of pollution under the bubble is no concern of the EPA. But it is vital to the firm, which can save money by cutting emissions in the least costly way. A striking example occurred in 1981 when a DuPont plant in New Jersey was ordered to reduce its emissions from 119 sources by 85 percent. Operating under a state bubble program, company engineers proposed instead that emissions from seven large stacks be reduced by 99 percent. The result? Pollution reduction exceeded the state's requirement by 2,300 tons per year

and DuPont saved $12 million in capital costs and $3 million per year in operating costs.

Partly because it was hampered by the courts, the bubble concept was little used at first. But bubbles have been growing rapidly since a crucial 1984 judicial decision. By October 1984, about seventy-five bubbles had been approved by the EPA and state authorities and hundreds more were under review or in various stages of development. The EPA estimated the cost savings from all these bubbles to be about $800 million per year. That may seem a small sum compared to the more than $70 billion we now spend on environmental protection. But remember that the whole program was still in the experimental stage, and these bubbles covered only a tiny fraction of the thousands of industrial plants in the United States.

The bubble program was made permanent only when EPA pronounced the experiment a success and issued final guidelines in November 1986. Economists greeted this announcement with joy. Environmentalist David Doniger... complained that, "The bubble concept is one of the most destructive impediments to the cleanup of unhealthy air." By now, many more bubbles have been approved or are in the works. Time will tell who was right.

The final step in the logical progression toward the economist's approach would be to make these "licenses to pollute" fully marketable so that firms best able to reduce emissions could sell their excess abatement to firms for which pollution abatement is too expensive. Little trading has taken place to date, though the EPA's November 1986 guidelines may encourage it. But at least one innovative state program is worth mentioning.

The state of Wisconsin found itself unable to achieve EPA-mandated levels of water quality along the polluted Fox and Wisconsin Rivers, even when it employed the prescribed technology. A team of engineers and economists then devised a sophisticated system of transferable discharge permits. Firms were issued an initial allocation of pollution permits (at no charge), based on historical levels of discharges. In total, these permits allow no more pollution than is consistent with EPA standards for water quality. But firms are allowed to trade pollution permits freely in the open market. Thus, in stark contrast to the standard regulatory approach, the Wisconsin system lets the firms along the river—not the regulators—decide how to reduce discharges. Little emissions trading has taken place to date because the entire scheme has been tied up in litigation. But one study estimated that pollution-control costs might eventually fall by as much as 80 percent compared to the alternative of ordering all firms along the river to reduce their discharges by a uniform percentage.

The state of Wisconsin thus came to the conclusion that economists have maintained all along: that applying a little economic horse sense makes it possible to clean up polluted rivers and reduce costs at the same time—a good bargain. That same bargain is available to the nation for the asking. . . .

A HARD-HEADED, SOFT-HEARTED ENVIRONMENTAL POLICY

Economists who specialize in environmental policy must occasionally harbor self-doubts. They find themselves lined up almost unanimously in favor of market-based approaches to pollu-

tion control with seemingly everyone else lined up on the other side. Are economists crazy or is everyone else wrong?

. . . I have argued the seemingly implausible proposition that environmental economists are right and everyone else really is wrong. I have tried to convey a sense of the frustration economists feel when they see obviously superior policies routinely spurned. By replacing our current command-and-control system with either marketable pollution permits or taxes on emissions, our environment can be made cleaner while the burden on industry is reduced. That is about as close to a free lunch as we are likely to encounter. And yet economists' recommendations are overwhelmed by an unholy alliance of ignorance, ideology, and self-interest.

This is a familiar story. The one novel aspect in the sphere of environmental policy is that the usual heavy hitter of this triumvirate—self-interest—is less powerful here than in many other contexts. To be sure, self-interested business lobbies oppose pollution fees. But, as I pointed out, they can be bought off by allowing some pollution free of charge. Doing so may outrage environmental purists, but it is precisely what we do now.

It is the possibility of finessing vested financial interests that holds out the hope that good environmental policy might one day drive out the bad. For we need only overcome ignorance and ideology, not avarice.

Ignorance is normally beaten by knowledge. Few Americans now realize that practical reforms of our environmental policies can reduce the national clean-up bill from more than $70 billion per year to less than $50 billion, and probably to much less. Even fewer understand the reasons why. If the case for market-based policies were better known, more and more people might ask the obvious question: Why is it better to pay more for something we can get for less? Environmental policy may be one area where William Blake's optimistic dictum —"Truth can never be told so as to be understood and not believed"—is germane.

Ideology is less easily rooted out, for it rarely succumbs to rational argument. Some environmentalists support the economist's case. Others understand it well and yet oppose it for what they perceive as moral reasons. I have argued at length that here, as elsewhere, thinking with the heart is less effective than thinking with the head; that the economist's case does not occupy the moral low ground; and that the environment is likely to be cleaner if we offer society clean-up at more reasonable cost. As more environmentalists come to realize that T-shirt slogans are retarding, not hastening, progress toward their goals, their objections may melt away.

The economist's approach to environmental protection is no panacea. It requires an investment in monitoring equipment that society has not yet made. It cannot work in cases where the sources of pollution are not readily identifiable, such as seepage into groundwater. And it will remain an imperfect antidote for environmental hazards until we know a great deal more than we do now about the diffusion of pollutants and the harm they cause.

But perfection is hardly the appropriate standard. As things stand now, our environmental policy may be a bigger mess than our environment. Market-based approaches that join the hard head of the accountant to the soft heart of the environmentalist offer the prospect of genuine improvement: more clean-up for less money. It is an offer society should not refuse.

NO

David Moberg

ENVIRONMENT AND MARKETS: A CRITIQUE OF "FREE MARKET" CLAIMS

The soot-darkened skies and fouled waters of Eastern Europe have given apologists for laissez-faire capitalism a new rallying cry: the "free market," far from being nature's enemy, is the environment's savior.

Some environmentalists have argued that there is no fundamental conflict between environmental responsibility and "free market" economics. Ecology, they contend, is ultimately sound, profitable business and environmental regulation must employ market forces if it is to succeed. They advocate giving business more flexibility and incentives, such as the right to buy and sell pollution rights, to increase efficiency and innovation so as to meet environmental goals.

Other environmentalists, however, continue to share a skepticism, with roots in both conservative and leftist traditions, about the compatibility of the market and the environment. This camp is also dissatisfied with the results of the first two decades of environmental regulation. Its advocates want a more aggressive democratic voice in what are usually private decisions. Ecological principles have become the basis for alternative models to capitalist markets, conflicting with or complementing the longstanding social class critiques. Ecologists have also opened another front criticizing not just the adequacy of market mechanisms but also market society in general and its exaltation of individual acquisitiveness and unbridled growth of commodity production.

All human societies have been shaped by interaction with nature, from the nomadism of hunters to the settled cultures of rich ecological niches, such as our own Northwest Coast or the slash-and-burn agriculture of tropical forests. Although earlier cultures undermined themselves by radically altering environments, stripping forests from the hills of Greece or raising the salinity of irrigated Mesopotamian soil, the worst depredation of the environment has come since the rise of capitalism. Now there is the prospect that human society has such an unsustainable relation with nature that both the future of humanity and the fate of thousands of other creatures is at stake.

From David Moberg, "Environment and Markets: A Critique of 'Free Market' Claims," *Dissent* (Fall 1991). Copyright © 1991 by David Moberg. Reprinted by permission.

But has capitalism itself been the cause of environmental damage or is the root problem industrial technologies or a growing population that consumes more and more goods?

Although the rapid growth of both population and global consumption magnifies every environmental impact, there are huge differences in environmental effects among nations, even the industrialized ones. The worst environmental insults are a result of modern industry, but not all industries degrade the environment equally. The nature of society, not just its size or technology, is largely responsible for the crisis in nature.

Obviously, the private market damages the natural environment because pollution is external to the balance sheets of private business. A factory owner doesn't pay to flush waste down the river or into the air; the costs are borne by nature as well as other people who share the environment. On the other hand, if a farmer preserves a marsh that cleans the stream's water, nourishes fish and wildlife, and prevents floods, he is paid nothing for those services. But if he sells it to be filled in for a shopping center, he will make money, and our accounting system evaluates this as economic growth, with no deductions for this loss of the wetland's natural functions. Likewise, nobody pays for the Amazon forest serving as "the lungs of the world" or preserving its diverse life forms for the future. So, the market doesn't adequately account for either negative or positive externalities.

If an ingenious entrepreneur devises a pollution-free production process that costs more than her competitor's, she will probably lose the market race: in most cases, nobody—except for a few generous souls—will pay the tab for her contribution to the common welfare. Now it is possible to level the playing field with taxes, fees, or penalties for the polluter, but it is difficult to assess the price of damage to the environment, especially if it is not a localized toxic spill but a global problem, like the greenhouse effect. Litigation over Exxon's Alaska oil spill or over compensation to the victims of Union Carbide's Bhopal disaster suggests the ethically and economically knotty problems.

WHO DETERMINES THE LOSSES?

There are similar problems if more direct environmental regulations are subjected to cost-benefit analysis: how much is a human life worth? Some economists argue that it's the person's likely future lifetime earnings. That makes an Indian peasant pretty expendable compared to a Connecticut executive. Such cost-benefit analyses illegitimately import values of the marketplace to answer questions that arise because of fundamental flaws in that same market system.

How much is a sea otter worth?, *Business Week* asked. Surveying people about how much the animals are worth to them or measuring lost income if sea otters disappeared may keep a few economists employed, but it does not answer the question. If only one respondent said it was of infinite value, that would throw off the survey. If you limit the response to how much a person would be willing to spend, the result would obviously be affected by how much money people have, a standard flaw of market preference analysis.

Nobody asks the sea otter how much otters are worth. But the presumption that human-kind's use of the world is the sole measure of its value is arrogant. Nor can anyone survey future generations on their valuations of nature. And trying to measure the environment in terms of clean-up costs makes the neat presumption, easy in economics but questionable in nature, that all processes are reversible.

So, correctly pricing the environmental effects of human activities is at best rough guesswork, an attempt to squeeze profound issues of value into a Procrustean bed of price. Ultimately, despite imported trappings of economic analysis, the decision is social: what does society value?

* * *

The market also fails to value adequately the depletion of nonrenewable resources. Again, future generations are largely ignored. How does the market allocate the right of a few generations in the twentieth and twenty-first centuries to use up most of the world's nonrenewable hydrocarbon resources? For a Brazilian gold miner or peasant, suffering in an economy burdened by huge external debts, short-term market rationality may dictate destroying the forest (just as the short-term rationality of the banks collecting their debts indirectly destroys the forest). But its resources of flora and fauna are lost, its land rendered useless. In different ways, then, the extreme inequities of income generated in the global market exhaust the planet —from the pressure of impoverished Third World masses on the land to the disproportionate consumption of nonrenewable resources and generation of waste in the richest countries....

Laissez-faire religion rests on the blind faith that maximizing profits will over time yield the most rational results. Yet even within a capitalist framework, far sighted investment at the expense of current profits often makes sense. Critics

have charged, with compelling evidence, that the short-term preoccupations of American business have weakened the American economy. With regard to nature, myopic economic calculation is even more devastating. Given the scale and toxicity of human activity today, waiting for the market to signal a need for change may result in catastrophic, even irreversible damage, such as global warming or extinction of valuable species. There is a fundamental conflict, Daly and Cobb argue, between short-term profit maximization and the real needs and concrete resources of the whole community far into the future.

DEFERRING GRATIFICATION

Again, the calculations of the market are inadequate. Economists often discount a future sum of money, figuring its present value as the amount that, if put in the bank at current interest rates, would yield the future sum. For the same reasons that bedevil other efforts to price nature, such discounting fails to assess the future value of the environment. From a free-market perspective, it may be rational for the private owner to kill the goose that lays the golden egg—if it can be sold now for more than its discounted future value and the proceeds invested. But thereby, Daly and Cobb argue, "society has lost a perpetual stream of golden eggs."

When we consider how long certain toxic substances and especially radioactive wastes are likely to remain threats, the problem is compounded: we rob the inheritance of future generations and leave them with a poisonous debt. If future people could be consulted, they would never sign the one-sided contract now being written. We can conclude that for several different reasons the market doesn't accurately price goods so as to take account of their environmental consequences. It ignores negative and positive externalities, ill accounts for depletion of natural resources, inappropriately measures income and welfare, and fails to take responsibility for future generations' welfare.

* * *

Since the defense of the market usually rests in large part on its ability to allocate resources efficiently and provide accurate information through prices, this failure to incorporate the environment is not a trifling flaw.

Can it be corrected? Increasingly some environmentalists argue for "green taxes" that would adjust prices upward to include uncounted environmental costs. U.S. energy users don't pay directly for as much as $300 billion a year in subsidies and tax credits (at least $50 billion a year, mainly to fossil fuels and nuclear power), environmental degradation, damage to health, military expenditures (the Gulf War alone would have added approximately $25 a barrel to imported oil), or employment effects of energy policies, according to Harold M. Hubbard, a scientist at Resources for the Future. By other calculations, we should now be paying more than $100 a barrel for oil if all costs were included. But Hubbard acknowledges that "calculating the actual cost of energy is not a simple matter.... The answers that economists derive may depend as much on social values as they do on analytical solutions to well-defined problems."

If consumers had to pay directly for the full price of energy, several things would happen. First, there would be economic shock and an increase in inequality. In general, the proportion of income spent on energy declines as income increases, although the use of energy increases (at the lowest income levels a decline in car ownership modifies this trend). Then there would be attempts to cope, by cutting back some use (much use is not very discretionary), and then, more important, by increasing efficiency. Also, other energy alternatives would become more competitive. And there would obviously be public clamor to do something—from unleashing nuclear power to promoting solar energy.

U.S. experience after the OPEC price increases of the 1970s illustrates the mixed record on market response to higher energy prices. Because the economy was ill-prepared to absorb the shocks, much of the stagflation of the decade can be attributed to everybody's efforts to pass on the costs to someone else. But the U.S. economy, with some governmental encouragement, also became more energy efficient. In little more than a decade after the first OPEC price increase, the energy intensity of the U.S. economy—energy per unit of GNP—dropped by about one-fourth. Energy production, including new sources of oil, increased in response to higher prices—but far less than mainstream economists predicted.

Much of the efficiency gain was driven by government regulation as well as by market factors. But what's remarkable is how limited the response was, considering the potential. After all, even before the OPEC price hikes, Germany and Japan used roughly half as much energy per unit of GNP as the United States and afterward still made efficiency gains nearly as great or greater than the United States did. Further, using technologies that are commercially available now, the United States could reduce its electric energy consumption by 70 percent at less than the present cost of generating electricity, according to analyses by efficiency guru Amory Lovins's Rocky Mountain Institute. Although the U.S. auto industry, forced by federal standards as much as by prices, made dramatic efficiency gains, the auto industry is still far from realizing the potential of diesel or gasoline engines, not to mention more advanced power sources.

Still, raising the price to some estimated real price would be a clumsy, slow, inequitable way of bringing about needed changes. First, there is nothing intrinsically good—and a lot bad—about high energy prices. What society needs is an inexpensive way to get necessary work done without the externalized costs. The question is: how do we get there in the most socially desirable way?

WILL GOVERNMENT REGULATION WORK?

Direct government intervention is, despite market mania, often the best route. Japanese industries have become leaders in efficiency because "the government spurred their enthusiasm through a carefully coordinated, long-range program that continues even today," the *Wall Street Journal* recently reported. "One clear lesson to learn from Japan is that forcing core industries to become more energy-efficient is one thing that government *can* do well." Other industrialized countries are more energy efficient than the United States because of public investment in their public mass transit systems or because of explicit government strategies, such as Danish support of wind power.

Why hasn't the price of energy—even taking into account the decline in real oil prices in the mid-eighties —spurred more response? Consumers often are ill-informed about alternatives and find it difficult to make lifetime energy cost assessments (cheap initial cost of a regular incandescent bulb is more persuasive than the argument that lifetime costs of an expensive compact fluorescent are lower, for example). Even many industries simply don't understand how energy efficiency can benefit them. They insist that they recover the entire cost of efficiency investments in a year or two, although they might plan on recovering other investments in five years. Sometimes consumers don't directly make decisions: developers or landlords may make choices based on their costs, leaving tenants with higher bills.

* * *

There are large-scale institutional obstacles to change as well. Automobile manufacturers are to some extent captives of tastes they have created, but like the rest of the auto-oil-highway complex, they have a huge stake in keeping changes incremental—only anticipation of direct governmental edicts on alternatives to gasoline engines is leading manufacturers to gear up for electric vehicles. And private companies are largely incapable of making the kinds of massive investments needed for expanded rail or mass transit.

There are countless other ways in which businesses and consumers would not respond rationally or quickly even to prices that fully reflect environmental costs. Especially in making a major transition, the market is sticky, chaotic, and inefficient. For example, many farmers would like to shift from a less chemically intensive regime, especially as they become aware that it is not only economically viable but much healthier. But making the transition can be too costly —for example, suffering severe losses for several years until alternative controls of pests and weeds begin to work well.

Or take the case of photovoltaic cells, clearly a much-needed technology of the near future. Even though deep-pockets energy corporations bought up solar cell firms in the seventies, U.S. companies have been abandoning the field, in some cases selling off to European firms. This highlights another limit to the market model of efficiency: there are significant cultural differences, especially regarding long-term investment, and differences in levels of government support for alternative energy policies. Both affect market responses.

REGULATION CAN HELP COMPETITION

Free-market enthusiasts insist that private businesses be allowed to innovate in response to market signals. But it is socially undesirable to treat the corporation as a black box, ignoring what goes on inside it and tinkering only with the price signals going in and then coping with what comes out. This is especially true in an era when large, multinational corporations dominate the global economy: their power, size, and internal governance distort idealized market responses to price signals.

Corporate policies vary significantly. At 3M Company, executives wisely instituted its "Pollution Prevention Pays" program and have saved $482 million since 1975, eliminated five hundred thousand tons of waste, and saved another $650 million through energy conservation. But what happens when a company compares polluting and nonpolluting alternatives and calculates that pollution does pay? Or take another example, representing a more familiar route in the eighties. Phillips Petroleum, under pressure of debt incurred in fighting off a hostile takeover, laid off experienced union workers and replaced them with ill-trained contract workers, took short-cuts on safety, and pushed production to the limit. The result was a major explosion in Pasadena, Texas, that killed twenty-six people and spread toxic materials throughout the environment.

Many businesses around the world have become more innovative and competitive as a result of strict environmental regulations. Both Germany and Japan have tougher standards than the United States and are growing faster. Some of the most strictly regulated U.S. industries, such as chemical, synthetics, and fabrics, have gained international competitiveness. Yet many businesses have chosen the path followed by a large segment of southern California's furniture industry: faced with tougher emissions standards, they fled to Mexico, where pollution laws are not enforced.

What makes one company prevent pollution while improving its ability to compete and another company endanger its employees and the surrounding community or flee abroad? Why does one business seize opportunities to become energy efficient and another respond to competitive pressures by shortchanging workers? How these distinct strategies emerge varies, but the general point is that when free marketeers talk about giving businesses flexibility and allowing the market to stimulate innovation, part of the flexibility and innovation will be socially good and part terrible. Why let private business make that momentous decision? Why should society wait until after the dirty deed is done to try to clean up the mess? ...

NIGHTMARE OF CONSUMPTION

Despite our own problems of inequality of consumption, which tear at the social fabric of the United States, an overemphasis on commodity consumption is the industrialized world's environmental nightmare. In mass-consumption societies self-fulfillment is defined in terms of buying more things, which leads to a disproportionate use of the world's resources and contributes to waste crises, from localized conflicts over municipal dumps to global destruction of the ozone layer. Of course, if raw materials were more accurately priced and if corporations were responsible for what happened to the waste they produced, there could be more reusable or at least recyclable packaging and less waste, all without a loss of meaningful consumption.

Environmentalists have contended that we must recognize limits to growth, a most unpopular prospect for both liberals and conservatives. Technically, the limit to a sustainable economy is the amount of solar energy falling on the earth that can reasonably be captured, even though there are much stricter limits on supplies of nonrenewable resources. The specter of global warming or holes in the ozone layer suggests that we could reach the limit of our use of nonrenewable fuels faster than we actually exhaust the earth's resources. Certainly there is no way that the earth can support the spread of wealthy, industrialized nations' current extravagant consumption to the world's poor. Environmentalists are divided over what are the limits to the earth's capacity, but markets have no way

of even considering the question: unending growth is both their assumption and goal.

The alternative does not have to be for the richer nations to take vows of poverty. Some of our problems come from relying on the dynamics of commodity production rather than considering what needs we have and how those can be best served. We want homes and offices that are comfortable and well-lighted. But electric utilities want to sell electricity. It would be better for everyone if they devoted their resources to promoting energy efficiency, but they will only do so, in most cases, if they are compensated for part of sales forgone through efficiency-reduced demand. Increasingly, public utility commissions are enforcing such policies, and municipally owned utilities have aggressively pursued this service-oriented alternative because they are not profit oriented.

Environmental concerns should be added to many other motivations—political, philosophical, religious—to challenge the model of "economic man" that market society helps to create. The highly individualistic, cost-minimizing, profit-seeking mentality of market society is not a result of "human nature" but a cultural construction that denies a place for many values and feelings that have appeared in most human societies. True, there are flaky manifestations of new-age spiritualism associated with the environmental movement, but the desire for a sense of human community and harmony with the world is widespread and authentic.

The logic of free-market economics creates untenable abstractions, as Daly and Cobb, following economic historian Karl Polanyi, emphasize. In the laissez-faire market vision, nature becomes land. Then land itself is left out of the calculation, with the assumption that it is interchangeable with humanly created capital. Life becomes labor, or abstract labor-power, and patrimony becomes capital. All values are reduced to prices. Time is not concrete history, incorporating natural biological processes, but rather an infinite series of equivalent seconds. Places with distinctive features disappear into an interchangeable abstract space. By contrast, ecology reminds us that we live in a concrete world, and that we often end up committing real, not just intellectual, violence upon nature, humanity, and history.

HOW DO WE DEAL WITH MARKETS?

So what do we do with markets? First, we must put them in their place, and that place is secondary to considerations of social values. The fundamental flaws in the market, from the environmental perspective alone, are enough to undo economists' claims for marketplace superiority. The market needs to be subordinated not only to nature but also to broader human values that form a limiting framework. That requires greater international cooperation. (This is already happening to a small extent with bans on whaling and the ivory trade and international agreements on reducing chlorofluorocarbons.) But ironically it also requires granting nations and communities power to enforce stronger standards to respond to their own local needs without having those undermined in the name of free trade.

Some environmentalists (including the Environmental Defense Fund and a group convened under senators Tim Wirth and the late John Heinz called Project 88) have argued that market-oriented regulations, such as tradable permits for discharges, will achieve environmental goals efficiently. The 1990 Clean Air Act revisions introduce such tradable permits, and the Chicago Board of Trade now plans a futures market in pollution permits. There are numerous objections: such trade *legitimates* pollution, it is likely to disadvantage the poor and powerless (especially if conducted on an international scale), regulatory regimes are already fairly flexible, and markets in such permits may be hard to establish and inefficient. The only evidence for efficiency so far comes from econometric studies already biased towards market solutions. Depending on the prices of permits or the level of taxes imposed, polluters could decide it was still cheaper to pollute.

Even more important, a focus on finding these market solutions diverts us from the main point. Nearly all these regulatory regimes represent attempts to control emissions, but as ecologist Barry Commoner argues in his book *Making Peace with the Planet*, regulatory efforts have at best slowed only slightly the rate of environmental deterioration. The real environmental successes have only come with outright bans of certain substances, such as lead in gasoline or paint. Instead of quibbling over how much toxic substance can be released, regulation should increasingly establish a standard of zero discharge. "The tax [on pollutants] can't work until you've done the wrong thing," Commoner says. "You can't have a market in pollutant rights until you have pollutants." The solution is prevention.

But prevention can't always be outright banning: for the foreseeable future, at least some hydrocarbons will be burned. In many cases, transitions to zero discharge may take time. During that period, using tradable permits or other market-oriented methods should be considered along with flexible regulation. But rather than a panacea, such devices represent an interesting gimmick of unproven value.

WHAT FORCES WILL WORK BEST?

There is increased interest in energy or carbon taxes to discourage fossil-fuel use and give better signals on the true costs of burning hydrocarbons, especially nonrenewable sources. Eliminating subsidies to dangerous or polluting sources, such as nuclear power, would also give more appropriate prices.

It's obvious that energy is mispriced and consequently misused, but relying on taxes to bring about a change through the market is likely to create great hardship for low-to-middle-income people and increase inequality. Ideally, a transition would not greatly increase energy bills but would increase energy prices steadily in tandem with changes to alternative, renewable energy sources, a different mix of technologies, and greater energy efficiency. If the government developed a strategy for transition to an essentially solar economy, then regular increases in energy taxes could be used for a variety of projects, including research. Federal, state, and local governments can have a tremendous impact: government purchases of solar cells or hydrogen- or electric-powered cars could speed the learning curve and cut prices quickly. Public investment would be needed to develop mass transit and railroads. A full-scale industrial extension service to promote energy efficiency and nonpolluting technologies could speed industrial transitions with less disruption. But

if energy taxes are going to work most effectively, it should not be simply through the indirect effect of higher prices but also through the investment of the new revenue in efficiency and alternatives.

* * *

Green consumerism and protest already have had some impact. McDonald's, responding to a campaign against its styrofoam clamshell, has switched packaging and is considering composting of its food wastes. Other businesses sense a good market, although many are as duplicitous as Mobil Chemical, whose representative said its "biodegradable" plastic trash bags "are not an answer to landfill crowding or littering.... Degradability is just a marketing tool.... We're talking out of both sides of our mouths because we want to sell bags." Green consumerism is an important phenomenon but is likely to remain marginal without other reinforcing measures.

There must first be clear public policy. A mixture of direct government actions (purchases, subsidies, prohibitions, research, and technical assistance) can be combined with changed market incentives (for example, taxes and markets in efficiency) in ways that complement each other. Public policy, however, should determine the direction.

The disastrous effects of centralized government control in the communist countries should remain a reminder that government is no guarantee of virtue. Clearly government in the United States and elsewhere has often been the captive of corporate interests. Environmental values, like other values, must be cultivated among the electorate if public policy is going to change. In the long run, altering the "economic man" outlook of market society will make environmental goals easier to attain.

Much of the progress toward environmental sanity in the United States has come as a result of grass-roots protest, environmental impact fights, and legal action over local issues. Often dismissed as NIMBYism—not-in-my-backyard—these movements are often concerned about other backyards as well. Even now the grass-roots protesters among environmentalists exert pressure on the bigger, established environmental groups that are entrapped in the rulemaking squabbles of federal legislation and tempted to form alliances with big corporations (at times having an influence, yet also subtly losing their independence).

Besides guaranteeing a free and full role for citizen protest, which big corporations especially want to eliminate, it is important that workers have broad powers to influence the safety and health of their work environment. Like the proverbial canaries in coal mines of the past, they are the first victims of pollution and toxicity. Giving them powers to protect themselves, with mandated worker health and safety committees in every workplace, protects everyone else.

Environmental values lead to a model of society that subordinates the market to nature, but environmentalists cannot claim nature as their model any more than the free marketeers can call their model "natural." No model of society is natural; all are historical, cultural creations. And nature itself has forever been altered by human culture.

A new model of society can aspire to respect nature and to make culture and nature as compatible as possible. The implications of the environmental critique go beyond traditional ecological issues. Many similar critiques of the market can be made on behalf of other cultural values. The market, for example, does not take into account the externalities of human poverty and inequality, economic dislocation, stunted work lives, and destruction of community. It gives the wrong price signals, the wrong information. In taming the market to protect nature, we should not forget the well-being of those most curious natural creatures—ourselves.

POSTSCRIPT

Should Pollution Be Put to the Market Test?

For the past 25 years a massive effort has been put forth in the United States to advance environmental protection by using laws and regulation. Efforts can be traced back to the 1970 National Environmental Policy Act (NEPA), the first modern environmental statute that required environmental impact statements on federal projects. That same year, Congress also passed the Clean Air Act, which replaced a weak environmental statute with enforceable, federal clean-air standards and timetables for industry to meet. Seven years later, the Clean Water Act (1977) was passed. This act established standards and permits, and it attempted to limit discharges in navigable waters and protect wetlands from exploration.

At first, federal action was directed toward air- and water-pollution control; this was accomplished by issuing regulations and permits. The second set of initiatives focused on cleaning up hazardous waste dumps. This action was first authorized by the Resource Conservation and Recovery Act (RCRA) of 1976, which established a permit system for disposal sites and regulated underground storage tanks. Later initiatives in this area were authorized by the Comprehensive Environmental Response, Compensation, and Liability Act (CERCLA) of 1980. This act, known as the Superfund, created a fund to finance the clean-up of hazardous waste sites.

What is significant is that, until recently, efforts to control, contain, and eliminate pollution and its effects have been accomplished largely by government regulation. Economists such as Blinder have argued for policies that captured and utilized the strength of the market. However, as Moberg so effectively argues, the opposition has been successful in warning public policy away from a free-market perspective that would allow "the private owner to kill the goose that lays the golden egg" and in the process deny society "a perpetual stream of golden eggs."

For a review of the legislation in the air pollution area, see Richard H. Schulze, "The 20-Year History of the Evolution of Air Pollution Control Legislation in the U.S.A.," *Atmospheric Environment* (March 1993). For a discussion of some of the ethical issues surrounding the pollution permits, see Paul Steichmeier, "The Morality of Pollution Permits," *Environmental Ethics* (Summer 1993). And for other economic interpretations see Dwight R. Lee, "An Economist's Perspective on Air Pollution," *Environmental Science and Technology* (October 1993) and Joe Alper, "Protecting the Environment with the Power of the Market," *Science* (June 25, 1993).

ISSUE 20

Has Capitalism Defeated Socialism?

YES: Malcolm S. Forbes, Jr., from "Three Cheers for Capitalism," *Forbes* (October 25, 1993)

NO: David McReynolds, from "Socialism Yes," *The Progressive* (April 1993)

ISSUE SUMMARY

YES: Publisher Malcolm S. Forbes, Jr., praises capitalism as the basis of human innovation and imagination, and he argues that it "works better than any of us can conceive."

NO: David McReynolds, cochair of the Socialist Party–U.S.A., remains committed to socialism because it "emphasizes cooperation rather than competition," and because it "is an effort to make every human being an end in himself or herself."

People generally agree that there are some functions that government should perform in the modern world. Almost everyone, for example, believes that national defense—the protection of a country from foreign invasion—is a legitimate function of government. Another generally accepted function is the establishment and maintenance of a code of laws that represent the ground rules for social and economic relationships and activities. Many also believe that government has the responsibility to provide systems and programs that will support those individuals in society who, through no fault of their own, are unable to care for themselves. Even the conservative Reagan administration accepted the notion of a "social safety net."

Narrowing the focus to the functions of government in the economic domain, the general rule is that government needs to ensure the efficient and equitable operation of the economy. Acceptance of this rule does not mean that there will be agreement on exactly what government should do and how extensive its involvement should be. At the one extreme are those who might be called *libertarians*, individuals who believe that government's involvement should be minimized. Whether in the economic domain or in the social domain, the libertarians argue that the government that governs least, governs best. At the other extreme are those who might be called *collectivists*, individuals who believe that government, especially in matters of economics, needs to play an active and pervasive role in society. The libertarians therefore support capitalism, while the collectivists support socialism.

This debate over the proper role of government has been played out at two levels. One level would be called intellectual, or academic. Here theorists debate the relative efficiency and equity of capitalism and socialism. The other level is more practical—and more important as countries modify their economies in accordance with the capitalist or socialist models. The former, of course, relies on private decision making and private ownership to generate efficiency and equity. The latter relies on collective decision making and collective ownership; so efficiency and equity can only be achieved if government plays the central role in the economic drama. There are distinctions in these models, including managed capitalism, democratic capitalism, communism, and democratic socialism.

In the post–World War II era, the list of countries employing the socialist/communist model included the Soviet Union, North Korea, Communist China, Cuba, and the Eastern European countries of Poland, East Germany, Bulgaria, Czechoslovakia, Hungary, and Romania. The United States, Japan, and the countries of Western Europe were considered the representatives of the capitalistic camp. In the late 1980s and early 1990s, with the collapse of the Soviet Union, the unification of East and West Germany, and the institution of economic and political reforms in the new Commonwealth of Independent States (the newly independent republics of the former Soviet Union) and the other Eastern European countries, many believed that the contest was over: the collapse and the reforms were proof that capitalism was superior to socialism.

But the fact of significant movement away from the socialist/communist model toward the capitalist model by the various countries raises several questions: Was the transformation a true sign of the victory of capitalism over socialism and communism, or was it a victory of capitalism over the particular version of socialism and communism practiced by these former socialist and communist countries? If the facts truly represent a victory of capitalism over socialism and communism, what were the reasons for the victory? If capitalism has now been embraced, does that mean that capitalism cannot be improved? These are the questions that are addressed by Malcolm S. Forbes, Jr., and David McReynolds in the following selections.

YES
Malcolm S. Forbes, Jr.

THREE CHEERS FOR CAPITALISM

Living in the 1990s, we are uniquely able to judge what the American economy has achieved in the 20th century. For this reason, we ought to give three cheers for capitalism. By this term I mean "democratic capitalism," which is as fundamentally different from the "managed capitalism" of modern-day central planners as it is from the "state capitalism" of old-style fascists, socialists and communists.

Capitalism works better than any of us can conceive. It is also the only truly *moral* system of exchange. It encourages individuals to freely devote their energies and impulses to peaceful pursuits, to the satisfaction of others' wants and needs and to constructive action for the welfare of all. The basis for capitalism is not greed. Misers don't create Wal-Marts and Microsofts.

Think about it for a moment. Capitalism is truly miraculous. What other system enables us to cooperate with millions of other ordinary people— people we never meet but whom we gladly provide with goods and services —in an incredible, complex web of commercial transactions? And what other system perpetuates itself, working every day, year in, year out, with no single hand guiding it?

Capitalism is a moral system if only because it is based on *trust.* When we turn on a light, we assume there will be electricity. When we drive into a service station, we assume there will be fuel. When we walk into a restaurant, we assume there will be food. If we were to make a list of all the basic things that capitalism provides—things we take for granted—it would fill an encyclopedia.

How do we become successful capitalists? The answer sounds simple but is often overlooked in places where it should be known: the government, the media and our most elite business schools and economics departments. We succeed as capitalists by offering goods and services that others are willing to buy. Many do not make correct assumptions about what to offer and, therefore, fail, but that is as it should be. There is no guarantee of success in any area of life, including business; there is always risk. The particular advantage of capitalism is that failed businesses don't necessarily equal a failed economy; they make way for successful businesses.

But even the most successful businesses can't afford to forget about market principles. AT&T is a case in point. In the 1970s fiber-optic technology was available, but AT&T decided that it would delay fully converting to it for 30 to 40 years. AT&T wanted to fully depreciate its old plants and equipment, and, because it enjoyed a virtual monopoly over its customers, it saw no reason to spend a lot of money on a new long-distance calling system. But then an upstart company, MCI, raised a couple billion dollars through the much-maligned "junk bonds" market and set up its own fiber-optic network. AT&T had no choice but to keep up with its competition, and, as a result, the U.S. experienced an enormous advance in communications that has put it ahead of its foreign competitors and that has benefited hundreds of millions of consumers.

About 25 years ago the federal government filed an antitrust suit against IBM because it had grown so successful that its name had become virtually synonymous with the computer industry. But the would-be trust busters underestimated the vitality of an open marketplace. IBM's dominance of mainframe computers, microchips and software did not prevent the rise of rival companies such as Digital Equipment, Apple Computer, Sun Microsystems and Microsoft. Today IBM's future is being questioned.

Around the same time John Kenneth Galbraith wrote *The New Industrial State*, in which he argued that though Ford Motor Co. was no longer the biggest of the auto companies (GM had roughly 50% of all sales), it was so large that it did not have to pay particular attention to its shareholders or customers. Apparently, Japanese automakers did not read John Kenneth Galbraith or the reports of countless other "experts" who claimed that it was impossible to compete against Ford, GM and Chrysler. They even ignored their own early failures to storm the U.S. market in the 1950s and early 1960s. Finally, after years of trying, Japanese automakers succeeded—to an extent no one could have predicted—in challenging the hegemony of the "giants" in Detroit.

Then there is Sears, Roebuck. What more mundane business could there be than retailing? Yet around the turn of the century, Sears made retailing truly exciting, reaching out to millions of people with new marketing methods and new products. By the end of the 1940s, it dwarfed all competitors. In the last several decades, however, the company lost its way and became a self-serving, insulated bureaucracy. Now it is closing its doors at numerous stores. Its market share has plunged, and its profits have almost disappeared.

Why, by contrast, has another retail firm, Wal-Mart, achieved its phenomenal success? Not because its founder Sam Walton used to ride around in a pickup truck visiting his stores, though that was good publicity. It was because he recognized the importance of computer technology and had systems devised that help store operators respond to inventory information on a weekly, even daily, basis. Sam Walton knew that success, even once it was achieved, was something that couldn't be taken for granted.

What should be clear from each of these examples is that capitalism is not a top-down system; it cannot be mandated or centrally planned. It operates from the bottom up, through individuals—individuals who take risks, who often "don't know any better," who venture into areas where, according to conventional wisdom, they have no business going, who see vast potential where others see nothing.

Often these individuals literally stumble across ideas that never would have occurred to them if they were forced to work in a top-down system, and they take supposedly "worthless" substances and turn them into infinitely valuable ones. Look at penicillin. Whoever thought that stale bread could be good for anything? The same goes for oil before the invention of the gasoline engine and the automobile and for sand before the invention of glass, fiber-optics and the microchip.

There is another important thing to remember about capitalism: Failure is not a stigma or a permanent obstacle. It is a spur to learn and try again. Edison invented the light bulb on, roughly, his *ten-thousandth* attempt. If we had depended on central planners to direct his experiments, we would all be sitting around in the dark today.

This leads to the next question regarding capitalism: What is the market? Central planners don't like the word; they prefer to say "market forces," as if describing aliens from outer space. But nothing could be further from the truth. The market is *people*. All of us. We decide what to do and what not to do, where to shop and where not to shop, what to buy and what not to buy. So when central planners trash "market forces," they are really trashing us.

Unfortunately, they are the ones who seem to be calling the shots today on a number of issues that should be left up to the market, i.e., us. One such issue

is the spiraling cost of health care. Not surprisingly, central planners advocate a top-down approach to reform. With unconscious irony, they call it "managed competition."

But we have *already* tried managed competition; in fact, it is managed competition that has caused so many problems in the health care industry in the first place. Specifically, the tax code penalizes individuals who want to buy medical insurance by making them pay for it with aftertax dollars, even if they are self-employed. Only 25% of their premiums are deductible. But companies may buy health insurance with pretax dollars. So they, instead of their employees, have become the primary purchasers of insurance. This drives a wedge between the real customers and the real providers and obscures the real costs of such features of the system as low deductibles. Imagine if every time you went to the supermarket you gave the cash register receipt to your employer, who then submitted it to the insurance company for a claim. What would happen to food prices? They would skyrocket, because you wouldn't care whether a bottle of soda cost $10, $100, or $1,000.

The problem doesn't stop there. Growth in demand and improvements in technology—key ingredients to success in any other business—have instead led to crisis in the health care industry. More people are receiving better treatment than ever before and leading longer, healthier lives. Perversely, this has sent costs up rather than down and has overloaded the delivery system.

If we want genuine health care reform, we must return to open competition. The tax code must be revised so that individuals can buy health insurance with pretax dollars and set up medical

IRAs for their families that can be used to finance routine medical expenses. There is no doubt that a majority of Americans would choose this option. They want to have control over their own health care decisions. Many would choose policies with higher deductibles. Premiums would go down and so would paperwork. Physicians and hospitals would see their patient load come under control and would be induced to offer competitive rates and services. The potential benefits are enormous.

Letting individuals make their own decisions is what capitalism is all about, but virtually all central planners (now in their heyday under the Clinton Administration) and a good many members of the U.S. Congress (Republicans as well as Democrats) fail to realize it. They do not realize that it is the decisions of individuals that really determine how much tax revenue the government collects and how well the economy prospers. Between 1982 and 1986 the American private sector created well over 18 million new jobs, including a record number of high-paying positions. Of these, 14 million were created by new businesses. But in 1987 Congress raised the capital gains tax to one of the highest levels in the industrial world. What happened? New business and job creation declined sharply. The nation was hit with a recession. And tax revenues, which were supposed to rise, went down. All this occurred because individuals made the decision *not* to invest. Today there is almost $7 *trillion* of unrealized capital gains that is going begging because of high taxes. If Congress lowered the capital gains tax rate, it would mean *more*, not *less*, tax revenue. It also would overwhelm any stimulus package Washington could concoct for revitalizing the economy.

Central planners also tend to be big fans of "industrial planning," whereby government picks the "winners" in the marketplace through subsidization of select companies and technologies. They ignore the fact that this obliterates incentives for companies to remain competitive, breeds corruption and special interests, and penalizes the small businesses that are the backbone of the economy.

And they want to micromanage the monetary system, knocking down the value of the dollar against the yen or raising it against some other currency in closed-door meetings with bureaucrats from other industrialized nations. One of the most important functions of money is to serve as a constant, reliable measure. A ruler is supposed to be 12 inches long, but they want to change it to 11 or 13 inches whenever it suits their political strategy. You and I might call this a swindle, but in Washington it is called sophisticated economic management.

Even such a simple word as "change" takes on a whole new definition in Washington, meaning change directed from above by well-intended central planners and politicians who think that they "know better" than most people when it comes to making decisions. But, in truth, the most revolutionary sweeping agent of change is capitalism. Look at what has happened in Eastern Europe, the former Soviet Union, Latin America and Asia. When people are free to make their own decisions, they have a stake in the economy; and when they have a stake in the economy, they have a stake in serving others; and when they have a stake in serving others, they have a stake in fighting for freedom.

Capitalism is the real enemy of tyranny. It stands not for accumulated wealth or greed but for human innovation, imagination and risk-taking. It cannot be measured in mathematical models or quantified in statistical terms, which is why central planners and politicians always underestimate it. As I noted at the outset, it is up to us, then, to give three cheers for capitalism. Who knows? If we cheer loud enough, perhaps even they will listen.

NO

David McReynolds

SOCIALISM YES

Socialism dead? An idea whose time it never was, a "project" of elitist intellectuals ending the century as ideological trash? Not quite so fast. Permit me, as one who consistently opposed the Soviet perversion of socialism, to say a few words over the body of this fallen dream.

I know the failure of the Soviet experiment has left the impression that socialism itself has been tried, and that it failed. It is not much good to mutter, "Yes, but it wasn't *my kind* of socialism," or, "It wasn't *really* socialism." It was sold to the world as socialism, and public opinion bought it. All socialists suffered in consequence.

But why should socialists give up their dreams? Think of the Christians, who practiced torture, burned heretics, engaged in the killing of "witches," expelled and hounded Jews, and gave their blessing to slavery and war (not to mention capitalism). What Christian leader would say there is no hope for Christianity in the future because the message of Jesus, the "experiment" he launched, has been so distorted?

We know communism failed in the Soviet Union, but look at the United States. Our unemployment rate has been rising by about 1 per cent a decade since 1950. When I was at UCLA about forty years ago, our economics courses taught that for the labor force to be "mobile," we had to have an unemployment rate of 3 per cent. That was one of the reasons I became a socialist; it seemed like an awful lot of people out of work just to keep the work force "mobile" and disciplined. But the figure has gone up: Today we not only have an unemployment rate of about 7 per cent, but our economists would be happy if that were an accurate statistic. Actual unemployment is substantially higher because people have given up looking and are not counted as unemployed, and many Americans are in the "underground" economy, paid "off the books" for a variety of reasons. Many economists believe the true unemployment rate is well above 10 per cent.

And what kind of employment? In the past fifteen years, we have seen a startling shift *downward* in the living standards of most Americans, including, for the first time, "middle-class" Americans. While the rich have, indeed, gotten a great deal richer, it isn't just the poor who have gotten poorer;

everyone except the rich has suffered a decline in real income. People are being forced out of productive work where wages had been high (steel production, for example) into service industries where wages are low (fast-food service, for example). The number of Americans who subsist on food stamps, or who have lost their medical coverage, or their homes, or who are actually living on the street (or in their cars) is higher than it has been since the Great Depression of the 1930s.

The Los Angeles "riots" after the Rodney King verdict were not about race but about class, as some Federal officials admitted at the time. People were hungry. A friend of mine reported seeing neighbors going back and forth from a store that had children's supplies, taking boxes of diapers or food.

But we have also seen a sharp increase in racial tensions in the urban areas—not just tension between black and white, but also tension *among* groups in the minority; Latino and Asian populations in conflict with each other or with the African-American population.

* * *

Our capitalism has, in the past fifteen years, failed to provide jobs, housing, and medical care for an increasing number of our people. The men who run this country can trot out academics to explain how well-off we are. Certainly most of America is in far better shape than the former Soviet bloc. But given the fact that the American experiment in capitalism suffered very little from the two world wars that devastated Europe, the reality here is grim for too many of our people —and with no economic excuse. If the homeless on our streets, the beggars who wordlessly shake their cups asking

for change, were victims of some war or natural disaster that had demolished much of our industrial base, that would be one thing. But this social breakdown comes at the end of a century when war did not directly touch this country and when the capitalist experiment faced few constraints.

It is time to try something different.

Capitalism is a system of enormous energy. It has a remarkable ability to mobilize productive forces. It is flexible and inventive. But it contains what Karl Marx called "contradictions," one of which is that the free market inevitably becomes less free, property becomes concentrated in fewer hands, the means of production become more highly centralized and collectivized.

On those points, Marx was correct. A free market is one that anyone can enter with a little help from his or her friends. But I doubt there is a single reader of *The Progressive* who is in a position to start a daily newspaper, a steel mill, or an airline. Those are enterprises that require enormous amounts of capital —far more than any combination of ordinary people can supply. Thus, as capitalism develops, more and more capital is required by anyone who seeks to enter the market, and the market becomes less and less "free." Competition continues, but usually not in terms of price; style, packaging, and advertising are decisive. Profit margins are artificially protected because the market has ceased to be free.

* * *

One area in which capitalism may be superior to socialism is its ability to generate "new things," some of which are quite useful. While I doubt that we need thirty-seven colors of toothbrushes,

I don't believe socialism would so swiftly have developed such advanced electronics that persons of even modest means could afford a television set. (Consider the humble digital wrist watch which, for a few dollars, gives to any person a timepiece whose accuracy would have been available in 1950 only to those of great wealth.)

Many socialists have underestimated the desire of people for variety, a desire that is human, not merely a result of capitalist advertising. To some socialists, it is enough that every citizen have a good gray dress or pair of pants, and a good gray blouse or work shirt, and good gray shoes. But people like variety and color, and socialists must take that human desire into account. So we must have a socialism in which the market plays some role, so that "central planners" can't impose a single model or a single color.

I support forms of socialism that are organized from below and involve workers in owning and running local factories —forms that involve setting up councils in which consumers and workers decide where plants should be located, what should be produced, and at what price.

Socialists have made several errors. First, we relied too much on the assumption that if the "State" took over a factory, the result would be socialism. It wasn't. It only shifted the employer confronting the worker from a private to a governmental bureaucracy. It did not lead to an increase of worker democracy. "State ownership" of the means of production is not at all the same as *social* ownership, which involves the workers and the community.

Second, socialists have too often spoken as if our job was simply to seize the wealth of the handful of multimillionaries and parcel it out to the poor. But distributive socialism would involve very marginal increases in anyone's wealth; we might be a few dollars richer for a year, but that is all. That is not what socialism is about. It must be about finding effective ways of organizing production and distribution of useful goods in a democratic way.

Third, we tended to think that everything could be planned—that the market played no role that couldn't be met by rational planning. However, as capitalists know, the best of planning can go haywire—and capitalists plan far more carefully than we may think, using market surveys, computer models, and other sophisticated techniques.

There are problems, of course, with allowing the "market" to determine all of our decisions. The "market" may have little demand for decent low-cost housing. *People* may want it most urgently, but a "market economy" supplies what people have money for, not what they want or need. Capitalist economists concede the free market cannot provide low-cost housing—construction costs are too high for a profit. But *the society as a whole* can afford low-cost housing because if we don't pay for it with a tax subsidy, we end up paying in other ways—through increased costs of police, prison, and welfare services.

Socialists have not always fully understood there is no such thing as a free lunch.

There is never enough money to do all the things we want done. That is just as true of us as a society as it is for us as individuals. Sometimes the choices are luxurious—I may not have enough money to choose both a new car and a new television set. Sometimes the choices are terrible—Cubans must choose today between medical care and new housing, between education and decent buses. But rich or poor, there are always choices.

The socialist wants those choices made democratically, by as many people as possible. Socialism is not about destroying the wealthy but about empowering the poor. The society we are out to build is one which would stress *relative* economic equality.

* * *

Capitalism has failed us on at least three counts. First, it is built on the assumption that "things are in the saddle and ride mankind." We are cogs in the corporate wheel, disenfranchised when it comes to such major decisions as whether a factory should leave our town —or be built there. Our communities have been polluted without consulting us. The cost of repairing the damage to the environment has been passed along to the consumer because there was no "profit" to be had in pollution controls. (In the old Soviet bloc, there was no civil society able to protest destruction of the environment. Planning, because it was centralized and not community-based, left no one to watch out for damage to the environment. We learned that simply removing "private profit" from production does not solve such problems.)

Second, because all basic economic decisions are based on what turns a profit for a sector of the economy, capitalists have not been concerned about the "profit" of the overall society. How do we weigh the shifting of a plant to Mexico, with the sharp increase in unemployment payments (a social cost to the whole society, not paid by the plant that moved), against the cost of saying that the plant should be worker-owned and controlled and might well accept a

much lower net profit if it meant the jobs stay in town? (The logic of the capitalist investor is inflexible—if a million dollars is drawing 5 per cent return at one place and a possible 15 per cent at another, the investor will shift the million dollars to maximize the profit. Yet that decision, so easily made by picking up a phone and calling the broker, can have a devastating impact on human beings. Socialism seeks to give to human life something of the value the investor gives to his or her money.)

Third, capitalism has undermined our democracy. (Granted, there has never been a "Golden Age" for our democracy, haunted from its early days by the Alien and Sedition Acts—and by the vastly larger fact of slavery.) For democracy to work, the "ordinary" citizen must be able to hold informed views and act on them. There was a time when dissenting publications (such as this one) would have had to confront the occasional mob because publishing truth at odds with the Government posed a threat. Today, however, the fact that *The Progressive* is published is offered as one proof of how "democratic" our society is, though in reality it is terribly difficult for any of us to be fully informed when so many vital decisions are made by such secret and quasi-secret agencies as the CIA.

Watergate was important not because it was the first time a governing party got caught committing illegal acts but because we had a brief glimpse of something more fearful than the Watergate burglary—an entire secret government. We have reached a point where *we* have our democracy, including the right to express ourselves freely, while *they* make the decisions, carry them out, and then manipulate the mass media to construct the needed supportive opinion. What I'm trying to get at is the problem we face when simply telling the truth is no longer a potent weapon against the ruling class.

Some Marxists once argued that "political democracy" was not so important as "economic democracy," but such thinking was sloppy, confusing "economic democracy" with having a job. A man in prison has a job (and food, housing, and shelter), yet no one would argue he is free. Economic democracy consists of far more than making sure people aren't hungry.

It is true that almost all of us who are socialists—certainly those of us who are Marxists—get impatient with a middle-class emphasis on morality and civil liberties, as if those could be separated from the economic reality. Something is wrong if our definition of freedom grants you the right to tell the President to go to hell but lets you be fired if you agitate for a union in your shop. Democracy must mean the full range of civil liberties. (Radicals who call for laws to suppress speech they don't like never seem to understand those laws will be used against them sooner or later.) Full freedom of speech, religion, press, conscience—the socialist does not want to diminish this but add to it. Democracy must also mean a voice in your workplace, some sense of daily involvement in the decisions which affect you, not just a routine vote every two years.

Finally, while in a political sense "socialism is not on the agenda"—there seems no prospect of making it a reality in the immediate future—it will never be on the agenda if we abandon the vision and surrender to a planet controlled by competing corporate structures. For socialism to become a reality, we must wage a political struggle for power, and

a far deeper struggle than the one we see every four years, for the struggle for socialism isn't about changing which party fills offices in Washington, D.C., but changing who has economic power. It would substitute for the present ruling class, which is a small minority, a government broadly based from the community up, more concerned about diffusing power than concentrating it.

Yes, there would be enormous problems with buying out the huge corporations and shifting ownership and control to regions and communities. (Probably there would be full compensation for stock bought and low taxes on investors who had little money—but confiscatory taxes on those who would be receiving millions from the buyout of such corporate giants as GM, IBM, and AT&T.) Some enterprises—banking, transportation, communications—are best operated centrally. For socialism to become workable, it must target the major corporations. Socialism should not even try to socialize small business; on the contrary, a healthy society would have a range of ownership patterns, including co-ops and small enterprises.

* * *

Socialism would strive to build a society that emphasizes cooperation rather than competition. In all of our history, most people have only been means to someone else's end. Socialism is an effort to make every human being an end in himself or herself.

Michael Harrington pointed out that the issue was not whether we would "collectivize the means of production" —capitalism has already collectivized them. They are privately owned, yes, but collectivized, and the only question is whether they remain in private hands. If they do, virtually all serious political decisions, including decisions about peace and war and about the fate of the environment, will rest in the hands of self-interested boards of directors. If we, the broader public, socially own and democratically control these massive concentrations of power, *we* can make the decisions that are now out of our hands.

Capitalism didn't create all human problems, and socialism can't solve all human problems. But moving toward a democratic socialist society is one step toward the discovery of what a human society might actually be. Socialism is not about a more efficient society at the economic level, but about a more fully human society. If capitalism were not a history in which wars and depressions were as much a part of the record as economic innovation and a sharp increase in the living standard, the issue of searching for alternatives would hardly arise. But as we approach the end of this century, during which a vast range of approaches has been used to "tame" capitalism, it is time to try the alternative of democratic socialism.

The Soviet experience showed us the limits of a command economy. The American experience has shown us the limits of a capitalist economy, in which the major decisions are made on the basis of what will benefit the smallest sector of the population, and in which that small sector of the population, by maintaining control over the political process, has stunted democracy.

POSTSCRIPT

Has Capitalism Defeated Socialism?

Forbes begins by distinguishing between managed capitalism and democratic capitalism; the former involves central planning while the latter does not. In giving "three cheers for capitalism," Forbes is cheering for *democratic* capitalism, and there are several reasons for cheering democratic capitalism. First, Forbes claims it is the only moral system, for it is the only system that allows individuals to make their own decisions—to be free. In this exercise of freedom, individuals will be serving others and enhancing social welfare. The second reason for cheering capitalism is that capitalism enables people to cooperate with one another and to provide the members of society with the goods and services they want. The third reason Forbes gives for cheering capitalism is that it is the enemy of tyranny. In this regard, capitalism allows and promotes human innovation, imagination, and risk taking.

McReynolds begins by admitting that communism failed in the Soviet Union. But, he argues, this does not mean that socialism cannot succeed or that capitalism is the best solution to all economic problems. McReynolds supports democratic socialism with workers owning and running local factories, and he believes that the adoption of such a system would redress a number of economic problems in the United States. He admits that socialists have made several mistakes. But he feels that capitalism has also failed society in several respects: the corporation is the master, while individuals are the servants; corporate profits, rather than social welfare, are the driving force in economic decisions; and capitalism has progressed only at the expense of democracy. In light of this, McReynolds believes that moving toward a democratic socialist society will be a move to a more fully human, and therefore better, society.

Milton Friedman presents a defense of capitalism in *Capitalism and Freedom* (University of Chicago Press, 1963). The preeminent spokesman for democratic socialism was Michael Harrington. He presents his case in *The Other America* (Macmillan, 1965). Two more recent books supporting capitalism are *The Capitalist Revolution* by Peter Berger (Basic Books, 1988) and *The Spirit of Democratic Capitalism* by Michael Novak (Madison Books, 1991). Also among the procapitalism readings is the article "Injecting Capitalism," by Julian L. Simon and Stephen K. Moore, *The Corporate Board* (May/June 1990). Other readings in support of socialism include "A New American Socialism," by Manning Marble, *The Progressive* (February 1993), and "The World, the Free Market and the Left," by Robert Pollin and Alexander Cockburn, *The Nation* (February 25, 1991).

CONTRIBUTORS
TO THIS VOLUME

EDITORS

THOMAS R. SWARTZ was born in Philadelphia in 1937. He received a B.A. from LaSalle University in 1960, an M.A. from Ohio University in 1962, and a Ph.D. from Indiana University in 1965. He is currently a professor of economics at the University of Notre Dame and the director of the Notre Dame Center for Economic Education. He writes in the areas of urban finance and economic education, and he and Frank J. Bonello have collaborated on a number of works, most recently *Urban Finance Under Siege* (M. E. Sharpe, 1993). In addition to *Taking Sides,* they have coedited *Alternative Decisions in Economic Policy* (Notre Dame Press, 1978) and *The Supply Side: Debating Current Economic Policies* (The Dushkin Publishing Group, 1983). Dr. Swartz is also the coeditor, with John E. Peck, of *The Changing Face of Fiscal Federalism* (M. E. Sharpe Press, 1990).

FRANK J. BONELLO was born in Detroit in 1939. He received a B.S. in 1961 and an M.A. in 1963 from the University of Detroit and a Ph.D. in 1968 from Michigan State University. He is currently an associate professor of economics and the Arts and Letters College Fellow at the University of Notre Dame. He writes in the areas of monetary economics and economic education, and in addition to those publications he has coedited with Thomas R. Swartz, he is the author of *The Formulation of Expected Interest Rates* and the coauthor, with William I. Davisson, of *Computer-Assisted Instruction in Economic Education: A Case Study* (University of Notre Dame Press, 1976).

STAFF

Mimi Egan   Publisher
Brenda S. Filley   Production Manager
Libra Ann Cusack   Typesetting Supervisor
Juliana Arbo   Typesetter
Lara Johnson   Graphics
Diane Barker   Proofreader
David Brackley   Copy Editor
David Dean   Administrative Editor
Richard Tietjen   Systems Manager

AUTHORS

RICHARD P. APPELBAUM is a professor in and the chair of the Department of Sociology at the University of California, Santa Barbara. He is the author of *Karl Marx* (Sage Publications, 1988) and the coauthor, with John I. Gilderbloom, of *Rethinking Rental Housing* (Temple University Press, 1988).

DOUG BANDOW is a senior fellow of the Cato Institute in Washington, D.C., a public policy research foundation, and a member of the State of California Bar Association and the U.S. Court of Appeals for the District of Columbia. He is the author of *Beyond Good Intentions* (Crossway Books, 1988) and *The Politics of Plunder: Misgovernment in Washington* (Transaction Publishers, 1990).

ALAN S. BLINDER is a member of the board of governors of the Federal Reserve System.

FRED BLOCK is a professor of sociology at the University of California, Davis. His publications include *Post-Industrial Possibilities: A Critique of Economic Discourse* (University of California Press, 1990).

JOHN E. CHUBB is a senior fellow in the Governmental Studies Program at the Brookings Institution in Washington, D.C., a private nonprofit organization devoted to research, education, and publication in economics, government, foreign policy, and the social sciences. He is also a partner in the Edison Project in Knoxville, Tennessee, and he has held academic appointments at Princeton University, the Johns Hopkins University, and Stanford University. His publications include *Can the Government Govern?* (Brookings Institution, 1989), co-authored with Paul E. Peterson, and *Politics, Markets, and America's Schools* (Brookings Institution, 1990), coauthored with Terry M. Moe.

STEPHEN D. COHEN, a former international economist for the U.S. Treasury Department and Visiting Fulbright Professor at the London School of Economics, is a professor of international economic relations in the School of International Service at American University in Washington, D.C. His publications include *Cowboys and Samurai: Why the United States Is Losing the Battle With the Japanese, and Why It Matters* (HarperCollins, 1991).

COUNCIL OF ECONOMIC ADVISERS was established by the provisions of the Employment Act of 1946 and the Full Employment and Balanced Growth Act of 1978 to advise the president on the current economic status of the United States.

GREG J. DUNCAN is a professor with the Survey Research Center at the University of Michigan in Ann Arbor, Michigan.

ROBERT EISNER, former president of the American Economic Association, is the William R. Kenan Professor of Economics at Northwestern University in Evanston, Illinois, and a fellow of the American Academy of Arts and Sciences and of the Econometric Society. His publications include *How Real Is the Federal Deficit?* (Free Press, 1986) and *The Total Incomes System of Accounts* (University of Chicago Press, 1989).

JEFF FAUX is the president of the Economic Policy Institute in Washington, D.C., which conducts research and provides a forum for the exchange of information on economic policy issues.

RANDALL K. FILER is an associate professor of economics in the Hunter College at the City University of New York, as well as in the university's Graduate Center. His research interests focus on wages, employment, discrimination, and financial markets.

MALCOLM S. FORBES, JR., is the editor in chief of *Forbes* magazine.

MILTON FRIEDMAN is a senior research fellow at the Stanford University Hoover Institution on War, Revolution, and Peace in Stanford, California. He received the 1976 Nobel Prize in economic science for his work in consumption analysis and monetary history and theory and for his demonstration of stabilization policy complexity.

DAVID F. GREENBERG is a professor in the Department of Sociology at New York University in New York City.

ALAN GREENSPAN is the chair of the Board of Governors of the Federal Reserve System and the chair of the Federal Open Market Committee, the Federal Reserve System's principal monetary policy-making body. He has served in a number of corporate and governmental positions, including chair of the Council of Economic Advisers under former president Gerald Ford.

ROBERT HEILBRONER is the Norman Thomas Professor of Economics at the New School for Social Research in New York City. His publications include *Inquiry Into the Human Prospect, Updated and Reconsidered for the Nineteen Nineties,* 2d ed. (W. W. Norton, 1991).

BILL HONIG is the superintendent of public instruction for California's State Department of Education in Sacramento.

W. LEE HOSKINS is the president and chief executive officer of the Huntington National Bank. He has also been president of the Federal Reserve Bank of Cleveland, a chief economist and senior vice president of PNC Financial Corporation, and a vice president and director of research at the Federal Reserve Bank of Philadelphia.

GARY CLYDE HUFBAUER is a senior fellow of the Institute for International Economics in Washington, D.C.

JERRY A. JACOBS is an associate professor of sociology and the chair of the graduate program in sociology at the University of Pennsylvania in Philadelphia, Pennsylvania. His research interests focus on the sex segregation of occupations and its intersection with gender inequality, and his recent projects include a study of women's entry into management, research on part-time employment, and an analysis of sex segregation trends in 56 countries.

ARTHUR L. KELLERMANN is a professor in the Departments of Internal Medicine, Preventive Medicine, and Biostatistics and Epidemiology at the University of Tennessee in Memphis, Tennessee.

MICHAEL KINSLEY is a senior editor for *The New Republic* magazine and the author of the weekly *New Republic* column "TRB from Washington," which also appears in the *Washington Post,* the *Los Angeles Times,* and the *Guardian of London.* He has also been the managing editor of the *Washington Monthly* and a columnist for the *Wall Street Journal.* His publications include *Curse of the Giant Muffins and Other Washington Maladies* (Summit Books, 1987).

ROBERT KUTTNER is a contributing editor for the *New Republic* magazine who writes on social and political subjects. His publications include *The Economic Illusion: False Choices Between Prosperity and Social Justice* (University of Pennsylvania Press, 1987) and *The Life of the Party: Democratic Prospects in 1988* (Penguin, 1988).

LESTER B. LAVE is the James H. Higgins Professor of Economics at Carnegie Mellon University in Pittsburgh, Pennsylvania, with appointments in the Graduate School of Industrial Administration, the School of Urban and Public Affairs, and the Department of Engineering and Public Policy. He received a Ph.D. in economics from Harvard University and was a senior fellow at the Brookings Institution from 1978 to 1982.

ELIZABETH McCAUGHEY is the John M. Olin Fellow of the Manhattan Institute for Policy Research in New York City, a coalition of corporations, foundations, and individuals that assists scholars, government officials, and the public in obtaining a better understanding of economic processes and the effect of government programs on the economic situation.

DAVID McREYNOLDS is a cochair of the Socialist Party–USA and a staff member of the War Resisters League.

MICHAEL MEEROPOL is a professor of economics at Western New England College in Springfield, Massachusetts, and a staff economist at the Center for Popular Economics in Amherst, Massachusetts.

DAVID MOBERG is the senior editor of *In These Times.*

TERRY M. MOE is a professor of political science at Stanford University in Stanford, California, where he has been teaching since 1981. His research interests generally focus on American political institutions, and he has written extensively on public bureaucracy, the presidency, interest groups, and the educational system. His book *Politics, Markets, and America's Schools* (Brookings Institution, 1990), coauthored with John E. Chubb, has received national attention for its institutional critique of the American school system and its market-based proposal for sweeping institutional change.

CHARLES MOSKOS is a professor of sociology and the chair of the intervarsity seminar on armed forces and society at Northwestern University in Evanston, Illinois. He also serves on the board of advisers of the Democratic Leadership Council, and he holds the Distinguished Service Medal, the U.S. Army's highest decoration for a civilian. His publications include *A Call to Civic Service* (Free Press, 1988).

WILLIAM D. NORDHAUS is the John Musser Professor of Economics and the chair of the Department of Economics at Yale University in New Haven, Connecticut. He is also a staff member of Yale University's Cowles Foundation for Research in Economics, a member of the American Economic Association, and a member and sometime senior advisor of the Brookings Panel on Economic Activity. His publications include *The Efficient Use of Energy Resources* (Yale University Press, 1979).

JOSEPH A. PECHMAN (d. 1989) was a senior fellow emeritus of the Brookings

Economic Studies program and a president of the American Economic Association.

DANIEL D. POLSBY is the Kirkland and Ellis Professor of Law at Northwestern University in Evanston, Illinois. He has also held academic positions at Cornell University, the University of Michigan, and the University of Southern California. He has published numerous articles on a number of subjects related to law, including employment law, voting rights, broadcast regulation, and weapons policy.

ROBERT RECTOR is policy analyst for social, welfare, and family issues at the Heritage Foundation in Washington, D.C., a public policy research and education institute whose programs are intended to apply a conservative philosophy to current policy questions.

WILLARD RODGERS is a professor with the Survey Research Center at the University of Michigan in Ann Arbor, Michigan.

JEFFREY J. SCHOTT is a senior fellow of the Institute for International Economics in Washington, D.C.

DONNA E. SHALALA is the secretary of health and human services for the United States.

CYNTHIA POLLOCK SHEA is a senior researcher with the Worldwatch Institute, a research organization with an interdisciplinary approach to global, environmental problem solving. She is a coauthor of the Worldwatch Institute's *State of the World* publication. Her principle interests include ozone depletion and energy and waste management technologies and policies.

TIMOTHY M. SMEEDING is a professor with the Metropolitan Studies Program at Syracuse University in Syracuse, New York.

RONNIE J. STEINBERG is a professor at Temple University in Philadelphia, Pennsylvania.

CHRISTOPHER D. STONE is the Roy P. Crocker Professor of Law at the University of Southern California in Los Angeles, California, where he has been teaching since 1965. His publications include *Earth and Other Ethics: The Case for Moral Pluralism* (Harper & Row, 1987).

PHILIP H. TREZISE, a former assistant secretary of state for economic affairs, is a senior fellow at the Brookings Institution in Washington, D.C., a private nonprofit organization devoted to research, education, and publication in economics, government, foreign policy, and the social sciences. He received the President's Award for Distinguished Federal Civilian Service and the Distinguished Honor Award from the U.S. Department of State. His publications include *Setting National Priorities: Agenda for the 1980s* (Brookings Institution, 1980) and *Japan and the United States: Economic and Political Adversaries* (Westview, 1980).

WILLIAM TUCKER, a writer and social critic, is a staff writer for *Forbes* magazine. His publications include *The Excluded Americans: Homelessness and Housing Policies* (Regnery Gateway, 1989), which is the winner of the 1991 Mencken Award for best nonfiction.

EDWIN W. ZEDLEWSKI is a staff economist for the U.S. Department of Justice's National Institute of Justice.

INDEX